ANIMAL RIGHTS AND WELFARE

ANIMAL RIGHTS AND WELFARE

A Documentary and Reference Guide

Lawrence W. Baker

Documentary and Reference Guides

GREENWOOD™

An Imprint of ABC-CLIO, LLC
Santa Barbara, California • Denver, Colorado

Library of Congress Cataloging-in-Publication Data

Animal rights and welfare : a documentary and reference guide / Lawrence W. Baker.
    pages cm. — (Documentary and reference guides)
    Includes bibliographical references and index.
    ISBN 978–1–61069–942–6 (hardback) — ISBN 978–1–61069–943–3 (ebook)
    1. Animal welfare—Law and legislation—United States 2. Animal welfare—Moral and ethical
aspects. I. Baker, Lawrence W., editor.
KF3841.A98   2015
179′.3—dc23   2014045694

ISBN: 978–1–61069–942–6
EISBN: 978–1–61069–943–3

19 18 17 16 15   1 2 3 4 5

This book is also available on the World Wide Web as an eBook.
Visit www.abc-clio.com for details.

ABC-CLIO, LLC
130 Cremona Drive, P.O. Box 1911
Santa Barbara, California 93116-1911

This book is printed on acid-free paper ∞

Manufactured in the United States of America

CONTENTS

READER'S GUIDE
TO RELATED DOCUMENTS

Animals Used in Entertainment

Environment and Climate Change

Laboratory Research Using Animals

Legislation and Government Statements/Testimony

Morality, Ethics, and Religion

Pain, Suffering, and Cruelty

PREFACE

Animal Rights and Welfare: A Documentary and Reference Guide presents 51 primary documents that address different aspects of the treatment of animals in American and world history, from ancient times to the present. Book excerpts, government acts and laws, presidential proclamations and comments, news articles, editorials, congressional hearings testimony, court documents, and press releases make up the multitude of primary source materials. The entries are presented in chronological order, beginning with Aristotle's thoughts on the differences between humans, plants, and animals (written in 322 BCE) and ending with an excerpt from a chapter on the impact of climate change on plants and animals from the U.S. Global Change Research Program's *Third National Climate Assessment* in May 2014.

It is important to highlight the difference between animal *rights* and animal *welfare*, which are wholly distinct concepts. According to the National Association for Biomedical Research (NABR), "animal rights . . . is based on the philosophical view that animals have similar, or the same rights as humans. As a result, animal rights advocates do not distinguish between human beings and animals. Animal rights proponents believe that humans do not have the right to use animals at all, including the use of dogs and cats as companion animals or pets. No matter how humane, animal rights proponents reject all animal use as exploitation, and therefore wish to ban all use of animals by humans." Representative animal rights organizations include People for the Ethical Treatment of Animals (PETA) and the Humane Society of the United States (HSUS).

On the other hand, according to NABR, "animal welfare is the desire to implement humane care and use standards for animals in research, testing, teaching, and exhibition. Animal welfare is based on the belief that animals can contribute to human welfare by providing food, fiber, work, companionship, entertainment, or by serving biomedical research or education, and humans have moral obligations to provide for the well-being of animals. Ensuring proper animal welfare requires adhering to responsible practices in all aspects of animal well-being, including proper housing, management, disease prevention and treatment, responsible care, humane handling, and, when necessary, humane euthanasia. In so doing, animal welfare supports the use of animals by humans, and seeks to improve their treatment and well-being." Well-known animal welfare groups include the American Society for the Prevention of Cruelty to Animals (ASPCA) and the American Humane Society (AHS). *Animal Rights and Welfare: A Documentary and Reference Guide* includes primary source material covering both animal rights and animal welfare interests.

Particular care has been paid to selecting primary source material from a wide variety of animal rights and welfare categories. For example:

Animals as machine-like creatures: In 1637, French writer René Descartes referred to an animal as "a machine made by the hands of God, which is incomparably better arranged, and adequate to movements more admirable than is any machine of human invention." French philosopher Voltaire countered that notion in 1764 by saying, "What a pitiful, what a sorry thing to have said that animals are machines bereft of understanding and feeling...."

Animals as food/support for vegetarianism: Physician William A. Alcott, who favored vegetarianism, was aghast at the idea of eating animal meat in 1838: "How shocking it must be to the inhabitants of Jupiter, or some other planet, who had never before witnessed these sad effects of the ingress of sin among us, to see the carcasses of animals, either whole or by piecemeal, hoisted upon our very tables before the faces of children of all ages, from the infant at the breast, to the child of ten or twelve, or fourteen, and carved, and swallowed; and this not merely once, but from day to day, through life!"

Wildlife protection: The Lacey Bird Law of 1900 was the first federal law enacted to address the protection of wildlife and the preservation of wild game. Presidential proclamations from Benjamin Harrison (1889), Theodore Roosevelt (1905), and Harry S. Truman (1947) dealt with the protection of seals in the Bering Sea, wildlife in Oklahoma, and plant and animal life in Florida's Everglades, respectively.

Animals as entertainment: An excerpt of court documents from 2007 surrounding the infamous dogfighting case involving NFL quarterback Michael Vick detail the cruelty of that form of "entertainment." Pro and con documents from 2010 point out the disagreements among experts on the benefits and disadvantages of marine-park entertainment for whales, dolphins, and other creatures of the sea.

Animal rights versus animal welfare: A number of documents from advocates in favor of animal rights or animal welfare from such organizations as Yum! Brands (parent company of Kentucky Fried Chicken), the Animal Liberation Front, and PETA point out the disparate and often extreme points of view in this area.

Many more areas of interest are covered, including agriculture, climate change's effect on animals, animal experimentation, and exotic animal protection.

ACKNOWLEDGMENTS

Much appreciation goes to contributing writers Tara Joffe, Julie Mellors, Max Valentine, and Jane Woychick. Their fine writing, adherence to deadlines, and good cheer helped immensely in the successful completion of this project. Many thanks also go to Kevin Hillstrom, whose gentle reins (and additional writing assistance) always moved the project along in the right direction.

1

A DEBATE WAGED
OVER THE CENTURIES

"ANIMALS ARE CREATED FOR THE SAKE OF MEN"

- **Document:** This document is an excerpt from a section of Aristotle's writing titled *Politics*, in which he discusses the differences between humans (men, women, and slaves), plants, and animals.
- **Date:** First published in English in 1912.
- **Where:** London, England.
- **Significance:** The excerpt shows Aristotle's opinions on the fundamental nature of all living things, including his conviction that animals exist to provide food and clothing for humans.

DOCUMENT

But whether any person is such by nature, and whether it is advantageous and just for any one to be a slave or no, or whether all slavery is contrary to nature, shall be considered hereafter; not that it is difficult to determine it upon general principles, or to understand it from matters of fact; for that some should govern, and others be governed, is not only necessary but useful, and from the hour of their birth some are marked out for those purposes, and others for the other, and there are many species of both sorts. And the better those are who are governed the better also is the government, as for instance of man, rather than the brute creation: for the more excellent the materials are with which the work is finished, the more excellent certainly is the work; and wherever there is a governor and a governed, there certainly is some work produced; for whatsoever is composed of many parts, which jointly become one, whether conjunct or separate, evidently show the marks of governing and governed; and this is true of every living thing in all nature; nay, even in some things which partake not of life, as in music; but this probably would be a disquisition too foreign to our present purpose. Every living thing in the first place is composed of soul and body, of these the one is by nature the governor, the other the governed; now if we would know what is natural, we ought to search for it in those subjects in which nature appears most perfect, and not in those which are corrupted; we should therefore examine into a man who is most perfectly formed both in soul and body, in whom this is evident, for in the depraved and vicious the body seems to rule rather than the soul, on account of their being corrupt and contrary to nature. We may then, as we affirm, perceive in an animal the first principles of herile and political government; for the soul governs the body as the master governs his slave; the mind governs the appetite with a political or a kingly power, which shows that it is both natural and advantageous that the body should be governed by the soul, and the pathetic part by the mind, and that part which is possessed of reason; but to have no ruling power, or an improper one, is hurtful to all; and this holds true not only of man, but of other animals also, for tame animals are naturally better than wild ones, and it is advantageous that both should be under subjection to man; for this is productive of their common safety: so is it naturally with the male and the female; the one is superior, the other inferior; the one governs, the other is governed; and the same rule must necessarily hold good with respect to all mankind. Those men therefore who are as much inferior to others as the body is to the soul, are to be thus disposed of, as the proper use of them is their bodies, in which their excellence consists; and if what I have said be true, they are slaves by nature, and it is advantageous to them to be always under government. He then is by nature formed a slave who is qualified to become the chattel of another person, and on that account is so, and who has just reason enough to know that there is such a faculty, without being indued with the use of it; for other animals have no perception of reason, but are entirely guided by appetite, and indeed they vary very little in their use from each other; for the advantage which we receive, both from slaves and tame animals, arises from their bodily strength administering to our necessities; for it is the intention of nature to make the bodies of slaves and freemen different from each other, that the one should be robust for their necessary purposes, the others erect, useless indeed for what slaves are employed in, but fit for civil life, which is divided into the duties of war and peace; though these rules do not always take place, for slaves have sometimes the bodies of freemen, sometimes the souls; if then it is evident that if some bodies are as much more excellent than others as the statues of the gods excel the human form, every one will allow that the inferior ought to be slaves to the superior; and if this is true with respect to the body, it is still juster to determine in the same manner, when we consider the soul; though it is not so easy to perceive the beauty of the soul as it is of the body. Since then some men are slaves by nature, and others are freemen, it is clear that where slavery is advantageous to any one, then it is just to make him a slave.

But as there are many sorts of provision, so are the methods of living both of man and the brute creation very various; and as it is impossible to live without food, the difference in that particular makes the lives of animals so different from each other. Of beasts, some live in herds, others separate, as is most convenient for procuring themselves food; as some of them live upon flesh, others on fruit, and others on whatsoever they light on, nature having so distinguished their course of life, that they can very easily procure themselves subsistence; and as the same things are not agreeable to all, but one animal likes one thing and another another, it follows that the lives of those beasts who live upon flesh must be different from the lives of those who live on fruits; so is it with men, their lives differ greatly from each other; and of all these the shepherd's is the idlest, for they live upon the flesh of tame animals, without any trouble, while they are obliged to change their habitations on account of their flocks, which they are compelled to follow, cultivating, as it were, a living farm. Others live exercising violence over living creatures, one pursuing this thing, another that, these preying upon men; those who live near lakes and marshes and rivers, or the sea itself, on fishing, while others are fowlers, or hunters of wild beasts; but the greater part of mankind live upon the produce of the earth and its cultivated fruits; and the manner in which all those live who follow the direction of nature, and labour for their own subsistence, is nearly the same, without ever thinking to procure any provision by way of exchange or merchandise, such are shepherds, husband-men, robbers, fishermen, and hunters: some join different employments together, and thus live very agreeably; supplying those deficiencies which were wanting to make their subsistence depend upon themselves only: thus, for instance, the same person shall be a shepherd and a robber, or a husbandman and a hunter; and so with respect to the rest, they pursue that mode of life which necessity points out. This provision then nature herself seems to have furnished all animals with, as well immediately upon their first origin as also when they are arrived at a state of maturity; for at the first of these periods some of them are provided in the womb with proper nourishment, which continues till that which is born can get food for itself, as is the case with worms and birds; and as to those which bring forth their young alive, they have the means for their subsistence for a certain time within themselves, namely milk. It is evident then that we may conclude of those things that are, that plants are created for the sake of animals, and animals for the sake of men; the tame for our use and provision; the wild, at least the greater part, for our provision also, or for some other advantageous purpose, as furnishing us with clothes, and the like. As nature therefore makes nothing either imperfect or in vain, it necessarily follows that she has made all these things for men: for which reason what we gain in war is in a certain degree a natural acquisition; for hunting is a part of it, which it is necessary for us to employ against wild beasts; and those men who being intended by nature for slavery are unwilling to submit to it, on which occasion such a war is by nature just: that species of acquisition then only which is according to nature is part of economy; and this ought to be at hand, or if not, immediately procured, namely, what is necessary to be kept in store to live upon, and which are useful as well for the state as the family.

Source: Aristotle. *The Politics of Government: A Treatise on Government.* Translated by William Ellis. London: Dent, 1912.

ANALYSIS

Greek philosopher and scientist Aristotle's (384–322 BCE) interests covered a vast array of subjects, ranging from the natural sciences to politics to theater and music. One of his areas of interest was animals, and he wrote several books about them. *History of Animals* looked at the physical makeup of animals, their reproduction processes, and their characteristics. *Generation of Animals* and *Parts of Animals* delved deeper into various elements of animals.

Aside from the biological and physical aspects of animals, Aristotle also wrote about their relationship with plants and human beings, as well as their comparison *with* plants and human beings. He viewed a hierarchy, largely pertaining to the role of food, in which plants served animals and humans, and then, logically, in his mind, animals served humans. This perspective of natural hierarchical thought—or what today might be referred to as the "natural food chain"—was prominent during Aristotle's time.

In the accompanying passage, Aristotle acknowledged that "every living thing in the first place is composed of soul and body." But he believed that one thing was made for the other. "It is evident . . . that plants are created for the sake of animals, and animals for the sake of men; the tame for our use and provision; the wild, at least the greater part, for our provision also, or for some other advantageous purpose, as furnishing us with clothes, and the like. As nature therefore makes nothing either imperfect or in vain, it necessarily follows that she has made all these things for men...."

Aristotle's hierarchical thinking also applied to tame animals versus wild animals, man versus woman, and nonslaves versus slaves. For instance: "... tame animals are naturally better than wild ones, and it is advantageous that both should be under subjection to man; for this is productive of their common safety: so is it naturally with the male and the female; the one is superior, the other inferior; the one governs, the other is governed...." And so it was with his views on slavery, as exemplified in *The Politics of Government*. As noted by moral philosopher Peter Singer in his milestone book *Animal Liberation*, "philosophy ought to question the basic assumptions of the age." But Singer points out that "philosophy does not always live up to its historic role. Aristotle's defense of slavery will always stand as a reminder that philosophers are human beings and are subject to all the preconceptions of the society to which they belong. Sometimes they succeed in breaking free of the prevailing ideology; more often they become its most sophisticated defenders" (Singer, 2002).

Aristotle's theories on the hierarchy of nature and living creatures held for a long time. Indeed,

Greek philosopher and scientist Aristotle believed that "every living thing in the first place is composed of soul and body," but that one thing was made for another. He said that plants were made for animals, and animals were made for humans. (Library of Congress)

Italian philosopher and religious figure Thomas Aquinas (1225–1274) adopted Aristotle's views into his own writings. He believed that since animals could not think for themselves, in the way that humans can, animals existed solely for the use of human beings. Furthermore, thought Aquinas, only the intellect of humans could appreciate and understand God, so with that void, all other beings exist only for humans.

FURTHER READING

Aristotle. *Generation of Animals*. Cambridge, MA: Harvard University Press, 1942.

Aristotle. *Parts of Animals*. Revised edition. Cambridge, MA: Harvard University Press, 2012.

Singer, Peter. *Animal Liberation*. Revised edition. New York: HarperCollins, 2002.

Wilson, Scott. "Animals and Ethics," in *Internet Encyclopedia of Philosophy*. n.d. http://www .iep.utm.edu/anim-eth/.

"[ANIMALS] ARE DESTITUTE OF REASON"

- **Document:** An excerpt from a section dealing with animals from René Descartes's *Discourse on the Method.*
- **Date:** 1637.
- **Where:** London, England.
- **Significance:** The excerpt exemplifies Descartes's views on animals as merely unfeeling machines.

DOCUMENT

I had expounded all these matters with sufficient minuteness in the Treatise which I formerly thought of publishing. And after these, I had shewn what must be the fabric of the nerves and muscles of the human body to give the animal spirits contained in it the power to move the members, as when we see heads shortly after they have been struck off still move and bite the earth, although no longer animated; what changes must take place in the brain to produce waking, sleep, and dreams; how light, sounds, odours, tastes, heat, and all the other qualities of external objects impress it with different ideas by means of the senses; how hunger, thirst, and the other internal affections can likewise impress upon it divers ideas; what must be understood by the common sense (*sensus communis*) in which these ideas are received, by the memory which retains them, by the fantasy which can change them in various ways, and out of them compose new ideas, and which, by the same means, distributing the animal spirits through the muscles, can cause the members of such a body to move in as many different ways, and in a manner as suited, whether to the objects that are presented to its senses or to its internal affections, as can take place in our own case apart from the guidance of the will. Nor will this appear at all strange to those who are acquainted with the variety of movements performed by the different automata, or moving machines fabricated by human industry, and that with help of but few pieces compared with the great multitude of bones, muscles, nerves, arteries, veins, and other parts that are found in the body of each animal. Such persons will look upon this body as a machine made by the hands of God, which is incomparably better arranged, and adequate to movements more admirable than is any machine of human invention. And here I specially stayed to show that, were there such machines exactly resembling in organs and outward form an ape or any other irrational animal, we could have no means of knowing that they were in any respect of a different nature from these animals; but if there were machines bearing the image of our bodies, and capable of imitating our actions as far as it is morally possible, there would still remain two most certain tests whereby to know that they were not therefore really men. Of these the first is that they could never use words or other signs arranged in such a manner as is competent to us in order to declare our thoughts to others; for we may easily conceive a machine to be so constructed that it emits vocables, and even that it emits some correspondent to the action upon it of external objects which cause a change in its organs; for example, if touched in a particular place it may demand what we wish to say to it; if in another it may cry out that it is hurt, and such like; but not that it should arrange them variously so as appositely to reply to what is said in its presence, as men of the lowest grade of intellect can do. The second test is, that although such machines might execute many things with equal or perhaps greater perfection than any of us, they would, without doubt, fail in certain others from which it could be discovered that they did not act from knowledge, but solely from the disposition of their organs: for while Reason is an universal instrument that is alike available on every occasion, these organs, on the contrary, need a particular arrangement for each particular action; whence it must be morally impossible that there should exist in any machine a diversity of organs sufficient to enable it to act in all the occurrences of life, in the way in which our reason enables us to act. Again, by means of these two tests we may likewise know the difference between men and brutes. For it is highly deserving of remark, that there are no men so dull and stupid, not even idiots, as to be incapable of joining together different words, and thereby constructing a declaration by which to make their thoughts understood; and that on the other hand, there is no other animal, however perfect or happily circumstanced which can do the like. Nor does this inability arise from want of organs: for we observe that magpies and parrots can utter words like ourselves, and are yet unable to speak as we do, that is, so as to show that they understand what they say; in place of which men born deaf and dumb, and thus not less, but rather more than the brutes, destitute of the organs which others use in speaking, are in the habit of spontaneously inventing certain signs by which they discover their thoughts to those who, being usually in their company, have leisure to learn their language. And this proves not only that the brutes have less Reason than man, but that they have none at all: for we see that very little is required to enable a person to speak; and since a certain inequality of capacity is observable among animals of the same species, as well as among men, and since some are more capable of being instructed than others, it is incredible that the most perfect ape or parrot of its species, should not in this be equal to the most stupid infant of its kind, or at least to one that was crack-brained, unless the soul of brutes were of a nature wholly different from ours. And we ought not to confound speech with the natural movements which indicate the passions, and can be imitated by machines as well as manifested by animals; nor must it be thought with certain of the ancients, that the brutes speak, although we do not understand their language. For if such were the case, since they are endowed with many organs analogous to ours, they could as easily communicate their thoughts to us as to their fellows. It is also very worthy of remark, that, though there are many animals which manifest more industry than we in certain of their actions, the same animals are yet observed to show none at all in many others: so that the circumstance that they do better than we does not prove that they are endowed with mind, for it would thence follow that they possessed greater Reason than any of us, and could surpass us in all things; on the contrary, it rather proves that they are destitute of Reason, and that it is Nature which acts in them according to the disposition of their organs: thus it is seen, that a clock composed only of wheels and weights can number the hours and measure time more exactly than we with all our skill.

I had after this described the Reasonable Soul, and shewn that it could by no means be educed from the power of matter, as the other things of which I had spoken but that it must be expressly created; and that it is not sufficient that it be lodged in the human body exactly like a pilot in a ship, unless perhaps to move its members, but that it is necessary for it to be joined and united more closely to the body, in order to have sensations and appetites similar to ours, and thus constitute a real man. I here entered, in conclusion, upon the subject of the soul at considerable length, because it is of the greatest moment: for after the error of those who deny the existence of God, an error which I think I have already sufficiently refuted, there is none that is more powerful in leading feeble minds astray from the straight path of virtue than the supposition that the soul of the brutes is of the same nature with our own; and consequently that after this life we have nothing to hope for or fear, more than flies and ants; in place of which, when we know how far they differ we much better comprehend the reasons which establish that the soul is of a nature wholly independent of the body, and that consequently it is not liable to die with the latter; and, finally, because no other causes are observed capable of destroying it, we are naturally led thence to judge that it is immortal.

Source: Descartes, René. "Animals as Automata," Part V, in *A Discourse on Method*, pp. 43–46. Everyman edition. Translated by John Veitch. London: Dent, 1912.

ANALYSIS

René Descartes (1596–1650) was a French writer, mathematician, and philosopher whose work on reason-based scientific study represented an important contribution to the progress made during the Scientific Revolution. Like many great thinkers before him, portions of Descartes's work addressed the mind's relationship to the body. His theories came to fruition in the form of Cartesian dualism—a theory positing that the physical space of the body existed separately from the intangible "mental substance" of the mind. The soul also existed within this nonphysical space of the mind, and both concurrently existed with the physical realm as a part of human experience. In order to justify this position, Descartes drew on evidence that the physical space of the body served a distinctly separate purpose from the mind in both form and function, and that humans, possessing both the capacity for coherent speech and logical application of knowledge, could distinctly possess both soul and mind. Animals, Descartes proposed, only possessed half of the mind-body picture, and thusly had neither soul nor mind.

In his fifth *Discourse on Method*, Descartes makes the distinction between beast and man and asserts that there are two main ways in which to discern that animals are equivalent to machines. The first reason he gives as evidence for the animals' lack of mind or soul is their inability to express linguistically their thoughts or inclinations: "For we may easily conceive a machine to be so constructed that it emits vocables ... but not that it should arrange them variously so as appositely to reply to what is said in its presence, as men of the lowest grade of intellect can do."

Descartes observes that even the least intelligent man is capable of linguistic expression, and posits that this distinguishing trait demonstrates the ability to apply cognition to achieve one's ends. He also expresses that while a parrot's request for food or repetition of human language may appear to be the result of cognizance, it is merely a mechanistically provoked behavior.

The second distinction is that men act from a place of thinking and knowledge that exists separately from the functions of their bodies. He further establishes that beasts, which are synonymous with machines, act from a place of neither learning nor knowledge: "Although such machines might execute many things with equal or perhaps greater perfection than any of us, they would, without doubt, fail in certain others from which it could be discovered that they did not act from knowledge, but solely from the disposition of their organs." Here again Descartes pulls from his conception of mind-body duality, in that he perceives animals as functioning solely as bodies, without the presence of the mind, which is attributed solely to humans. Where the mind does not exist in beasts, neither does the soul, and thus none must exist, according to Descartes. He suggests that it might be concluded that the rights of animals are inconsequential in accordance with his Cartesian perspective, as they are merely machines without conscious thought and thus not an object of moral consideration.

FURTHER READING

"Animals and Ethics." *Internet Encyclopedia of Philosophy*. n.d. http://www.iep.utm.edu/anim-eth/.

Battuello, Patrick. "The Infamous Rene Descartes." Examiner.com. August 7, 2010. http://www.examiner.com/article/the-infamous-rene-descartes.

Clark, Desmond M. *Descartes: A Biography*. Cambridge: Cambridge University Press, 2006.

Cottingham, John. " 'A Brute to the Brutes?': Descartes' Treatment of Animals." *Philosophy* 53 (1978). http://people.whitman.edu/~herbrawt/classes/339/Descartes.pdf.

Panaman, Roger, "Descartes and Animal Rights," *How to Do Animal Rights* (blog). April 2008. http://www.animalethics.org.uk/descartes.html.

"BE TENDER TO ALL SENSIBLE CREATURES"

- **Document:** An excerpt from *Some Thoughts Concerning Education* by English philosopher John Locke on the subject of cruelty to animals.
- **Date:** 1693.
- **Where:** London, England.
- **Significance:** The excerpt shows Locke's concern about treating living creatures with compassion. Locke also discusses the importance of instilling that attitude of kindness in children, whom he describes as otherwise all too disposed toward treating "poor creatures" with brutality and malice.

DOCUMENT

One thing I have frequently observed in children, that, when they have got possession of any poor creature, they are apt to use it ill; they often torment and treat very roughly young birds, butterflies, and such other poor animals, which fall into their hands, and that with a seeming kind of pleasure. This, I think, should be watched in them; and if they incline to any such cruelty, they should be taught the contrary usage. For the custom of tormenting and killing beasts, will, by degrees, harden their minds even towards men; and they who delight in the suffering and destruction of inferior creatures, will not be apt to be very compassionate or benign to those of their own kind. Our practice takes notice of this, in the exclusion of butchers from juries of life and death. Children should from the beginning be bred up in an abhorrence of killing or tormenting any living creature, and be taught not to spoil or destroy any thing unless it be for the preservation or advantage of some other that is nobler. And truly, if the preservation of all mankind, as much as in him lies, were every one's persuasion, as indeed it is every one's duty, and the true principle to regulate our religion, politics, and morality by, the world would be much quieter, and better-natured, than it is. But to return to our present business; I cannot but commend both the kindness and prudence of a mother I knew, who was wont always to indulge her daughters, when any of them desired dogs, squirrels, birds, or any such things, as young girls use to be delighted with: but then, when they had them, they must be sure to keep them well, and look diligently after them, that they wanted nothing, or were not ill used; for, if they were negligent in their care of them, it was counted a great fault, which often forfeited their possession: or at least they failed not to be rebuked for it, whereby they were early taught diligence and good-nature. And indeed I think people should be accustomed, from their cradles, to be tender to all sensible creatures, and to spoil or waste nothing at all.

This delight they take in doing of mischief (whereby I mean spoiling of any thing to no purpose, but more especially the pleasure they take to put any thing in pain, that is capable of it) I cannot persuade myself to be any other than a foreign and introduced disposition, an habit borrowed from custom and conversation. People teach children to strike, and laugh when they hurt, or see harm come to others; and they have the examples of most about them to confirm them in it. All the entertainment and talk of history is of nothing almost but fighting and killing; and the honour and renown that is bestowed on conquerors (who for the most part are but the great butchers of mankind) farther mislead growing youths, who by this means come to think slaughter the laudable business of mankind, and the most heroic of virtues. By these steps unnatural cruelty is planted in us; and what humanity abhors, custom reconciles and recommends to us, by laying it in the way to honour. Thus by fashion and opinion, that comes to be a pleasure, which in itself neither is, nor can be any. This ought carefully to be watched, and early remedied, so as to settle and cherish the contrary and more natural temper of benignity and compassion in the room of it; but still by the same gentle methods, which are to be applied to the other two faults before mentioned. It may not perhaps be unreasonable here to add this farther caution, viz. that the mischiefs or harms that come by play, inadvertency, or ignorance, and were not known to be harms, or designed for mischief's sake, though they may perhaps be sometimes of considerable damage, yet are not at all, or but very gently to be taken notice of. For this, I think, I cannot too often inculcate, that whatever miscarriage a child is guilty of, and whatever be the consequence of it, the thing to be regarded in taking notice of it, is only what root it springs from, and what habit it is likely to establish; and to that the correction ought to be directed, and the child not to suffer any punishment for any harm which may have come by his play or inadvertency. The faults to be amended lie in the mind; and if they are such as either age will cure, or no ill habits will follow from, the present action, whatever displeasing circumstances it may have, is to be passed by without any animadversions.

Another way to instil sentiments of humanity, and to keep them lively in young folks, will be, to accustom them to civility, in their language and deportment towards their inferiors, and the meaner sort of people, particularly servants. It is not unusual to observe the children, in gentlemen's families, treat the servants of the house with domineering words, names of contempt, and an imperious carriage; as if they were of another race, and species beneath them. Whether ill example, the advantage of fortune, or their natural vanity, inspire this haughtiness, it should be prevented, or weeded out; and a gentle, courteous, affable carriage towards to the lower ranks of men, placed in the room of it. No part of their superiority will be hereby lost, but the distinction increased, and their authority strengthened, when love in inferiors is joined to outward respect, and an esteem of the person has a share in their submission; and domestics will pay a more ready and cheerful service, when they find themselves not spurned, because fortune has laid them below level of others, at their master's feet. Children should not be suffered to lose the consideration of human nature in the shufflings of outward conditions: the more they have, the better-humoured they should be taught to be, and the more compassionate and gentle to those of their brethren, who are placed lower, and have scantier portions. If they are suffered from their cradles to treat men ill and rudely, because, by their father's title, they think they have a little power over them; at best it is ill-bred;

and, if care be not taken, will, by degrees, nurse up their natural pride into an habitual contempt of those beneath them: and where will that probably end, but in oppression and cruelty?

Source: Locke, John. "Cruelty Is Not Natural," from *The Works of John Locke in Ten Volumes*, 10th ed. (London: Johnson, 1801), vol. 9, pp. 112–15.

ANALYSIS

The mid-1600s brought with them an entirely transcendent philosophical tune. This period of Enlightenment in seventeenth-century Europe was accompanied by a radical adjustment in societal values and traditions. This philosophical revolution was preceded by a system of governance that depended on religion and tradition to justify its authority and behavior. Enlightenment thinkers pushed to challenge these ideologies and replace religious mores—and the political and social order they had produced—with tools like rational thought. The minds behind the Enlightenment sought to instill these principles of logic in the minds of the European people, many of whom still held tightly to the religious dogmas to which they were accustomed. This radical shift toward rational thought produced a popular ethic that rejected the use of brutality and cruelty as means of interacting with the natural world and one another. One of the intellectuals who held most tightly to this notion of rationality was John Locke (1632–1704).

Locke, an English physician and philosopher, wrote on a range of topics, including the scope of human rights and liberties, the proper role and function of government, and the human psyche; his work in the area of political theory remains relevant and influential today. He perceived humans at birth as a *tabula rasa*, or blank slate, born without inclinations toward good or evil to govern their actions. Rather, Locke's conceptualized man was shaped by interactions with his fellow man and with his environment. This philosophy entwined with his later address of animal rights, which contradicted pre-Enlightenment philosophies favoring violence and brutality as a means of controlling beasts and men alike. Locke, in his famous writing *Some Thoughts Concerning Education*, asserted that animals are capable of feeling pain and suffering. His position stood in stark contrast with his philosophical predecessor René Descartes, who denied the existence of the mind or soul in animals. According to Locke, though, the primary tragedy of animal cruelty derives not from the animal's own suffering but instead from the perpetrators' brutality, which lowers their own morality and their capacity for rational and just interactions with fellow human beings.

Children, Locke says, were taught from a young age to view cruelty as a virtue: "People teach children to strike, and laugh when they hurt, or see harm come to others; and they have the examples of most about them to confirm them in it. All the entertainment and talk of history is of nothing almost but fighting and killing." Locke believed that the impressionable child must be taught to make reasonable judgments of what is right and wrong, especially in regard to the treatment of other living creatures, and that while history had taught them to revere doing harm, strong guidance should teach them to adopt attitudes that more strongly aligned with peace and gentleness. The temperament of violence "ought carefully to be watched, and early remedied, so as to settle and cherish the contrary and more natural temper of benignity and compassion in the room of it; but still by the same gentle methods, which are to be applied to the other two faults before mentioned"—meaning that gentle teaching methods would result in more gentle practices.

Locke asserted that if these tendencies toward cruelty were allowed—or even encouraged—then the acceptance or promotion of the mistreatment of animals would later manifest itself in cruelty toward one's fellow man. If, however, strong parental guidance sought to deter the child from cruelty toward innocent animals, this would result in a fundamental shift in attitude to one that valued peace and cooperation. Humanity, Locke suggested, is at its best when in cooperation, when no man seeks to subjugate another or trod on the rights of either man or beast. Animals, being both inferiors and servants (especially when used in agricultural work and as a source of nourishment), should be regarded with kindness, so as to end the cycle of cruelty that otherwise flourished. Locke regarded animals as emotive, semi-cognizant beings and encouraged their equitable treatment as a means by which to foster harmonious conduct between men and prevent moral destitution.

FURTHER READING

Cranston, Maurice. *John Locke: A Biography*. Oxford: Oxford University Press, 1985.

Johnson, Philip, "Reverend Arthur Broomer Founder of RSPCA (Part One)," *Animals Matter to God* (blog), June 16, 2012. http://animalsmattertogod.com/tag/john-locke-and-cruelty-to-animals/.

Katz, Jon. "John Locke and the Carriage Horses: Protecting Freedom and Human Rights." May 28, 2014. Bedlamfarm.com. http://www.bedlamfarm.com/2014/05/28/john-locke-and-the-carriage-horses-protecting-freedom-and-human-rights/.

Locke, John. "Some Thoughts Concerning Education." London, 1693. Animal Rights History. http://www.animalrightshistory.org/animal-rights-c1660-1785/enlightenment-l/loc-john-locke/1693-education-cruelty.htm.

"WHAT A PITIFUL, WHAT A SORRY THING TO HAVE SAID THAT ANIMALS ARE MACHINES BEREFT OF UNDERSTANDING AND FEELING...."

- **Document:** "Beasts" entry in *Voltaire's Philosophical Dictionary*, written by the French philosopher and writer Voltaire.
- **Date:** 1764.
- **Where:** France.
- **Significance:** In this essay, the famous philosopher of the French Enlightenment, best known for his views on politics and religion, weighs in on the feelings and souls of animals.

DOCUMENT

What a pitiful, what a sorry thing to have said that animals are machines bereft of understanding and feeling, which perform their operations always in the same way, which learn nothing, perfect nothing, etc.!

What! That bird which makes its nest in a semi-circle when it is attaching it to a wall, which builds it in a quarter circle when it is in an angle, in a circle upon a tree; that bird acts always in the same way? That hunting-dog which you have disciplined for three months, does it not know more at the end of this time than it knew before your lessons? Does the canary to which you teach a tune repeat it at once? Do you not spend a considerable time in teaching it? Have you not seen that it has made a mistake and that it corrects itself?

Is it because I speak to you, that you judge that I have feeling, memory, ideas? Well, I do not speak to you; you see me going home looking disconsolate, seeking a paper anxiously, opening the desk where I remember having shut it, finding it, reading it joyfully. You judge that I have experienced the feeling of distress and that of pleasure, that I have memory and understanding.

Bring the same judgment to bear on this dog which has lost its master, which has sought him on every road with sorrowful cries, which enters the house agitated, uneasy, which goes down the stairs, up the stairs, from room to room, which at last finds in his study the master it loves, and which shows him its joy by its cries of delight, by its leaps, by its caresses.

Barbarians seize this dog, which in friendship surpasses man so prodigiously; they nail it on a table, and they dissect it alive in order to show the mesenteric veins. You discover in it all the same organs of feeling that are in yourself. Answer me, machinist, has nature arranged all the means of feeling in this animal, so that it may not feel? Has it nerves in order to be impassible? Do not suppose this impertinent contradiction in nature.

But the schoolmasters ask what the soul of animals is? I do not understand this question. A tree has the faculty of receiving in its fibres its sap which circulates, of unfolding the buds of its leaves and its fruit; will you ask what the soul of this tree is? It has received these gifts; the animal has received those of feeling, of memory, of a certain number of ideas. Who has bestowed these gifts? Who has given these faculties? He who has made the grass of the fields to grow, and who makes the earth gravitate toward the sun.

"Animals' souls are substantial forms," said Aristotle, and after Aristotle, the Arab school, and after the Arab school, the angelical school, and after the angelical school, the Sorbonne, and after the Sorbonne, nobody at all.

"Animals' souls are material," cry other philosophers. These have not been in any better fortune than the others. In vain have they been asked what a material soul is; they have to admit that it is matter which has sensation: but what has given it this sensation? It is a material soul, that is to say that it is matter which gives sensation to matter; they cannot issue from this circle.

Listen to other brutes reasoning about the brutes; their soul is a spiritual soul which dies with the body; but what proof have you of it? what idea have you of this spiritual soul, which, in truth, has feeling, memory, and its measure of ideas and ingenuity; but which will never be able to know what a child of six knows? On what ground do you imagine that this being, which is not body, dies with the body? The greatest fools are those who have advanced that this soul is neither body nor spirit. There is a fine system. By spirit we can understand only some unknown thing which is not body. Thus these gentlemen's system comes back to this, that the animals' soul is a substance which is neither body nor something which is not body.

Whence can come so many contradictory errors? From the habit men have always had of examining what a thing is, before knowing if it exists. The clapper, the valve of a bellows, is called in French the "soul" of a bellows. What is this soul? It is a name that I have given to this valve which falls, lets air enter, rises again, and thrusts it through a pipe, when I make the bellows move.

There is not there a distinct soul in the machine: but what makes animals' bellows move? I have already told you, what makes the stars move. The philosopher who said, *"Deus est anima brutorum,"* was right; but he should go further.

Source: Voltaire. *Voltaire's Philosophical Dictionary*. Selected and translated by H. I. Woolf. New York: Knopf, 1924.

ANALYSIS

Voltaire was the pen name for French writer and philosopher François-Marie Arouet, who was born November 21, 1694, and died May 20, 1778. He was best known for his satire, his social and political commentary, and his criticism of religious intolerance. He wrote thousands of books, plays, letters, poems, and other literary works, including such influential and controversial works as *Letters Concerning the English Nation* (1733), *Essay on the Customs and the Spirit of the Nations* (1756), *Plato's Dream* (1756), and the satirical novella *Candide* (1759).

Another of his major works was *Voltaire's Philosophical Dictionary* (*Dictionnaire Philosophique*), first published in 1764. An important distillation of Enlightenment thought, it first consisted of 73 articles, later expanded to 120 articles. Entries were presented alphabetically and consisted of themes that covered such topics as the Catholic Church, tolerance, and morality. One smaller theme, however, touched upon Voltaire's views on the souls of "beasts" and their treatment by humans.

Voltaire bristles at the notion of animals being merely machines—"bereft of understanding and feeling." He notes that animals are capable of learning, giving as examples birds that build nests differently depending on whether they are in a tree or against a wall; hunting-dogs that process three months of discipline from their masters with successful results; and canaries that learn to repeat tunes they hear.

Animals have feelings and souls, too, Voltaire posits. For instance, a "dog which has lost its master, which has sought him on every road with sorrowful cries, which enters the house agitated, uneasy, which goes down the stairs, up the stairs, from room to room, which at last finds in his study the master it loves, and which shows him its joy by its cries of delight, by its leaps, by its caresses."

Voltaire lambastes "barbarians [who] seize this dog, which in friendship surpasses man so prodigiously; they nail it on a table, and they dissect it alive in order to show the mesenteric veins. You discover in it all the same organs of feeling that are in yourself. Answer me, machinist, has nature arranged all the means of feeling in this animal, so that it may not feel?" The philosopher further defends the "gifts" possessed by animals—gifts, he reminds readers, that are not bestowed by humans: "A tree has the faculty of receiving in its fibres its sap which circulates, of unfolding the buds of its leaves and its fruit; will you ask what the soul of this tree is? It has received these gifts; the animal has received those of feeling, of memory, of a certain number of ideas. Who has bestowed these gifts? Who has given these faculties? He who has made the grass of the fields to grow, and who makes the earth gravitate toward the sun."

Otherwise, there are very few examples of Voltaire's views on animals in his writings. But his well-known wit came through in a whimsical quote in which he favorably compared the experiences of animals over humans on the subject of death: "Animals have these advantages over man: they never hear the clock strike, they die without any idea of death, they have no theologians to instruct them, their last moments are not disturbed by unwelcome and unpleasant ceremonies, their funerals cost them nothing, and no one starts lawsuits over their wills."

FURTHER READING

Davidson, Ian. *Voltaire: A Life*. New York: Pegasus Books, 2010.

Kowalski, Gary A. *The Souls of Animals*. 2nd ed. Novato, CA: New World Library, 2007.

Mastin, Luke, 2008, "Voltaire," *The Basics of Philosophy* (blog). http://www.philosophybasics.com/philosophers_voltaire.html.

Pearson, Roger. *Voltaire Almighty: A Life in Pursuit of Freedom*. New York: Bloomsbury, 2005.

Preece, Rod. *Brute Souls, Happy Beasts, and Evolution: The Historical Status of Animals*. Vancouver, BC: University of British Columbia Press, 2005.

Tompkins, Ptolemy. *The Divine Life of Animals: One Man's Quest to Discover Whether the Souls of Animals Live On*. New York: Crown, 2010.

"... [N]EITHER MORE NOR LESS THAN GOD MADE THEM, THERE IS NO MORE DEMERIT IN A BEAST BEING A BEAST, THAN THERE IS MERIT IN A MAN BEING A MAN"

- **Document:** Anglican clergyman Humphrey Primatt's *Dissertation on the Duty of Mercy and the Sin of Cruelty to Brute Animals.*
- **Date:** 1776.
- **Where:** London, England.
- **Significance:** While the issue of cruelty to animals had been addressed by other people of Primatt's time, his status as a cleric brought additional attention to his thoughts on the issue.

DOCUMENT

I presume there is no Man of feeling, that has any idea of Justice, but would confess upon the principles of reason and common sense, that if he were to be put to unnecessary and unmerited pain by another man, his tormentor would do him an act of injustice; and from a sense of the injustice in his *own* case, now that He is the sufferer, he must naturally infer, that if he were to put another man of feeling to the same unnecessary and unmerited pain which He now suffers, the injustice in himself to the other would be exactly the same as the injustice in his tormentor to Him. Therefore the man of feeling and justice will not put another man to unmerited pain, because he will not do that to another, which he is unwilling should be done to himself. Nor will he take any advantage of his own superiority of strength, or of the accidents of fortune, to abuse them to the oppression of his inferior; because he knows that in the article of feeling all men are equal; and that the differences of strength or station are as much the gifts and appointments of God, as the differences of understanding, colour, or stature. Superiority of rank or station may give ability to communicate happiness, and seems so intended; but it can give no right to inflict unnecessary or unmerited pain. A wise man would impeach his own wisdom, and be unworthy of the blessing of a good understanding, if he were to infer from thence that he had a right to despise or make game of a fool, or put him to any degree of pain. The folly of the fool ought rather to excite his compassion, and demands the wise man's care and attention to one that cannot take care of himself.

It has pleased God the Father of all men, to cover some men with white skins, and others with black skins; but as there is neither merit nor demerit in complexion, the white man, notwithstanding the barbarity of custom and prejudice, can have no right, by virtue of his colour, to enslave and tyrannize over a black man; nor has a fair man any right to despise, abuse, and insult a brown man. Nor do I believe that a tall man, by virtue of his stature, has any legal right to trample a dwarf under his foot. For, whether a man is wise or foolish, white or black, fair or brown, tall or short, and I might add, rich or poor, for it is no more a man's choice to be poor, than it is to be a fool, or a dwarf, or black, or tawny—such he is by God's appointment; and, abstractedly considered, is neither a subject for pride, nor an object of contempt. Now, if amongst men, the differences of their powers of the mind, and of their complexion, stature, and accidents of fortune, do not give to any one man a right to abuse or insult any other man on account of these differences; for the same reason, a man can have no natural right to abuse and torment a beast, merely because a beast has not the mental powers of a man. For, such as the man is, he is but as God made him; and the very same is true of the beast. Neither of them can lay claim to any intrinsic Merit, for being such as they are; for, before they were created, it was impossible that either of them could deserve; and at their creation, their shapes, perfections, or defects were invariably fixed, and their bounds set which they cannot pass. And being such, neither more nor less than God made them, there is no more demerit in a beast being a beast, than there is merit in a man being a man; that is, there is neither merit nor demerit in either of them.

A Brute is an animal no less sensible of pain than a Man. He has similar nerves and organs of sensation; and his cries and groans, in case of violent impressions upon his body, though he cannot utter his complaints by speech, or human voice, are as strong indications to us of his sensibility of pain, as the cries and groans of a human being, whose language we do not understand. Now, as pain is what we are all averse to, our own sensibility of pain should teach us to commiserate it in others, to alleviate it if possible, but never wantonly or unmeritedly to inflict it. As the differences amongst men in the above particulars are no bars to their feelings, so neither does the difference of the shape of a brute from that of a man exempt the brute from feeling; at least; we have no ground to suppose it. But shape or figure is as much the appointment of God, as complexion or stature. And if the difference of complexion or stature does not convey to one man a right to despise and abuse another man, the difference of shape between a man and a brute, cannot give to a man any right to abuse and torment a brute. For he that made man and man to differ in complexion or stature, made man and brute to differ in shape or figure. And in this case likewise there is neither merit nor demerit; every creature, whether man or brute, bearing that shape which the supreme Wisdom judged most expedient to answer the end for which the creature was ordained.

Source: Primatt, Humphrey. *A Dissertation on the Duty of Mercy and the Sin of Cruelty to Brute Animals* [1776]. Edinburgh: T. Constable, 1834, pp. 15–21.

ANALYSIS

The Industrial Revolution ushered in massive transformations in the structure of British society. Attracted by the higher-paying jobs and improved standards of living promised by new technology, millions of traditionally bucolic Englanders descended upon major industrial centers like Manchester, Bristol, and London to form sprawling urban areas. The nation's explosive population growth and social reorganization were reflected in changes to political, philosophical, and economic thought—capitalism provided the impetus for industry's stately progress, while the first strains of socialism developed in response to its perceived trespasses; likewise, harsh working and living conditions and an empowered populace produced one of the world's first participatory governments.

Much of the innovation, both intellectual and technological, that characterized the Industrial Revolution was rooted in the philosophical movements known as the Enlightenment and Scientific Revolution. Both movements emphasized the application of rationality, logic, reason, and empiricism in determining the proper conduct of man and properties of the natural world, eschewing the dependence on tradition, dogmatism, emotion, superstition, and imagination that had typified past European beliefs. Thinkers such as Emmanuel Kant, John Locke, and David Hume established an intellectual tradition that transcended the traditional, stratified categories of thought by encouraging cross-disciplinary study and exploring the interrelation of all aspects of existence. By the late eighteenth century, no belief or cultural practice was safe from examination under the lens of Enlightened thought—not even Christianity.

While there were certainly religious hard-liners who denounced attempts to shed new light on the Bible's teachings, they were unable to silence a growing faction within the Anglican Church that sought to reconcile the messages contained in the Scriptures with their personal beliefs in the tenets of the Enlightenment. To that effect, a number of Industrial Revolution–era Episcopal theologians and Christian philosophers dedicated their minds to modernizing the Church. One of the many topics toward which they directed their attention was that of animal welfare, on which the Bible has very little to say. Lacking any clear direction from God on the subject of man's relationship with animals, these intellectuals turned to logic and reason to parse a satisfying conclusion on the matter.

Contemporary scientific examination had revealed that animals possessed personalities, the capacity to experience pleasure and pain, directed wills, and other traits indicating similarities between humanity and the lower animal kingdom. These findings, according to some observers, supported claims that animals possessed souls and should be the subject of moral treatment. Using the Bible as a foundation, theologians and clergymen such as Bishop Joseph Butler, Augustus Montague Troplady, John Wesley, and Richard Dean made claims asserting that animals would be included in the Resurrection, and that their ability to feel pain and emotional suffering proved that inflicting harm upon them constituted the injustice of brutality, a sin.

That is the reasoning employed by Anglican Reverend Doctor Humphrey Primatt (baptized 1735, d. 1776–1777) in his 1776 *Dissertation on the Duty of Mercy and the Sin of Cruelty to Brute Animals* to argue against cruelty and mistreatment of animals, which he calls "brutes." The *Dissertation* reflects its status as a product of Enlightened thought in its structure and language. Rather than depending on platitudes or emotional appeals, Primatt's work reads like a philosophical treatise, building upon the simple, indisputable premise that "the man of feeling and justice will not put another man to unmerited pain, because he will not do that to another, which he is unwilling should be done to himself." From there, he reasons that God created men of different capabilities, races, and statures not to justify the mistreatment of one at the hand of another, but to encourage the exercise of virtue, noting that no man or beast is more or less deserving of equitable treatment than another because their attributes are predetermined by God. He extrapolates that animals are different from mankind in no way but their physical and mental constitutions and are thus undeserving of cruelty by the same reasoning.

Primatt's position is best expressed in the passage, "Pain is pain, whether it be inflicted on man o[r] on beast; and the creature that suffers it, whether man or beast, being sensible of the misery of it whilst it lasts, suffers evil; and the sufferance of evil, unmeritedly, unprovokedly, where no offense has been given; and no good end can possibly be answered by it, but merely, to exhibit power or gratify malice, is Cruelty and Injustice in him that occasions it.... We may pretend to what religion we please, but cruelty is atheism. We may make our boast of Christianity, but cruelty is infidelity. We may trust to our orthodoxy, but cruelty is the worst of heresies." This ethic formed the basis for the genesis of the modern animal rights movement, which would manifest over the course of the following 50 years in the form of the Royal Society for the Prevention of Cruelty to Animals and the implementation of the world's first laws prohibiting cruelty to animals. Although it was not particularly influential or popular, Primatt's work perfectly encapsulates the ideological position toward animals shared by much of England during the Industrial Revolution.

FURTHER READING

"Animal Rights History Timeline: Enlightenment." Animal Rights History, accessed June 15, 2014. http://www.animalrightshistory.org/animal-rights-enlightenment.htm.

"Christianity: Animal Rights." BBC. http://www.bbc.co.uk/religion/religions/christianity/christianethics/animals_1.shtml.

Morris, Jan. "Book Review/On the Animal Revelation Front: 'The Duty of Mercy'—Humphrey Primatt: Centaur Press, 8.99 Pounds: Jan Morris Applauds an 18th-Century Anglican Vicar and His Unusual Early Enthusiasm for Animal Rights." *The Independent*, March 20, 1993. http://www.independent.co.uk/arts-entertainment/books/book-review—on-the-animal-revelation-front-the-duty-of-mercy—humphrey-primatt-centaur-press-899-pounds-jan-morris-applauds-an-18thcentury-anglican-vicar-and-his-unusual-early-enthusiasm-for-animal-rights-1498795.html.

Primatt, Humphrey. All-Creatures.org. http://www.all-creatures.org/quotes/primatt_humphrey.html.

Primatt, Humphrey. *Duty of Mercy and Sin of Cruelty to Brute Animals*. Animal Rights History. http://www.animalrightshistory.org/animal-rights-c1660-1785/enlightenment-p/pri-humphrey-primatt/1776-mercy-cruelty-reviews.htm.

"THE QUESTION IS NOT, CAN THEY REASON? NOR, CAN THEY TALK? BUT, CAN THEY SUFFER?"

- **Document:** These two documents are from English philosopher Jeremy Bentham. The first is an excerpt from *A Fragment on Government and an Introduction to the Principles of Morals and Legislation*; the second is a letter to the editor of the *Morning Chronicle*, a London newspaper.
- **Date:** The first passage was written in 1789; the letter to the editor was written in 1825.
- **Where:** England.
- **Significance:** Both documents express Bentham's concern over the amount of pain and suffering animals can experience, as well as his conviction that humans who play a role in generating such pain and suffering are engaging in acts of cruelty.

DOCUMENT

What other agents then are there, which, at the same time that they are under the influence of man's direction, are susceptible of happiness? They are of two sorts: (1) other human beings who are styled persons, (2) other animals, which on account of their interests having been neglected by the insensibility of the ancient jurists, stand degraded into the class of things.

Under the Gentoo and Mahometan religions, the interests of the rest of the animal creation seem to have met with some attention. Why have they not, universally, with as much as those of human creatures, allowance made for the difference in point of sensibility? Because the laws that are have been the work of mutual fear; a sentiment which the less rational animals have not had the same means as man has of turning to account. Why ought they not? No reason can be given. If the being eaten were all, there is very good reason why we should be suffered to eat such of them as we like to eat: we are the better for it, and they are never the worse. They have none of those long protracted anticipations of future misery which we have. The death they suffer in our hands commonly is, and always may be, a speedier, and by that means a less painful one, than that which would await them in the inevitable course of nature. If the being killed were all, there is very good reason why we should be suffered to kill such as molest us; we should be the worse for their living, and they are never the worse for being dead. But is there any reason why we should be suffered to torment them? Not any that I can see. Are there any why we should not be suffered to torment them? Yes, several. The day has been, I grieve to say in many places it is not yet past, in which the greater part of the species, under the denomination of slaves, have been treated by the law exactly upon the same footing, as, in England for example, the inferior races of animals are still.

The day may come, when the rest of the animal creation may acquire those rights which never could have been withholden from them but by the hand of tyranny. The French have already discovered that the blackness of the skin is no reason why a human being should be abandoned without redress to the caprice of a tormentor. It may come one day to be recognized, that the number of the legs, the villosity of the skin, or the termination of the *os sacrum*, are reasons equally insufficient for abandoning a sensitive being to the same fate. What else is it that should trace the insuperable line? Is it the faculty of reason, or, perhaps, the faculty of discourse? But a full-grown horse or dog is beyond comparison a more rational, as well as a more conversable animal, than an infant of a day, or a week, or even a month, old. But suppose the case were otherwise, what would it avail? The question is not, Can they reason? nor, Can they talk? but, Can they suffer?

Source: Bentham, Jeremy. "An Introduction to the Principles of Morals and Legislation." In *A Fragment on Government and an Introduction to the Principles of Morals and Legislation.* Edited by Wilfred Harrison, 1823 edition. Oxford: Blackwell, 1948.

English philosopher Jeremy Bentham fought against cruelty to animals. He believed they experienced pain, suffering, and sadness, though he was an advocate of using animals for medical research purposes. (Library of Congress)

DOCUMENT

Sir, I have never seen, nor ever can see, any objection to the putting of dogs and other inferior animals to pain, in the way of medical experiment, when that experiment has a determinate object, beneficial to mankind, accompanied with a fair prospect of the accomplishment of it. But I have a decided and insuperable objection to the putting of them to pain without any such view. To my apprehension, every act by which, without prospect of preponderant good, pain is knowingly and willingly produced in any being whatsoever, is an act of cruelty: and like other bad habits, the more the correspondent habit is indulged in, the stronger it grows, and the more frequently productive of its bad fruit. I am unable to comprehend how it should be, that to him, to whom it is a matter of amusement to see a dog or horse suffer, it should not be a matter of like amusement to see a man suffer; and seeing, as I do, how much more morality, as well as intelligence, an adult quadruped of those and many other species has in him, than any biped has for some months after he has been brought into existence: nor does it appear to me, how it should be, that a person to whom the production of pain, either in the one or the other instance, is a source of amusement, would scruple to give himself that amusement when he could do so under an assurance of impunity.

To one who is in this way of thinking, you will judge, Sir, whether it be possible to believe that the desire and endeavour to lessen the sum of pain on the part of the species inferior to man, and subject to his dominion, can afford any tolerably grounded presumption of an indifference to human suffering, in the instance of any part of the human species. Judge then, Sir, again, of the surprise and affliction with which, being, as I am, one of the sincerest admirers and most zealous friends of the *Morning Chronicle*, I have for such a length of time been beholding the endeavours so repeatedly and zealously employed in it, to oppose and frustrate, if it be possible, the exertions making in Parliament to repress antisocial propensities, by imposing restraints on the wanton and useless manifestation of them.

Of these ungracious endeavours, the morality and the logic seem to me pretty equally in unison. Thus persevering in the exertions which the Parliamentary men in question have been, ergo, they are insincere. In sympathy towards the animals inferior to man, thus they have been abundant, ergo, in sympathy, good will, and good deeds, as towards men, they are deficient. With concern I say it, the exertions made in the *Morning Chronicle* to encourage and promote barbarity, have equalled, at least, in ardour and perseveringness, those made in Parliament for the repression of it. By nothing but by fallacies could an argument such as this have been supported. Accordingly, what a tissue of them is that which I have been witnessing. Such a tissue of fallacies, all of them so trite and so transparent; fallacies forming so marked a contrast with the close and genuine reasoning which I have been accustomed to witness with admiration and delight. All this, too, from so powerful and successful a champion of the cause of the people, with the laurels won by the discomfiture of the would-be conqueror of Naboth's vineyard still fresh upon his head. Were it not for that inconsistency which ever has been, and for a long time will continue to be, so unhappily abundant even in the best specimens of the human species, that such opposite exhibitions should have been made in so short a time, by the same individual, would have been altogether inconceivable.

In the ardent wish to see a stop put to a warfare, in my own view of it, so much more dangerous to the reputation of the *Morning Chronicle*, than to that of the public men whom it has taken for its objects—I remain, Sir, your sincere and sorrowing friend, J. B.

Source: Bentham, Jeremy. Letter to the Editor. *Morning Chronicle*, March 4, 1825.

ANALYSIS

Perhaps one of the most iconoclastic figures of his time, theorist Jeremy Bentham (1748–1832) entertained no sentimentality or reverence toward the institutions that comprised Romantic society in his native England. From the privileged position as beneficiary to his father's inheritance, Bentham was able to direct his substantial intellect toward whatever matters interested him—which, as it would turn out, were almost all of them. He wrote at great length on all manner of social, legal, political, and philosophical subjects, never mincing words in asserting that the implementation of his beliefs would produce a harmonious British society and eliminate the world's ills. His most famous criticisms included advocating the legalization of homosexuality and divorce, granting full legal equality to women, and abolishing corporal punishment, executions, and slavery; they also included his ardent campaign to codify all of England's convoluted common-law system and his position against unwarranted animal cruelty.

The foundation for Bentham's confident critiques was an early form of utilitarianism, the philosophical position that the best course of action in any scenario is that which maximizes the benefit to the agents involved and minimizes their suffering, which he is credited with originating. Utilitarianism is best explained in his simple adage, "it is the greatest happiness of the greatest number that is the measure of right and wrong," representing an analytical and rational approach to government and exchange that was decidedly a product of the principals of the Enlightenment. From this standpoint, which marked a radical departure from the political and moral thought that had characterized British society in the past, Bentham asserted that a simple calculus of pleasure and pain could be used to sort past all the historical and cultural ephemera to establish objectively ideal systems of law, government, and ethics.

Among Bentham's favorite causes was a crusade against cruelty to animals. Asserting that they possess the capacities to experience pain, suffering, and sadness, the philosopher claims in his 1789 "Introduction to the Principles of Morals and Legislation" that, in accordance with the fundamental tenet of utilitarianism, the unnecessary infliction of brutality against them is morally wrong. He goes on to assault the prevailing conception of animals as nonmoral agents directly, claiming that it is the ability to experience suffering—rather than the capability to speak or utilize reason—that ought to determine the moral consideration given to an entity. The simple truth of that statement, he reasons, can be most easily surmised by examining human infants, or those afflicted with certain mental disabilities. Although they display absolutely no propensity for rational thought or speech, few would dare suggest that they are in any way deserving of unnecessary pain.

In an 1825 letter to the editors of the *Morning Chronicle*, Bentham altered his position toward animal cruelty with an important caveat. Adopting a utilitarian perspective, he stated that there is nothing immoral or unjust about causing animals to suffer in the pursuit of legitimate medical research, wherein the potential good to humanity outweighs the suffering experienced by the animals.

The letter also affirms Bentham's agreement with fellow English philosopher John Locke that cruelty toward animals is unadvisable because it promotes generally cruel behavior: "I am unable to comprehend how it should be, that to him, to whom it is a matter of amusement to see a dog or horse suffer, it should not be a matter of like amusement to see a man suffer." While the works of his successors and students in the field of political philosophy enjoy more contemporary influence than his own, Bentham's contributions to public discourse on the subject of animal cruelty have earned him a permanent position of celebrity among animal rights activists.

FURTHER READING

Bentham, Jeremy. "Principles of the Penal Code," in *Theory of Legislation*. Animal Rights History. 1802. http://www.animalrightshistory.org/animal-rights-c1785-1837/romantic-b/ben-jeremy-bentham/1802-theory-penal-code.htm.

Everett, Charles Warren. *Jeremy Bentham*. London: Weidenfeld & Nicolson, 1966.

Gruen, Lori. "The Moral Status of Animals," in *Stanford Encyclopedia of Philosophy*. http://plato.stanford.edu/entries/moral-animal/.

Rosen, F. *Jeremy Bentham*. Burlington, VT: Ashgate, 2007.

Singer, Peter. *The Animal Liberation Movement: Its Philosophy, Its Achievements, and Its Future*. Nottingham, England: Old Hammond Press, 1985.

"Who Was Jeremy Bentham?" UCL Bentham Project. n.d. http://www.ucl.ac.uk/Bentham -Project/who.

"EDUCATION, HABIT, PREJUDICE, FASHION, AND INTEREST, HAVE BLINDED THE EYES OF MEN, AND SEARED THEIR HEARTS"

- **Document:** "Remarks on Defences of Flesh-Eating," from *On the Primeval Diet of Man* by George Nicholson.
- **Date:** 1801.
- **Where:** Poughnill, England.
- **Significance:** English printer and writer George Nicholson produced a number of works that are regarded today as important contributions to the vegetarian canon. An outspoken advocate for a wide variety of liberal causes, including women's rights, public education, and an end to slavery, he was also an implacable critic of "flesh-eating," which he saw as morally repugnant. The following excerpt from his 1801 *On the Primeval Diet of Man* details his deepest objections.

DOCUMENT

The reflecting reader will not expect a formal refutation of common-place objections, which *mean nothing*, as, "There would be more unhappiness and slaughter among animals did we not keep them under proper regulations and government. Where would they find pasture did we not manure and enclose the land for them? &c." The following objection, however may deserve notice: "Animals must die, and is it not better for them to live a short time in plenty and ease, than be exposed to their enemies, and suffered in old age to drag on a miserable life?" The lives of animals in a *state of nature* are very rarely miserable, and it argues a barbarous and savage disposition to cut them *prematurely* off in the midst of an agreeable and happy existence; especially when we reflect on the *motives* which induce it. Instead of a friendly concern for promoting their happiness, your aim is the gratification of your own sensual appetites. How inconsistent is your conduct with the fundamental principle of pure morality and true-goodness (which some of you ridiculously profess)—*whatsoever you would that others should do to you, do you even so to them.* No man would willingly become the food of other animals; he ought not therefore to prey on *them*. Men who consider themselves to be members of universal nature, and links in the great chain of Being, ought not to usurp power and tyranny over others, beings naturally free and independent, however such beings may be inferior in intellect or strength. . . . It is that argued "man has a permission, proved by the practice of mankind, to eat the flesh of other animals, and consequently to kill them; and as there are many animals which subsist wholly on the bodies of other animals, the practice is sanctioned among mankind." By reason of the at present very low state of morality of the human race, there are many evils which it is the duty and business of enlightened ages to eradicate. The various refinements of civil society, the numerous improvements in the arts and sciences, and the different reformations in the laws, policy, and government of nations, are proofs of this assertion. That mankind, in the present stage of *polished* life, act in direct violation of the principles of justice, mercy, tenderness, sympathy, and humanity, in the practice of eating flesh, is obvious. To take away the life of any happy being, to commit acts of depredation and outrage, and to abandon every refined feeling and sensibility, is to degrade the human kind beneath his professed dignity of character; but to *devour* or eat any animal is an additional violation of those principles, because it is the *extreme* of brutal ferocity. Such is the conduct of the most savage of wild beasts, and of the most uncultivated and barbarous of our own species. Where is the person who, with calmness, can hear himself compared in disposition to a lion, a hyena, a tiger or a wolf? And yet, how exactly similar is his disposition.

Mankind affect to revolt at murders, at the shedding of blood, and yet eagerly, and without remorse, feed on the corpse after it has undergone the culinary process. What mental blindness pervades the human race, when they do not perceive that every feast of blood is a *tacit encouragement* and licence to the very crime their *pretended* delicacy abhors! I say pretended delicacy, for that it is pretended is most evident. The profession of sensibility, humanity, &c., in such persons, therefore, is egregious folly. And yet there are respectable persons among everyone's acquaintance, amiable in other dispositions, and advocates of what is commonly termed the cause of humanity, who are weak or prejudiced enough to be satisfied with such arguments, on which they ground apologies for their practice! Education, habit, prejudice, fashion, and interest, have blinded the eyes of men, and seared their hearts.

Opposers of compassion urge: "If we should live on vegetable food, what shall we do with our *cattle*? What would become of them? They would grow up so numerous they would be prejudicial to us—they would eat us up if we did not kill and eat them." But there is abundance of animals in the world whom men do not kill and eat; and yet we hear not of their injuring mankind, and sufficient room is found for their abode. Horses are not usually killed to be eaten, and yet we have not heard of any country overstocked with them. The raven and redbreast are seldom killed, and yet they do not become too numerous. If a decrease of cows, sheep and others were required, mankind would readily find means of reducing them. Cattle are at present an article of trade, and their numbers are *industriously* promoted. If cows are kept solely for the sake of milk, and if their young should become too numerous, let the evil be nipped in the bud. Scarcely suffer the innocent young to feel the pleasure of breathing. Let the least pain possible be inflicted; let its body be deposited entire in the ground, and let a sigh have vent for the calamitous necessity that induced the painful act. . . . Self-preservation justifies a man in putting noxious animals to death, yet cannot warrant the least act of cruelty to any being. By suddenly despatching one when in extreme misery, we do a kind office, an office which reason approves, and which accords with our best and kindest feelings, but which (such is the force of custom) we are denied to show, though solicited, to our own species. When they can no longer enjoy happiness, they may perhaps be deprived of life. Do not suppose that in this reasoning an intention is included of *perverting* nature. No! some animals are savage and unfeeling; but let not *their* ferocity and brutality be the standard pattern of the conduct of *man*. Because *some* of them have no compassion, feeling, or reason, are *we* to possess no compassion, feeling, or reason? . . .

The inconsistencies of the conduct and opinions of mankind in general are evident and notorious; but when ingenious writers fall into the same glaring errors, our regret and surprise are justly and strongly excited. Annexed to the impressive remarks by Soame Jenyns, to be inserted hereafter, in examining the conduct of man to [other] animals, we meet with the following passage:

> God has been pleased to create numberless animals intended for our sustenance, and that they are so intended, the agreeable flavour of their flesh to our palates, and the wholesome nutriment which it administers to our stomachs, are sufficient proofs; these, as they are formed for our use, propagated by our culture, and fed by our care, we have certainly a right to deprive of life, because it is given and preserved to them on that *condition*.

But it has already been argued that the bodies of animals are *not* intended for the sustenance of man; and the decided opinions of several eminent medical writers and others sufficiently disprove assertions in favour of the wholesomeness of the flesh of animals. The *agreeable taste* of food is not always a proof of its *nourishing* or *wholesome* properties. This truth is too frequently experienced in mistakes, ignorantly or accidentally made, particularly by children, in eating the fruit of the deadly nightshade, the taste of which resembles black currants, and is extremely inviting by the beauty of its colour and shape.

That we have a right to make attacks on the existence of any being *because* we have assisted and fed such being, is an assertion opposed to every established principle of justice and morality. A "condition" cannot be made without the mutual consent of parties, and, therefore, what this writer terms "a condition," is nothing less than an unjust, arbitrary, and deceitful imposition. "Such is the deadly and stupefying influence of habit or custom," says Mr. Lawrence, "of so poisonous and brutalising a quality is prejudice, that men, perhaps no way inclined by nature to acts of barbarity, may yet live insensible of the constant commission of the most flagrant deeds." . . . A cook-maid will weep at a tale of woe, while she is skinning a living eel, and the devotee will mock the Deity by asking a blessing on food supplied by murderous outrages against nature and religion! Even women of education, who readily weep while reading an affecting moral tale, will clear away clotted blood, still warm with departed life, cut the flesh, disjoint the bones, and tear out the intestines of an animal, without sensibility, without sympathy, without fear, without remorse. What is more common than to hear this *softer* sex talk of, and assist in, the cookery of a deer, a hare, a lamb or a calf (those acknowledged emblems of innocence) with perfect composure? Thus the female character, by nature soft, delicate, and susceptible of tender impressions, is debated and sunk. It will be maintained that in other respects they still possess the characteristics of their sex, and are humane and sympathising. The inconsistency then is the more glaring. To be virtuous in some instances does not constitute the moral character, but to be uniformly so.

Source: Nicholson, George. "Remarks on Defenses of Flesh-Eating," in *On the Primeval Diet of Man: Arguments in Favour of Vegetable Food; with Remarks on Man's*

Conduct to [Other] Animals. Poughnill, UK: G. Nicholson, 1801. Reprinted in Howard Williams, *The Ethics of Diet: A Catena of Authorities Deprecatory of the Practice of Flesh-Eating.* London and Manchester: F. Pittman and John Haywood, 1883, pp. 192–95.

ANALYSIS

Nicholson, who was born in Yorkshire in 1760 and died in 1825, was one of England's best-known printers of the late-eighteenth and early-nineteenth centuries. According to historian Harriet Guest, in fact, "Nicholson achieved a remarkable degree of metropolitan recognition for a provincial printer, and his work was distributed by prominent London booksellers" (Guest 2013, p. 114). Among his best known works were his *Literary Miscellany,* an anthology of essays and literature that featured selections from other authors as well as himself, and his own *On the Conduct of Man to Inferior Animals* (1797). In this latter work, he lamented that any entreaties for improved treatment of animals would be disregarded by any "who is capable of enslaving his own species. . . . No arguments of truth or justice can affect such a hardened mind." But he expressed hope that "the truly independent and sympathizing mind" might be swayed to "recognize and to respect, in other animals, the feelings which vibrate in *ourselves!*" Nicholson also published several other tracts that reflected his own feelings about vegetarianism, slavery, and other prominent topics of debate.

Nicholson's 1801 *On the Primeval Diet of Man* was perhaps his most important proselytizing work on animal welfare and vegetarianism. In his "Remarks on Defences of Flesh-Eating" excerpted above, Nicholson squarely confronts various arguments advanced for eating animals, from the need to keep animal populations in check to ensure healthy woodlands and pastures to the sheer tastiness of beef, pork, and poultry. He dismisses the former argument as a false and transparently self-serving rationalization for the "gratification of your own sensual appetites," and he addresses the latter by caustically observing that "*agreeable taste* of food is not always a proof of its *nourishing* or *wholesome* properties." Again and again, though, "Remarks on Defences of Flesh-Eating" returns to the book's central thesis—that killing and dismembering other creatures for our own selfish ends, when a vegetarian diet would render such "savagery" unnecessary, is an exercise in depravity. "Some animals are savage and unfeeling," he admits. "but let not *their* ferocity and brutality be the standard pattern of the conduct of *man.*"

FURTHER READING

Guest, Harriet. *Unbounded Attachment: Sentiment and Politics in the Age of the French Revolution.* Oxford: Oxford University Press, 2013.

Preece, Rod. "George Nicholson." *Sins of the Flesh: A History of Ethical Vegetarian Thought.* Vancouver: University of British Columbia Press, 2008.

Salt, Henry. *Animals' Rights, Considered in Relation to Social Progress.* New York: Macmillan, 1894.

2

ANIMAL WELFARE AND
THE NEW CONSERVATION ETHIC

"IT IS EXPEDIENT TO PREVENT THE CRUEL AND IMPROPER TREATMENT OF HORSES, MARES, GELDINGS, MULES, ASSES, COWS, HEIFERS, STEERS, OXEN, SHEEP, AND OTHER CATTLE"

- **Document:** The Cruel and Improper Treatment of Cattle Act.
- **Date:** July 22, 1822.
- **Where:** London, England.
- **Significance:** This law has been described as the first ever national law passed by a democratically elected legislature to deal specifically and entirely with the issue of animal cruelty.

DOCUMENT

Whereas it is expedient to prevent the cruel and improper Treatment of Horses, Mares, Geldings, Mules, Asses, Cows, Heifers, Steers, Oxen, Sheep, and other Cattle: May it therefore please Your Majesty, by and with the Advice and Consent of the Lords Spiritual and Temporal, and Commons, in this present Parliament assembled, and by the Authority of the same, That if any person or persons shall wantonly and cruelly beat, abuse, or ill-treat any Horse, Mare, Gelding, Mule, Ass, Ox, Cow, Heifer, Steer, Sheep, or other Cattle, and Complaint on Oath thereof be made to any Justice of the Peace or other Magistrate within whose Jurisdiction such Offence shall be committed, it shall be lawful for such Justice of the Peace or other Magistrate to issue his Summons or Warrant, at his Discretion, to bring the party or parties so complained of before him, or any other Justice of the Peace or other Magistrate of the County, City, or place within which such Justice of the Peace or other Magistrate has Jurisdiction, who shall examine upon Oath any Witness or Witnesses who shall appear or be produced to give Information touching such Offence, (which Oath the said Justice of the Peace or other Magistrate is hereby authorized and required to administer); and if the party or parties accused shall be convicted of any such Offence, either by his, her, or their own Confession, or upon such Information as aforesaid, he, she, or they so convicted shall forfeit and pay any Sum not exceeding Five Pounds, not less than Ten Shillings, to His Majesty, His Heirs and Successors; and if the person or persons so convicted shall refuse or not be able forthwith to pay the Sum forfeited, every such Offender shall, by Warrant under the Hand and Seal of some Justice or Justices of the Peace or other Magistrate within whose Jurisdiction the person offending shall be Convicted, be committed to the House of Correction or some other Prison within the Jurisdiction within which the Offence shall have been committed, there to be kept without Bail or Main prize for any Time not exceeding Three Months.

[No Persons to be punished, unless Complaint made within Ten Days after the Offence.]

II. Provided always, and be it enacted by the Authority aforesaid, That no Person shall suffer any Punishment for any Offence committed against this Act, unless the Prosecution for the same be commenced within Ten Days after the Offence shall be committed; and that when any Person shall suffer Imprisonment pursuant to this Act, for any Offence contrary thereto, in Default of Payment of any Penalty hereby imposed, such Person shall not be liable afterwards to any such Penalty.

[Proceedings not to be quashed for want of Form.]

III. Provided also, and be it further enacted, that not Order or Proceedings to be made or had by or before any Justice of the Peace or other Magistrate by virtue of this Act shall be quashed or vacated for want of Form, and that the Order of such Justice or other Magistrate shall be final; and that no proceedings of any such Justice or other Magistrate in pursuance of this Act shall be removable by Certiorari or otherwise.

[Form of Conviction]

IV. And for the more easy and speedy Conviction of Offenders under this Act, be it further enacted, That all and every the Justice and Justices of the Peace or other Magistrate or Magistrates, before whom any Person or Persons shall be convicted of any offence against this Act, shall and may cause the Conviction to be drawn up in the following Form of Words to the same effect as the Case shall happen; (*videlicet*)

"Be it remembered, That on the day of in the year of our Lord, A. B. is convicted before me, One of His Majesty's Justices of the Peace for or Mayor or other Magistrate of [*as the case may be*] either by his own Confession, or on the Oath of One or more credible witness or Witnesses [*as the case may be*] by virtue of an Act made in the Third Year of the Reign of his Majesty King George the Fourth, intitled *An Act to prevent the cruel and improper Treatment of Cattle, [specifying the Offence, and Time and Place where the same was committed, as the Case may be.*] Given under my Hand and Seal, the Day and Year above written."

[Justices to Order Compensation to Persons vexatiously complained against.]

V. And be it further enacted, That if on hearing any such Complaint as is hereinbefore mentioned, the Justice of the Peace or other Magistrate who shall hear the same shall be of opinion that such Complaint was frivolous or vexatious then and in every such Case it shall be lawful for such Justice of the Peace or other Magistrate to order, adjudge, and direct the Person or Persons making such Complaint, to pay the Party complained of, any Sum of Money not exceeding the Sum of Twenty Shillings, as Compensation for the Trouble and Expense to which such Party may have been put to by such Complaint; such Order or Adjudgment to be final between the said Parties, and the Sum thereby ordered or adjudged to be paid and levied in manner as is herein before provided for enforcing Payment of the Sums of Money to be forfeited by the person convicted of the Offence herein-before mentioned.

[Limitation of Actions.]

VI. And be it further enacted by the Authority aforesaid, That if any Action or Suit shall be brought or commenced against any person or persons, for any thing done in pursuance of this Act, it shall be brought or commenced within Six Calender Months next after ever such Case of Action shall have accrued, and not afterwards, and shall be brought, laid, and tried in the County, City, or place in which such Offence shall have been committed, and not elsewhere; and the Defendant or Defendants in such Action or Suit may plead the General Issue, and give this Act and the special Matter in Evidence at any Trial or Trials to be had thereon, and that the same was done in pursuance and by authority of this Act; and if the same shall appear to have been so done, or if any such Action or Suit shall not be commenced within the Time before limited, or shall be laid or brought in any other Country, City, or place than where the Offence shall have been committed, than and in any such Case the Jury or Juries shall find for the Defendant or Defendants; of if the Plaintiff or Plaintiffs shall become nonsuit, or shall discontinue his Action or Actions, or if Judgment shall be given for the Defendant or Defendants therein, then and in any of the Cases aforesaid such Defendant or Defendants shall have Treble Costs, and shall have such Remedy for recovering the same as any Defendant of Defendants hath or may have for his, her, or their Costs in any other Cases by Law.

Source: The Statutes of the United Kingdom of Great Britain and Ireland, 3 George IV. 1822. London: His Majesty's Statute and Law Printers; J. Butterworth and Son, Law Booksellers, 1822, pp. 403–5.

ANALYSIS

Passage of the landmark Cruel and Improper Treatment of Cattle Act was largely attributable to the efforts of Richard Martin, who was a Member of Parliament (MP) in England when the law was passed in 1822. Martin was known for his love of animals, and he especially worked hard combating bear-baiting and dog fighting. Editorial cartoons of that era often showed Martin with donkey ears. He was so essential in shaping the act and lobbying for its passage, in fact, that it is often referred to as Martin's Act.

Martin was one of the founders of the Society for the Prevention of Cruelty to Animals, which was established in 1824 and still exists today (Martin's portrait still hangs in the society's board room in London.) The society obtained royal status from Queen Victoria in 1840 and has been known as the Royal Society for the Prevention of Cruelty to Animals ever since. It is an important lobbying organization in England, creating and helping to enforce animal welfare legislation.

As a result of lobbying on behalf of the society, the original act was amended in 1835 to include bulls, dogs, and bears among the animals for which cruel behavior and abuse were banned. It specified that "fighting or baiting of Bears, Cock-fighting, baiting or fighting of Badgers or other Animals" would be subject to a fine or imprisonment. The 1835 act prompted further animal rights action, including the creation of shelters, veterinary hospitals, and legislation pertaining to humane slaughter and transportation.

The 1822 and 1835 acts were repealed in 1849 and replaced by An Act for the More Effectual Prevention of Cruelty to Animals. Parliament amended the 1849 act in August 1876 to address the subject of animal experimentation. Animals could be used "for medical, physiological, or scientific purposes"; issues of pain and anesthesia were dealt with as well. The act maintained that an "experiment must be performed with a view to the advancement by new discovery of physiological knowledge or of knowledge which will be useful for saving or prolonging life or alleviating suffering; . . . the animal must during the whole of the experiment be under the influence of some anaesthetic of sufficient power to prevent the animal feeling pain; and . . . the animal must, if the pain is likely to continue after the effect of the anaesthetic has ceased, or if any serious injury has been inflicted on the animal, be killed before it recovers from the influence of the anaesthetic which has been administered." The 1876 act was repealed in 1911 by the Protection of Animals Act, and then replaced and repealed in 2006 by the Animal Welfare Act.

FURTHER READING

Courtney, William Prideaux. "Martin, Richard (1754–1834)." *Dictionary of National Biography, 1885–1900.* Vol. 36. London: Smith, Elder & Co., 1885–1901.

"Cruelty to Animals Act, 1835." Animal Rights History. http://www.animalrightshistory .org/animal-rights-law/romantic-legislation/1835-uk-act-cruelty-to-animals.htm.

"HOW DO YOU PROVE THAT MANKIND IS INVESTED WITH THE RIGHT OF KILLING THEM, AND THAT BRUTES HAVE BEEN CREATED FOR THE PURPOSE YOU ASSERT THEM TO BE?"

- **Document:** Excerpt from *Moral Inquiries on the Situation of Man and of Brutes* by Lewis Gompertz.
- **Date:** 1824.
- **Where:** London, England.
- **Significance:** Early nineteenth-century animal rights/welfare advocate Lewis Gompertz wrote an exhaustive tome that expressed his opinions—from both moral and health vantage points—against the slaughtering of animals.

DOCUMENT

Y: I understand that you act in opposition to the laws of God, of nature, and of man; that you deny the very first elements of those laws by which the world is governed; that through a pretended or mistaken aim at perfection, and in attempting to compass things far beyond your reach, you misapply your exertions and fail in your grasp; you set your face against the precepts of your forefathers, and of the most learned of all ages in every civilized country in the world, and set up your own judgement in opposition to them all. Scarcely with the support of a single partisan to share in your presumptuous innovations on the established principles of society, do you attack, and wish to overturn them, without having any thing to offer in lieu, but vain chimeras, the produce of vitiated feelings, and a diseased brain. Thus, while you attempt to create new theories, you only breed confusion, and lose yourself in the labyrinth where you have undertaken to lead others.

Z: These are serious accusations! But though I confess that my laws differ in many points from those of the generality of mankind, I trust that they are not of opposition to the purpose of God. If you blame me for not paying blind obedience to the established customs of man, I own to the charge; but how much more culpable should I be, were I to adopt those tenets which are in contrariety to my own conscience! God has furnished every man with reason, and God *demands* him to exert it in the regulation of his conduct. If then he commit an error while following the guidance of others, the fault is still his own; and consists in not using that judgment by which his own actions should first be weighed. Besides, even in pursuing the dictates of others, his judgment must first give the assent to one of the various opinions of others whereby he is to be led; and thus in spite of himself his reason will have its way, whether he consults it or not. If I endeavor to compass more than I am able, I may find where I am stopped; if I attempt less, I remain ignorant of my strength.

I confess I cannot always see clearly: but it seems that though you act differently, your sight is as treacherous as mine. However, where are your charges? I will yield to demonstration, but not to assertion.

Y: In the first place, you dispute the right invested in mankind of slaughtering other animals for food, and of compelling them to labour for his benefit, for which purpose they have been created, their flesh and their services have been made palatable and necessary to man, without the nourishment of which he would soon grow sickly and unfit for his station—his life would be painful—his death premature.

Z: First, how do you prove that mankind is invested with the right of killing them, and that brutes have been created for the purpose you assert them to be? Secondly, is it to be observed that the flesh of man himself possesses the same nourishing and palatable qualities? And are we then to become cannibals for that reason? I grant that the health of man requires animal food, and it is not to be expected that the strength and faculties of either the body or the mind can be near as great with the privation of it, as with its aid; but that is nothing to the animals; a robber would not be so rich if he were not to steal; it is not therefore right to steal, when the laws can be evaded.

Y: It is evident that the right has been invested in man; first, because he has been furnished with the power, and because his life is of the most importance. Secondly, it is better for the animals themselves; they would otherwise grow so numerous as not only to destroy each other; there would be nothing to be seen but animals starving and dying of all manner of diseases, without receiving any succor or attention from their own kind. Is it not better that we should cause them to have a short and happy life, than a long and miserable one?

Z: Then it is right for one to kill another, if he fear not the laws of his country, and if he fancy that it is to the benefit of the other. It is besides not quite proved to me that his life is more important. ... But even allowing it to be so, the two are unconnected with each other, and I do not see what right one animal has to deprive another of its small importance, to prevent himself from losing more: if this theory be generally admitted, a young man might kill an old man, to save his own longer expectant life. And are we authorized to kill one animal for the benefit of another of its species? If they should overstock the world, it will then be time to begin to destroy them. It seems however more just that nature should take her course, and that man should be neutral till provoked. It is certainly easier for him to destroy others than to suffer inconvenience himself; but that does not make it right. We have not however at present any reason to complain of the too great fecundity of those animals we use for food, etc., and we even take great pains to produce them, not for their own enjoyment, but for the good and pleasure we derive by destroying and tormenting them.

Source: Gompertz, Lewis. *Moral Inquiries on the Situation of Man and of Brutes.* London: Westley and Parrish, 1824.

ANALYSIS

Lewis Gompertz was the cofounder of the Society for the Prevention of Cruelty of Animals (later known as the Royal Society for the Prevention of Cruelty to

Animals). A retired diamond merchant, Gompertz was also an inventor, but his primary interest was in the area of animal rights and welfare.

Gompertz wrote two books that covered his views on animals: *Moral Inquiries on the Situation of Man and of Brutes* (1824) and *Fragments in Defence of Animals and Essays on Morals, Soul, and Future State* (1852). In *Moral Inquiries*, excerpted here, Gompertz approaches the rights of animals from two perspectives: a moral objection to killing animals and the healthy benefits to humans of not eating animal meat. A large part of *Moral Inquiries* has Gompertz writing in dialogue style, in which Person Y and Person Z (presumably Gompertz himself) engage in a conversation about an issue or ask and answer each other's questions. The excerpt here exemplifies this style with a discussion of the merits of slaughtering animals. He also offered his opinions against the practice of vivisection (dissection of animals for scientific purposes) and hunting. Of the latter, Gompertz wrote:

> Who can dispute the inhumanity of the sport of hunting, of pursuing a poor defenceless creature for mere amusement, till it becomes exhausted by terror and fatigue, and of then causing it to be torn to pieces by a pack of dogs? From what kind of instruction can men, and even women, imbibe such principles as these? How is it possible they can justify it? And what can their pleasure in it consist of? Is it not solely in the agony they produce to the animal? They will pretend that it is not, and try to make us believe so too, that it is merely in the pursuit. But what is the object of their pursuit? Is there any other than to torment and destroy?

Much of his concern for the treatment of animals concerned horses. Indeed, Gompertz had at one time said, "I admit it as an axiom, that every animal has more right to the use of its own body than others have to use it." In Gompertz's era, horses were the primary means of transportation, both for human and work purposes. Horses pulled carriages in which citizens were passengers as they traveled to and fro. Horses also pulled wagons containing bricks, consumer goods, and other items. Gompertz felt that horses were the equivalent of slaves when forced to pull the combined weight of carriage and humans. He believed horses should live freely. An inventor by trade, Gompertz worked on producing a bicycle that had no pedals or brakes—a bike rider would move only by using his or her feet. He viewed this type of bicycle as an alternative to the use of horses as a transportation method. When he realized that a ban on using animals in this way would likely never occur, he worked at making sure animals were at least treated humanely.

The same year *Moral Inquiries* was published, Gompertz and 11 others formed the Society for the Prevention of Cruelty of Animals, in large part to recruit inspectors who would enforce a recently passed (but often ignored) British Parliament law that outlawed the abuse of cattle and other four-legged animals. The group, which met the evening of June 16, 1824, in London's Old Slaughter's Coffee House, sought to enforce the law but also to further educate the public on the benefits of animal welfare. One of the 12 men, British Member of Parliament Richard Martin, campaigned for better treatment of animals, especially given the popularity at the time of the use of animals for sport, such as dogfighting and cockfighting. Another cofounder,

William Wilberforce, was known for his involvement in many charitable and social causes, perhaps the most famous of which was abolitionism.

Gompertz stayed with the group for eight years—six of them as the group's secretary, during which he spent much of his time fixing the financial errors made by another founder. He worked hard to advance the rights of animals; he participated in debates, arranged fundraisers, broke up dogfights, and worked with law officials to establish a legal limit on the maximum amount of weight a horse could pull. Eventually Gompertz left to form his own group, the Animals' Friend Society, after disagreements with fellow members over the issue of animal meat-eating. His new group embraced the membership of Quakers and evangelicals.

Gompertz ran the Animals' Friend Society until 1846, when he resigned to tend to his terminally ill wife, Ann. He spent the rest of his life speaking and writing about animal rights and welfare, as well as continuing to come up with new inventions (for instance, he invented a drill with an expanding chuck). Gompertz died in 1861.

FURTHER READING

Brisack, Mikaela. "Lewis Gompertz: Animal's Friend." August 30, 2013. PlanetGreen.org. http://www.planetgreen.org/2013/08/lewis-gompertz-animals-friend.html.

Davis, John. "Lewis Gompertz—Jewish 'Vegan' and Co-Founder of the RSPCA in 1824." VegSource.com, accessed December 6, 2014. http://www.vegsource.com/john-davis/lewis-gompertz—-jewish-vegan-and-co-founder-of-the-rspca-in-1824.html.

Gompertz, Lewis. *Fragments in Defence of Animals and Essays on Morals, Soul, and Future State*.London: Horsell, 1852.

Kemmerer, Lisa. *Animals and World Religions*. New York: Oxford University Press, 2012.

Renier, Hannah. "An Early Vegan: Lewis Gompertz." March 15, 2012. London Historians. http://www.londonhistorians.org/index.php?s=file_download&id=55.

"THE DESTRUCTION OF ANIMALS FOR FOOD … INVOLVES SO MUCH OF CRUELTY AS TO CAUSE EVERY REFLECTING INDIVIDUAL—NOT DESTITUTE OF THE ORDINARY SENSIBILITIES OF OUR NATURE—TO SHUDDER"

- **Document:** "The World Is a Mighty Slaughterhouse," by William A. Alcott, the founder of the American Vegetarian Society and the American Physiological Society.
- **Date:** 1838.
- **Where:** New York City.
- **Significance:** An influential physician and education reformer expresses both moral and health-related concerns related to the consumption of animal flesh and endorses vegetarianism. Alcott's many writings on these subjects are regarded as important contributions to the evolution of animal rights philosophy and the vegetarian movement.

DOCUMENT

In one point of view, nearly every argument which can be brought to show the superiority of a vegetable diet over one that includes flesh or fish, is a moral argument.

Thus, if man is so constituted by his structure, and by the laws of his animal economy, that all the functions of the body, and of course all the faculties of the mind, and the affections of the soul, are in better condition—better subserve our own purposes, and the purposes of the great Creator—as well as hold out longer, on the vegetable system—then it is desirable, in a moral point of view, to adopt it. If mankind lose, upon the average, two years of their lives by sickness, as some have estimated it, saying nothing of the pain and suffering undergone, or of the mental anguish and soul torment which grow out of it, and often render life a burden; and if the simple primitive custom of living on vegetables and fruits, along with other good physical and mental habits, which seem naturally connected with it, will, in time, nearly if not wholly remove or prevent this amazing loss, then is the argument deduced therefrom … a moral argument.

If, as I have endeavored to show [in earlier sections], the adoption of the vegetable system by nations and individuals, would greatly advance the happiness of all, in every known respect, and if, on this account, such a change in our flesh-eating countries would be sound policy, and good economy—then we have another moral argument in its favor.

But, again: if it be true that all nations have been the most virtuous and flourishing, other things being equal, in the days of their simplicity in regard to food, drink, etc.; and if we can, in every instance, connect the decline of a nation with the period of their departure, as a nation, into the maze of luxurious and enervating habits; and if this doctrine is, as a general rule, obviously applicable to smaller classes of men, down to single families, then is the argument we derive from it in its nature a moral one. Whatever really tends, without the possibility of mistake, to the promotion of human happiness, here and hereafter, is, without doubt, moral.

But this, though much, is not all. The destruction of animals for food, in its details and tendencies, involves so much of cruelty as to cause every reflecting individual—not destitute of the ordinary sensibilities of our nature—to shudder. I recall: daily observation shows that such is not the fact; nor should it, upon second thought, be expected. Where all are dark, the color is not perceived; and so universally are the moral sensibilities which really belong to human nature deadened by the customs which prevail among us, that few, if any, know how to estimate, rightly, the evil of which I speak. They have no more a correct idea of a true sensibility—not a *morbid* one—on this subject, than a blind man has of colors; and for nearly the same reasons. And on this account it is, that I seem to shrink from presenting, at this time, those considerations which, I know, cannot, from the very nature of the case, be properly understood or appreciated, except by a very few.

Still, there are some things which, I trust, may be made plain. It must be obvious that the custom of rendering children familiar with the taking away of life, even when it is done with a good degree of tenderness, cannot have a very happy effect. But, when this is done, not only without tenderness or sympathy, but often with manifestations of great pleasure, and when children, as in some cases, are almost constant witnesses of such scenes, how dreadful must be the results!

In this view, the world, I mean our own portion of it, sometimes seems to me like one mighty slaughterhouse—one grand school for the suppression of every kind, and tender, and brotherly feeling—one grand process of education to the entire destitution of all moral principle—one vast scene of destruction to all moral sensibility, and all sympathy with the woes of those around us. Is it not so?

I have seen many boys who shuddered, at first, at the thought of taking the life, even of a snake, until compelled to it by what they conceived to be duty; and who shuddered still more at taking the life of a lamb, a calf, a pig, or a fowl. And yet I have seen these same boys, in subsequent life, become so changed, that they could look on such scenes not merely with indifference, but with gratification. Is this change of feeling desirable? How long is it after we begin to look with indifference on pain and suffering in brutes, before we begin to be less affected than before by human suffering?

I am not ignorant that sentiments like these are either regarded as morbid, and therefore pitiable, or as affected, and therefore ridiculous. . . .

I am not prepared to maintain, strongly, the old-fashioned doctrine, that a butcher who commences his employment at adult age, is necessarily rendered hard-hearted or unfeeling; or, that they who eat flesh have their sensibilities deadened, and their passions inflamed by it—though I am not sure that there is not some truth in it. I only maintain, that to render children familiar with the taking away of animal life—especially the lives of our own domestic animals, often endeared to us by many interesting circumstances of their history, or of our own, in relation to them—cannot be otherwise than unhappy in its tendency.

How shocking it must be to the inhabitants of Jupiter, or some other planet, who had never before witnessed these sad effects of the ingress of sin among us, to see the carcasses of animals, either whole or by piecemeal, hoisted upon our very tables before the faces of children of all ages, from the infant at the breast, to the child of ten or twelve, or fourteen, and carved, and swallowed; and this not merely once, but from day to day, through life! What could they—what would they—expect from such an education of the young mind and heart? What, indeed, but mourning, desolation, and woe!

On this subject the First Annual Report of the American Physiological Society thus remarks—and I wish the remark might have its due weight on the mind of the reader:

> How can it be right to be instrumental in so much unnecessary slaughter? How can it be right, especially for a country of vegetable abundance like ours, to give daily employment to twenty thousand or thirty thousand butchers? How can it be right to train our children to behold such slaughter? How can it be right to blunt the edge of their moral sensibilities, by placing before them, at almost every meal, the mangled corpses of the slain; and not only placing them there, but rejoicing while we feast upon them?

One striking evidence of the tendency which an habitual shedding of blood has on the mind and heart, is found in the fact that females are generally so reluctant to take away life, that notwithstanding they are trained to a fondness for all sorts of animal food, very few are willing to gratify their desires for a stimulating diet, by becoming their own butchers. I have indeed seen females who would kill a fowl or a lamb rather than go without it; but they are exceedingly rare. And who would not regard female character as tarnished by a familiarity with such scenes as those to which I have referred? But if the keen edge of female delicacy and sensibility would be blunted by scenes of bloodshed, are not the moral sensibilities of our own sex affected in a similar way? And must it not, then, have a deteriorating tendency?

It cannot be otherwise than that the circumstances of which I have spoken, which so universally surround infancy and childhood, should take off, gradually, the keen edge of moral sensibility, and lessen every virtuous or holy sympathy. I have watched—I believe impartially—the effect on certain sensitive young persons in the circle of my acquaintance. I have watched myself. The result has confirmed the opinion I have just expressed. No child, I think, can walk through a common market or slaughterhouse without receiving a moral injury; nor am I quite sure that any virtuous adult can.

How have I been struck with the change produced in the young mind by that merriment which often accompanies the slaughter of an innocent fowl, or lamb, or pig! How can the Christian, with the Bible in hand, and the merciful doctrines of its pages for his text, "Teach me to feel another's woe,"—the beast's not excepted—and yet, having laid down that Bible, go at once from the domestic altar to make light of the convulsions and exit of a poor domestic animal?

Is it said that these remarks apply only to the *abuse* of a thing which, in its place, is proper? Is it said, that there is no necessity of levity on these occasions? Grant that there is none; still the result is almost inevitable. But there is, in any event, one way of avoiding, or rather preventing both the abuse and the occasion for abuse, by ceasing to kill animals for food; and I venture to predict that the evil never will be prevented otherwise.

The usual apology for hunting and fishing, in all their various and often cruel forms—whereby so many of our youth, from the setters of snares for birds, and the anglers for trout, to the whalemen, are educated to cruelty, and steeled to every virtuous and holy sympathy—is, the necessity of the animals whom we pursue for food. I know, indeed, that this is not, in most cases, the true reason, but it *is* the reason given—it is the substance of the reason. It serves as an apology. They who make it may often be ignorant of the true reason, or they or others may wish to conceal it; and, true to human nature, they are ready to give every reason for their conduct, but the real and most efficient one.

It must not, indeed, be concealed that there is one more apology usually made for these cruel sports; and made too, in some instances, by good men; I mean, by men whose intentions are in the main pure and excellent. These sports are healthy, they tell us. They are a relief to mind and body. Perhaps no good man, in our own country, had defended them with more ingenuity, or with more show of reason and good sense, than Dr. Comstock, in his recent popular work on human physiology. And yet, there is scarcely a single advantage which he has pointed out, as being derived from the "pleasures of the chase," that may not be gained in a way which savors less of blood. The doctor himself is too much in love with botany, geology, mineralogy, and the various branches of natural history, not to know what I mean when I say this. He knows full well the excitement, and, on his own principles, the consequent relief of body and mind from their accustomed and often painful round, which grows out of clambering over mountains and hills, and fording streams, and climbing trees and rocks, to need any very broad hints on the subject; to say nothing of the delights of agriculture and horticulture. How could he, then, give currency to practices which, to say the least—and by his own concessions, too—are doubtful in regard to their moral tendencies, by inserting his opinions in favor of sports, for which he himself happens to be partial, in a schoolbook? Is this worthy of those who would educate the youth of our land on the principles of the Bible?

Source: Alcott, William A. *Vegetable Diet: As Sanctioned by Medical Men, and by Experience in All Ages.* 2nd ed. New York: Fowlers & Wells, 1848, pp. 276–83.

ANALYSIS

William Andrus Alcott was born on August 6, 1798. He was an educator, author, and physician who embraced the concept of vegetarianism. He was the second cousin of philosopher Amos Bronson Alcott, an advocate of transcendentalism and the father of popular novelist Louisa May Alcott. William Alcott was the founder of both the American Physiological Society (1837) and the American Vegetarian Society (1850).

According to an article penned by Alcott for the April 1850 issue of *Vegetarian Advocate*, he developed a discomfort with eating meat at a very early age: "From the age of two or three years I had a natural and strong aversion to most kinds of animal food, and ate very little of any. But bred to hard labour, and in a region where it was thought vegetarians could have the strength to work, I was urged at the age of fourteen or fifteen, to the moderate use of flesh and fish. In the year 1839, I fell in with Rev. Wm. C. Woodbridge, the great American geographer, who having travelled in nearly every quarter of the world, had become, theoretically at least, a vegetarian. Partly through his influence and partly from conviction beforehand, I abandoned animal food in the summer of this year." He and Woodbridge became good friends, and they both wrote for *Annals of Education*.

Alcott wrote over 100 books during his life on a variety of subjects related to education, health, nutrition, and marriage. *Vegetable Diet: As Sanctioned by Medical Men, and by Experience in All Ages* ranked among his best-known works. In this work, Alcott expressed grave concern about the moral effects on humans of killing animals: "I have seen many boys who shuddered, at first, at the thought of taking the life, even of a snake, until compelled to it by what they conceived to be duty; and who shuddered still more at taking the life of a lamb, a calf, a pig, or a fowl. And yet I have seen these same boys, in subsequent life, become so changed, that they could look on such scenes not merely with indifference, but with gratification. Is this change of feeling desirable? How long is it after we begin to look with indifference on pain and suffering in brutes, before we begin to be less affected than before by human suffering?"

Once Alcott embraced vegetarianism, he never strayed from its path. To the contrary, he remained an outspoken advocate for the vegetarian lifestyle, which he believed was a key to a happier, healthier, and more spiritually advanced life. According to one history of vegetarianism, Alcott believed that by "abstaining from animal food, vegetarians would not have to engage in acts of violence against animals and thus would avoid any temptation to give in to the baser passions. Thus, a vegetarian could move beyond the simple human need of obtaining food and instead focus on the higher things, including cultivating morality and a spiritual life" (Rivers 2010). Alcott, who was married and had three children, died of tuberculosis on March 29, 1859, in Massachusetts.

FURTHER READING

Alcott, William A. "Vegetarianism in the United States." *Vegetarian Advocate* (April 1850). http://www.ivu.org/congress/1850/history.html.

Iacobbo, Karen. *Vegetarian America: A History*. Westport, CT: Praeger, 2004.

Rivers, Gwynne K. Langley. "Alcott, William A. (1789–1859)," in *Cultural Encyclopedia of Vegetarianism*. Edited by Margaret Puskar-Pasewicz. Santa Barbara, CA: ABC-Clio, 2010, pp. 19–20.

Shprintzen, Adam D. *The Vegetarian Crusade: The Rise of an American Reform Movement, 1817–1821*. Chapel Hill: University of North Carolina Press, 2013.

"TO PREVENT CRUELTY TO ANIMALS WHILE IN TRANSIT"

- **Document:** The Twenty-Eight Hour Law, the first federal protection law for animals.
- **Date:** Enacted in 1873, repealed and supplanted in 1906, and amended in 1994.
- **Where:** Washington, D.C.
- **Significance:** This federal law, which established regulations for the humane treatment of animals who were being transported across state lines for long periods of time, was the first to address livestock welfare in the United States.

DOCUMENT

AN ACT to prevent cruelty to animals while in transit by railroad or other means of transportation from one State or Territory or the District of Columbia into or through another State or Territory or the District of Columbia . . .

Be it enacted by the Senate and House of Representatives of the United States of America in Congress assembled, That no railroad, express company, car company, common carrier other than by water, or the receive, trustee, or lessee of any of them, whose road forms any part of a line of road over which cattle, sheep, swine, or other animals shall be conveyed from one State or Territory or the District of Columbia into or through another State or Territory or the District of Columbia, or the owners or masters of steam, sailing, or other vessels carrying or transporting cattle, sheep, swine, or other animals from one State or Territory or the District of Columbia into or through another State or Territory of the District of Columbia, shall confine the same in cars, boats, or vessels of any description for a period longer than twenty-eight consecutive hours without unloading the same in a humane manner, into properly equipped pens for rest, water, and feeding, for a period of at least five consecutive hours, unless prevented by storm or by other accidental or unavoidable causes which can not be anticipated or avoided by the exercise of due diligence and foresight: *Provided,* That upon the written request of the owner or person in custody of that particular shipment, which written request shall be separate and apart from any printed bill of lading, or other railroad form, the time of confinement may be extended to thirty-six hours. In estimating such confinement, the time consumed in loading and unloading shall not be considered, but the time during which the animals have been confined without such rest or food or water on connecting roads shall be included, it being the intent of this act to prohibit their continuous confinement beyond the period of twenty-eight hours, except upon the contingencies hereinbefore stated: *Provided,* That it shall not be required that sheep be unloaded in the nighttime, but where the time expires in the nighttime in case of sheep the same may continue in transit to a suitable place for unloading, subject to the aforesaid limitation of thirty-six hours.

SEC. 2. That animals so unloaded shall be properly fed and watered during such rest either by the owner or person having the custody thereof, or in case of his default in so doing, then by the railroad, express company, car company, common carrier other than by water, or the receiver, trustee, or lessee of any of them, or by the owners or masters of boats or vessels transporting the same, at the reasonable expense of the owner or person in custody thereof, and such railroad, express company, car company, common carrier other than by water, receiver, trustee, or lessee of any of them, owners or masters, shall in such case have a lien upon such animals for food, care, and custody furnished, collectible at their destination in the same manner as the transportation charges are collected, and shall not be liable for any detention of such animals, when such detention is of reasonable duration, to enable compliance with section one of this act; but nothing in this section shall be construed to prevent the owner or shipper of animals from furnishing food therefor, if he so desires.

SEC. 3. That any railroad, express company, car company, common carrier other than by water, or the receiver, trustee, or lessee of any of them, or the master or owner of any steam, sailing, or other vessel who knowingly and willfully fails to comply with the provisions of the two preceding sections shall for every such failure be liable for and forfeit and pay a penalty of not less than one hundred nor more than five hundred dollars: *Provided,* That when animals are carried in cars, boats, or other vessels in which they can and do have proper food, water, space and opportunity to rest the provisions in regard to their being unloaded shall not apply . . .

Approved, June 29, 1906.

Source: The Twenty-Eight Hour Law Annotated. Act of Congress Approved June 29, 1906, C. 3594, 34 Stat. 607. Washington, DC: U.S. Department of Agriculture, Office of the Solicitor, 1909, pp. 7–8.

DOCUMENT

49 USC, Section 80502. Transportation of Animals

(a) Confinement – (1) Except as provided in this section, a rail carrier, express carrier, or common carrier (except by air or water), a receiver, trustee, or lessee of one of those carriers, or an owner or master of a vessel transporting animals from a place in a State, the District of Columbia, or a territory or possession of the United States through or to a place in another State, the District of Columbia, or a territory or possession, may not confine animals in a vehicle or vessel for more than 28 consecutive hours without unloading the animals for feeding, water, and rest.

(2) Sheep may be confined for an additional 8 consecutive hours without being unloaded when the 28-hour period of confinement ends at night. Animals may be confined for—

(A) more than 28 hours when the animals cannot be unloaded because of accidental or unavoidable causes that could not have been anticipated or avoided when being careful; and

(B) 36 consecutive hours when the owner or person having custody of animals being transported requests, in writing and separate from a bill of lading or other rail form, that the 28-hour period be extended to 36 hours.

(3) Time spent in loading and unloading animals is not included as part of a period of confinement under this subsection.

(b) Unloading, Feeding, Watering, and Rest – Animals being transported shall be unloaded in a humane way into pens equipped for feeding, water, and rest for at least 5 consecutive hours. The owner or person having custody of the animals shall feed and water the animals. When the animals are not fed and watered by the owner or person having custody, the rail carrier, express carrier, or common carrier (except by air or water), the receiver, trustee, or lessee of one of those carriers, or the owner or master of a vessel transporting the animals—

(1) shall feed and water the animals at the reasonable expense of the owner or person having custody, except that the owner or shipper may provide food;

(2) has a lien on the animals for providing food, care, and custody that may be collected at the destination in the same way that a transportation charge is collected; and

(3) is not liable for detaining the animals for a reasonable period to comply with subsection (a) of this section.

(c) Non-application –This section does not apply when animals are transported in a vehicle or vessel in which the animals have food, water, space, and an opportunity for rest.

(d) Civil Penalty – A rail carrier, express carrier, or common carrier (except by air or water), a receiver, trustee, or lessee of one of those carriers, or an owner or master of a vessel that knowingly and willfully violates this section is liable to the United States Government for a civil penalty of at least $100 but not more than $500 for each violation. On learning of a violation, the Attorney General shall bring a civil action to collect the penalty in the district court of the United States for the judicial district in which the violation occurred or the defendant resides or does business.

Source: "49 U.S. Code Section 80502—Transportation of Animals." *Legal Information Institute*. Cornell University Law School, accessed December 10, 2014. http://www.law.cornell.edu/uscode/text/49/80502.

ANALYSIS

The nation's first federal protection law in regard to animals, most commonly referred to as the Twenty-Eight Hour Law, was passed by Congress on March 3, 1873, and repealed and supplanted on June 29, 1906. It states that animals being transported domestically (at the time of its passage, this referred to trains and barges transporting livestock to stockyards) must be given a five-hour break every 28 hours of transport. This break included unloading the animals and allowing them to exercise, feeding them, providing them with water, and letting them rest. This was the first major act by Congress to address animal welfare concerns. The law is also referred to as the Cruelty to Animals Act, the Live Stock Transportation Act, and the Food and Rest Law.

There are several exceptions to the law, which were added years after its enactment. Sheep can be kept in confinement longer if it is nighttime when the 28-hour period ends. Animals also can be kept penned for longer periods if there is an unforeseen problem and unloading is not possible. An example of this is a storm or other natural disaster that is out of the control of the carrier. The animals can also be kept longer if that is acceptable to the owner. Finally, the law does not apply to birds, according to the U.S. Department of Agriculture. Moreover, the law does not apply when the vehicle that the animals are traveling in includes food, water, space to move around, and an opportunity for rest.

In 1994, the Twenty-Eight Hour Law was amended to include "vehicles and vessels," and in September 2006, the Department of Agriculture agreed that "vehicles" could apply to trucks. Previously, trucks had not been covered by the law. However, animal rights activists say that truck drivers rarely adhere to this rule and it is rarely enforced.

From a legal standpoint, there are liabilities attached to this law if someone is found in violation of one or more of its mandates. There is a civil penalty of at least $100 but not more than $500 for each violation. The attorney general can also bring a civil action to the district courts in order to collect the penalty if a payment is not made.

The Twenty-Eight Hour Law has some controversies associated with it. At the time of the law's original passage, there was not much improvement in the treatment of the animals. The law was not often enforced, and railroad companies eventually ignored it completely. For many years after the law was approved, animals continued to be kept in rail cars or other tight confinement for very long periods of time. As a result, many died in transit or were maimed. Real enforcement of the law by the Department of Agriculture, the federal agency authorized under its provisions, did not begin until the early 1900s.

The continued exclusion of birds from the law is another point of controversy. This means that chickens, which make up more than 90 percent of the animals farmed for food in the United States, are not subject to the law. Animal rights activists feel that chickens should be treated as humanely as possible and should be included in the law. They also feel that trucks need to be inspected more frequently to ensure that they are in appropriate condition for the transportation of these animals.

The humane treatment of pigs is a top priority of the pork industry as well. Top concerns include reducing stress levels, making sure that weather conditions are taken into consideration when animal transportation is taking place (not too hot in the summer, not too cold in the winter), and that proper cleanliness is adhered to since these animals are being transported and then inspected to ensure that they are safe for human consumption. Members of the pork industry, however, have expressed some concerns with the Twenty-Eight Hour Law. In particular, they have cited problems with biosecurity—protecting animals from infectious agents—at sites where pigs are frequently unloaded and loaded to comply with the law.

The Twenty-Eight Hour Law was introduced into law in an effort to ensure that animals are treated as decently and humanely as possible. Throughout the years, it has had its share of critics and controversies, but it is generally acknowledged to have helped improve conditions for livestock animals.

FURTHER READING

"Farmed Animals and the Law." Animal Legal Defense Fund, accessed December 10, 2014. http://aldf.org/resources/advocating-for-animals/farmed-animals-and-the-law/.

"Treatment of Farm Animals." American Humane Association, accessed December 10, 2014. http://www.americanhumane.org/about-us/who-we-are/history/treatment-of-farm-animals.html.

"Twenty-Eight-Hour Law." National Pork Producers Council, accessed December 10, 2014. http://www.nppc.org/issues/animal-health-safety/28-hour-law/.

"Twenty-Eight Hour Law." U.S. Department of Agriculture, National Agricultural Library, accessed December 10, 2014. http://awic.nal.usda.gov/government-and-professional-resources/federal-laws/twenty-eight-hour-law.

"NO PERSON SHALL KILL ANY OTTER, MINK, MARTEN, SABLE, OR FUR SEAL, OR OTHER FUR-BEARING ANIMAL WITHIN THE LIMITS OF ALASKA TERRITORY"

- **Document:** Proclamation 287—President Benjamin Harrison's "Prohibition of Hunting Fur-Bearing Animals in Alaska and Bering Sea."
- **Date:** March 21, 1889.
- **Where:** Washington, D.C.
- **Significance:** The president's proclamation expressed concern for the well-being of seals, whose widespread slaughter in the Bering Sea in the nineteenth century for their valuable furs caused some to believe that they might be completely exterminated without the implementation of federal conservation measures.

DOCUMENT

The following provisions of the laws of the United States are hereby published for the information of all concerned:

Section 1956, Revised Statutes, chapter 3, Title XXIII, enacts that—

No person shall kill any otter, mink, marten, sable, or fur seal, or other fur-bearing animal within the limits of Alaska Territory or in the waters thereof; and every person guilty thereof shall for each offense be fined not less than $200 nor more than $1,000, or imprisoned not more than six months, or both; and all vessels, their tackle, apparel, furniture, and cargo, found engaged in violation of this section shall be forfeited; but the Secretary of the Treasury shall have power to authorize the killing of any such mink, marten, sable, or other fur-bearing animal, except fur seals, under such regulations as he may prescribe; and it shall be the duty of the Secretary to prevent the killing of any fur seal and to provide for the execution of the provisions of this section until it is otherwise provided by law, nor shall he grant any special privileges under this section.

Section 3 of the act entitled "An act to provide for the protection of the salmon fisheries of Alaska," approved March 2, 1889, provides that—

SEC. 3. That section 1956 of the Revised Statutes of the United States is hereby declared to include and apply to all the dominion of the United States in the waters of Bering Sea, and it shall be the duty of the President at a timely season in each year to issue his proclamation, and cause the same to be published for one month in at least one newspaper (if any such there be) published at each United States port of entry on the Pacific coast, warning all persons against entering such waters for the purpose of violating the provisions of said section, and he shall also cause one or more vessels of the United States to diligently cruise said waters and arrest all persons and seize all vessels found to be or to have been engaged in any violation of the laws of the United States therein.

Now, therefore, I, Benjamin Harrison, President of the United States, pursuant to the above-recited statutes, hereby warn all persons against entering the waters of Bering Sea within the dominion of the United States for the purpose of violating the provisions of said section 1956, Revised Statutes; and I hereby proclaim that all persons found to be or have been engaged in any violation of the laws of the United States in said waters will be arrested and punished as above provided, and that all vessels so employed, their tackle, apparel, furniture, and cargoes, will be seized and forfeited.

In testimony whereof I have hereunto set my hand and caused the seal of the United States to be affixed.

Done at the city of Washington, this 21st day of March, 1889, and of the Independence of the United States the one hundred and thirteenth.

BENJ. HARRISON
By the President:
JAMES G. BLAINE,
Secretary of State.

Source: Harrison, Benjamin. "Proclamation 287—Prohibition of Hunting Fur-Bearing Animals in Alaska and Bering Sea," March 21, 1889. Online by Gerhard Peters and John T. Woolley, *The American Presidency Project.* http://www.presidency.ucsb.edu/ws/?pid=71168.

ANALYSIS

During the late nineteenth century, sealskin coats and muffs were extremely popular among American and European women. The fashion trend, however, sparked a diplomatic incident between the United States, Great Britain, and the British dominion of Canada. Eager to meet demand for sealskins, seal hunters began killing seals—both male and female—in the waters of the Bering Sea near the U.S.-owned Alaska Territory. Some viewed the slaughter as so malicious and widespread that the seal population was being threatened with extermination. According to Thomas A. Bailey in *A Diplomatic History of the American People*, "Swimming [seal] females cannot be distinguished from males, and the death of a female ordinarily meant the loss of a nursing pup on the land, and an unborn pup in the seal. Since about half of the animals shot in the water were not recovered, every skin obtained in the open sea represented the death of approximately four seals." The number of seal herds decreased as the number of poaching boats increased. As supplies dwindled and demand rose, the price of the sealskins increased even more, triggering even more intensive hunting.

This seal-poaching activity led to the United States seizing Canadian schooners. The Canadians claimed that the United States did not have jurisdiction in the open seas, beyond the three-mile limit that was established in 1794 (at that time, even the most advanced artillery could not hit targets more than three miles distant, so the three-mile limit was a tacit acknowledgement of the limitations of coastal armaments). The United States claimed that the destruction of seals was a corruption of public morals and sought exclusive jurisdiction with regard to the sealing industry in that part of the Bering Sea. Neither President Benjamin Harrison nor Secretary of State James G. Blaine disputed the three-mile limit, but they also believed that "the law of the sea is not lawlessness."

On March 21, 1889, President Harrison issued Proclamation 287, which warned "all persons against entering the waters of Bering Sea within the dominion of the United States for the purpose" of killing "any otter, mink, marten, sable, or fur seal, or other fur-bearing animal...." Despite the president's proclamation, the British government continued its dispute, and it even sent warships to the Bering Sea to protect Canadian sealing ships against threats from American military vessels.

Harrison's concern for the well-being of the seals (and the economic well-being of American sealskin traders) was clear. But British officials continued to dispute the legitimacy of his proclamation, and the two governments finally agreed to arbitration by third parties. International arbiters in Paris ruled in favor of the British (and their Canadian subjects) on August 15, 1893. The tribunal also directed the U.S. government to pay more than $400,000 in compensation to various Canadian plaintiffs for unlawful seizures of their property. The *Report of the Benjamin Harrison Memorial Commission* subsequently adopted a philosophical stance toward this setback. It stated that "the United States adopted an untenable position, from which she was at last obliged to retire ... [but she] obtained a primary objective, namely the protection of the fur seals."

FURTHER READING

Morris, Richard B., ed. *Encyclopedia of American History*. 5th ed. New York: Harper and Row, 1953.

Newsom, David D. "Why the Three-Mile Limit Sank." *Christian Science Monitor*, January 26, 1989.

Roberts, Callum. *The Unnatural History of the Sea*. Washington, DC: Shearwater, 2007.

Sievers, Harry J. *Benjamin Harrison: Hoosier President*. Indianapolis, IN: Bobbs-Merrill, 1952.

Thompson, John Herd, and Stephen J. Randall. *Canada and the United States: Ambivalent Allies*. 4th ed. Athens: University of Georgia Press, 2008.

"WHEN I TOLD HIM THAT EATING FLESH IS NOT NECESSARY, BUT IS ONLY A LUXURY, HE AGREED"

- **Document:** "The First Step," an essay by Russian philosopher and writer Leo Tolstoy.
- **Date:** 1892.
- **Where:** Russia.
- **Significance:** In this essay, written seven years after he became a vegetarian, Tolstoy describes in graphic detail his experiences visiting a slaughterhouse and provides moral and health reasons for humans to refrain from killing animals for food.

DOCUMENT

Fasting is an indispensable condition of a good life; but in fasting, as in self-control in general, the question arises, with what shall we begin—how to fast, how often to eat, what to eat, what to avoid eating?

Fasting! And even an analysis of how to fast, and where to begin! The notion seems ridiculous and wild to the majority of men.

I remember how, with pride at his originality, an Evangelical preacher, who was attacking monastic asceticism, once said to me, "Ours is not a Christianity of fasting and privations, but of beefsteaks." Christianity, or virtue in general—and beefsteaks!

During a long period of darkness and lack of all guidance, Pagan or Christian, so many wild, immoral ideas have made their way into our life (especially into that lower region of the first steps toward a good life—our relation to food, to which no one paid any attention), that it is difficult for us even to understand the audacity and senselessness of upholding, in our days, Christianity or virtue with beefsteaks.

We are not horrified by this association, solely because a strange thing has befallen us. We look and see not: listen and hear not. There is no bad odor, no sound, no monstrosity, to which man cannot become so accustomed that he ceases to remark what would strike a man unaccustomed to it. Precisely so it is in the moral region. Christianity and morality with beefsteaks!

A few days ago I visited the slaughter house in our town of Toula. It is built on the new and improved system practised in large towns, with a view to causing the animals as little suffering as possible. It was on a Friday, two days before Trinity Sunday. There were many cattle there. . . .

Long before this . . . I had wished to visit a slaughter house, in order to see with my own eyes the reality of the question raised when vegetarianism is discussed. But at first I felt ashamed to do so, as one is always ashamed of going to look at suffering which one knows is about to take place, but which one cannot avert; and so I kept putting off my visit.

But a little while ago I met on the road a butcher returning to Toula after a visit to his home. He is not yet an experienced butcher, and his duty is to stab with a knife. I asked him whether he did not feel sorry for the animals that he killed. He gave me the usual answer: "Why should I feel sorry? It is necessary." But when I told him that eating flesh is not necessary, but is only a luxury, he agreed; and then he admitted that he was sorry for the animals.

"But what can I do? I must earn my bread," he said. "At first I was *afraid* to kill. My father, he never even killed a chicken in all his life." The majority of Russians cannot kill; they feel pity, and express the feeling by the word "fear." This man had also been "afraid," but he was so no longer. He told me that most of the work was done on Fridays, when it continues until the evening.

Not long ago I also had a talk with a retired soldier, a butcher, and he, too, was surprised at my assertion that it was a pity to kill, and said the usual things about its being ordained; but afterwards he agreed with me: "Especially when they are quiet, tame cattle. They come, poor things! trusting you. It is very pitiful."

This is dreadful! Not the suffering and death of the animals, but that man suppresses in himself, unnecessarily, the highest spiritual capacity—that of sympathy and pity toward living creatures like himself—and by violating his own feelings becomes cruel. And how deeply seated in the human heart is the injunction not to take life!

Once, when walking from Moscow, I was offered a lift by some carters who were going from Serpouh to a neighboring forest to fetch wood. It was the Thursday before Easter. I was seated in the first cart, with a strong, red, coarse carman, who evidently drank. On entering a village we saw a well-fed, naked, pink pig being dragged out of the first yard to be slaughtered. It squealed in a dreadful voice, resembling the shriek of a man. Just as we were passing they began to kill it. A man gashed its throat with a knife. The pig squealed still more loudly and piercingly, broke away from the men, and ran off covered with blood. Being near-sighted I did not see all the details. I saw only the human-looking pink body of the pig and heard its desperate squeal; but the carter saw all the details and watched closely. They caught the pig, knocked it down, and finished cutting its throat. When its squeals ceased the carter sighed heavily. "Do men really not have to answer for such things?" he said.

So strong is man's aversion to all killing. But by example, by encouraging greediness, by the assertion that God has allowed it, and, above all, by habit, people entirely lose this natural feeling.

On Friday I decided to go to Toula, and, meeting a meek, kind acquaintance of mine, I invited him to accompany me.

"Yes, I have heard that the arrangements are good, and have been wishing to go and see it; but if they are slaughtering I will not go in."

"Why not? That's just what I want to see! If we eat flesh it must be killed."

"No, no, I cannot!"

It is worth remarking that this man is a sportsman and himself kills animals and birds.

So we went to the slaughter house. Even at the entrance one noticed the heavy, disgusting, fetid smell, as of carpenter's glue, or paint on glue. The nearer we approached, the stronger became the smell. The building is of red brick, very large, with vaults and high chimneys. We entered the gates. To the right was a spacious enclosed yard, three-quarters of an acre in extent—twice a week cattle are driven in here for sale—and adjoining this enclosure was the porter's lodge. To the left were the chambers, as they are called—i.e., rooms with arched entrances, sloping asphalt floors, and contrivances for moving and hanging up the carcasses. On a bench against the wall of the porter's lodge were seated half a dozen butchers, in aprons covered with blood, their tucked-up sleeves disclosing their muscular arms also besmeared with blood. They had finished their work half an hour before, so that day we could only see the empty chambers. Though these chambers were open on both sides, there was an oppressive smell of warm blood; the floor was brown and shining, with congealed black blood in the cavities.

One of the butchers described the process of slaughtering, and showed us the place where it was done. I did not quite understand him, and formed a wrong, but very horrible, idea of the way the animals are slaughtered; and I fancied that, as is often the case, the reality would very likely produce upon me a weaker impression than the imagination. But in this I was mistaken.

The next time I visited the slaughter house I went in good time. It was the Friday before Trinity—a warm day in June. The smell of glue and blood was even stronger and more penetrating than on my first visit. The work was at its height. The duty yard was full of cattle, and animals had been driven into all the enclosures beside the chambers.

In the street, before the entrance, stood carts to which oxen, calves, and cows were tied. Other carts drawn by good horses and filled with live calves, whose heads hung down and swayed about, drew up and were unloaded; and similar carts containing the carcasses of oxen, with trembling legs sticking out, with heads and bright red lungs and brown livers, drove away from the slaughter house. The dealers themselves, in their long coats, with their whips and knouts in their hands, were walking about the yard, either marking with tar cattle belonging to the same owner, or bargaining, or else guiding oxen and bulls from the great yard into the enclosures which lead into the chambers. These men were evidently all preoccupied with money matters and calculations, and any thought as to whether it was right or wrong to kill these animals was as far from their minds as were questions about the chemical composition of the blood that covered the floor of the chambers.

No butchers were to be seen in the yard; they were all in the chambers at work. That day about a hundred head of cattle were slaughtered. I was on the point of entering one of the chambers, but stopped short at the door. I stopped both because the chamber was crowded with carcasses which were being moved about, and also because blood was flowing on the floor and dripping from above. All the butchers present were besmeared with blood, and had I entered I, too, should certainly have been covered with it. One suspended carcass was being taken down, another was being moved toward the door, a third, a slaughtered ox, was lying with its white legs raised, while a butcher with strong hand was ripping up its tight-stretched hide.

Through the door opposite the one at which I was standing, a big, red, well-fed ox was led in. Two men were dragging it, and hardly had it entered when I saw a butcher raise a knife above its neck and stab it. The ox, as if all four legs had suddenly given way, fell heavily upon its belly, immediately turned over on one side, and began to work its legs and all its hind-quarters. Another butcher at once threw himself upon the ox from the side opposite to the twitching legs, caught its horns and twisted its head down to the ground, while another butcher cut its throat with a knife. From beneath the head there flowed a stream of blackish-red blood, which a besmeared boy caught in a tin basin. All the time this was going on the ox kept incessantly twitching its head as if trying to get up, and waved its four legs in the air. The basin was quickly filling, but the ox still lived, and, its stomach heaving heavily, both hind and fore legs worked so violently that the butchers held aloof. When one basin was full, the boy carried it away on his head to the albumen factory, while another boy placed a fresh basin, which also soon began to fill up. But still the ox heaved its body and worked its hind legs.

When the blood ceased to flow the butcher raised the animal's head and began to skin it. The ox continued to writhe. The head, stripped of its skin, showed red with white veins, and kept the position given it by the butcher; on both sides hung the skin. Still the animal did not cease to writhe. Than another butcher caught hold of one of the legs, broke it, and cut it off. In the remaining legs and the stomach the convulsions still continued. The other legs were cut off and thrown aside, together with those of other oxen belonging to the same owner. Then the carcass was dragged to the hoist and hung up, and the convulsions were over.

Thus I looked on from the door at the second, third, fourth ox. It was the same with each: the same cutting off of the head with bitten tongue, and the same convulsed members. The only difference was that the butcher did not always strike at once so as to cause the animal's fall. Sometimes he missed his aim, whereupon the ox leaped up, bellowed, and, covered with blood, tried to escape. But then his head was pulled under a bar, struck a second time, and he fell.

I afterwards entered by the door at which the oxen were led in. Here I saw the same thing, only nearer, and therefore more plainly. But chiefly I saw here, what I had not seen before, how the oxen were forced to enter this door. Each time an ox was seized in the enclosure and pulled forward by a rope tied to its horns, the animal, smelling blood, refused to advance, and sometimes bellowed and drew back. It would have been beyond the strength of two men to drag it in by force, so one of the butchers went round each time, grasped the animal's tail and twisted it so violently that the gristle crackled, and the ox advanced.

When they had finished with the cattle of one owner, they brought in those of another. The first animal of his next lot was not an ox, but a bull—a fine, well-bred creature, black, with white spots on its legs, young, muscular, full of energy. He was dragged forward, but he lowered his head and resisted sturdily. Then the butcher who followed behind seized the tail, like an engine-driver grasping the handle of a whistle, twisted it, the gristle crackled, and the bull rushed forward, upsetting the men who held the rope. Then it stopped, looking sideways with its black eyes, the whites of which had filled with blood. But again the tail crackled, and the bull sprang forward and reached the required spot. The striker approached, took aim, and struck. But the blow missed the mark. The bull leaped up, shook his head, bellowed, and, covered with blood, broke free and rushed back. The men at the doorway all sprang aside: but the experienced butchers, with the dash of men inured to danger, quickly caught the rope; again the tail operation was repeated, and again the bull was in the chamber, where he was dragged under the bar, from which he did not again escape. The striker quickly took aim at the spot where the hair divides like a star, and, notwithstanding the blood, found it, struck, and the fine animal, full of life, collapsed, its head and legs writhing while it was bled and the head skinned.

"There, the cursed devil hasn't even fallen the right way!" grumbled the butcher as he cut the skin from the head.

Five minutes later the head was stuck up, red instead of black, without skin; the eyes that had shone with such splendid color five minutes before, fixed and glassy.

Afterwards I went into the compartment where small animals are slaughtered—a very large chamber with asphalt floor, and tables with backs, on which sheep and calves are killed. Here the work was already finished; in the long room, impregnated with the smell of blood, were only two butchers. One was blowing into the leg of a dead lamb and patting the swollen stomach with his hand; the other, a young fellow in an apron besmeared with blood, was smoking a bent cigarette. There was no one else in the long, dark chamber, filled with a heavy smell. After me there entered a man, apparently an ex-soldier, bringing in a young yearling ram, black with a white mark on its neck, and its legs tied. This animal he placed upon one of the tables, as if upon a bed. The old soldier greeted the butchers, with whom he was evidently acquainted, and began to ask when their master allowed them leave. The fellow with the cigarette approached with a knife, sharpened it on the edge of the table, and answered that they were free on holidays. The live ram was lying as quietly as the dead inflated one, except that it was briskly wagging its short little tail and its sides were heaving more quickly than usual. The soldier pressed down its uplifted head gently, without effort; the butcher, still continuing the conversation, grasped with his left hand the head of the ram and cut its throat. The ram quivered, and the little tail stiffened and ceased to wave. The fellow, while waiting for the blood to flow, began to relight his cigarette, which had gone out. The blood flowed and the ram began to writhe. The conversation continued without the slightest interruption. It was horribly revolting. . . .

[A]nd how about those hens and chickens which daily, in thousands of kitchens, with heads cut off and streaming with blood, comically, dreadfully, flop about, jerking their wings?

And see, a kind, refined lady will devour the carcasses of these animals with full assurance that she is doing right, at the same time asserting two contradictory propositions:

First, that she is, as her doctor assures her, so delicate that she cannot be sustained by vegetable food alone, and that for her feeble organism flesh is indispensable; and, secondly, that she is so sensitive that she is unable, not only herself to inflict suffering on animals, but even to bear the sight of suffering.

Whereas the poor lady is weak precisely because she has been taught to live upon food unnatural to man; and she cannot avoid causing suffering to animals—for she eats them.

[W]e cannot pretend that we do not know this. We are not ostriches, and cannot believe that if we refuse to look at what we do not wish to see, it will not exist. This is especially the case when what we do not wish to see is what we wish to eat. If it were really indispensable, or, if not indispensable, at least in some way useful! But it is quite unnecessary, and only serves to develop animal feelings, to excite desire, and to promote fornication and drunkenness. And this is continually being confirmed by the fact that young, kind, undepraved people—especially women and girls—without knowing how it logically follows, feel that virtue is incompatible with beefsteaks, and, as soon as they wish to be good, give up eating flesh.

What, then, do I wish to say? That in order to be moral people must cease to eat meat? Not at all.

I only wish to say that for a good life a certain order of good actions is indispensable; that if a man's aspirations toward right living be serious they will inevitably follow one definite sequence; and that in this sequence the first virtue a man will strive after will be self-control, self-restraint. And in seeking for self-control a man will inevitably follow one definite sequence, and in this sequence the first thing will be self-control in food—fasting. And in fasting, if he be really and seriously seeking to live a good life, the first thing from which he will abstain will always be the use of animal, food, because, to say nothing of the excitation of the passions caused by such food, its use is simply immoral, as it involves the performance of an act which is contrary to the moral feeling – killing; and is called forth only by greediness and the desire for tasty food.

Source: Tolstoy, Leo. "The First Step." In *Essays and Letters*. Translated by Aylmer Maude. New York: H. Frowde, 1909, pp. 82–91.

ANALYSIS

Leo Tolstoy was a Russian philosopher and writer who was best known for his authorship of two epic novels: *War and Peace* (1869) and *Anna Karenina* (1877). Tolstoy's political and social views focused on morality, nonviolence, and simplicity. These perspectives on life informed his views on humankind's treatment of animals and eventually led him to practice vegetarianism.

Tolstoy loved nature and expressed deep appreciation for the flora and fauna that inhabited the world. In a diary entry in July 1857, Tolstoy exclaimed: "I love it when you do not exult and rejoice alone in Nature, but when around you myriads of insects buzz and whirl, and beetles, clinging together, creep about, and all around you birds overflow with song." Even if insects became annoying to Tolstoy, his philosophy was "to act as to free ourselves from them without having recourse to killing them, and to be rid of them by means of cleanliness."

The concept of vegetarianism entered his life when he met with Russian-born American social reformer William Frey, who spoke positively about the benefits of vegetarianism to one's diet. It did not take long for Tolstoy to endorse vegetarianism, but the writer's embrace of vegetarianism was less related to the health benefits of not eating meat and more to the moral benefits of not taking the life an animal. Eating animal flesh, Tolstoy believed, was "simply immoral, as it involves the performance of an act which is contrary to moral feeling—killing."

Tolstoy's "The First Step" essay, which described his visit to a slaughterhouse and his observations of both the animals whose lives were being taken and the humans who were doing the killing, was an attempt to grapple with the moral dimensions of killing animals for food. He provided many graphic details of the blood and squealing and pain that he witnessed from the animals whose lives were being taken for their "flesh-meat." But he also recounted a conversation he had about killing animals with a butcher who, from Tolstoy's perspective, "suppresses in himself, unnecessarily, the highest spiritual capacity—that of sympathy and pity toward living creatures like himself—and by violating his own feelings becomes cruel. And how deeply seated in the human heart is the injunction not to take life!"

Despite Tolstoy's views on killing animals and vegetarianism in general, he held the view that each person's attitude toward eating meat was their own to make. Two of his children became vegetarians, but his wife and aunt did not. As Gregory B. Betts noted in "History of Vegetarianism: Leo Tolstoy," Tolstoy "deeply believed that an individual is accountable for themselves, and possesses infinite influence over the world. It is therefore necessary to concentrate on our own beings, and correct the hypocrisies that lie within before turning potential venom outwards."

Tolstoy even had a little fun with a sister-in-law who ate meat. As his relative sat at a table awaiting lunch, Tolstoy arranged for a live fowl to be tied near where she was sitting and an empty plate and large knife to be set nearby. Tolstoy then said to his sister-in-law, "We all know, dear, . . . how fond you are of flesh and we should like to provide you with what you wish; but the difficulty is that none of us can bring himself to slay the bird for you. Therefore, there seems to be no other way but to ask that you should do it for yourself." Reportedly, she was none too amused by his attempt at humor.

Tolstoy's private secretary, Valentin Bulgakov, wrote that "Tolstoy always declared that he was a Christian, by which he meant he had no new teaching to promulgate, his business being simply to translate the teachings of the gospels into modern speech and practice. Man, he held, though confined within the limits of the flesh, yet remains the expression of an eternal Principle. In a word, he is a son of God, and by inference all men are brothers. The natural bond between them is the bond of love, and this should extend also to all living creatures. One and the same 'soul' is common to all, and, realising this, it becomes impossible that men should either slay or hurt animals."

FURTHER READING

Betts, Gregory B. "History of Vegetarianism: Leo Tolstoy." *Lifelines*, September/October 1998. http://veg.ca/1998/09/07/history-of-vegetarianism-leo-tolstoy-author-of-war-and-peace/.

Bulgakov, Valentin. "Leo Tolstoy and Vegetarianism." *Vegetarian News*, September 1932. http://www.ivu.org/congress/wvc32/bulgakov.html.

Donovan, Josephine. "Tolstoy's Animals." *Society and Animals* 17, no. 1 (2009): 38–52. http://www.animalsandsociety.net/assets/library/863_tolstoysanimals.pdf.

Spencer, Colin. *The Heretic's Feast: A History of Vegetarianism*. Hanover, NH: University Press of New England, 1995.

Tolstoy, Leo. *Forbidden Words: On God, Alcohol, Vegetarianism, and Violence*. Edited by Simon Parke. Guildford, England: White Crow Books, 2009.

"THIS ANIMALIZING OF THE HUMAN BODY, INSTEAD OF ENSOULING AND SPIRITUALIZING IT ... KEEP[S] THE PLANE OF HUMANITY LOWER BY THIS CONSTANT DEGRADATION OF THE ANIMAL SELF"

- **Document:** Excerpt from a speech delivered by British theosophist and activist Annie Besant. It was later published as a pamphlet.
- **Date:** 1894.
- **Where:** Madras, India.
- **Significance:** Annie Besant spoke out on and wrote about a wide range of social issues, including women's rights, marriage, and birth control. She was scorned by many due to her outspoken nature and controversial beliefs, both of which were unusual for women of that era. Besant was also a fierce animal welfare advocate, as the following excerpt illustrates.

DOCUMENT

From the Theosophical standpoint there are arguments to be adduced other than those which deal with the nourishment of the body, with chemical or physiological questions, or even with its bearing on the drink traffic. ... The vegetarianism that I am going to argue about tonight is that which will be familiar to all of you as the abstinence from all those kinds of food which imply the slaying of the animal or cruelty inflicted upon the animal ... and I am going to try to show the reasons for such abstinence which may be drawn from the teachings of Theosophy. ... You will understand that in speaking I am not committing the Society. The views that I speak are drawn from the Philosophy which may or may not be held by any individual member of our union. ...

Theosophy regards man's place in the world as a link in a mighty chain ... which has its first link in manifestation in the divine life itself. ... Man ... is, at it were, the highest expression of this evolving life: he ought, therefore, also to be the most perfect expression of this continually growing manifestation of law. ... Man has a double possibility, a greater responsibility, a higher or a more degraded destiny. He has this power of choice. ... Man has the power of setting himself against law and holding his own ... for a while against it. In the long run the law will crush him. Always when he sets himself against it, the law justifies itself by the pain it inflicts: he cannot really break it. But he can cause disorder, he can cause disharmony, he can, by this will of his, refuse to follow out the highest and the best, and deliberately choose the lower and the worse road. Man, wherever he goes, should be the friend of all, the helper of all, the lover of all, expressing his nature that is love in his daily life, and bringing to every lower creature not only the control that may be used to educate, but the love also that may be used to lift that lower creature in the scale of being.

Man, Vicegerent of God

Apply then that principle of man's place in the world, vicegerent in a very real sense, ruler and monarch of the world, but with the power of being either a bad monarch or a good, and responsible to the whole of the universe for the use that he makes of the power. Take then man in relation to the lower animals from this standpoint. Clearly, if we are to look at him in this position, slaying them for his own gratification is at once placed out of court. He is not to go amongst the happy creatures of the woods, and bring there the misery of fear, of terror, of horror by carrying destruction wherever he goes: he is not to arm himself with hook and with other weapons which he is able to make, remember, only by virtue of the mind which is developed within him. Prostituting those higher powers of mind to make himself the more deadly enemy of the other sentient creatures that share the world with him, he uses the mind, that should be there to help and to train the lower, to carry fresh forms of misery and destructive energy in every direction. When you see a man go amongst, the lower animals they fly from his face, when experience has taught them what it means to meet a man. If he goes into some secluded part of the earth where human foot has rarely trodden, there he will find the animals fearless and friendly, and he can go about amongst crowds of them and they shrink not from his touch. Take the accounts you will read of a traveller who has gone into some district where man has not hitherto penetrated, and you will read how he can walk among crowds of birds and other creatures as friends. And it is only when he begins to take advantage of their confidence to strike them down, only then, by experience of what the presence of man moans to them do they learn the lesson of distrust, of fear, of flying from his presence. So that in every civilized country, wherever there is a man, in field or in wood, all living things fly at the sound of his footstep, and he is not the friend of every creature but the one who brings terror and alarm, and they fly from his presence. And yet there have been some men from whom there has rayed out so strongly the spirit of love, that the living things of field and forest crowded around them wherever they went: men like St. Francis of Assisi, of whom it was told that as he walked the woods the birds would fly to him and perch on his body, so strongly did they feel the sense of love that was around him as a halo wherever he trod. So in India you will find man after man in whom this same spirit of love and compassion is seen, and in the woods and the jungle, on the mountain and in the desert, these men may go wherever they will, and even the wild beasts will not touch them. I could tell you stories of Yogis there, harmless in every act of thought and life, who will go through jungles where tigers are crouching, and the tiger will sometimes come and lie at their feet and lick their feet, harmless as a kitten might be in the face of the spirit of love. And though, in truth, it would now take many a century to undo the evil of a bloodstained past, still the undoing is possible, the friendliness might be made, and each man, each woman, who in life is friendly to the lower creatures, is adding his quota to the love in the world, which ultimately will subdue all things to itself.

A Terror-Laden Atmosphere

Pass from that duty of man, as monarch of the world to the next point which in Theosophical teachings forbids the slaughter of living things. ... The physical world is interpenetrated and surrounded by a subtler world of matter that we speak of as "astral"; that in that subtle matter ... *forces* especially have their home. ... The thought world, full of the thoughts of men, sends down these potent energies into the astral world: there they take image, which reacts upon the physical. It is this which is so often felt by the "sensitive. ..." Think of astral matter for a moment from the standpoint of Theosophy as inter-penetrating and surrounding our world; then carry your thoughts to a slaughter-house. Try and estimate, if you can, by imagination—if you have not been unfortunate enough to see it in reality—something of the passions and emotions which there are aroused, not for the moment in the man who is slaying—I will deal with him presently—but in the animals that are being slain! Notice the terror that strikes them as they come within scent of the blood! See the misery, and the fright, and the horror which they struggle to get away even from the turning, down which they are being driven! Follow them, if you have the courage to do it, right into the slaughter-house, and see them as they are being slain, and then let your imagination go a step further, or, if you have the subtle power of sensing astral vibrations, look, and remember what you see: images of terror, of fear, of horror, as the life is suddenly wrenched out of the body, and the animal soul with its terror, with its horror, goes out into the astral world to remain there for a considerable period before it breaks up and perishes. And remember that wherever this slaughtering of animals goes on the material world, that these react on the minds of men, and that anyone who is sensitive, coming into the neighbourhood of such a place sees and feels these terrible vibrations, suffers under them, and knows whence they are.

Now, suppose, that you went to Chicago—I take that illustration, because it is one where I myself particularly noticed this effect. Chicago, as you know, is preeminently a slaughtering city, it is the city where they have, I suppose, the most elaborate arrangements for the killing of animals which human ingenuity has yet devised, where it is done by machinery very largely, and where myriads upon myriads of creatures are slaughtered week by week. No one who is the least sensitive, far less anyone who by training has had some of these inner senses awakened, can pass not only within Chicago, but within miles of Chicago, without being conscious of a profound sense of depression that comes down upon him, a sense of shrinking, as it were, from pollution, a sense of horror which at first is not clearly recognised not is its source at once seen. Now, here I am speaking only of what I know. And as it happened, when I went to Chicago, I was reading, as I am in the habit of doing, in the train, and I did not even know that I was coming within a considerable distance of the town—for the place is so enormous that it stretches far farther than a stranger would imagine, and it takes far longer to reach the centre than one has any notion of—and I was conscious suddenly as I sat there in the train of this sense of oppression that came upon me; I did not recognize it at first, my thoughts were anywhere but in the city; but it made itself so strongly felt that I found very soon what the reason of it was, and then I remembered that I was coming into the great slaughter-house of the United States. It was as though one came within a physical pall of blackness and of misery—this psychic or astral result being, as it were; the covering that over-spreads that mighty town. And I say to you that for those who know anything of the invisible world, this constant slaughtering of animals takes on a very serious aspect apart from all other questions which may be brought to elucidate it; for this continual throwing down of these magnetic influences of fear, of horror, and of anger, passion, and revenge, work on the people amongst whom they play, and tends to degrade, tends to pollute. It is not only the body that is soiled by the flesh of animals, it is the subtler forces of the man that also come within this area of population, and much, very much of the coarser side of city life, of the coarser side of the life of those who are concerned in the slaughtering, comes directly from this reflection from the astral world, and the whole of this terrible protest comes from the escaped lives of the slaughtered beasts.

The Fatal Slaughter-House "Twist"

But I said that there was this apart from the men who slaughter. But can we rightly leave them out of consideration when we're dealing with the question of flesh-eating? It is clear that neither you nor I can eat flesh unless we either slay it for ourselves or get somebody else to do it for us; therefore, we are directly responsible for any amount of deterioration in the moral character of the man on whom we throw that work of slaughtering, because we are too delicate and refined to perform it for ourselves. Now take the class of the slaughterer. I suppose no one will contend that it is in a form of business which he himself would very gladly take up, if he be either an educated or refined man or woman—for I do not know why women should be left out of this, as they figure largely amongst meat-eaters. I presume that very few men and very few women would be willing to go and catch hold either of sheep or of oxen and themselves slaughter the creature in order that they may eat. They admit that if it has on the person who does it a certain coarsening influence. So much is that recognized by law that certainly in the United States—I don't know if the law is the same here—no butcher is permitted to sit on a jury in a murder trial; he is not permitted to take part in such a trial, simply because his continual contact with slaughter is held to somewhat blunt his susceptibilities in that connection, so that all through the States no man of the trade of butcher is permitted to take part as juryman in a trial for murder. This is very clear and definite: that if you go to a city like Chicago, and if you take the class of slaughtermen there, you will find that the number of crimes of violence in that class is greater than among any other class of the community; that the use of the knife is far more common, and this has been observed—I am speaking now of facts that I gathered at Chicago—it has been observed that this use of the knife is marked by one peculiar feature, namely, that the blow struck in anger by them, these trained slaughtermen, is almost invariably fatal, because instinctively they give it the peculiar twist of hand to which they are continually habituated in their daily killing of the lower animals. Now that in Chicago is recognized as fact, but it does not seem to imply in the minds of the people any moral responsibility for their share in the evolution of this very uncomfortable type of human being. And so with the whole question of slaughtering in this city and anywhere else. Has it ever struck you as a rule in ethics that you have no right to put upon another human being for your own advantage a duty that you are not prepared to discharge yourself? It is all very well for some fine and delicate and refined lady to be proud of her delicacy and refinement, to shrink from any notion, say, of going to tea with a butcher, to certainly strongly object to the notion of his coming into her drawing-room, to shrink altogether from the idea of consorting with such persons, "so coarse, you know, and so unpleasant." Quite go, but why? In order that she may eat meat, in order that she may gratify her appetite; and she puts on another the coarsening and the brutalizing which she escapes from herself in her refinement, while she takes for the gratification of her own appetite the fruits of the brutalization of her fellow-man. Now I venture to submit that if people want to eat meat, they should kill the animals for themselves, that they have no right to degrade other people by work of that sort. Nor should they say that if they did not do it the slaughter would still go on. That is no sort of way of evading a moral responsibility. Every person who eats meat takes a share in that degradation of their fellow-men; on him and on her personally lies the share, in personally lies the responsibility. And if this world be a world of law, if it be true that law obtains not only in the physical, but also in the mental and the moral and the spiritual world, then every person who has share in the crime has a share also in the penalty that follows on the heels of the crime, and so in his own nature is brutalized by the brutality that he makes necessary by his share in the results that come therefrom.

We Rise and Fall Together

There is another point for which people are responsible in addition to their responsibility to the slaughtering class. They are responsible for all the pain that grows out of meat-eating, and which is necessitated by the use of sentient animals as food; not only the horrors of the slaughter-house, but also all the preliminary horrors of the railway traffic, of the steamboat and ship traffic; all the starvation and the thirst, and the prolonged misery of fear which these unhappy creatures have to pass through for the gratification of the appetite of man. If you want to know something of it, go down and see the creatures brought off some of the ships, and you will see the fear, you will see the pain which is marked on the faces of these our lower fellow-creatures. I say you have no right to inflict it, that you have no right to be party to it, that all that pain acts as a record against humanity and slackens and retards the whole of human growth; for you cannot separate yourself while you are trampling others down. Those that you trample on retard your own progress. The misery that you cause is as it were mire that clings round your feet when you would ascend; for we have to rise together or to fall together, and all the misery we inflict on sentient beings slackens our human evolution and makes the progress of humanity slower towards the ideal that it is seeking to realize.

Looking at the thing from this broad standpoint, we get away from all the smaller arguments on which discussion arises, away from all questions as to whether meat nourishes or not, whether it helps the human body or not; and we take our ground fundamentally on this solid position; that nothing that retards the growth and the progress of the world, nothing that adds to its suffering, nothing that increases its misery, nothing that prevents its evolution towards higher forms of life, can possibly be justified, even if it could be shown that the physical vigour of man's body were increased by passing along that road. So that we get a sound standpoint from which to argue. Then you may go on, if you will, to argue that as a matter of fact the physical vigour does not need these articles of food; but I would rather rake my solid stand on a higher ground; that is, on the evolution of the higher nature everywhere, and the harmony which it is man's duty to increase, and finally to render perfect in the world.

Polluting the Life-Stream

You may notice on all these points I have been arguing outside as it were, the individual meat-eater; I am not, therefore, urging abstinence for the sake of personal development, for the sake of personal growth. I have been putting it on the higher basis of duty, of compassion, of altruism, on those essential qualities which mark the higher evolution of the world. But we have a right also to turn to the individual and see the bearing on himself, on his body, on his mind, on his spiritual growth, which this question of meat-eating or abstinence from meat may have. And it has a very real bearing. It is perfectly true, as regards the body, when you look upon it as an instrument of the mind, when you look on it as that which is to develop into an instrument of the Spirit, it is perfectly true that it is a matter of very great importance what particular kind of nourishment you contribute to the body that you have in charge. And here Theosophy comes in and says: This body that the Soul is inhabiting is an exceedingly fleeting thing; it is made up of minute particles, each one of which is a life, and these lives are continually changing, continually passing from body to body and affecting, as they fall on all these bodies, affecting them either for good or for evil. Science, remember, is also coming to recognize that as truth. Science studying disease has found that disease is constantly propagated by these minute organisms that it speaks of as microbes; it has not yet recognized that the whole body is made of minute living creatures that come and go with every hour of our life, that build our body today, the body of someone else tomorrow, passing away and coming continually, a constant interchange going on between these bodies of men, women, animals, children, and so on. Now, suppose for a moment you look on the body from that standpoint, first again will come your responsibility to your fellows. These tiny lives that are building your body take on themselves the stamp that you put upon them while they are yours; you feed them and nourish them and that affects their characteristics; you give them either pure or foul food; you either poison them or you render them healthy; and as you feed them they pass away from you, and carry from you to the bodies of others these characteristics that they have gained while living in your charge; so that what a man eats, what a man drinks is not a matter for himself alone but for the whole community of which that man is a part and any man who in his drinking is not careful to be pure, restrained, and temperate, becomes a focus of physical evil in the place where he is, and tends to poison his brothers-men and to make their vitality less pure than it ought to be. Here both in flesh and in drink the great responsibility comes in. It is clear that the nature of the food very largely affects the physical organism, and gives, as it were, a physical apparatus for the throwing out of one quality or another. Now the qualities reside in the Soul, but they are manifested through the brain and the body; therefore the materials of which the brain and the body are made up is a matter of very considerable importance, for just as the light that shines through a coloured window comes through it coloured and no longer white, so do the qualities of the Soul working through the brain and the body take up something of the qualities of brain and body, and manifest their condition by the characteristics of that brain and that body alike.

As We Eat So We Are

Now, suppose that you look for a moment at some of the lower animals in connection with their food, you find that according to their food so are the characteristics that they show. Nay, if you even take a dog, you find that you can make that dog either gentle or fierce according to the nature of the food with which you supply him. Now, while it is perfectly true that the animal is much more under the control of the physical body than the man; while it is quite true that the animal is more plastic to these outer influences than the man with the stronger self determining will; still it is also true that, inasmuch as the man has a body and can only work through that body in the material world, he makes his task either harder or easier as regards the qualities of the Soul according to the nature of the physical apparatus which that Soul is forced to use in its manifestations in the outer world. And if in feeding the body he feeds these tiny lives, which make it up, with food which brings into action with them the passions of the lower animals and their lower nature, then he is making a grosser and a more animal body, more apt to respond to animal impulses and less apt to respond to the higher impulses of the mind. For when he uses in the building of his own body these tiny lives from the body of the lower animals, he is there giving his Soul to work with a body that vibrates most easily under animal impulses. Is it not hard enough to grow pure in thought? Is it not hard enough to control the passions of the body? Is it not hard enough to be temperate in food, drink, and in all the appetites that belong to the physical frame? Has not the Soul already a difficult task enough, that we should make its task harder by polluting the instrument through which it has to work, and by giving it material that will not answer to its subtler impulses, but that answers readily to all the lower passions of the animal nature to which the Soul is bound? And then, when you remember that you pass it on, that as you eat meat and so strengthen these animal and lower passions you are printing on the molecules of your own body the power of thus responding, you ought surely to train and purify your body, and not continually help it, as it were, to remain so responsive to these vibrations belonging to the animal kingdom. And as you do you send them out abroad as your ambassadors to your fellow-men, you make their task harder as well as your own by training these tiny lives for evil and not for good;

and so the task of every man who is struggling upwards is also rendered harder by this increase of the molecules that vibrate to the lower passions. And while that is true in the most terrible degree of the taking of alcohol—which acts as an active poison, going forth from everyone who takes it—it is also true of this animalizing of the human body, instead of ensouling and spiritualizing it, and we are keeping the plane of humanity lower by this constant degradation of the animal self.

The Evolution of the World Depends upon Us

When you come then to think of the evolution of the Soul in yourself, what is your object in life? Why are you here? For what are you living? There is only one thing which justifies the life of man, only one thing that answers to all that is noblest in him and gives him a sense of satisfaction and of duty done; and that is when he makes his life a constant offering for the helping of the world, and when every part of his life is so regulated that the world may be the better for his presence in it and not the worse. In Soul, in thought, in body, a man is responsible for the use he makes of his life. We cannot tear ourselves apart from our brothers; we ought not to wish to do it, even if we could, for this world is climbing upwards slowly towards a divine ideal, and every Soul that recognizes the fact should lend its own hand to the raising of the world. You and I are either helping the world upward or pulling the world downward; with every day of our life we are either giving it a force for the upward climbing or we are clogs on that upward growth; and every true Soul desires to be a help and not a hindrance, to be a blessing and not a curse, to be amongst the raisers of the world and not amongst those who degrade it. Every true Soul wishes it, whether or not it is strong enough always to carry the wish into act. And shall we not at least put before us as an ideal that sublime conception of helping, and blame ourselves whenever we fall below it, whether in the feeding of the body or in the training of the mind? For it seems to me, looking at man in the light of Theosophy, that all that makes his life worth having is this cooperation with the divine life in nature, which is gradually moulding the world into a nobler image, and making it grow ever nearer and nearer to a perfect ideal. If we could make men and women see it, if only we could make them respond to the thought of such power on their own side, if only they would recognize this divine strength that is in them to help in the making of a world, to share in the evolution of a universe, if they could under-stand that this world is theirs, placed as it mere in their hands and in their charge, the growth of the world depends upon them, that if they will not help, the divine life itself cannot find instrument whereby to work on this material plane. If they would realize that, then, with very many falls, their faces would be set upward; with very many mistakes and blunders and weaknesses, still they would be turned in the right direction, and they would be gazing at the ideal that they long to realize. And so in mind and in body, in their work in the inner world of force as in the outer world of action, the one ruling idea would be: Will this act and thought of mine make the world better or worse, will it raise it or lower it, will it help my fellow-men or hinder them? Shall the power of my Soul be used to raise or to lower? If that thought were the central force of life, even though forgetting it or failing, the Soul would again take up the effort and refuse to yield because it had so often failed. If we could all do that and think that, and win others to do it too, then sorrow would pass away from earth, the cries and the anguish and the misery of sentient existence would lessen; then from man, become one with divine law, would love radiate through the world and bring it into nobler harmony. And each who turns his face in that direction, each who purifies his own body, his own life, is a fellow-worker with the inner life of the world, and the development of his own Spirit shall come as guerdon for the work he does for the helping of the world.

Source: Besant, Annie. *Vegetarianism in the Light of Theosophy.* Adyar, India: Theosophical Publishing House, 1913.

ANALYSIS

Annie Besant (1847–1933) was a British activist who focused much of her considerable energy on women's rights, India, and free thought. Born Annie Wood, she had a difficult and unhappy childhood, especially after her father died when she was five years old. Unable to raise her daughter by herself, young Annie's mother recruited a friend who raised and home-schooled her. At the age of 19, Besant married Reverend Frank Besant and had a son and a daughter. She was a willing helper to parishioners in need, but she soon came to believe that broader social changes were needed to address poverty and other ills afflicting England. When her religious views began to change, she and her Christian clergyman husband legally separated.

In her mid-twenties, Besant, now an atheist, joined two groups: the National Secular Society, which endorsed free thought, and the Fabian Society, a socialist organization. She became the coeditor of the *National Reformer*, which addressed such topics as national education, trade unions, women's suffrage, and birth control. She and fellow *National Reformer* editor Charles Bradlaugh wrote a pamphlet advocating birth control that resulted in a six-month prison sentence (later overturned) for publishing "obscene libel." Undeterred by this experience, she soon wrote a book about birth control, leading newspapers to criticize her; the *Times*, for example, called her book "indecent, lewd, filthy, bawdy and obscene."

In the 1880s Besant helped organize a strike for better working and health conditions by women workers at a match company. She is perhaps best known, however, for her involvement in India in the Theosophy movement, a belief system based on Hindu ideas of karma and reincarnation. She joined the Theosophical Society in 1889. She subsequently divided her time between social reform campaigns and writings about her Theosophical beliefs. She also became a prominent orator, prompting one colleague to comment: "Mrs. Besant transfixed me; her superb control of voice, her whole-souled devotion to the cause she was advocating, her love of the downtrodden, and her appeal on behalf of a sound education for all children, created such an impression upon me."

Theosophy also led her into the realm of vegetarianism. She cared deeply for animals and found the concept of slaughtering animals for human consumption to be abhorrent, as exemplified by her references in the accompanying excerpt to Chicago slaughterhouses. She believed that those who ate animal flesh, even if they were not involved in the actual killing of the animal, were committing acts of great immorality.

As the above excerpt makes clear, Besant experienced great distress in imagining the pain that animals went through not only during the actual slaughter, but during the time leading up to it:

> We find amongst animals, as amongst men, power of feeling pleasure, power of feeling pain; we see them moved by love and by hate; we see them feeling terror and attraction; we recognize in them powers of sensation closely akin to our own, and while we transcend them immensely in intellect, yet, in mere passional characteristics our natures and the animals' are closely allied. We know that when they feel terror, that terror means suffering. We know that when a wound is inflicted, that wound means pain to them. We know that threats bring to them suffering; they have a feeling of shrinking, of fear, of absence of friendly relations, and at once we begin to see that in our relations to the animal kingdom a duty arises which all thoughtful and compassionate minds should recognize—the duty that because we are stronger in mind than the animals, we are or ought to be their guardians and helpers, not their tyrants and oppressors.

FURTHER READING

"Annie Besant (1847–1933)." BBC, accessed December 8, 2014. http://www.bbc.co.uk/history/historic_figures/besant_annie.shtml.

"Annie Besant (1847–1933)." Theosophical Society, accessed December 8, 2014. http://www.ts-adyar.org/content/annie-besant-1847-1933.

"Annie Besant (1847–1933): Text of a Speech." International Vegetarian Union, accessed December 8, 2014. http://www.ivu.org/history/besant/text.html.

Bennett, Olivia. *Annie Besant*. London: Hamilton, 1988.

Besant, Annie. *Autobiographical Sketches*. Edited by Carol Hanbery MacKay. Buffalo, NY: Broadview Press, 2009.

Besant, Annie. *An Autobiography*. Reprint edition. Whitefish, MT: Kessinger Publishing, 2003.

Besant, Annie. "Vegetarianism in the Light of Theosophy." From 15th IVU World Vegetarian Congress 1957 collection. International Vegetarian Union (IVU). http://www.ivu.org/congress/wvc57/souvenir/.

Dinnage, Rosemary. *Annie Besant*. New York: Penguin Books, 1986.

Lewis, Jone Johnson. "Annie Besant, Heretic." About.com, accessed December 9, 2014. http://womenshistory.about.com/od/freethought/a/annie_besant.htm.

West, Geoffrey. *The Life of Annie Besant*. New York: Viking Press, 1928.

"ANIMALS HAVE ALSO THE RIGHT TO BE TREATED WITH GENTLENESS AND CONSIDERATION"

- **Document:** A book presenting the pro–animal rights views of English writer, social reformer, and vegetarian Henry S. Salt.
- **Date:** 1894.
- **Where:** Copublished in London and New York City.
- **Significance:** This excerpt comes from a seminal book on animal rights, one that prominent animal rights advocate Peter Singer called "the best of the eighteenth- and nineteenth-century works on the rights of animals."

DOCUMENT

Have the lower animals "rights?" Undoubtedly—if men have. That is the point I wish to make evident.

But have men rights? Let it be stated at the outset that I have no intention of discussing the abstract theory of natural rights, which, at the present time, is looked upon with suspicion and disfavour by many social reformers, since it has not unfrequently been made to cover the most extravagant and contradictory assertions. But though its phraseology is confessedly vague and perilous, there is nevertheless a solid truth underlying it—a truth which has always been clearly apprehended by the moral faculty, however difficult it may be to establish it on an unassailable logical basis. If men have not "rights"—well, they have an unmistakable intimation of something very similar; a sense of justice which marks the boundary-line where acquiescence ceases and resistance begins; a demand for freedom to live their own life, subject to the necessity of respecting the equal freedom of other people.

Such is the doctrine of rights as formulated by [nineteenth-century English philosopher] Herbert Spencer. "Every man," he says, "is free to do that which he wills, provided he infringes not the equal liberty of any other man." And again, "Whoever admits that each man must have a certain restricted freedom, asserts that it is *right* he should have this restricted freedom. ... And hence the several particular freedoms deducible may fitly be called, as they commonly are called, his *rights*."

The fitness of this nomenclature is disputed, but the existence of some real principle of the kind can hardly be called in question; so that the controversy concerning "rights" is little else than an academic battle over words, which leads to no practical conclusion. I shall assume, therefore, that men are possessed of "rights" in the sense of Herbert Spencer's definition; and if any of my readers object to this qualified use of the term, I can only say that I shall be perfectly willing to change the word as soon as a more appropriate one is forthcoming. The immediate question that claims our attention is this—if men have rights, have animals their rights also?

From the earliest times there have been thinkers who, directly or indirectly, answered this question with an affirmative. The Buddhist and Pythagorean canons, dominated perhaps by the creed of reincarnation, included the maxim "not to kill or injure any innocent animal." The humanitarian philosophers of the Roman empire, among whom Seneca and Plutarch and Porphyry were the most conspicuous, took still higher ground in preaching humanity on the broadest principle of universal benevolence. "Since justice is due to rational beings," wrote Porphyry, "how is it possible to evade the admission that we are bound also to act justly towards the races below us?"

It is a lamentable fact that during the churchdom of the middle ages, from the fourth century to the sixteenth, from the time of Porphyry to the time of Montaigne, little or no attention was paid to the question of the rights and wrongs of the lower races. Then, with the Reformation and the revival of learning, came a revival also of humanitarian feeling, as may be seen in many passages of Erasmus and More, Shakespeare and [Francis] Bacon; but it was not until the eighteenth century, the age of enlightenment and "sensibility," of which Voltaire and Rousseau were the spokesmen, that the rights of animals obtained more deliberate recognition. From the great Revolution of 1789 dates the period when the world-wide spirit of humanitarianism, which had hitherto been felt by but one man in a million—the thesis of the philosopher or the vision of the poet—began to disclose itself, gradually and dimly at first, as an essential feature of democracy.

A great and far-reaching effect was produced in England at this time by the publication of such revolutionary works as [Thomas] Paine's *Rights of Man*, and Mary Wollstonecraft's *Vindication of the Rights of Women*; and looking back now, after the lapse of a hundred years, we can see that a still wider extension of the theory of rights was thenceforth inevitable. In fact, such a claim was anticipated—if only in bitter jest—by a contemporary writer, who furnishes us with a notable instance of how the mockery of one generation may become the reality of the next. There was published anonymously in 1792 a little volume entitled *A Vindication of the Rights of Brutes*, a *reductio ad absurdum* of Mary Wollstonecraft's essay, written, as the author informs us, "to evince by demonstrative arguments the perfect equality of what is called the irrational species to the human." The further opinion is expressed that "after those wonderful productions of Mr. Paine and Mrs. Wollstonecraft, such a theory as the present seems to be necessary." It *was* necessary; and a very short term of years sufficed to bring it into effect; indeed, the theory had already been put forward by several English pioneers of nineteenth-century humanitarianism.

To [English jurist and philosopher] Jeremy Bentham, in particular, belongs the high honour of first asserting the rights of animals with authority and persistence. "The legislator," he wrote, "ought to interdict everything which may serve to lead to cruelty.…. Why should the law refuse its protection to any sensitive being? The time will come when humanity will extend its mantle over everything which breathes. We have begun by attending to the condition of slaves; we shall finish by softening that of all the animals which assist our labours or supply our wants."

So, too, wrote one of Bentham's contemporaries [John Lawrence]: "The grand source of the unmerited and superfluous misery of beasts exists in a defect in the constitution of all communities. No human government, I believe, has ever recognized the *jus animalium*, which ought surely to form a part of the jurisprudence of every system founded on the principles of justice and humanity." A large number of later moralists have followed on the same lines, with the result that the rights of animals have already, to a certain limited extent, been established both in private usage and by legal enactment.

It is interesting to note the exact commencement of this new principle in law. When Lord Erskine, speaking in the House of Lords in 1811, advocated the cause of justice to the lower animals, he was greeted with loud cries of insult and derision. But eleven years later the efforts of the despised humanitarians, and especially of Richard Martin, of Galway, were rewarded by their first success. The passing of the Ill-treatment of Cattle Bill, commonly known as "Martin's Act," in June, 1822, is a memorable date in the history of humane legislation, less on account of the positive protection afforded by it, for it applied only to cattle and "beasts of burden," than for the invaluable precedent which it created. From 1822 onward, the principle of that *jus animalium* for which Bentham had pleaded, was recognized, however partially and tentatively at first, by English law, and the animals included in the Act ceased to be the mere property of their owners; moreover the Act has been several times supplemented and extended during the past half century. It is scarcely possible, in the face of this legislation, to maintain that "rights" are a privilege with which none but human beings can be invested; for if *some* animals are already included within the pale of protection, why should not more and more be so included in the future?

For the present, however, what is most urgently needed is some comprehensive and intelligible principle, which shall indicate, in a more consistent manner, the true lines of man's moral relation towards the lower animals. And here, it must be admitted, our position is still far from satisfactory; for though certain very important concessions have been made, as we have seen, to the demand for the *jus animalium*, they have been made for the most part in a grudging, unwilling spirit, and rather in the interests of property than of principle; while even the leading advocates of animals' rights seem to have shrunk from basing their claim on the only argument which can ultimately be held to be a really sufficient one—the assertion that animals, as well as men, though, of course, to a far less extent than men, are possessed of a distinctive individuality, and, therefore, are in justice entitled to live their lives with a due measure of that "restricted freedom" to which Herbert Spencer alludes. It is of little use to claim "rights" for animals in a vague general way, if with the same breath we explicitly show our determination to subordinate those rights to anything and everything that can be construed into a human "want"; nor will it ever be possible to obtain full justice for the lower races so long as we continue to regard them as beings of a wholly different order, and to ignore the significance of their numberless points of kinship with mankind.

For example, it has been said by a well-known writer on the subject of humanity to animals that "the life of a brute, having no moral purpose, can best be understood ethically as representing the sum of its pleasures; and the obligation, therefore, of producing the pleasures of sentient creatures must be reduced, in their case, to the abstinence from unnecessary destruction of life." Now, with respect to this statement, I must say that the notion of the life of an animal having "no moral purpose," belongs to a class of ideas which cannot possibly be accepted by the advanced humanitarian thought of the present day—it is a purely arbitrary assumption, at variance with our best instincts, at variance with our best science, and absolutely fatal (if the subject be clearly thought out) to any full realization of animals' rights. If we are ever going to do justice to the lower races, we must get rid of the antiquated notion of a "great gulf" fixed between them and mankind, and must recognize the common bond of humanity that unites all living beings in one universal brotherhood.

As far as any excuses can be alleged, in explanation of the insensibility or inhumanity of the western nations in their treatment of animals, these excuses may be mostly traced back to one or the other of two theoretical contentions, wholly different in origin, yet alike in this—that both postulate an absolute difference of nature between men and the lower kinds.

The first is the so-called "religious" notion, which awards immortality to man, but to man alone, thereby furnishing (especially in Catholic countries) a quibbling justification for acts of cruelty to animals, on the plea that they "have no souls."...

The second and not less fruitful source of modern inhumanity is to be found in the "Cartesian" doctrine—the theory of Descartes and his followers—that the lower animals are devoid of consciousness and feeling; a theory which carried the "religious" notion a step further, and deprived the animals not only of their claim to a life hereafter, but of anything that could, without mockery, be called a life in the present, since mere "animated machines," as they were thus affirmed to be, could in no real sense be said to *live* at all!...

Yet no human being is justified in regarding any animal whatsoever as a meaningless automaton, to be worked, or tortured, or eaten, as the case may be, for the mere object of satisfying the wants or whims of mankind. Together with the destinies and duties that are laid on them and fulfilled by them, animals have also the right to be treated with gentleness and consideration, and the man who does not so treat them, however great his learning or influence may be, is, in that respect, an ignorant and foolish man, devoid of the highest and noblest culture of which the human mind is capable.

Something must here be said on the important subject of nomenclature. It is to be feared that the ill-treatment of animals is largely due—or at any rate the difficulty of amending that treatment is largely increased—by the common use of such terms as "brute-beast," "live-stock," etc., which implicitly deny to the lower races that intelligent individuality which is most undoubtedly possessed by them. It was long ago remarked by Bentham, in his *Introduction to Principles of Morals and Legislation*, that, whereas human beings are styled *persons*, "other animals, on account of their interests having been neglected by the insensibility of the ancient jurists, stand degraded into the class of *things;*" and [Arthur] Schopenhauer [a German philosopher] also has commented on the mischievous absurdity of the idiom which applies the neuter pronoun "it" to such highly organized primates as the dog and the ape.

A word of protest is needed also against such an expression as "dumb animals," which, though often cited as "an immense exhortation to pity," has in reality a tendency to influence ordinary people in quite the contrary direction, inasmuch as it fosters the idea of an impassable barrier between mankind and their dependents. It is convenient to us men to be deaf to the entreaties of the victims of our injustice;

and, by a sort of grim irony, we therefore assume that it is *they* who are afflicted by some organic incapacity—they are "dumb animals," forsooth! although a moment's consideration must prove that they have innumerable ways, often quite human in variety and suggestiveness, of uttering their thoughts and emotions. Even the term "animals," as applied to the lower races, is incorrect, and not wholly unobjectionable, since it ignores the fact that *man* is an animal no less than they. My only excuse for using it in this volume is that there is absolutely no other brief term available.

So anomalous is the attitude of man towards the lower animals, that it is no marvel if many humane thinkers have wellnigh despaired over this question. "The whole subject of the brute creation," wrote Dr. [Thomas] Arnold, "is to me one of such painful mystery, that I dare not approach it;" and this (to put the most charitable interpretation on their silence) appears to be the position of the majority of moralists and teachers at the present time. Yet there is urgent need of some key to the solution of the problem; and in no other way can this key be found than by the full inclusion of the lower races within the pale of human sympathy. All the promptings of our best and surest instincts point us in this direction. "It is abundantly evident," says [William Edward Hartpole] Lecky, "both from history and from present experience, that the instinctive shock, or natural feelings of disgust, caused by the sight of the sufferings of men, is not generically different from that which is caused by the sight of the suffering of animals."

If this be so—and the admission is a momentous one—can it be seriously contended that the same humanitarian tendency which has already emancipated the slave, will not ultimately benefit the lower races also? Here, again, the historian of *European Morals* [Lecky] has a significant remark: "At one time," he says, "the benevolent affections embrace merely the family, soon the circle expanding includes first a class, then a nation, then a coalition of nations, then all humanity; and finally its influence is felt in the dealings of man with the animal world. In each of these cases a standard is formed, different from that of the preceding stage, but in each case the same tendency is recognized as virtue."

But, it may be argued, vague sympathy with the lower animals is one thing, and a definite recognition of their "rights" is another; what reason is there to suppose that we shall advance from the former phase to the latter? Just this; that every great liberating movement has proceeded exactly on these lines. Oppression and cruelty are invariably founded on a lack of imaginative sympathy; the tyrant or tormentor can have no true sense of kinship with the victim of his injustice. When once the sense of affinity is awakened, the knell of tyranny is sounded, and the ultimate concession of "rights" is simply a matter of time. The present condition of the more highly organized domestic animals is in many ways very analogous to that of the negro slaves of a hundred years ago; look back, and you will find in their case precisely the same exclusion from the common pale of humanity; the same hypocritical fallacies, to justify that exclusion; and, as a consequence, the same deliberate stubborn denial of their social "rights." Look back—for it is well to do so—and then look forward, and the moral can hardly be mistaken.

We find so great a thinker and writer as Aristotle seriously pondering whether a slave may be considered as in any sense a *man*. In emphasizing the point that friendship is founded on propinquity, he expresses himself as follows: "Neither can men have friendships with horses, cattle, or slaves, considered merely as such; for a slave is merely a living instrument, and an instrument a living slave. Yet, considered as a man, a slave may be an object of friendship, for certain rights seem to belong to all those capable of participating in law and engagement. A slave, then, considered as a man, may be treated justly or unjustly." "Slaves," says Bentham, "have been treated by the law exactly upon the same footing as in England, for example, the inferior races of animals are still. The day *may* come when the rest of the animal creation may acquire those rights which could never have been withholden from them but by the hand of tyranny."

Let us unreservedly admit the immense difficulties that stand in the way of this animal enfranchisement. Our relation towards the animals is complicated and embittered by innumerable habits handed down through centuries of mistrust and brutality; we cannot, in all cases, suddenly relax these habits, or do full justice even where we see that justice will have to be done. A perfect ethic of humaneness is therefore impracticable, if not unthinkable; and we can attempt to do no more than to indicate in a general way the main principle of animals' rights, noting at the same time the most flagrant particular violations of those rights, and the lines on which the only valid reform can hereafter be effected. But, on the other hand, it may be remembered, for the comfort and encouragement of humanitarian workers, that these obstacles are, after all, only such as are inevitable in each branch of social improvement; for at every stage of every great reformation it has been repeatedly argued, by indifferent or hostile observers, that further progress is impossible; indeed, when the opponents of a great cause begin to demonstrate its "impossibility," experience teaches us that that cause is already on the high road to fulfilment. . . .

Our main principle is now clear. If "rights" exist at all—and both feeling and usage indubitably prove that they do exist—they cannot be consistently awarded to men and denied to animals, since the same sense of justice and compassion apply in both cases. "Pain is pain," says an honest old writer [Humphrey Primatt], "whether it be inflicted on man or on beast; and the creature that suffers it, whether man or beast, being sensible of the misery of it while it lasts, suffers evil; and the sufferance of evil, unmeritedly, unprovokedly, where no offence has been given, and no good can possibly be answered by it, but merely to exhibit power or gratify malice, is Cruelty and Injustice in him that occasions it."

I commend this outspoken utterance to the attention of those ingenious moralists who quibble about the "discipline" of the suffering, and deprecate immediate attempts to redress what, it is alleged, may be a necessary instrument for the attainment of human welfare. It is, perhaps, a mere coincidence, but it has been observed that those who are most forward to disallow the rights of others, and to argue that suffering and subjection are the natural lot of all living things, are usually themselves exempt from the operation of this beneficent law, and that the beauty of self-sacrifice is most loudly belauded by those who profit most largely at the expense of their fellow creatures.

But "nature is one with rapine," [a quotation from Alfred Tennyson's poem "Maud"] say some, and this utopian theory of "rights," if too widely extended, must come in conflict with that iron rule of internecine competition, by which the universe is regulated. But is the universe so regulated? We note that this very objection, which was confidently relied on a few years back by many opponents of the emancipation of the working classes, is not heard of in that connection now! Our learned economists and men of science, who set themselves to play the defenders of the social *status quo*, have seen their own weapons of "natural selection," "survival of the fittest," and what not, snatched from their hands and turned against them, and are therefore beginning to explain to us, in a scientific manner, what we untutored humanitarians had previously felt to be true, viz. that competition is not by any means the sole governing law among the human race. We are not greatly dismayed, then, to find the same old bugbear trotted out as an argument against animals' rights—indeed, we see already unmistakable signs of a similar complete reversal of the scientific judgment.

The charge of "sentimentalism" is frequently brought against those who plead for animals' rights. Now "sentimentalism," if any meaning at all can be attached to the word, must signify an inequality, an ill balance of sentiment, an inconsistency which leads men into attacking one abuse, while they ignore or condone another where a reform is equally desirable. That this weakness is often observable among "philanthropists" on the one hand, and "friends of animals" on the other, and most of all among those acute "men of the world," whose regard is only for themselves, I am not concerned to deny; what I wish to point out is, that the only real safeguard against sentimentality is to take up a consistent position towards the rights of men and of the lower animals alike, and to cultivate a broad sense of universal justice (not "mercy") for all living things. Herein, and herein alone, is to be sought the true sanity of temperament.

It is an entire mistake to suppose that the rights of animals are in any way antagonistic to the rights of men. Let us not be betrayed for a moment into the specious fallacy that we must study human rights first, and leave the animal question to solve itself hereafter; for it is only by a wide and disinterested study of *both* subjects that a solution of either is possible. "For he who loves all animated nature," says Porphyry, "will not hate any one tribe of innocent beings, and by how much greater his love for the whole, by so much the more will he cultivate justice towards a part of them, and that part to which he is most allied." To omit all worthier reasons, it is too late in the day to suggest the indefinite postponement of a consideration of animals' rights, for from a moral point of view, and even from a legislative point of view, we are daily confronted with this momentous problem, and the so-called "practical" people who affect to ignore it are simply shutting their eyes to facts which they find it disagreeable to confront.

Once more then, animals have rights, and these rights consist in the "restricted freedom" to live a natural life—a life, that is, which permits of the individual development—subject to the limitations imposed by the permanent needs and interests of the community. There is nothing quixotic or visionary in this assertion; it is perfectly compatible with a readiness to look the sternest laws of existence fully and honestly in the face. If we must kill, whether it be man or animal, let us kill and have done with it; if we must inflict pain, let us do what is inevitable, without hypocrisy, or evasion, or cant. But (here is the cardinal point) let us first be assured that it *is* necessary; let us not wantonly trade on the needless miseries of other beings, and then attempt to lull our consciences by a series of shuffling excuses which cannot endure a moment's candid investigation. As [English poet] Leigh Hunt well says:

That there is pain and evil, is no rule
That I should make it greater, like a fool.

Source: Salt, Henry S. *Animals' Rights Considered in Relation to Social Progress.*
New York and London: Macmillan, 1894.

ANALYSIS

Some scholars consider Englishman Henry Salt (1851–1939) to be the first writer
who made a clear distinction between animal welfare and animal rights. However,
in this passage, Salt mentions many earlier writers who contributed to the idea of
animal rights. By describing their work, he provides a prehistory of the animal rights
movement. Using an elaborate writing style that was typical of his era, Salt discusses
philosophical and religious ideas that promoted animal welfare but ignored animal
rights. He notes that support for animal rights (along with support for democracy
and early feminist ideas) grew from "the world-wide spirit of humanitarianism" that
followed the French Revolution (1789). Scientific discoveries in the mid-1800s—
specifically, Charles Darwin's theories about the origins of life—confirmed Salt's
belief that human beings share "numberless points of kinship" with nonhuman animals. By the time Salt wrote this passage, he had a strong foundation to begin building the case for animal rights.

   The excerpt includes many of the ideas and arguments that later writers would
use in favor of animal rights. In particular, Salt describes the concept of rights as
"a sense of justice . . . a demand for freedom to live [one's] own life." He then argues
that both human and nonhuman animals "are possessed of a distinctive individuality, and, therefore, are in justice entitled to live their lives with a due measure
of . . . 'restricted freedom' [i.e., rights]." This is the "main principle" Salt tries to
establish in the excerpt. His principle is echoed in Albert Schweitzer's excerpt from
Civilisation and Ethics (especially in Schweitzer's concept of "will to live") and in
Tom Regan's "Philosophy of Animal Rights." There, Regan states that human
beings and nonhuman animals both "have a life of their own that is of importance
to them. . . . What happens to them matters to them. . . . And so it is that the ethics
of our dealings with them . . . must acknowledge the same fundamental moral principles."

   Almost a 100 years before Regan and others began to link animal rights and
human rights, Salt understood animal rights as part of a larger, broader movement
toward progressive change. He was a social reformer who was involved in various
causes besides animal rights, including socialism and nature conservation. He disagreed with the teachings of organized religion but professed a "creed of kinship,"
which included the belief "that the basis of any real morality must be the sense of
Kinship between all living beings." Like the modern animal rights advocates who
followed in his footsteps, Salt emphasized that animal rights and human rights can
be pursued together, with no loss to either cause.

Near the end of the passage, Salt summarizes his position: Humans and nonhumans are both entitled to rights, because "the same sense of justice and compassion apply in both cases." Then, to bolster that thought, Salt quotes Humphrey Primatt (see "Differences between Humans and Animals"): "Pain is pain, whether it be inflicted on man or on beast; and the creature that suffers it . . . suffers evil." Salt goes on to say that people who try to ignore the suffering of nonhuman animals "are simply shutting their eyes to facts which they find it disagreeable to confront." In effect, he is saying that these human beings are avoiding their own pain—painful feelings such as sorrow, disgust, or guilt about the poor treatment of animals. Like his other ideas on animal rights, Salt's comments on this point remain relevant in the twenty-first century, as animal rights advocates continue to exhort people to open their eyes to the suffering of nonhuman animals.

FURTHER READING

"Animal Rights." Henry S. Salt, accessed December 9, 2014. http://www.henrysalt.co.uk/reformer/animal-rights.

Hendrick, George. *Henry Salt: Humanitarian Reformer and Man of Letters.* Urbana: University of Illinois Press, 1977.

"Henry Salt: Animals' Rights." Animal Rights History, accessed December 9, 2014. http://www.animalrightshistory.org/animal-rights-c1837-1901/victorian-s/sal-henry-salt/1892-animals-rights.htm.

"History of Vegetarianism: Henry S. Salt (1851–1939)." International Vegetarian Union, accessed December 9, 2014. http://www.ivu.org/history/salt/.

Manley, Deborah, and Peter Ree. *Henry Salt: Artist, Traveller, Diplomat, Egyptologist.* London: Libri, 2001.

Panaman, Roger, "Henry Salt (1851–1939)," *How to Do Animal Rights* (blog), April 2008. http://www.animalethics.org.uk/i-ch6-8-salt.html.

Pipe, Sheryl L. "Animal Rights and Animal Welfare." Learning to Give, accessed December 9, 2014. http://learningtogive.org/papers/paper360.html.

Salt, Henry S. *The Savour of Salt: A Henry Salt Anthology.* Edited by George Hendrick and Willene Hendrick. Fontwell: Centaur, 1989.

"TO AID IN THE RESTORATION OF SUCH BIRDS ... [THAT] HAVE BECOME SCARCE OR EXTINCT"

- **Document:** Excerpt of the Lacey Bird Law, a congressional law from 1900, enacted to protect wildlife.
- **Date:** Enacted May 18, 1900.
- **Where:** Washington, D.C.
- **Significance:** This law was the first federal act to address the protection of wildlife and the preservation of wild game.

DOCUMENT

An Act to enlarge the Powers of the Department of Agriculture, prohibit the transportation by Interstate Commerce of Game killed in Violation of Local Laws, and for other Purposes.

Be it enacted by the Senate and House of Representatives in the United States of America in Congress assembled, That the duties and powers of the Department of Agriculture are hereby enlarged so as to include the preservation, distribution, introduction, and restoration of game-birds and other wild birds. The Secretary of Agriculture is hereby authorized to adopt such measures as may be necessary to carry out the purposes of this act and to purchase such game-birds and other wild birds as may be required therefor, subject, however, to the laws of the various States and Territories. The object and purpose of this act is to aid in the restoration of such birds in those parts of the United States adapted thereto where the same have become scarce or extinct, and also to regulate the introduction of American or foreign birds or animals in localities where they have not heretofore existed.

The Secretary of Agriculture shall from time to time collect and publish useful information as to the propagation, uses, and preservation of such birds. And the Secretary of Agriculture shall make and publish all needful rules and regulations for carrying out the purposes of this act, and shall expend for said purposes such sums as Congress may appropriate therefor.

SEC. 2. — That it shall be unlawful for any person or persons to import into the United States any foreign wild animal or bird except under special permit from the United States Department of Agriculture: Provided, That nothing in this section shall restrict the importation of natural history specimens for museums or scientific collections or the importation of certain cage birds, such as domesticated canaries, parrots, or such other species as the Secretary of Agriculture may designate.

The importation of the mongoose, the so-called "flying-foxes" or fruit bats, the English sparrow, the starling, or such other birds or animals as the Secretary of Agriculture may from time to time declare injurious to the interest of agriculture

Decorating hats with bird feathers, and sometimes the entire bird, was fashionable during the late-nineteenth century and early-twentieth century. The market for the plumes of various birds led to the indiscriminate killing of many species in Florida, which prompted the passage of the Lacey Act to prohibit the feather trade. The act also led to increased public awareness of natural conservation issues. (E. O. Hoppe/Corbis)

or horticulture is hereby prohibited, and such species upon arrival at any of the ports of the United States shall be destroyed or returned at the expense of the owner. The Secretary of the Treasury is hereby authorized to make regulations for carrying into effect the provisions of this section.

SEC. 3. — That it shall be unlawful for any person or persons to deliver to any common carrier or for any common carrier to transport from one State or Territory to another State or Territory, or from the District of Columbia or Alaska to any State or Territory, or from any State or Territory to the District of Columbia or Alaska, any foreign animals or birds the importation of which is prohibited, or the dead bodies or parts thereof of any wild animals or birds where such animals or birds have been killed in violation of the laws of the State, Territory, or District in which the same were killed: Provided, That nothing herein shall prevent the transportation of any dead birds or animals killed during the season when the same may be lawfully captured and the export of which is not prohibited by law in the State, Territory, or District in which the same are killed.

SEC. 4. — That all packages containing such dead animals, birds, or parts thereof, when shipped by interstate commerce, as provided in Section 1 of this act, shall be plainly and clearly marked, so that the name and address of the shipper and the nature of the contents may be readily ascertained on inspection of the outside of such packages. For each evasion or violation of this act the shipper shall, upon conviction, pay a fine of not exceeding two hundred dollars; and the consignee knowingly receiving such articles so shipped and transported in violation of this act shall, upon conviction, pay a fine of not exceeding two hundred dollars; and the carrier knowingly carrying or transporting the same shall, upon conviction, pay a fine of not exceeding two hundred dollars.

SEC. 5. — That all dead bodies, or parts thereof, of any foreign game-animals or game- or song-birds, the importation of which is prohibited, or the dead bodies or parts thereof of any wild game-animals or game- or song-birds transported into any State or Territory, or remaining therein for use, consumption, sale, or storage therein, shall, upon arrival in such State or Territory, be subject to the operation and effect of the laws of such State or Territory enacted in the exercise of its police powers, to the same extent and in the same manner as though such animals and birds had been produced in such State or Territory, and shall not be exempt therefrom by reason of being introduced therein in original packages or otherwise. This act shall not prevent the importation, transportation, or sale of birds or bird plumage manufactured from the feathers of barn-yard fowl.

Source: "The Lacey Bird Law." In *Birds in Their Relations to Man: A Manual of Economic Ornithology for the United States and Canada.* Edited by Clarence M. Weed and Ned Dearborn. Philadelphia: J. B. Lippincott, 1903, pp. 320–22.

ANALYSIS

The first comprehensive federal legislation enacted to protect wildlife, the Lacey Bird Law was passed by the U.S. Congress on May 18, 1900. It was signed into law by President William McKinley on May 25, 1900. The law was named after Congressman John F. Lacey (R-Iowa), who was instrumental in getting the law passed.

The Lacey Bird Law protects both plants and wildlife by invoking penalties for a wide variety of violations. The penalties are both civil and criminal, typically involving a fine and/or jail time if the violation is large enough. It also allows government officials to step in and restore game and birds in parts of the country where they have become extinct or are rare. The law also seeks to prevent birds and other animals from being introduced into parts of the country where they have never existed before.

The most notable part of the law protects plants, wildlife, and fish that have been illegally taken from one state, in violation of state laws, from being traded in another state. This part of the law largely impacted market hunters, who relied heavily on trade across state borders to earn money. A crucial benefit of the law was that it helped to expand awareness of natural resource conservation issues among a populace that had long taken the inexhaustibility of America's land, water, timber, and wildlife for granted.

The venerable law remains an important one today. As the U.S. Fish & Wildlife Service has noted, it still "regulates the import of any species protected by international or domestic law and prevents the spread of invasive, or non-native, species," which is critical to the health of society.

The law has been amended several times. In 1969 it was amended to add amphibians, reptiles, mollusks, and crustaceans to the protected species list. In 1981, indigenous plants were added. The wording of the law has also been modified slightly over the years. The Lacey Bird Law was most recently amended in 2008 to include penalties for illegal logging and to prohibit the sale of plants and plant products (including wood) that have been taken or traded illegally. The addition of illegal logging provisions has had a big impact on the international timber industry, which until this amendment, had gone largely unregulated. Amending the law was seen as a way to address forest ecosystem degradation, especially in countries that could not afford to lose valuable commodities. Now, importers must specify the type of species that they are bringing into the country, the country where the species originated, and any other relevant information so everyone is aware of the origin of the wood.

One of the most high-profile cases that occurred as a result of the 2008 amendment was the Gibson Guitar Corporation case. A raid on the company by the U.S. Department of Justice took place in 2009 and pieces of wood originating from Madagascar and India were seized. This wood was believed to be illegally imported by the instrument company. U.S. assistant attorney general Ignacia Moreno of the Environment and Natural Resources Division of the Justice Department said in a statement that "Gibson has acknowledged that it failed to act on information that the Madagascar ebony it was purchasing [which is banned from exporting] may have violated laws intended to limit over-harvesting and conserve valuable wood species from Madagascar, a country which has been severely impacted by deforestation." Gibson agreed to pay a penalty, forfeit claims to the wood seized in the raids, and make a contribution to the National Fish and Wildlife Foundation.

FURTHER READING

Bennett-Smith, Meredith. "Gibson Guitar Settles with Federal Investigators, Acknowledges Exotic Wood Violation." *Huffington Post*. August 8, 2012. http://www.huffingtonpost.com/2012/08/08/gibson-guitar-settles-admits-exotic-wood-violation_n_1756969.html.

Clarke, Caitlin, and Adam Grant. "Gibson Guitar Logging Bust Demonstrates Lacey Act's Effectiveness." World Resources Institute. August 10, 2012. http://www.wri.org/blog/2012/08/gibson-guitar-logging-bust-demonstrates-lacey-act%E2%80%99s-effectiveness.

"Editorial: Gibson Axed Up by Lacey Act." *Washington Times*, August 14, 2012. http://www.washingtontimes.com/news/2012/aug/14/gibson-axed-up-by-lacey-act/.

"Gibson Guitar Corp. Agrees to Resolve Investigation into Lacey Act Violations." U.S. Department of Justice, August 6, 2012. http://www.justice.gov/opa/pr/2012/August/12-enrd-976.html.

Havighurst, Craig. "Why Gibson Guitar Was Raided by the Justice Department." *The Record*. NPR. August 31, 2011. http://www.npr.org/blogs/therecord/2011/08/31/140090116/why-gibson-guitar-was-raided-by-the-justice-department.

"Lacey Act." U.S. Fish & Wildlife Service International Affairs, accessed December 10, 2014. http://www.fws.gov/international/laws-treaties-agreements/us-conservation-laws/lacey-act.html.

Morgan, Gilbert E., and Deavon Hill, eds. *The Lacey Act: Federal Regulation and Protection of Wildlife and Plants*. New York: Nova Science Publishers, 2012.

Revkin, Andrew. "A Closer Look at Gibson Guitar's Legal Troubles." *New York Times*, August 13, 2012. http://dotearth.blogs.nytimes.com/2012/08/10/a-closer-look-at-gibson-guitars-legal-troubles/.

"U.S. Lacey Act." Environmental Investigation Agency, accessed December 10, 2014. http://eia-global.org/lacey/.

"VEGETARIANISM IS A COMMENDABLE DEPARTURE FROM THE ESTABLISHED BARBAROUS HABIT"

- **Document:** An excerpt from "The Problem of Increasing Human Energy," an essay by Serbian-American inventor Nikola Tesla.
- **Date:** 1900.
- **Where:** Published in New York City.
- **Significance:** In this article by the famed inventor, Tesla posits that an embrace of vegetarianism—which necessitates the rejection of consuming animal flesh for nourishment—is a natural part of the evolution of the human race into a more advanced form, both morally and physiologically.

DOCUMENT

Man . . . is not an ordinary mass, consisting of spinning atoms and molecules, and containing merely heat-energy. He is a mass possessed of certain higher qualities by reason of the creative principle of life with which he is endowed. His mass, as the water in an ocean wave, is being continuously exchanged, new taking the place of the old. Not only this, but he grows, propagates, and dies, thus altering his mass independently, both in bulk and density. What is most wonderful of all, he is capable of increasing or diminishing his velocity of movement by the mysterious power he possesses of appropriating more or less energy from other substance, and turning it into motive energy.

Whiskey, wine, tea, coffee, tobacco, and other such stimulants are responsible for the shortening of the lives of many, and ought to be used with moderation. But I do not think that rigorous measures of suppression of habits followed through many generations are commendable. It is wiser to preach moderation than abstinence. We have become accustomed to these stimulants, and if such reforms are to be effected, they must be slow and gradual. Those who are devoting their energies to such ends could make themselves far more useful by turning their efforts in other directions, as, for instance, toward providing pure water.

For every person who perishes from the effects of a stimulant, at least a thousand die from the consequences of drinking impure water. This precious fluid, which daily infuses new life into us, is likewise the chief vehicle through which disease and death enter our bodies. The germs of destruction it conveys are enemies all the more terrible as they perform their fatal work unperceived. They seal our doom while we live and enjoy. The majority of people are so ignorant or careless in drinking water, and the consequences of this are so disastrous, that a philanthropist can scarcely use his efforts better than by endeavoring to enlighten those who are thus injuring themselves. By systematic purification and sterilization of the drinking water the human mass would be very considerably increased. It should be made a rigid rule—which might be enforced by law—to boil or to sterilize otherwise the drinking water in every household and public place. The mere filtering does not afford sufficient security against infection. All ice for internal uses should be artificially prepared from water thoroughly sterilized. The importance of eliminating germs of disease from the city water is generally recognized, but little is being done to improve the existing conditions, as no satisfactory method of sterilizing great quantities of water has yet been brought forward. . . .

Gambling, business rush, and excitement, particularly on the exchanges, are causes of much mass reduction, all the more so because the individuals concerned represent units of higher value. Incapacity of observing the first symptoms of an illness, and careless neglect of the same, are important factors of mortality. In noting carefully every new sign of approaching danger, and making conscientiously every possible effort to avert it, we are not only following wise laws of hygiene in the interest of our well-being and the success of our labors, but we are also complying with a higher moral duty. Everyone should consider his body as a priceless gift from one whom he loves above all, as a marvelous work of art, of indescribable beauty and mastery beyond human conception, and so delicate and frail that a word, a breath, a look, nay, a thought, may injure it. Uncleanliness, which breeds disease and death, is not only a self destructive but highly immoral habit. In keeping our bodies free from infection, healthful, and pure, we are expressing our reverence for the high principle with which they are endowed. He who follows the precepts of hygiene in this spirit is proving himself, so far, truly religious. Laxity of morals is a terrible evil, which poisons both mind and body, and which is responsible for a great reduction of the human mass in some countries. Many of the present customs and tendencies are productive of similar hurtful results. For example, the society life, modern education and pursuits of women, tending to draw them away from their household duties and make men out of them, must needs detract from the elevating ideal they represent, diminish the artistic creative power, and cause sterility and a general weakening of the race. A thousand other evils might be mentioned, but all put together, in their bearing upon the problem under discussion, they could not equal a single one, the want of food, brought on by poverty, destitution, and famine. Millions of individuals die yearly for want of food, thus keeping down the mass. Even in our enlightened communities, and not withstanding the many charitable efforts, this is still, in all probability, the chief evil. I do not mean here absolute want of food, but want of healthful nutriment.

How to provide good and plentiful food is, therefore, a most important question of the day. On the general principles the raising of cattle as a means of providing food is objectionable, because, in the sense interpreted above, it must undoubtedly tend to the addition of mass of a "smaller velocity." It is certainly preferable to raise vegetables, and I think, therefore, that vegetarianism is a commendable departure from the established barbarous habit. That we can subsist on plant food and perform our work even to advantage is not a theory, but a well-demonstrated fact. Many races living almost exclusively on vegetables are of superior physique and strength. There is no doubt that some plant food, such as oatmeal, is more economical than meat, and superior to it in regard to both mechanical and mental performance. Such food, moreover, taxes our digestive organs decidedly less, and, in making us more contented and sociable, produces an amount of good difficult to estimate. In view of these facts every effort should be made to stop the wanton and cruel slaughter of animals, which must be destructive to our morals. To free ourselves from animal instincts and appetites, which keep us down, we should begin at the very root from which we spring: we should effect a radical reform in the character of the food.

Source: Tesla, Nikola. "The Problem of Increasing Human Energy." *The Century Illustrated Magazine*, June 1900, Volume 60 (New Series Volume 38), pp. 179–80.

ANALYSIS

Several of the world's most famous inventors and scientists of the nineteenth and twentieth centuries expressed varying degrees of support for vegetarianism, both on moral grounds and for health reasons. Thomas Alva Edison and Albert Einstein both explored the vegetarian lifestyle, and they were outspoken in support of the idea of abandoning meat consumption. However, neither man made the purported health benefits of a vegetarian diet or the ethics of sparing animals from the dinner table a central focus of their research, writings, or public pronouncements.

A similar pattern can be detected in the life and work of Nikola Tesla, the Serbian-born inventor who was both collaborator and competitor to Edison in the late 1800s. Tesla was born on July 10, 1856, in a region of the Balkans within the Austro-Hungarian Empire that is now within the borders of Croatia. Mesmerized by the subjects of science and mathematics from an early age, young Tesla was also influenced by the example of his mother, Djuda, who was adept at inventing modest but helpful little devices to aid with chores around the home and farm. He successfully resisted the calls from his father, Milutin, to follow him into the priesthood. Instead, he enrolled at the prestigious Austrian Polytechnic School at Graz and immersed himself in science, mathematics, and engineering coursework.

Tesla became particularly interested in alternating current (AC) as a means of generating electricity, but growing boredom with his studies (which he found unchallenging) and an irresponsible gambling fling led him to leave school without graduating. He worked across Europe as an electrical engineer for the next several years, gaining a reputation as a brilliant young scientific mind. In 1884 he crossed the Atlantic to the United States where, armed with a note of introduction from a mutual colleague, he came under the employ of Edison. Their collaboration was a brief one, however, as Edison came to view Tesla's AC research as a threat to his own preferred direct current (DC)–based method for generating electricity. The two men parted ways after a matter of months under a cloud of tension.

Over the next several years Tesla continued to develop his ideas, often working on only two or three hours of sleep. "He can invent with his hands tied behind his back!" marveled Robert Underwood Johnson, editor of *Century Illustrated Magazine* and a close friend to Tesla. "He is superior to all laws of hygiene and human energy. He is a vegetarian that doesn't know how to vegetate" (quoted in Seifer 1996, p. 236).

During the late 1880s and early 1890s he developed the so-called Tesla coil, which became an integral part of radio technology. He also sold several patents for AC electricity generation to businessman George Westinghouse. The Westinghouse Corporation subsequently used Tesla's AC concepts to power the famed 1893 Chicago World's Columbian Exposition, an enormous "city of light" that attracted tens of millions of Americans and hundreds of thousands of people from around the globe during its five-month run. The fair, which was powered by a dozen 1,000-horsepower AC generators made it "dramatically clear that the power of the future was AC. From that point forward more than 80 percent of all the electrical devices ordered in the United States were for alternating current" ("Tesla: Master of Lightning," 2004).

The City of Light made such an impression on financier J. P. Morgan that he embarked on a ruthless campaign to wrest control of the Tesla patents from Westinghouse. With Westinghouse on the brink of collapse, Tesla agreed to slash the royalties that the company owed him for his inventions. Tesla's gesture enabled Westinghouse to withstand Morgan's predations, but it also deprived the inventor of the financial security that had once appeared to be his.

In the late 1890s Tesla became involved in a competition with Italian inventor Guglielmo Marconi to develop a wireless telegraphy system. At first it appeared that Tesla occupied the high legal ground in the battle. Armed with a range of radio patent applications, Tesla initially expressed unconcern over the fact that Marconi had appropriated some of the Serbian inventor's own devices and work to advance his wireless ideas. In 1901, though, Marconi became the first person to transmit and receive signals across the Atlantic Ocean, a feat that brought a flood of investors. Marconi's company became a politically formidable one, and in 1904 the U.S. Patent Office, after years of denying Marconi's patent applications as duplications of patents held by Tesla and others, suddenly recognized the Italian scientist as the inventor of radio.

This blow came at the same time that another Tesla research initiative into the wireless transmission of energy was tottering. Back in 1900, Tesla wrote an article titled "The Problem of Increasing Human Energy" for publication in Johnson's magazine. In his essay, excerpted above, Tesla speculated about a future of instantaneous global communication unconstrained by wire, limitless energy drawn from the sun, and electrical innovations capable of controlling the weather. He characterized all of these possibilities as part of a general, inexorable march of advancement by mankind (and he definitely meant "mankind"—the essay included harsh criticism of the education of women for drawing them away from their "household duties" and "mak[ing] men out of them").

Tesla warned, however, that a thousand "evils" posed a threat to this advancement, the most serious being the difficulty in maintaining a prosperous and nutritious food supply capable of feeding the globe. It is here that the inventor ventured forth with a ringing endorsement of vegetarianism on both utilitarian and moral grounds. He asserted that societies that embrace vegetarian diets are not only making more economical use of their resources, but that they also benefit in terms of health and vitality: "Many races living almost exclusively on vegetables are of superior physique and strength." Tesla further pressed his case by arguing that vegetarianism would be of moral benefit because it would wean humans from its carnivorous state, which he saw as a vestige of primitive man.

Tesla's comments on vegetarianism attracted relatively little attention, but his musings about wireless global communication and solar energy drew wide comment and interest. One of his intrigued readers was Morgan, who agreed to bankroll Tesla's efforts to build such a system via a massive electrical tower. The tower project, called Wardenclyffe, was located on Long Island, New York. Over the next few years, though, Morgan's interest in the project waned, and in 1905 he pulled his financial support. Tesla was forced to walk away from Wardenclyffe, to his considerable distress.

Tesla faded from public view over the next few decades, although occasional statements and writings still attracted some attention. He lived modestly in a New York hotel and spent larger and larger blocs of time feeding pigeons at nearby parks. "All told, Tesla had 111 American patents, and there were apparently many other inventions he never bothered to register," wrote one biographer. "But lacking any major backer, most of his inventions remained either completely theoretical or were never fully developed for real commercial use. More and more, Tesla lived in his own world, as big a romantic as ever, and as eccentric. He had his vegetarian meals specially cooked by the hotel chef and insisted that the help not get closer to him than a few feet, part of his phobia of germs."

Tesla died on January 7, 1943, in New York City. A few months after his death, the U.S. Supreme Court ruled that Tesla's half-century-old radio patent actually superseded that of Marconi. This decision has since become a key talking point to historians who insist that Tesla was the true father of radio.

FURTHER READING

Carlson, W. Bernard. *Tesla: Inventor of the Electrical Age.* Princeton, NJ: Princeton University Press, 2013.

Cheney, Margaret. *Tesla: Man Out of Time.* 1981. New York: Touchstone, 2001.

Jonnes, Jill. *Empires of Light: Edison, Tesla, Westinghouse, and the Race to Electrify the World.* New York: Random House, 2003.

"Nikola Tesla."Biography.com, 2014, accessed September 8, 2014.http://www.biography .com/people/nikola-tesla-9504443.

Seifer, Marc. *Wizard: The Life and Times of Nikola Tesla.* New York: Citadel Press, 1998.

"Tesla: Master of Lightning." PBS.com, 2004, accessed September 8, 2014.http://www.pbs .org/tesla/index.html.

"I, THEODORE ROOSEVELT, ... DO HEREBY MAKE KNOWN AND PROCLAIM THAT THE WICHITA FOREST RESERVE ... IS DESIGNATED AND SET ASIDE FOR THE PROTECTION OF GAME ANIMALS AND BIRDS"

- **Document:** Presidential Proclamation 563—Redesignating the Wichita Forest Reserve, Oklahoma, as a Game Preserve.
- **Date:** June 2, 1905.
- **Where:** Washington, D.C.
- **Significance:** President Theodore Roosevelt's proclamation designating a region in Oklahoma as a game preserve was the first time such an area was so established by the U.S. government.

DOCUMENT

Whereas, it is provided by the Act of Congress, approved January twenty-fourth, nineteen hundred and five, entitled, "An Act for the protection of wild animals and birds in the Wichita Forest Reserve," "That the President of the United States is hereby authorized to designate such areas in the Wichita Forest Reserve as should, in his opinion, be set aside for the protection of game animals and birds and be recognized as a breeding place therefor.

"Sec. 2. That when such areas have been designated as provided for in section one of this Act, hunting, trapping, killing, or capturing of game animals and birds upon the lands of the United States within the limits of said areas shall be unlawful, except under such regulations as may be prescribed from time to time, by the Secretary of Agriculture; and any person violating such regulations or the provisions of this Act shall be deemed guilty of a misdemeanor, and shall, upon conviction in any United States court of competent jurisdiction, be fined in a sum not exceeding one thousand dollars or be imprisoned for a period not exceeding one year, or shall suffer both fine and imprisonment, in the discretion of the court.

"Sec. 3. That it is the purpose of this Act to protect from trespass the public lands of the United States and the game animals and birds which may be thereon, and not to interfere with the operation of the local game laws as affecting private, State, or Territorial lands";

And Whereas, for the purpose of giving this Act effect, it appears desirable that the entire Wichita Forest Reserve be declared a Game Preserve;

Now, Therefore, I, Theodore Roosevelt, President of the United States, by virtue of the power in me vested by the aforesaid Act of Congress, do hereby make known and proclaim that the Wichita Forest Reserve, in the Territory of Oklahoma, is designated and set aside for the protection of game animals and birds, and shall be recognized as a breeding place therefor, and that the hunting, trapping, killing or capturing of game animals and birds upon the lands of the United States within the limits of said area is unlawful, except under such regulations as may be prescribed from time to time by the Secretary of Agriculture.

In Witness Whereof, I have hereunto set my hand and caused the seal of the United States to be affixed.

Done at the city of Washington this 2d day of June, in the year of our Lord one thousand nine hundred and five, and of the Independence of the United States the one hundred and twenty-ninth.

THEODORE ROOSEVELT.
By the President:
FRANCIS B. LOOMIS,
Acting Secretary of State.

Source: Roosevelt, Theodore. "Proclamation 563—Redesignating the Wichita Forest Reserve, Oklahoma, as a Game Preserve," June 2, 1905. Online by Gerhard Peters and John T. Woolley, *The American Presidency Project.* http://www.presidency.ucsb.edu/ws/?pid=69581.

ANALYSIS

The Wichita Mountains National Wildlife Refuge is located in Comanche County, Oklahoma, in the southwestern part of the state. With a total size of 59,000 acres, it is Oklahoma's largest wildlife refuge. The area includes many different animals: antelope, bobcats, chickens, coyotes, elk, hawks, longhorn cattle, otters, prairie dogs, rabbits, raccoons, sheep, turkeys, and various species of migratory birds.

In 1901 President William McKinley set aside a portion of the mountains as the Wichita Forest Reserve and gave the responsibility of its management to the Forestry Division of the U.S. Department of the Interior's General Land Office. In 1905 the Wichita Forest Reserve was transferred to the U.S. Department of Agriculture's Bureau of Forestry. That same year Congress passed a bill that authorized the establishment of a national wildlife refuge. Seizing on the opportunity, President Theodore Roosevelt issued Proclamation 563, which redesignated the Wichita Forest Reserve as a game preserve, on June 2, 1905. Roosevelt, who was an avid hunter and outdoorsman, took this step after personally visiting the reserve. As noted by the National Audubon Society, the Wichita Game Preserve became "the first managed and fenced preserve for big game animals to be established by the federal government."

A key aspect of Wichita's designation as a game preserve was the hope that it might be a sanctuary for the nation's bison population, which had been devastated by rapacious hunting practices through the second half of the nineteenth century. The same year of the president's proclamation, the New York Zoological Park (later known as the Bronx Zoo) offered to donate 15 bison to the refuge. According to a Congressional report in 1905, "in view of the well-known fact that no large species of quadruped [animal with four feet] can be bred and perpetuated for centuries in the confinement of zoological gardens and parks—even where the enclosures are as large as those in the New York Zoological Park—it seemed reasonably certain that the only way to insure the perpetuation of the bison species for centuries to come lies in the creation of several national herds, maintained by the Government on large areas of grazing grounds. It seemed desirable that for the encouragement of the National Government in the perpetuation of the bison species the scientific institutions of the country and private individuals also should do more than offer advice and exhortations to Congress." The selection process and analysis and preparation of the range for the animals took two years. New, safe, and proper crates were built, the animals were loaded in New York, and the bison eventually were delivered safely to their new home in 1907. This successful transfer led to the formation of the American Bison Society, which in 1908 urged Congress to establish the National Bison Range in the northern plains of Montana. These events helped spur a modest recovery of the bison population. In the twenty-first century, approximately 550 bison roam the Wichita Refuge. (Elk were also transferred to the same region from Wyoming shortly after the bison debuted.)

Roosevelt's creation of the Wichita Game Preserve reflected his comfort with using the full power of the Oval Office to preserve wildlife, forests, and other natural resources that, by the time he reached the White House, had been under decades of intensive pressure from logging operations, market hunters, and agricultural interests. According to author Robert Fischman, the president viewed conservation "as a moral issue as well as a necessary condition for sustaining national prosperity."

Roosevelt's first use of official powers specifically for the protection of threatened wildlife actually came on March 14, 1903, when he issued a presidential proclamation designating Pelican Island, Florida, as a "preserve and breeding ground for native birds." A lawyer with the government subsequently paid Roosevelt a visit and informed him that "I cannot find a law that will allow you to do this, Mr. President." Unruffled, Roosevelt countered by asking, "Is there a law that will prevent it?" When the lawyer granted that there was no such law, Roosevelt responded, "Very well, I so declare it" (quoted in Wilkinson, 1987). The result was a bird reserve—the first time the U.S. government had identified land exclusively for wildlife.

Beginning with his Pelican Island proclamation through the end of his presidency in 1909, Roosevelt established 52 bird reserves and four big game reserves. In the specific case of the Wichita reserve, Roosevelt added another 3,680 acres to that designated region in 1906. A year later, all U.S. forest reserves were reclassified as national forests, prompting a name change to the Wichita National Forest and Game Preserve.

During his presidency, Roosevelt also established five national parks and four national monuments. In fact, on the same day he issued the Wichita Game Refuge proclamation, he also issued Proclamation 564, which established the Lassen Peak Forest Reserve (now Lassen National Forest) in northeastern California, and Proclamation 565, which established the Maury Mountain Forest Reserve in Oregon (now divided up among many forests).

FURTHER READING

Brinkley, Douglas. *Wilderness Warrior: Theodore Roosevelt and the Crusade for America.* New York: HarperCollins, 2009.

Cutright, Paul Russell. *Theodore Roosevelt: The Making of a Conservationist.* Urbana: University of Illinois Press, 1985.

Fischman, Robert. *The National Wildlife Refuges: Coordinating a Conservation System Through Law.* Washington, DC: Island Press, 2003.

"Frequently Asked Questions." *Wichita Mountains.* U.S. Fish & Wildlife Services, accessed December 10, 2014. http://www.fws.gov/refuge/Wichita_Mountains/FAQs.html.

"History of Pelican Island." *Pelican Island National Wildlife Refuge.* U.S. Fish & Wildlife Refuge, accessed December 10, 2014. http://www.fws.gov/pelicanisland/history.html.

Hornaday, William T. "The Founding of the Wichita National Bison Herd." *United States Congressional Serial Set.* Issue 5219, accessed December 10, 2014. Washington, DC: Government Printing Office, 1900s.

Morris, Edmund. *Theodore Rex.* New York: Random House, 2001.

O'Dell, Larry. "Wichita Mountains National Wildlife Refuge." *Encyclopedia of Oklahoma History & Culture.* Oklahoma Historical Society, accessed December 10, 2014. http://digital.library.okstate.edu/encyclopedia/entries/W/WI003.html.

"Theodore Roosevelt and the National Park System." *Theodore Roosevelt Birthplace.* National Park Service, accessed December 31, 2014. http://www.nps.gov/thrb/historyculture/trandthenpsystem.htm.

Wilkinson, Charles F. *Land and Resource Planning in the National Forests.* Washington, DC: Island Press, 1987.

Wilson, Randall K. *America's Public Lands: From Yellowstone to Yogi Bear and Beyond.* Lanham, MD: Rowman & Littlefield, 2014.

"[THE HOGS] WERE SO VERY HUMAN IN THEIR PROTESTS—AND SO PERFECTLY WITHIN THEIR RIGHTS!"

- **Document:** Excerpt from Chapter 3 of the muckraking novel *The Jungle* by Upton Sinclair.
- **Date:** 1906.
- **Where:** *The Jungle* is set in the stockyards of Chicago.
- **Significance:** One of the great muckraking works of the Progressive Era, *The Jungle* cast an unsparing eye on the filth and corruption of the operations of America's early twentieth-century "beef trust," or meatpacking industry. Upton Sinclair's exposé of the dehumanizing conditions in Chicago's stockyards and slaughterhouses, the brutal treatment of animals, the filth and poverty in which the industry's immigrant laborers lived, and the nauseating ingredients in the nation's food supply caused a tremendous uproar across the United States. Public outrage about Sinclair's revelations was so great that Congress defied the politically influential beef trust and passed both the Federal Meat Inspection Act and the Pure Food and Drug Act in 1906. President Theodore Roosevelt signed both measures, and the latter in particular forced improvements in the safety and quality of the nation's food supply.

  Sinclair, however, expressed considerable frustration that the outrage generated by *The Jungle* only seemed to extend to his accounts of diseased, spoiled, and contaminated meat being packaged for sale to an unsuspecting public. He had also meant for the book to elicit sympathy for the exploited workers who toiled on the "killing floor" of the dank slaughterhouses, where terrified animals were routinely killed in brutal fashion. "I aimed at the public's heart," he later said, "and by accident hit its stomach." In the following excerpt, Sinclair describes how pigs and cattle are killed in the slaughterhouses, emphasizing the terror they must have felt in their final moments.

DOCUMENT

. . . There being no more to be done that day, the shop was left under the care of Lucija, and her husband sallied forth to show his friends the sights of Packingtown. Jokubas did this with the air of a country gentleman escorting a party of visitors over his estate; he was an old-time resident, and all these wonders had grown up under his eyes, and he had a personal pride in them. The packers might own the land, but he claimed the landscape, and there was no one to say nay to this.

They passed down the busy street that led to the yards. It was still early morning, and everything was at its high tide of activity. A steady stream of employees was

pouring through the gate—employees of the higher sort, at this hour, clerks and ste-
nographers and such. For the women there were waiting big two-horse wagons,
which set off at a gallop as fast as they were filled. In the distance there was heard
again the lowing of the cattle, a sound as of a far-off ocean calling. They followed
it, this time, as eager as children in sight of a circus menagerie—which, indeed,
the scene a good deal resembled. They crossed the railroad tracks, and then on each
side of the street were the pens full of cattle; they would have stopped to look, but
Jokubas hurried them on, to where there was a stairway and a raised gallery, from
which everything could be seen. Here they stood, staring, breathless with wonder.

There is over a square mile of space in the yards, and more than half of it is occupied by cattle pens; north and south as far as the eye can reach there stretches a sea
of pens. And they were all filled—so many cattle no one had ever dreamed existed in
the world. Red cattle, black, white, and yellow cattle; old cattle and young cattle;
great bellowing bulls and little calves not an hour born; meek-eyed milch cows
and fierce, long-horned Texas steers. The sound of them here was as of all the barn-
yards of the universe; and as for counting them—it would have taken all day simply
to count the pens. Here and there ran long alleys, blocked at intervals by gates; and
Jokubas told them that the number of these gates was twenty-five thousand. Jokubas
had recently been reading a newspaper article which was full of statistics such as
that, and he was very proud as he repeated them and made his guests cry out with
wonder. Jurgis too had a little of this sense of pride. Had he not just gotten a job,
and become a sharer in all this activity, a cog in this marvelous machine? Here
and there about the alleys galloped men upon horseback, booted, and carrying long
whips; they were very busy, calling to each other, and to those who were driving the
cattle. They were drovers and stock raisers, who had come from far states, and
brokers and commission merchants, and buyers for all the big packing houses.

. . . Then Jokubas pointed out the place where the cattle were driven to be
weighed, upon a great scale that would weigh a hundred thousand pounds at once
and record it automatically. It was near to the east entrance that they stood, and
all along this east side of the yards ran the railroad tracks, into which the cars were
run, loaded with cattle. All night long this had been going on, and now the pens
were full; by tonight they would all be empty, and the same thing would be done
again.

"And what will become of all these creatures?" cried Teta Elzbieta.

"By tonight," Jokubas answered, "they will all be killed and cut up; and over there
on the other side of the packing houses are more railroad tracks, where the cars come
to take them away."

There were two hundred and fifty miles of track within the yards, their guide went
on to tell them. They brought about ten thousand head of cattle every day, and as
many hogs, and half as many sheep—which meant some eight or ten million live
creatures turned into food every year. One stood and watched, and little by little
caught the drift of the tide, as it set in the direction of the packing houses. There
were groups of cattle being driven to the chutes, which were roadways about fifteen
feet wide, raised high above the pens. In these chutes the stream of animals was continuous; it was quite uncanny to watch them, pressing on to their fate, all unsuspi-
cious, a very river of death. Our friends were not poetical, and the sight suggested

to them no metaphors of human destiny; they thought only of the wonderful efficiency of it all. The chutes into which the hogs went climbed high up—to the very top of the distant buildings; and Jokubas explained that the hogs went up by the power of their own legs, and then their weight carried them back through all the processes necessary to make them into pork.

"They don't waste anything here," said the guide, and then he laughed and added a witticism, which he was pleased that his unsophisticated friends should take to be his own: "They use everything about the hog except the squeal." In front of Brown's General Office building there grows a tiny plot of grass, and this, you may learn, is the only bit of green thing in Packingtown; likewise this jest about the hog and his squeal, the stock in trade of all the guides, is the one gleam of humor that you will find there.

After they had seen enough of the pens, the party went up the street, to the mass of buildings which occupy the center of the yards. These buildings, made of brick and stained with innumerable layers of Packingtown smoke, were painted all over with advertising signs, from which the visitor realized suddenly that he had come to the home of many of the torments of his life. It was here that they made those products with the wonders of which they pestered him so—by placards that defaced the landscape when he traveled, and by staring advertisements in the newspapers and magazines—by silly little jingles that he could not get out of his mind, and gaudy pictures that lurked for him around every street corner. Here was where they made Brown's Imperial Hams and Bacon, Brown's Dressed Beef, Brown's Excelsior Sausages! Here was the headquarters of Durham's Pure Leaf Lard, of Durham's Breakfast Bacon, Durham's Canned Beef, Potted Ham, Deviled Chicken, Peerless Fertilizer!

Entering one of the Durham buildings, they found a number of other visitors waiting; and before long there came a guide, to escort them through the place. They make a great feature of showing strangers through the packing plants, for it is a good advertisement. But Ponas Jokubas whispered maliciously that the visitors did not see any more than the packers wanted them to. They climbed a long series of stairways outside of the building, to the top of its five or six stories. Here was the chute, with its river of hogs, all patiently toiling upward; there was a place for them to rest to cool off, and then through another passageway they went into a room from which there is no returning for hogs.

It was a long, narrow room, with a gallery along it for visitors. At the head there was a great iron wheel, about twenty feet in circumference, with rings here and there along its edge. Upon both sides of this wheel there was a narrow space, into which came the hogs at the end of their journey; in the midst of them stood a great burly Negro, bare-armed and bare-chested. He was resting for the moment, for the wheel had stopped while men were cleaning up. In a minute or two, however, it began slowly to revolve, and then the men upon each side of it sprang to work. They had chains which they fastened about the leg of the nearest hog, and the other end of the chain they hooked into one of the rings upon the wheel. So, as the wheel turned, a hog was suddenly jerked off his feet and borne aloft.

At the same instant the car was assailed by a most terrifying shriek; the visitors started in alarm, the women turned pale and shrank back. The shriek was followed

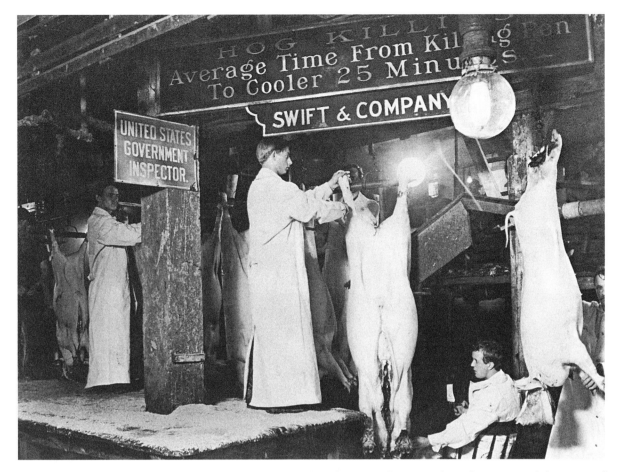

Meat inspectors examine hogs at the Swift & Company packing house in Chicago in the early 1900s. Both hygiene and labor conditions within the meatpacking industry came under close scrutiny by "muckraking" journalists. Perhaps the most prominent report about the industry came from writer Upton Sinclair, whose 1906 novel *The Jungle* helped lead to the passage of the 1906 Federal Meat Inspection Act. (Corbis)

by another, louder and yet more agonizing—for once started upon that journey, the hog never came back; at the top of the wheel he was shunted off upon a trolley, and went sailing down the room. And meantime another was swung up, and then another, and another, until there was a double line of them, each dangling by a foot and kicking in frenzy—and squealing. The uproar was appalling, perilous to the eardrums; one feared there was too much sound for the room to hold—that the walls must give way or the ceiling crack. There were high squeals and low squeals, grunts, and wails of agony; there would come a momentary lull, and then a fresh outburst, louder than ever, surging up to a deafening climax. It was too much for some of the visitors—the men would look at each other, laughing nervously, and the women would stand with hands clenched, and the blood rushing to their faces, and the tears starting in their eyes.

Meantime, heedless of all these things, the men upon the floor were going about their work. Neither squeals of hogs nor tears of visitors made any difference to them; one by one they hooked up the hogs, and one by one with a swift stroke they slit their throats. There was a long line of hogs, with squeals and lifeblood ebbing away together; until at last each started again, and vanished with a splash into a huge vat of boiling water.

It was all so very businesslike that one watched it fascinated. It was porkmaking by machinery, porkmaking by applied mathematics. And yet somehow the most matter-of-fact person could not help thinking of the hogs; they were so innocent, they came so very trustingly; and they were so very human in their protests—and so perfectly within their rights! They had done nothing to deserve it; and it was adding insult to injury, as the thing was done here, swinging them up in this cold-blooded, impersonal way, without a pretense of apology, without the homage of a tear. Now and then a visitor wept, to be sure; but this slaughtering machine ran on, visitors or no visitors. It was like some horrible crime committed in a dungeon, all unseen and unheeded, buried out of sight and of memory.

One could not stand and watch very long without becoming philosophical, without beginning to deal in symbols and similes, and to hear the hog squeal of the universe. Was it permitted to believe that there was nowhere upon the earth, or above the earth, a heaven for hogs, where they were requited for all this suffering? Each one of these hogs was a separate creature. Some were white hogs, some were black; some were brown, some were spotted; some were old, some young; some were long and lean, some were monstrous. And each of them had an individuality of his own, a will of his own, a hope and a heart's desire; each was full of self-confidence, of self-importance, and a sense of dignity. And trusting and strong in faith he had gone about his business, the while a black shadow hung over him and a horrid Fate waited in his pathway. Now suddenly it had swooped upon him, and had seized him by the leg. Relentless, remorseless, it was; all his protests, his screams, were nothing to it—it did its cruel will with him, as if his wishes, his feelings, had simply no existence at all; it cut his throat and watched him gasp out his life. And now was one to believe that there was nowhere a god of hogs, to whom this hog personality was precious, to whom these hog squeals and agonies had a meaning? Who would take this hog into his arms and comfort him, reward him for his work well done, and show him the meaning of his sacrifice? Perhaps some glimpse of all this was in the thoughts of our humble-minded Jurgis, as he turned to go on with the rest of the party, and muttered: "Dieve—but I'm glad I'm not a hog!"

The carcass hog was scooped out of the vat by machinery, and then it fell to the second floor, passing on the way through a wonderful machine with numerous scrapers, which adjusted themselves to the size and shape of the animal, and sent it out at the other end with nearly all of its bristles removed. It was then again strung up by machinery, and sent upon another trolley ride; this time passing between two lines of men, who sat upon a raised platform, each doing a certain single thing to the carcass as it came to him. One scraped the outside of a leg; another scraped the inside of the same leg. One with a swift stroke cut the throat; another with two swift strokes severed the head, which fell to the floor and vanished through a hole. Another made a slit down the body; a second opened the body wider; a third with a saw cut the breastbone; a fourth loosened the entrails; a fifth pulled them out—and they also slid through a hole in the floor. There were men to scrape each side and men to scrape the back; there were men to clean the carcass inside, to trim it and wash it. Looking down this room, one saw, creeping slowly, a line of dangling hogs a hundred yards in length; and for every yard there was a man, working as if a demon were after him. At the end of this hog's progress every inch of the carcass had been gone over several times; and then it was rolled into the chilling room, where it stayed for twenty-four hours, and where a stranger might lose himself in a forest of freezing hogs.

Before the carcass was admitted here, however, it had to pass a government inspector, who sat in the doorway and felt of the glands in the neck for tuberculosis. This government inspector did not have the manner of a man who was worked to death; he was apparently not haunted by a fear that the hog might get by him before he had finished his testing. If you were a sociable person, he was quite willing to enter into conversation with you, and to explain to you the deadly nature of the ptomaines which are found in tubercular pork; and while he was talking with you you could hardly be so ungrateful as to notice that a dozen carcasses were passing him untouched. This inspector wore a blue uniform, with brass buttons, and he gave an atmosphere of authority to the scene, and, as it were, put the stamp of official approval upon the things which were done in Durham's.

Jurgis went down the line with the rest of the visitors, staring open-mouthed, lost in wonder. He had dressed hogs himself in the forest of Lithuania; but he had never expected to live to see one hog dressed by several hundred men. It was like a wonderful poem to him, and he took it all in guilelessly—even to the conspicuous signs demanding immaculate cleanliness of the employees. Jurgis was vexed when the cynical Jokubas translated these signs with sarcastic comments, offering to take them to the secret rooms where the spoiled meats went to be doctored.

The party descended to the next floor, where the various waste materials were treated. Here came the entrails, to be scraped and washed clean for sausage casings; men and women worked here in the midst of a sickening stench, which caused the visitors to hasten by, gasping. To another room came all the scraps to be "tanked," which meant boiling and pumping off the grease to make soap and lard; below they took out the refuse, and this, too, was a region in which the visitors did not linger. In still other places men were engaged in cutting up the carcasses that had been through the chilling rooms. First there were the "splitters," the most expert workmen in the plant, who earned as high as fifty cents an hour, and did not a thing all day except chop hogs down the middle. Then there were "cleaver men," great giants with muscles of iron; each had two men to attend him—to slide the half carcass in front of him on the table, and hold it while he chopped it, and then turn each piece so that he might chop it once more. His cleaver had a blade about two feet long, and he never made but one cut; he made it so neatly, too, that his implement did not smite through and dull itself—there was just enough force for a perfect cut, and no more. So through various yawning holes there slipped to the floor below—to one room hams, to another forequarters, to another sides of pork. One might go down to this floor and see the pickling rooms, where the hams were put into vats, and the great smoke rooms, with their airtight iron doors. In other rooms they prepared salt pork—there were whole cellars full of it, built up in great towers to the ceiling. In yet other rooms they were putting up meats in boxes and barrels, and wrapping hams and bacon in oiled paper, sealing and labeling and sewing them. From the doors of these rooms went men with loaded trucks, to the platform where freight cars were waiting to be filled; and one went out there and realized with a start that he had come at last to the ground floor of this enormous building.

Then the party went across the street to where they did the killing of beef—where every hour they turned four or five hundred cattle into meat. Unlike the place they had left, all this work was done on one floor; and instead of there being one line of carcasses which moved to the workmen, there were fifteen or twenty lines, and the men moved from one to another of these. This made a scene of intense activity, a picture of human power wonderful to watch. It was all in one great room, like a circus amphitheater, with a gallery for visitors running over the center.

Along one side of the room ran a narrow gallery, a few feet from the floor; into which gallery the cattle were driven by men with goads which gave them electric shocks. Once crowded in here, the creatures were prisoned, each in a separate pen, by gates that shut, leaving them no room to turn around; and while they stood bellowing and plunging, over the top of the pen there leaned one of the "knockers," armed with a sledge hammer, and watching for a chance to deal a blow. The room echoed with the thuds in quick succession, and the stamping and kicking of the steers. The instant the animal had fallen, the "knocker" passed on to another; while a second man raised a lever, and the side of the pen was raised, and the animal, still kicking and struggling, slid out to the "killing bed." Here a man put shackles about one leg, and pressed another lever, and the body was jerked up into the air. There were fifteen or twenty such pens, and it was a matter of only a couple of minutes to knock fifteen or twenty cattle and roll them out. Then once more the gates were opened, and another lot rushed in; and so out of each pen there rolled a steady stream of carcasses, which the men upon the killing beds had to get out of the way.

The manner in which they did this was something to be seen and never forgotten. They worked with furious intensity, literally upon the run—at a pace with which there is nothing to be compared except a football game. It was all highly specialized labor, each man having his task to do; generally this would consist of only two or three specific cuts, and he would pass down the line of fifteen or twenty carcasses, making these cuts upon each. First there came the "butcher," to bleed them; this meant one swift stroke, so swift that you could not see it—only the flash of the knife; and before you could realize it, the man had darted on to the next line, and a stream of bright red was pouring out upon the floor. This floor was half an inch deep with blood, in spite of the best efforts of men who kept shoveling it through holes; it must have made the floor slippery, but no one could have guessed this by watching the men at work.

The carcass hung for a few minutes to bleed; there was no time lost, however, for there were several hanging in each line, and one was always ready. It was let down to the ground, and there came the "headsman," whose task it was to sever the head, with two or three swift strokes. Then came the "floorsman," to make the first cut in the skin; and then another to finish ripping the skin down the center; and then half a dozen more in swift succession, to finish the skinning. After they were through, the carcass was again swung up; and while a man with a stick examined the skin, to make sure that it had not been cut, and another rolled it up and tumbled it through one of the inevitable holes in the floor, the beef proceeded on its journey.

There were men to cut it, and men to split it, and men to gut it and scrape it clean inside. There were some with hose which threw jets of boiling water upon it, and others who removed the feet and added the final touches. In the end, as with the hogs, the finished beef was run into the chilling room, to hang its appointed time.

Source: Sinclair, Upton. *The Jungle*. New York: Doubleday, 1906. http://www .gutenberg.org/files/140/140-h/140-h.htm.

ANALYSIS

This passage from *The Jungle* reveals some of the horrors visited upon hogs and cattle killed in early twentieth-century slaughterhouses to produce bacon, ham, steaks, and hamburger for American families. Sinclair's narrative displays a clear revulsion with the brutality of the process—and especially with the callous disregard exhibited by the processing operations for the pain and terror that the animals felt during their last moments of life. The author wrote that these "cold-blooded" executions, undertaken without a "pretense of apology," added "insult to injury" to the animals herded into the slaughterhouses.

Sinclair then proceeds to speculate whether the pigs meeting their demise, each with "an individuality of his own, a will of his own, a hope and a heart's desire," might find a more peaceful and comforting existence in an afterlife presided over by a "god of hogs." Years later, however, Sinclair insisted that his musings about a possible hog heaven and hog deity were not meant to be taken seriously. Writing in his 1962 autobiography, he asserted that "for fifty-six years I have been ridiculed for a passage in *The Jungle* that deals with the moral claims of dying hogs—which passage was intended as hilarious farce" (quoted in Lundblad, 2013, p. 109). This protest underscores how the author's main point in writing his thinly fictionalized novel was to shine a spotlight on the exploitation of human workers, not animals. In fact, "many literary critics have read Sinclair's sections on animal killings as metaphors for capitalism's brutalization of workers" (Warren, 2007, p. 127).

Sinclair experimented with vegetarianism and other dietary regimens through much of his adult life, but in 1911 he indicated that his dalliances with a vegetarian diet did not stem from any outrage at the treatment of animals in America's slaughterhouses. "I had never taken any stock in the arguments for vegetarianism upon the moral side. It has always seemed to me that human beings have a right to eat meat, if meat is necessary for their best development, either physical or mental. I have never had any sympathy with that 'humanitarianism' which tells us that it is our duty to regard pigs and chickens as our brothers" (Sinclair, 1911, pp. 86–87).

Sinclair's comments notwithstanding, passages from *The Jungle* such as the one excerpted here became important tools for people and organizations calling for more humane treatment of animals. More than a century after its publication, in fact, Sinclair's muckraking novel is regarded not only as a work that hit America's stomach but also as one that contributed to the growth of a coherent animal welfare movement in the United States.

FURTHER READING

Arthur, Anthony. *Radical Innocent: Upton Sinclair*. New York: Random House, 2006.

Gallagher, Aileen. *The Muckrakers: American Journalism during the Age of Reform*. New York: Rosen Publishing, 2006.

Jones, Dena. "Crimes Unseen." *Orion*, July/August 2004. http://www.orionmagazine.org/index.php/articles/article/144/.

Lundblad, Michael. *The Birth of a Jungle: Animality in Progressive-Era U.S. Literature and Culture*. New York: Oxford University Press, 2013.

Sinclair, Upton. *The Fasting Cure*. New York and London: Mitchell Kennerly, 1911.

Warren, Wilson J. *Tied to the Great Packing Machine: The Midwest and Meatpacking*. Iowa City: University of Iowa Press, 2007.

"ETHICS ... WITHOUT LIMITS TOWARDS ALL THAT LIVES"

- **Document:** *Civilisation and Ethics* by philosopher and physician Albert Schweitzer.
- **Date:** 1923.
- **Where:** Published in London, England.
- **Significance:** The excerpt demonstrates Schweitzer's philosophical stance regarding moral interactions with all living creatures and the extent to which he would follow his beliefs. Schweitzer's perspective became an important one in the development of theories of animal rights, and his legacy is still evident in many aspects of the animal rights movement.

DOCUMENT

Complicated and laborious are the roads along which ethical thought, which has mistaken its way and taken too high a flight, must be brought back. Its course, however, maps itself out quite simply if, instead of taking apparently convenient short cuts, it keeps to its right direction from the very beginning. For this three things are necessary: It must have nothing to do with an ethical interpretation of the world; it must become cosmic and mystical, that is to say, it must seek to conceive all the self-devotion which rules in ethics as a manifestation of an inward, spiritual relation to the world; it must not lapse into abstract thinking, but must remain elemental, understanding self-devotion to the world to be self-devotion of human life to every form of living being with which it can come into relation.

The origin of ethics is that I think out the full meaning of the world-affirmation which, together with the life-affirmation in my will-to-live, is given by nature, and try to make it a reality.

To become ethical means to begin to think sincerely.

Thinking is the argument between willing and knowing which goes on within me. Its course is a naïve one, if the will demands of knowledge to be shown a world which corresponds to the impulses which it carries within itself, and if knowledge attempts to satisfy this requirement. This dialogue, which is doomed to produce no result, must give place to a debate of the right kind, in which the will demands from knowledge only what it really knows.

If knowledge answers solely with what it knows, it is always teaching the will one and the same fact, namely, that in and behind all phenomena there is a will-to-live. Knowledge, though ever becoming deeper and more comprehensive, can do nothing except take us ever deeper and ever further into the mystery that all that is, is will-to-live. Progress in science consists only in increasingly accurate description of the phenomena in which life in its innumerable forms appears and passes, letting us discover life where we did not previously expect it, and putting us in a position to turn to our own use in this or that way what we have learnt of the course of the will-to-live in nature. But what life is, no science can tell us.

For our conception of the universe and of life, then, the gain derived from knowledge is only that it makes it harder for us to be thoughtless, because it ever more forcibly compels our attention to the mystery of the will-to-live which we see stirring everywhere. Hence the difference between learned and unlearned is entirely relative. The unlearned man who, at the sight of a tree in flower, is overpowered by the mystery of the will-to-live which is stirring all round him, knows more than the scientist who studies under the microscope or in physical and chemical activity a thousand forms of the will-to-live, but, with all his knowledge of the life-course of these manifestations of the will-to-live, is unmoved by the mystery that everything which exists is will-to-live while he is puffed up with vanity at being able to describe exactly a fragment of the course of life.

All true knowledge passes on into experience. The nature of the manifestations I do not know, but I form a conception of it in analogy to the will-to-live which is within myself. Thus my knowledge of the world becomes experience of the world. The knowledge which is becoming experience does not allow me to remain in face of the world a man who merely knows, but forces upon me an inward relation to the world, and fills me with reverence for the mysterious will-to-live which is in all things. By making me think and wonder, it leads me ever upwards to the heights of reverence for life. There it lets my hand go. It cannot accompany me further. My will-to-live must now find its way about the world by itself.

It is not by informing me what this or that manifestation of life means in the sumtotal of the world that knowledge brings me into connection with the world. It goes about with me not in outer circles, but in the inner ones. From within outwards it puts me in relation to the world by making my will-to-live feel everything around it as also will-to-live.

With Descartes, philosophy starts from the dogma: "I think, therefore I exist." With this paltry, arbitrarily chosen beginning, philosophy it is landed irretrievably on the road to the abstract. It never finds the right approach to ethics, and remains entangled in a dead world—and life—view. True philosophy must start from the most immediate and comprehensive fact of consciousness, which says: "I am life which wills to live, in the midst of life which will to live." This is not an ingenious dogmatic formula. Day by day, hour by hour, I live and move in it. At every moment of reflection it stands fresh before me. There bursts forth from it again and again, as from roots that can never dry up, a living world- and life-view which can deal with all the facts of Being. A mysticism of ethical union with Being grows out of it.

As in my own will-to-live there is a longing for wider life and for the mysterious exaltation of the will-to-live which we call pleasure, with dread of annihilation and of the mysterious depreciation of the will-to-live which we call pain; so is it also in the will-to-live all around me, whether it can express itself before me, or remains dumb.

Ethics consists, therefore, in my experiencing the compulsion to show to all will-to-live the same reverence as I do to my own. There we have given us that basic principle of the morals which is a necessity of thought. It is good to maintain and to encourage life; it is bad to destroy life or to obstruct it.

As a matter of fact, everything which in the ordinary ethical valuation of the relations of men to each other ranks as good can be brought under the description of material and spiritual maintenance or promotion of human life, and of effort to bring it to its highest value. Conversely, everything which ranks as bad in human relations is in the last analysis material or spiritual destruction or obstruction of human life, and negligence in the endeavour to bring it to its highest value. Separate individual categories of good and evil which lie far apart and have apparently no connection at all with one another fit together like the pieces of a jig-saw puzzle, as soon as they are comprehended and deepened in this the most universal definition of good and evil.

The basic principle of the moral which is a necessity of thought means, however, not only an ordering and deepening, but also a widening of the current views of good and evil. A man is truly ethical only when he obeys the compulsion to help all life which he is able to assist, and shrinks from injuring anything that lives. He does not ask how far this or that life deserves one's sympathy as being valuable, nor, beyond that, whether and to what degree it is capable of feeling. Life as such is sacred to him. He tears no leaf from a tree, plucks no flower, and takes care to crush no insect. If in summer he is working by lamplight, he prefers to keep his window shut and breathe a stuffy atmosphere rather than see one insect after another fall with singed wings upon his table.

If he walks on the road after a shower and sees an earthworm which has strayed on to it, he bethinks himself that it must get dried up on the sun, if it does not return soon enough to ground into which it can burrow, so he lifts it from the deadly stone surface, and puts it on the grass. If he comes across an insect which has fallen into a puddle, he stops a moment in order to hold out a leaf or a stalk on which it can save itself.

He is not afraid of being laughed at as sentimental. It is the fate of every truth to be a subject for laughter until it is generally recognised. Once it was considered folly to assume that men of colour were really men and ought to be treated as such, but the folly has become an accepted truth. To-day it is thought to be going too far to declare that constant regard for everything that lives, down to the lowest manifestations of life, is a demand made by rational ethics. The time is coming, however, when people will be astonished that mankind needed so long a time to learn to regard thoughtless injury to life as incompatible with ethics.

Ethics are responsibility without limit towards all that lives.

As a general proposition the definition of ethics as a relationship within a disposition to reverence for life, does not make a very moving impression. But it is the only complete one. Compassion is too narrow to rank as the total essence of the ethical. It denotes, of course, only interest in the suffering will-to-live. But ethics include also feeling as one's own all the circumstances and all the aspirations of the will-to-live, its pleasure, too, and its longing to live itself out to the full, as well as its urge to self-perfecting.

Love means more, since it includes fellowship in suffering, in joy, and in effort, but it shows the ethical only in a simile, although in a simile that is natural and profound. It makes the solidarity produced by ethics analogous to that which nature calls forth on the physical side, for more or less temporary purposes between two beings which complete each other sexually, or between them and their offspring.

Thought must strive to bring to expression the nature of the ethical in itself. To effect this it arrives at defining ethics as devotion to life inspired by reverence for life. Even if the phrase reverence for life sounds so general as to seem somewhat lifeless, what is meant by it is nevertheless something which never lets go of the man into whose thought it has made its way. Sympathy, and love, and every kind of valuable enthusiasm are given within it. With restless living force reverence for life works upon the mind into which it has entered, and throws it into the unrest of a feeling of responsibility which at no place and at no time ceases to affect it. Just as the screw which churns its way through the water drives the ship along, so does reverence for life drive the man. . . .

Source: Schweitzer, Albert. *Civilisation and Ethics.* London: A. & C. Black, 1923.

ANALYSIS

Albert Schweitzer (1875–1965) studied music, philosophy, and theology before ultimately deciding to become a physician. He did not merely dabble in these subjects. He fully committed himself to each one and achieved many impressive accomplishments, including a doctorate degree in philosophy.

By the time Schweitzer wrote *Civilisation and Ethics*, he had been working as a doctor for about 10 years. He spent some of that time establishing a hospital in Africa as part of a missionary group. There, Schweitzer endured primitive conditions and a heavy workload but still found enough energy to contemplate questions of philosophy. One day, while he was gazing at hippopotamuses, the phrase "reverence for life" came into his mind. For Schweitzer, that phrase summarized the guiding principle behind all of his ideas about ethics and moral behavior. Specifically, he believed that reverence for life should include *all* forms of life, not just human life. Schweitzer developed this idea at length in *Civilisation and Ethics*.

In the selected passage, Schweitzer rejects the idea that animals are inferior to human beings, a belief held by many earlier philosophers (for example, see "[Animals] Are Destitute of Reason" by Descartes and "Animals Are Created for the Sake of Men" by Aristotle). Schweitzer believed that people, animals, and all other forms of life should be treated with equal reverence and respect. In the excerpted passage, he states that the philosophy of Descartes—"I think, therefore I am"—is the wrong way to approach a discussion about ethics and the relationship between human beings and animals. In Schweitzer's view, the ability to think or reason does not determine the value of a living being. Instead, as he puts it, "Life as such is sacred."

Schweitzer states that humans, animals, and all other forms of life are united by an obvious, observable fact: the will to live. He describes this will as "the most immediate and comprehensive fact of consciousness." Schweitzer believed that because human beings can observe and understand the will to live, they ought to honor it equally in all life forms, both human and nonhuman. Schweitzer believed that the ability to reason gives people an ethical responsibility to avoid causing injury or death to any living being.

Schweitzer also believed that humans ought to actively help or protect nonhuman life—for example, by rescuing a drowning insect or a stranded earthworm. And he tried to live up to his own ideals, as noted by Ann Cottrell in *Animals, Nature, and Albert Schweitzer*. According to Cottrell, while Schweitzer was working in Africa, he was once so concerned for an overworked animal pulling a cart in the street that he decided to help by pushing the cart from behind.

Schweitzer acknowledged that people of his era might think he was "going too far" in his concern for animals. At that time, a few modest animal protection and anti-cruelty laws had already been passed, reflecting general sympathy for reducing animal suffering. However, what sets Schweitzer apart was his stated belief that "ethics are responsibility without limit towards all that lives." Schweitzer's views went beyond the limitations of any legislation and challenged the common view that humans are superior to other beings. Schweitzer challenged people to extend their understanding of ethics beyond their own species.

FURTHER READING

"Animal Rights: A History: Albert Schweitzer." Think Differently About Sheep, accessed December 10, 2014. http://www.think-differently-about-sheep.com/Animal_Rights _Albert_Schweitzer.htm.

"Dr. Albert Schweitzer." International Vegetarian Union, accessed December 19, 2014. http://www.ivu.org/history/europe20a/schweitzer.html.

Fenner, Jack N. "The Albert Schweitzer Page," accessed December 10, 2014. http://home .pcisys.net/~jnf/schabout/ra3.html.

Schweitzer, Albert. *Albert Schweitzer's Ethical Vision: A Sourcebook*. Edited by Predrag Cicovacki. New York: Oxford University Press, 2009.

Schweitzer, Albert. *Animal World of Albert Schweitzer: Jungle Insights into Reverence for Life*. Boston: Beacon Press, 1950.

Schweitzer, Albert. **Animals, Nature, and Albert Schweitzer.** Edited by Ann Cottrell Free. New York: Albert Schweitzer Fellowship, 1982.

Shapiro, Caroline. "Albert Schweitzer: A Life Lived in Reverence." National Museum of Animals & Society, accessed December 10, 2014. http://www.museumofanimals.org/ albert-schweitzer/3863804.

"WE SHALL PROTECT HUNDREDS OF ALL KINDS OF WILDLIFE WHICH MIGHT OTHERWISE SOON BE EXTINCT"

- **Document:** Proclamation 231—President Harry S. Truman's Address on Conservation at the Dedication of Everglades National Park.
- **Date:** December 6, 1947.
- **Where:** Everglades City, Florida.
- **Significance:** President Truman's dedication of Everglades National Park in Florida reflected an evolution in attitudes toward the national park system. His remarks made clear that extending federal protection to the Everglades was prompted not only by a desire to preserve and highlight natural beauty for parkgoers but also by the urgent need to protect plants, animals, and other precious aspects of America's natural heritage.

DOCUMENT

I can't tell you what a great pleasure it is to me to be with you today. You know, I have a White House down in Key West. It is very conveniently located for this occasion.

Not often in these demanding days are we able to lay aside the problems of the times, and turn to a project whose great value lies in the enrichment of the human spirit. Today we mark the achievement of another great conservation victory. We have permanently safeguarded an irreplaceable primitive area. We have assembled to dedicate to the use of all the people for all time, the Everglades National Park.

Here in Everglades City we have the atmosphere of this beautiful tropical area. Southeast of us lies the coast of the Everglades Park, cut by islands and estuaries of the Gulf of Mexico. Here are deep rivers, giant groves of colorful trees, prairie marshes, and a great many lakes and streams.

In this park we shall preserve tarpon and trout, pompano, bear, deer, crocodiles and alligators—and rare birds of great beauty. We shall protect hundreds of all kinds of wildlife which might otherwise soon be extinct.

The benefits our Nation will derive from this dedication will outlast the youngest of us. They will increase with the passage of the years. Few actions could make a more lasting contribution to the enjoyment of the American people than the establishment of the Everglades National Park.

Our national park system is a dear expression of the idealism of the American people. Without regard for sectional rivalries or for party politics, the Nation has advanced constantly in the last 75 years in the protection of its natural beauties and wonders.

The success of our efforts to conserve the scenery and wildlife of the country can be measured in popular use. The national park system covers but a fraction of 1 percent of the area of the United States, but over 25 million of our fellow countrymen have visited our national parks within the last year. Each citizen returned to his home with a refreshed spirit and a greater appreciation of the majesty and beauty of our country.

These are the people's parks, owned by young and old, by those in the cities and those on the farms. Most of them are ours today because there were Americans many years ago who exercised vision, patience, and unselfish devotion in the battle for conservation.

Each national park possesses qualities distinctive enough to make its preservation a matter of concern to the whole Nation. Certainly, this Everglades area has more than its share of features unique to these United States. Here are no lofty peaks seeking the sky, no mighty glaciers or rushing streams wearing away the uplifted land. Here is land, tranquil in its quiet beauty, serving not as the source of water but as the last receiver of it. To its natural abundance we owe the spectacular plant and animal life that distinguishes this place from all others in the country.

Our park system also embraces such national shrines as Jamestown Island, the Statue of Liberty, and the battlefields of Yorktown and Gettysburg. These historic places—as much as the scenic areas—also need to be protected with all the devotion at our command in these days when we are learning again the importance of an understanding loyalty to our national heritage.

Our parks are but one part of the national effort to conserve our natural resources. Upon these resources our life as a nation depends. Our high level of employment and our extraordinary production are being limited by scarcities in some items of our natural wealth. This is the time to develop and replenish our basic resources.

Conservation has been practiced for many decades and preached for many more, yet only in recent years has it become plain that we cannot afford to conserve in a haphazard or piecemeal manner. No part of our conservation program can be slighted if we want to make full use of our resources and have full protection against future emergencies.

If we waste our minerals by careless mining and processing, we shall not be able to build the machinery to till the land. If we waste the forests by careless lumbering, we shall lack housing and construction materials for factory, farm, and mine. If we waste the water through failure to build hydroelectric plants, we shall burn our reserves of coal and oil needlessly. If we waste our soil through erosion and failure to replenish our fields, we shall destroy the source of our people's food.

Each conservation need is dependent upon the others. A slashed and burned forest brings erosion of the uplands and fills downstream reservoirs with silt so that water power is lessened and irrigated farms lose their water supplies. Eroded farmlands contribute to devastating floods. Uncontrolled rivers means lost electricity, farms without water, and perennial, increasing flood danger.

To maintain our natural wealth we must engage in full and complete conservation of all our resources.

Full conservation of our energy resources can be accomplished by continued construction of dams, hydroelectric plants, and transmission lines; by greater use of natural gas, by research for more efficient methods of extraction of coal and oil, and by exploration for new reserves.

In forests, conservation can be achieved by adhering to the principle of sustained yield and forest management so that timber is harvested each year just as other crops are. This should be true for both privately owned and publicly owned forest lands.

In farmland, conservation can be achieved by expanding and intensifying the many soil conservation practices developed by our agricultural technicians to sustain productivity. The area of irrigated land can be expanded materially by new reclamation projects. Range lands in the West can be protected by the control of erosion and by the enforcement of safe limits on the number of grazing stock.

In minerals, we can come closer to the proper balance with increased efficiency in extraction and with scientific exploration of new reserves. When ores contain several minerals, we should extract all the useful products and waste none. Despite a bounteous nature, this country has never been self-sufficient in all minerals. We have always imported minerals to meet these deficiencies and we must continue to do so.

In water, we need to prevent further dropping of the water table, which in many areas is dangerously low. Surface water must be stored, and ground water used in such a way as to cause the least depletion. Although the water level is high now here in the Everglades, there has been damage from a lowered fresh-water table, and, during the war, fires raged through the glades—fires fed by dry grass which should have been covered by water.

The battle for conservation cannot be limited to the winning of new conquests. Like liberty itself, conservation must be fought for unceasingly to protect earlier victories. There are always plenty of hogs who are trying to get natural resources for their own personal benefit!

Public lands and parks, our forests and our mineral reserves, are subject to many destructive influences. We have to remain constantly vigilant to prevent raids by those who would selfishly exploit our common heritage for their private gain. Such raids on our natural resources are not examples of enterprise and initiative. They are attempts to take from all the people just for the benefit of a few.

As always in the past when the people's property has been threatened, men and women whose primary concern has been their country's welfare have risen to oppose these selfish attacks. We can be thankful for their efforts, as we can be grateful for the efforts of citizens, private groups, local governments, and the State of Florida which, joined in the common purpose, have made possible the establishment of the Everglades National Park.

The establishment of this park is an object lesson and an example to the entire Nation that sound conservation depends upon the joint endeavors of the people and their several governments. Responsibility is shared by town and State and the Federal Government, by societies and legislatures and all lovers of nature.

No man can know every element that makes a nation great. Certainly the lofty spirit of its people, the daily cooperation, the helpfulness of one citizen to another are elements. A nation's ability to provide a good living for its people in industry, in business, and on the farm is another. Intelligent recognition by its citizens of a nation's responsibility for world order, world peace, and world recovery is still another.

Wise use of our natural resources is the foundation of our effectiveness in all these efforts.

The problems of peace, like those of war, require courage and sustained effort. If we wish this Nation to remain prosperous, if we wish it still to be "the home of the free," we can have it so. But, if we fail to heed the lesson of other nations which have permitted their natural resources to be wasted and destroyed, then we shall reap a sorry harvest.

For conservation of the human spirit, we need places such as Everglades National Park where we may be more keenly aware of our Creator's infinitely varied, infinitely beautiful, and infinitely bountiful handiwork. Here we may draw strength and peace of mind from our surroundings.

Here we can truly understand what that great Israelitist Psalmist meant when he sang: "He maketh me to lie down in green pastures, He leadeth me beside still waters; He restoreth my soul."

Source: Truman, Harry S. "Address on Conservation at the Dedication of Everglades National Park." December 6, 1947. Online by Gerhard Peters and John T. Woolley, *The American Presidency Project.* http://www.presidency.ucsb.edu/ws/?pid=12798.

ANALYSIS

Everglades National Park is a series of mangrove swamps, pine forests, and sawgrass prairie that cover 1.5 million acres in the state of Florida. More than 300 species of birds call the Everglades home, and alligators, manatees, and Florida panthers also inhabit the watery region.

The present-day Everglades is but a remnant of its former size. According to the National Park Service, "water in south Florida once flowed freely from the Kissimmee River to Lake Okeechobee and southward over low-lying lands to the estuaries of Biscayne Bay, the Ten Thousand Islands, and Florida Bay. This shallow, slow-moving sheet of water covered almost 11,000 square miles, creating a mosaic of ponds, sloughs, sawgrass marshes, hardwood hammock, and forested uplands. For thousands of years this intricate system evolved into a finely balanced ecosystem that formed the biological infrastructure for the southern half of the state."

The great vastness that was the Everglades area remained that way for thousands of years, until the early twentieth century, when developers looked at the region for agricultural opportunities. In 1905 Florida governor Napoleon Bonaparte Broward set in motion a drainage process in order to convert wetlands into farmland and other development. Such coastal cities as Miami and Fort Lauderdale emerged and expanded as well.

This development, which seemed to pick up speed with each passing year, wreaked major changes on the regional ecosystem and the wildlife that resided therein. In the 1920s, a transplanted New Englander, landscape architect Ernest F. Coe, became interested in the future of the Everglades region. Together with University of Miami president Bowman Foster Ashe and freelance writer and former

Miami Herald journalist Marjory Stoneman Douglas, Coe established the Everglades Tropical National Park Association in 1928. Through the subsequent years, Coe and his allies worked hard to make the Everglades a national park, lobbying Washington politicians with a combination of relentlessness and good cheer (at one point the group even sent coconuts from the Everglades to President Herbert Hoover). Success finally came in 1934 when national park status was approved, and then in 1947 when the park was officially dedicated. Of the Everglades, Coe said: "It's the spirit of the thing that holds you. The appeal is to your heart, and arouses a deep feeling of wonder and reference."

Truman's dedication of the Everglades National Park marked a new type of protection for national land. Whereas in the past, most national parks had been set aside for their scenic beauty and value, the designation of the Everglades as a national park was also meant to protect and benefit the rich variety of unique plant and animal life found there.

Everglades National Park contains nine distinct ecosystems. The most common habitat is the freshwater marsh, where such wildlife as alligators, brown pelicans, eastern diamondback rattlesnakes, egrets, and herons prosper. The tropical hardwood hammock habitats support such creatures as the Florida panther, white-tailed deer, and woodpeckers. Another notable ecosystem type is the coastal lowlands, which is home to such animal species as Cape Sable sparrows, eastern indigo snakes, mice, and rabbits. The marine and estuary habitats in the Everglades, which include the large Florida Bay, support barracudas, crustaceans, mollusks, and sharks.

Truman's central role in the dedication of the Everglades was appropriate, given his love for the state of Florida. The president enjoyed the sun and warmth of Florida and even set up a vacation spot in Key West, a home that became known as the Little White House. He visited Key West eleven times (covering a total of 175 days) as president, and another five times after he left office. Family members later said that Truman's visits to southern Florida often reenergized him, especially during troubling and turbulent periods of his presidency.

Scholars have pointed out that Truman does not have a stellar environmental legacy. A former Missouri farmer, his administration was generally friendly to developers and resource-extraction industries and sympathetic to businesses that preferred light environmental regulation. As one scholar put it, Truman's overall environmental legacy "endures as a tangible heritage of concrete and steel and asphalt throughout the nation" (Brooks, 2009). The establishment of Everglades National Park, then, stands as a true landmark in Truman's environmental record. "For conservation of the human spirit," Truman said, "we need places such as Everglades National Park where we may be more keenly aware of our Creator's infinitely varied, infinitely beautiful, and infinitely bountiful handiwork. Here we may draw strength and peace of mind from our surroundings."

FURTHER READING

"Brief History of the Everglades." Florida Department of Environmental Protection, accessed December 10, 2014. http://www.dep.state.fl.us/evergladesforever/about/.

Brooks, Karl Boyd. *The Environmental Legacy of Harry S. Truman*. Kirksville, MO: Truman State University Press, 2009.

Douglas, Marjory Stoneman. *The Everglades: River of Grass*. New York: Rinehart & Co., 1947.

"Everglades Ecosystem." Everglades National Park Museum Collections, accessed December 10, 2014. http://www.nps.gov/museum/exhibits/ever/ecosystem.html.

"Everglades National Park." RedOrbit, accessed December 10, 2014. http://www.redorbit .com/education/reference_library/earth/national-parks/1112825359/everglades-national -park/.

Grunwald, Michael. *The Swamp: The Everglades, Florida, and the Politics of Paradise*. New York: Simon and Schuster, 2006.

"History & Culture." National Park Service, U.S. Department of the Interior, accessed December 10, 2014. http://www.nps.gov/ever/historyculture/index.htm.

"Little White House." National Park Service, U.S. Department of the Interior, accessed December 10, 2014. http://www.nps.gov/nr/travel/presidents/trumans_little_white _house.html.

"Natural Features & Ecosystems." National Park Service, U.S. Department of the Interior, accessed December 10, 2014. http://www.nps.gov/ever/naturescience/naturalfeatures andecosystems.htm.

Taylor, Jon E. "The Environmental Legacy of Harry Truman." Reviews in History, accessed December 10, 2014. July 2010. http://www.history.ac.uk/reviews/review/929.

Truman, Margaret. *Bess W. Truman*. New York: Macmillan, 1986.

3

REGULATING ANIMAL RIGHTS AND WELFARE IN AN INDUSTRIALIZED ECONOMY

"SLAUGHTERING OF LIVESTOCK...SHALL BE CARRIED OUT ONLY BY HUMANE METHODS"

- **Document:** An excerpt from the Humane Methods of Slaughter Act, or Humane Slaughter Act.
- **Date:** Enacted on August 27, 1958.
- **Where:** Washington, D.C.
- **Significance:** This law recognized the benefits of treating livestock humanely during slaughter.

DOCUMENT

Sec. 1901. Findings and Declaration of Policy

The Congress finds that the use of humane methods in the slaughter of livestock prevents needless suffering; results in safer and better working conditions for persons engaged in the slaughtering industry; brings about improvement of products and economies in slaughtering operations; and produces other benefits for producers, processors, and consumers which tend to expedite an orderly flow of livestock and livestock products in interstate and foreign commerce. It is therefore declared to be the policy of the United States that the slaughtering of livestock and the handling of livestock in connection with slaughter shall be carried out only by humane methods.

Sec. 1902. Humane methods

No method of slaughtering or handling in connection with slaughtering shall be deemed to comply with the public policy of the United States unless it is humane. Either of the following two methods of slaughtering and handling are hereby found to be humane:

(a) in the case of cattle, calves, horses, mules, sheep, swine, and other livestock, all animals are rendered insensible to pain by a single blow or gunshot or an electrical, chemical or other means that is rapid and effective, before being shackled, hoisted, thrown, cast, or cut; or

(b) by slaughtering in accordance with the ritual requirements of the Jewish faith or any other religious faith that prescribes a method of slaughter whereby the animal suffers loss of consciousness by anemia of the brain caused by the simultaneous and instantaneous severance of the carotid arteries with a sharp instrument and handling in connection with such slaughtering.

Sec. 1903. Repealed.

Sec. 1904. Methods research; designation of methods

In furtherance of the policy expressed herein the Secretary is authorized and directed—

(a) to conduct, assist, and foster research, investigation, and experimentation to develop and determine methods of slaughter and the handling of livestock in connection with slaughter which are practicable with reference to the speed and scope of slaughtering operations and humane with reference to other existing methods and then current scientific knowledge; and

(b) on or before March 1, 1959, and at such times thereafter as he deems advisable, to designate methods of slaughter and of handling in connection with slaughter which, with respect to each species of livestock, conform to the policy stated in this chapter. If he deems it more effective, the Secretary may make any such designation by designating methods which are not in conformity with such policy. Designations by the Secretary subsequent to March 1, 1959, shall become effective 180 days after their publication in the Federal Register. . . .

Sec. 1905. Repealed.

Sec. 1906. Exemption of ritual slaughter

Nothing in this chapter shall be construed to prohibit, abridge, or in any way hinder the religious freedom of any person or group. Notwithstanding any other provision of this chapter, in order to protect freedom of religion, ritual slaughter and the handling or other preparation of livestock for ritual slaughter are exempted from the terms of this chapter. For the purposes of this section the term "ritual slaughter" means slaughter in accordance with section 1902(b) of this title.

Sec. 1907. Practices involving nonambulatory livestock

(a) Report

The Secretary of Agriculture shall investigate and submit to Congress a report on—

(1) the scope of nonambulatory livestock;

(2) the causes that render livestock nonambulatory;

(3) the humane treatment of nonambulatory livestock; and

(4) the extent to which nonambulatory livestock may present handling and disposition problems for stockyards, market agencies, and dealers.

(b) Authority

Based on the findings of the report, if the Secretary determines it necessary, the Secretary shall promulgate regulations to provide for the humane treatment, handling, and disposition of nonambulatory livestock by stockyards, market agencies, and dealers.

(c) Administration and enforcement

For the purpose of administering and enforcing any regulations promulgated under subsection (b) of this section, the authorities provided under sections 10414 [7 U.S.C. 8313] and 10415 [7 U.S.C. 8314] shall apply to the regulations in a similar manner as those sections apply to the Animal Health Protection Act [7 U.S.C. 8301 et seq.]. Any person that violates regulations promulgated under subsection (b) of this section shall be subject to penalties provided in section 10414.

Source: "Humane Methods of Slaughter Act." *United States Code,* accessed December 11, 2014. http://uscode.regstoday.com/7USC_CHAPTER48.aspx.

ANALYSIS

In the late 1950s, a number of individuals and groups sought to enact the first legislation to protect domestic animals since 1873, when the passage of the Twenty-Eight Hour Law required transporters of certain livestock to provide food, water, rest, and exercise after 28 hours of transport confinement. U.S. senator Hubert Humphrey (D-Minnesota), the Animal Welfare Institute, and the Humane Society of the United States were all prominent sponsors or interested parties of the Humane Slaughter Act. Indeed, the Humane Society, at the time known as the American Humane Association, fought vigorously for this bill. The eventual passage of the legislation was viewed as an early success for the relatively new organization, which had just been founded four years earlier by Larry Andrews, Marcia Glaser, Helen Jones, and Fred Myers. Public interest in the bill was so high that President Dwight D. Eisenhower jokingly commented that "if I went by mail, I'd think no one was interested in anything but humane slaughter."

Public interest in the issue of humane animal slaughter occurred partially because of a film that was released in the 1950s that showed workers in slaughterhouses abusing animals. The undercover film made by Arthur P. Redman, of Seattle, Washington, showed inhumane treatment of hogs during slaughter. The film was shown during a congressional hearing in 1957 and led Senator Humphrey to comment: "We are morally compelled, here in this hour, to try to imagine—to try to feel in our own nerves—the totality of the suffering of 100 million tortured animals. The issue before us today is pain, agony and cruelty—and what a moral man must do about it in view of his own conscience."

One part of the law required slaughterhouses doing business with the government to ensure that livestock were insensitive to any kind of pain during the slaughtering procedure. This could be done by anesthetization, a gunshot, or a single blow. But it could not include the work of "knockers," employees who used sledgehammers to stun animal. As Humphrey stated, this resulted in animals being "hammered into unconsciousness. . . . The hammer knocks off horns, mashes noses, breaks jaws, pounds out eyes."

There was some discussion in Congress over whether the bill addressed concerns the Jewish community might have over whether *shechita*, a form of slaughter consistent with the kosher dietary laws, was endangered. Senator Humphrey read a letter from former U.S. senator Herbert H. Lehman (D-New York) that said that the bill with "adequate protection for Jewish ritual slaughter not only represents no real threat to the sensibilities of my faith, but is, indeed, consistent with the objectives of humaneness which are honored in the Jewish faith and tradition as well as in others." Amendments to the language of the law offered by U.S. senator Jacob Javits (R-New York) and U.S. senator Wayne Morse (D-Oregon) satisfied their fellow senators, and the Senate approved the bill 72–9; President Eisenhower signed the law less than a month later.

The Humane Methods of Slaughter Act of 1958 has been amended twice since its original enactment: once in 1978 and once in 2002. The 1978 amendment required that livestock (other than poultry) imported into the United States for meat be slaughtered humanely. Inspectors from the U.S. Department of Agriculture

(USDA) would be allowed to stop any slaughtering operations where those standards were not being met. The 2002 amendment included a resolution requiring that the Humane Methods of Slaughter Act of 1958 be strictly enforced.

FURTHER READING

"Cabinet Members May Urge Eisenhower to Veto Slaughter Bill." *JTA: The Global Jewish News Source*, July 21, 1958. http://www.jta.org/1958/07/31/archive/cabinet-members -may-urge-eisenhower-to-veto-slaughter-bill.

"Fred Myers: Co-Founder of the HSUS." Humane Society of the United States, February 16, 2005. http://www.humanesociety.org/about/history/fred_myers.html.

Frommer, Frederic J. "Film Prompted First Humane Slaughter Law." *USA Today*, February 27, 2008. http://usatoday30.usatoday.com/news/washington/2008-02-27 -2035066042_x.htm.

"Humane Methods of Slaughter Act." Animal Welfare Institute, accessed December 11, 2014. https://awionline.org/content/humane-methods-slaughter-act.

Pacelle, Wayne. "Farm Animal Protection, Past and Present." *A Humane Nation* (blog). Humane Society of the United States, August 27, 2008. blog.humanesociety.org/ wayne/2008/08/humaneslaughter.html.

Ray, Daryll E., and Harwood D. Schaffer. "Humane Livestock Handling and Slaughter Regs Through the Years." *NFU Blog* (blog). National Farmers Union, December 31, 2014. http://www.nfu.org/blog/?p=1157.

"WHOEVER USES AN AIRCRAFT OR A MOTOR VEHICLE TO HUNT ... ANY WILD UNBRANDED HORSE, MARE, COLT, OR BURRO ... SHALL BE FINED NOT MORE THAN $500, OR IMPRISONED NOT MORE THAN SIX MONTHS"

- **Document:** The Wild Horse Annie Act of 1959.
- **Date:** This bill was enacted on September 9, 1959.
- **Where:** Washington, D.C.
- **Significance:** This law prohibited the use of motor vehicles (ground or air) to hunt wild burros and horses on public land.

DOCUMENT

18 U.S.C. 47. Use of aircraft or motor vehicles to hunt certain wild horses or burros; pollution of watering holes

(a) Whoever uses an aircraft or a motor vehicle to hunt, for the purpose of capturing or killing, any wild unbranded horse, mare, colt, or burro running at large on any of the public land or ranges shall be fined not more than $500, or imprisoned not more than six months, or both.

(b) Whoever pollutes or causes the pollution of any watering hole on any of the public land or ranges for the purpose of trapping, killing, wounding, or maiming any of the animals referred to in subsection (a) of this section shall be fined not more than $500, or imprisoned not more than six months, or both.

(c) As used in subsection (a) of this section—

(1) The term "aircraft" means any contrivance used for flight in the air; and

(2) The term "motor vehicle" includes an automobile, automobile truck, automobile wagon, motorcycle, or any other self-propelled vehicle designed for running on land.

(b) The analysis of such chapter 3, immediately preceding section 41, is amended by adding at the end thereof the following new item:

"47. Use of aircraft or motor vehicles to hunt certain wild horses or burros."

Approved September 8, 1959.

Source: Public Law 86-234. U.S. Government Printing Office. Washington, DC. September 8, 1959.

ANALYSIS

During the 1950s, a Nevada rancher named Velma Bronn Johnston, later known as Wild Horse Annie, launched a public relations campaign to end cruel and inhumane treatment of wild horses by ranchers and hunters on public lands across the American West. Many ranchers and hunters were only interested in the horses for commercial purposes and were indifferent to how they were treated or if their capture led to mutilation or death. They just wanted to capture them as quickly and easily as possible. To this end, they employed airplanes and trucks to identify and pursue them, often chasing them until they were so tired that they collapsed. Once they were captured they were packed into trucks so tightly that they could barely move. If they fell they were sometimes trampled and left to die. The final destination of these grim caravans was the local slaughterhouse, where their meat was used for dog and chicken food.

Johnston's deep affection and empathy for animals dated back to her childhood. When she was 11 years old, she contracted polio and became disfigured as a result of her illness. Her appearance led to ridicule from her peers, so she spent a lot of time being around and caring for animals on the ranch where her family lived. As an adult, she and her husband also ran a dude ranch for children, so she spent time with animals constantly. She started her grassroots campaign to bring awareness to the public about the plight of these wild horses in 1950, after following a truck full of live mustangs that was dripping blood as it cruised down the road.

Wild ponies walk along the shoreline on Assateague Island National Seashore in Maryland and Virginia. In 1959, Congress passed the Wild Horse Annie Act that made it illegal to use motorized vehicles or aircraft to hunt or capture wild horses and burros on all public lands. The act was named after Velma Bronn Johnston (also known as Wild Horse Annie), an animal lover who brought public awareness to the plight of wild horses. (Wendy Farrington/Shutterstock.com)

In the beginning of Johnston's campaign, she was diligent about gathering evidence and taking careful notes about prevailing horse-capturing practices and the abuses they suffered during confinement. Schoolchildren were among her leading allies in this crusade, but as word spread, the general public soon became involved as well.

Johnston's first tangible victory came in 1952, when her home county of Storey County banned the use of aircraft to capture wild horses. That same year, Johnston and Nevada state senator James Slattery led a successful effort to pass a state law outlawing wild horse capture by aircraft or motor vehicles on private lands.

Federal property under the Bureau of Land Management (BLM) was exempted from that law, however. That exemption was significant, given that about 67 percent of Nevada's total land area is BLM land. Determined to close that gaping loophole, Johnston—or "Wild Horse Annie," as she had come to be known by friend and foe alike—recruited U.S. representative Walter Baring (D-Nevada) to her cause. Baring created a bill that made it illegal to use motorized vehicles or aircraft to hunt or capture wild horses and burros on all public lands. The bill also made it illegal to pollute water holes in order to capture wild horses. The bill passed the House of Representatives unanimously. It became a law on September 8, 1959.

Wild Horse Annie also was instrumental in getting the Wild Free-Roaming Horses and Burros Act of 1971 passed into law. This legislation protected wild horses and burros from capture, injury, or being disturbed on public lands and even included a provision to transfer wild horses and burros from overpopulated rangelands to lightly populated regions. It was signed into law on December 15, 1971, by President Richard Nixon. Wild Horse Annie is also credited with establishing wild horse refuges throughout the state of Nevada and across several other states.

FURTHER READING

Cruise, David, and Alison Griffiths. *Wild Horse Annie and the Last of the Mustangs*. New York: Scribner, 2010.

"Earthkeeper Hero: Velma Bronn Johnston." My Hero, accessed December 11, 2014. http://www.myhero.com/go/hero.asp?hero=V_Johnston_stclair_US_2011.

"History of the Program." *National Wild Horse and Burro Program*. U.S. Department of the Interior. Bureau of Land Management, accessed December 11, 2014. http://www.blm.gov/wo/st/en/prog/wild_horse_and_burro/wh_b_information_center/facts_and_stats/history_of_the_program.html.

Kania, Alan J. *Wild Horse Annie: Velma Johnston and Her Fight to Save the Mustang*. Reno: University of Nevada Press, 2013.

"The Wild Horse Annie Act." American Wild Horse Preservation, accessed December 11, 2014. http://wildhorsepreservation.org/wild-horse-annie-act.

"The Wild Horse Annie Act." Return to Freedom: American Wild Horse Preservation and Sanctuary, accessed December 11, 2014. http://www.returntofreedom.org/about-wild-horses/the-wild-horse-annie-act/.

"Women's Biographies: Velma Bronn Johnston a.k.a. 'Wild Horse Annie.'" Nevada Women's History Project, accessed December 11, 2014. http://www.unr.edu/nwhp/bios/women/johnston.htm.

"TO END THE BUSINESS OF STEALING DOGS AND CATS FOR SALE TO RESEARCH FACILITIES"

- **Document:** Public Law 89-544, better known as the Animal Welfare Act, and President Lyndon B. Johnson's comments following his signing of the bill.
- **Date:** August 24, 1966.
- **Where:** Washington, D.C.
- **Significance:** This law established new regulations for the treatment of certain animals used in research, experiments, and exhibition. Among its most important provisions were regulations that required animal dealers to be registered, licensed, and subject to oversight by federal agencies.

DOCUMENT

Summary: Enacted August 24, 1966, Public Law 89-544 is what commonly is referred to as The Animal Welfare Act although that title is not mentioned within the law. It authorizes the Secretary of Agriculture to regulate transport, sale, and handling of dogs, cats, nonhuman primates, guinea pigs, hamsters, and rabbits intended to be used in research or "for other purposes." It also introduced licensing and inspection requirements of dog and cat dealers and humane handling of animals at auction sales.

89th Congress, H.R. 13881
August 24, 1966
An Act

To authorize the Secretary of Agriculture to regulate the transportation, sale, and handling of dogs, cats, and certain other animals intended to be used for purposes of research or experimentation, and for other purposes.

Be it enacted by the Senate and House of Representatives of the United States of America in Congress assembled. That, in order to protect the owners of dogs and cats from theft of such pets, to prevent the sale or use of dogs and cats which have been stolen, and to insure that certain animals intended for use in research facilities are provided humane care and treatment, it is essential to regulate the transportation, purchase, sale, housing, care, handling, and treatment of such animals by persons or organizations engaged in using them for research or experimental purposes or in transporting, buying, or selling them for such use.

SEC. 2. When used in this Act—

(a) The term "person" includes any individual, partnership, firm, joint stock company, corporation, association, trust, estate, or other legal entity;

(b) The term "Secretary" means the Secretary of Agriculture;

(c) The term "commerce" means commerce between any State, territory, possession, or the District of Columbia, or the Commonwealth of Puerto Rico, but through any place outside thereof; or within any territory, possession, or the District of Columbia;

(d) The term "dog" means any live dog (*Canis familiaris*);

(e) The term "cat" means any live cat (*Felis catus*);

(f) The term "research facility" means any school, institution, organization, or person that uses or intends to use dogs or cats in research, tests, or experiments, and that (1) purchases or transports dogs or cats in commerce, or (2) receives funds under a grant, award, loan, or contract from a department, agency, or instrumentality of the United States for the purpose of carrying out research, tests, or experiments;

[80 *STAT. 350.*] (g) The term "dealer" means any person who for compensation or profit delivers for transportation, or transports, except as a common carrier, buys, or sells dogs or cats in commerce for research purposes;

[80 *STAT. 351.*] (h) The term "animal" means live dogs, cats, monkeys (nonhuman primate mammals), guinea pigs, hamsters, and rabbits.

SEC. 3. The Secretary shall issue licenses to dealers upon application therefor in such form and manner as he may prescribe and upon payment of such fee established pursuant to section 23 of this Act: *Provided*, That no such license shall be issued until the dealer shall have demonstrated that his facilities comply with the standards promulgated by the Secretary pursuant to section 13 of this Act: *Provided, however,* That any person who derives less than a substantial portion of his income (as determined by the Secretary) from the breeding and raising of dogs or cats on his own premises and sells any such dog or cat to a dealer or research facility shall not be required to obtain a license as a dealer under this Act. The Secretary is further authorized to license, as dealers within the meaning of this Act upon such persons' complying with the requirements specified above and agreeing, in writing, to comply with all the requirements of this Act and the regulations promulgated by the Secretary hereunder.

SEC. 4. No dealer shall sell or offer to sell or transport or offer for transportation to any research facility any dog or cat, or buy, sell, offer to buy or sell, transport or offer for transportation in commerce to or from another dealer under this Act any dog or cat, unless and until such dealer shall have obtained a license from the Secretary and such license shall not have been suspended or revoked.

SEC. 5. No dealer shall sell or otherwise dispose of any dog or cat within a period of five business days after the acquisition of such animal or within such other period as may be specified by the Secretary.

SEC. 6. Every research facility shall register with the Secretary in accordance with such rules and regulations as he may prescribe.

SEC. 7. It shall be unlawful for any research facility to purchase any dog or cat from any person except a person holding a valid license as a dealer issued by the Secretary pursuant to this Act unless such person is exempted from obtaining such license under section 3 of this Act.

SEC. 8. No department, agency, or instrumentality of the United States which uses animals for research or experimentation shall purchase or otherwise acquire any dog or cat for such purposes from any person except a person holding a valid license as a dealer issued by the Secretary pursuant to this Act unless such person is exempted from obtaining such license under section 3 of this Act.

SEC. 9. When construing or enforcing the provisions of this Act, the act, omission, or failure of any individual action for or employed by a research facility or a dealer, or a person licensed as a dealer pursuant to the second sentence of section 3, within the scope of his employment or office, shall be deemed the act, omission, or failure of such research facility, dealer, or other person as well as of such individual.

SEC. 10. Research facilities and dealers shall make, and retain for such reasonable period of time as the Secretary may prescribe, such records with respect to the purchase, sale, transportation, identification, and previous ownership of dogs and cats but not monkeys, guinea pigs, hamsters, or rabbits as the Secretary may prescribe, upon forms supplied by the Secretary. Such records shall be made available at all reasonable times for inspection by the Secretary, by any Federal officer or employee designated by the Secretary.

SEC. 11. All dogs and cats delivered for transportation, transported, purchased, or sold in commerce by any dealer shall be marked or identified at such time and in such humane manner as the Secretary may prescribe.

SEC. 12. The Secretary is authorized to promulgate humane standards and recordkeeping requirements governing the purchase, handling, or sale of dogs or cats by dealers or research facilities at auction sales.

SEC. 13. The Secretary shall establish and promulgate standards to govern the humane handling, care, treatment, and transportation of animals by dealers and research facilities. Such standards shall include minimum requirements with respect to the housing, feeding, watering, sanitation, ventilation, shelter from extremes of weather and temperature, separation by species, and adequate veterinary care. The foregoing shall not be construed as authorizing the Secretary to prescribe standards for the handling, care, or treatment of animals during actual research or experimentation by research facility as determined by such research facility.

SEC. 14. Any department, agency, or instrumentality of the United States having laboratory animal facilities shall comply with the standards promulgated by the Secretary for a research facility under section 13.

SEC. 15. (a) The Secretary shall consult and cooperate with other Federal departments, agencies, or instrumentalities concerned with the welfare of animals used for research or experimentation when establishing standards pursuant to section 13 and in carrying out the purposes of this Act.

(b) The Secretary is authorized to cooperate with the officials of the various States or political subdivisions thereof in effectuating the purposes of this Act and of any State, local, or municipal legislation or ordinance on the same subject.

SEC. 16. The Secretary shall make such investigations or inspections as he deems necessary to determine whether any dealer or research facility has violated or is violating any provision of this Act or any regulation issued thereunder. The Secretary shall promulgate such rules and regulations as he deems necessary to permit inspectors to confiscate or destroy in a humane manner any animals found to be suffering as a result of a failure to comply with any provision of this Act or any regulation issued thereunder if (1) such animals are held by a dealer, or (2) such animals are held by a research facility and are no longer required by such research facility to carry out the research, test, or experiment for which such animals have been utilized.

SEC. 17. The Secretary shall issue rules and regulations requiring licensed dealers and research facilities to permit inspection of their animals and records at reasonable hours upon request by legally constituted law enforcement agencies in search of lost animals.

SEC. 18. Nothing in this Act shall be construed as authorizing the Secretary to promulgate rules, regulations, or orders for the handling, care, treatment, or inspection of animals during actual research or experimentation by a research facility as determined by such research facility.

SEC. 19.

(a) If the Secretary has reason to believe that any person licensed as a dealer has violated or is violating any provision of this Act or any of the rules or regulations promulgated by the Secretary hereunder, the Secretary may suspend such person's license temporarily, but not to exceed twenty-one days, and, after notice and opportunity for hearing, may suspend for such additional period as he may specify or revoke such license, if such violation is determined to have occurred and may make an order that such person shall cease and desist from continuing such violation.

(b) Any dealer aggrieved by a final order of the Secretary issued pursuant to subsection (a) of this section may, within sixty days after entry of such an order, seek review of such order in the manner provided in section 10 of the Administrative Procedure Act (5 U.S.C. 1009).

(c) Any dealer who violates any provision of this Act shall, on conviction thereof, be subject to imprisonment for not more than one year or a fine of not more than $1,000, or both.

SEC. 20.

(a) If the Secretary has reason to believe that any research facility has violated or is violating any provision of this Act or any of the rules or regulations promulgated by the Secretary hereunder and if, after notice and opportunity for hearing, he finds a violation, he may make an order that such research facility shall cease and desist from continuing such violation. Such cease and desist order shall become effective fifteen days after issuance of the order. Any research facility which knowingly fails to obey a cease-and-desist order made by the Secretary under this section shall be subject to a civil penalty of $500 for each offense, and each day during which such failure continues shall be deemed a separate offense.

(b) Any research facility aggrieved by a final order of the Secretary issued pursuant to subsection (a) of this section may, within sixty days after entry of such order, seek review of such order in the district court for the district in which such research facility is located in the manner provided in section 10 of the Administrative Procedure Act (5 U.S.C. 1009).

SEC. 21. The Secretary is authorized to promulgate such rules, regulations, and orders as he may deem necessary in order to effectuate the purposes of this Act.

SEC. 22. If any provision of this Act or the application of any such provision to any person of circumstances shall be held invalid, the remainder of this Act and the application of any such provision to persons or circumstances other than those as to which it is held invalid shall not be affected thereby.

SEC. 23. The Secretary shall charge, assess, and cause to be collected reasonable fees for licenses issued. Such fees shall be adjusted on an equitable basis taking into consideration the type and nature of the operations to be licensed and shall be deposited and covered into the Treasury as miscellaneous receipts. There are hereby authorized to be appropriated such funds as Congress may from time to time provide.

SEC. 24. The regulations referred to in section 10 and section 13 shall be prescribed by the Secretary as soon as reasonable but not later than six months from the date of enactment of this Act. Additions and amendments thereto may be prescribed from time to time as may be necessary or advisable. Compliance by dealers with the provisions of this Act and such regulations shall commence ninety days after the promulgation of such regulation. Compliance by research facilities with the provisions of this Act and such regulations shall commence six months after the promulgation of such regulations, except that the Secretary may grant extensions of time to research facilities which do not comply with the standards prescribed by the Secretary pursuant to section 13 of this Act provided that the Secretary determines that there is evidence that the research facilities will meet such standards within a reasonable time.

Approved August 24, 1966.

Source: National Archives. Act of August 24, 1966, Public Law 89-544. http://research.archives.gov/description/299931.

DOCUMENT

I am delighted to see my friends from the Congress and others here this morning to witness the signing of the bill that the Congress has passed to end the business of stealing dogs and cats for sale to research facilities and to provide for humane handling and treatment of animals by dealers and research facilities.

As Dr. Schweitzer has reminded us: "The quality of a culture is measured by its reverence for all life."

Progress, particularly in science and medicine, does require the use of animals for research and this bill does not interfere with that. But science and research do not compel us to tolerate the kind of inhumanity which has been involved in the business of supplying stolen animals to laboratories or which is sometimes involved in the careless and callous handling of animals in some of our laboratories.

This bill will put an end to these abuses. At the same time the bill does not authorize any sort of interference with actual research or experimentation. They just must go on.

But I am sure that all of us are very glad that the Congress has wisely seen fit to make provision for decent and humane standards in the procurement and handling of the animals that are necessarily involved.

I thank those of you who are here for coming for this ceremony. I appreciate the efforts that you have made to make this event possible, and I have no doubt but what with the passing of the years, the wisdom of your action will be thoroughly demonstrated.

Thank you.

Source: Johnson, Lyndon B. "Remarks upon Signing the Animal Welfare Bill." August 24, 1966. Online by Gerhard Peters and John T. Woolley. *The American Presidency Project.* http://www.presidency.ucsb.edu/ws/?pid=27796.

ANALYSIS

The United States was slower than several countries in Europe to pass laws pertaining to the welfare of animals used for experimental purposes. The Cruelty to Animals Act passed in the United Kingdom in 1876, for instance, set up a board that monitored the treatment of animals used in research. It was not until two American magazines, *Sports Illustrated* and *LIFE*, published articles about animal experimentation and animal dealers in 1965 and 1966, respectively, that the U.S. Congress took action and sponsored legislation that resulted in the Animal Welfare Act (AWA).

In the first instance, *Sports Illustrated* recounted the story of Pepper, a Dalmatian owned by the Lakavage family, who lived on 82 acres near Slatington, Pennsylvania. When the children let Pepper outside and she failed to return nearly a half hour later (as the well-trained dog had always done in the past), the Lakavages knew something was wrong. Many phone calls and visits to animal shelters and truck rides eventually led to the discovery that Pepper had been dognapped under the cover of darkness. Sold to medical researchers in the Bronx, Pepper died after undergoing a failed procedure involving the implantation of a cardiac pacemaker.

In the second instance, *LIFE* photographer Stan Wayman's eight-page spread of photographs showing mistreated and neglected animals on the property of a White Hall, Maryland, animal dealer named Lester Brown elicited widespread public shock and outrage. The *LIFE* story acted as another important catalyst in the successful passage of a federal animal welfare bill written to address both Pepper's sad end and Brown's callous business operations.

The law, originally introduced to Congress by U.S. representative Joseph Resnick (D-New York) and passed on August 24, 1966, requires that businesses that buy or sell warm-blooded animals, exhibit them, transport them, or use them in experiments must be licensed. The law also formally placed the U.S. Department of Agriculture (including the Animal and Plant Health Inspection Service [APHIS], a USDA agency) in charge of enforcement of its various provisions.

The law further requires licensed animal dealers to be monitored by a committee (which includes a veterinarian) that inspects dealers twice a year to assess the care and treatment of the animals. According to the original law, "animal" is defined as "live dogs, cats, monkeys (nonhuman primate mammals), guinea pigs, hamsters, and rabbits."

When President Lyndon B. Johnson signed the bill on August 24, 1966, he made some brief remarks to members of Congress and other guests. The president was fond of animals and had a number of dogs during his stay in the White House from 1963 to 1969. He even had the White House doghouse redesigned and enlarged for his dogs. According to the LBJ Presidential Library in Austin, Texas, Him and Her were the two most popular of the presidential canine collection. The president frequently walked the two beagles on the grounds of the White House. A controversial moment involving Johnson lifting Him by his ears was photographed by *LIFE*. Him sired a litter of puppies, including Kim and Freckles. Other dogs owned by Johnson during his presidency included J. Edgar, Blanco, and Yuki.

The AWA has been amended seven times since its original enactment in 1966. In 1970 its legal protections were expanded to include all warm-blooded animals. Fines for lawbreakers were also increased. In 1976 the act provided further regulations to increase the safety and care of animals undergoing transportation. In 1985 the Food Security Act provided an amendment to the AWA that outlawed multiple experiments on individual animals. Another provision contained in that same act instituted new regulations to ensure proper exercise for animals. In 1990 the Food, Agriculture, Conservation, and Trade Act included an amendment to the AWA that instituted a holding period of five days before sales of animals could be completed. This language was inserted to give original owners of animals more time to recover their animals. In 2002 the Farm Security and Rural Investment Act included an amendment to the AWA to reduce animal fighting operations. Five years later, the Animal Fighting Prohibition Enforcement Act further strengthened animal fighting prohibitions, and in 2008, the Food, Conservation, and Energy Act amended the AWA by increasing fines and prison time for people convicted of animal fighting offenses.

FURTHER READING

"Animal Welfare Act." United States Department of Agriculture, accessed December 11, 2014. http://awic.nal.usda.gov/government-and-professional-resources/federal-laws/animal-welfare-act.

Babb, Earl B., Leonard C. Hare, and Tadlock Cowan. *Animal Welfare: Select Issues and Management Considerations*. New York: Nova Science Publishers, 2013.

Engber, Daniel. "Where's Pepper?" *Slate*, June 1, 2009. http://www.slate.com/articles/health _and_science/pepper/2009/06/wheres_pepper.html.

Phinizy, Coles. "The Lost Pets That Stray to the Labs." *Sports Illustrated*, November 29, 1965. http://sportsillustrated.cnn.com/vault/article/magazine/MAG1077956/1/index.htm.

"President Johnson's Dogs." LBJ Presidential Library, accessed December 11, 2014. http://www.lbjlib.utexas.edu/johnson/archives.hom/faqs/dog/doghouse.asp

Unti, Bernard. "Concentration Camps for Lost and Stolen Pets." Humane Society of the United States, accessed December 11, 2014. http://archive.today/FEmvu.

Wayman, Stan, photographer. "Concentration Camps for Dogs." *LIFE*, February 4, 1966.

"NOTHING IS MORE PRICELESS AND MORE WORTHY OF PRESERVATION THAN THE RICH ARRAY OF ANIMAL LIFE WITH WHICH OUR COUNTRY HAS BEEN BLESSED"

- **Document:** President Richard Nixon's comments following his signing of the Endangered Species Act.
- **Date:** December 28, 1973.
- **Where:** Washington, D.C.
- **Significance:** The Endangered Species Act was crafted to protect imperiled plants and animals in the United States from extinction. It remains the legal cornerstone of efforts to preserve and restore endangered species and protect associated wildlife habitat from development or degradation.

DOCUMENT

I have today signed S. 1983, the Endangered Species Act of 1973. At a time when Americans are more concerned than ever with conserving our natural resources, this legislation provides the Federal Government with needed authority to protect an irreplaceable part of our national heritage—threatened wildlife.

This important measure grants the Government both the authority to make early identification of endangered species and the means to act quickly and thoroughly to save them from extinction. It also puts into effect the Convention on International Trade in Endangered Species of Wild Fauna and Flora signed in Washington on March 3, 1973.

Nothing is more priceless and more worthy of preservation than the rich array of animal life with which our country has been blessed. It is a many-faceted treasure, of value to scholars, scientists, and nature lovers alike, and it forms a vital part of the heritage we all share as Americans. I congratulate the 93d Congress for taking this important step toward protecting a heritage which we hold in trust to countless future generations of our fellow citizens. Their lives will be richer, and America will be more beautiful in the years ahead, thanks to the measure that I have the pleasure of signing into law today.

Source: Nixon, Richard. "Statement on Signing the Endangered Species Act of 1973." December 28, 1973. Public Papers of the Presidents: Richard Nixon, 1973. Washington, DC: Government Printing Office, 1975, p. 1027.

ANALYSIS

The Endangered Species Act (ESA) is the strongest, most comprehensive law ever passed in the United States for the protection of animals. Enacted in December 1973, this legislation aims to protect animal species that are at risk for extinction, the habitats of those species, and at-risk plant species and their habitats. By passing the ESA, Congress committed the United States to policies that attempt to honor the intrinsic worth of all species.

As noted by President Richard Nixon in the selected passage, enactment of the ESA also honored and codified U.S. commitment to the Convention on International Trade in Endangered Species of Wild Fauna and Flora (also known as CITES). CITES is an agreement among nations worldwide to regulate wildlife trade (including live plants and animals as well as products made from plants or animals). Cooperation with CITES regulations is voluntary, but passage of the ESA signaled strong U.S. commitment to the agreement.

In the selected passage, President Nixon mentions both "threatened" and "endangered" wildlife species. According to the ESA, " 'endangered species' means any species which is in danger of extinction throughout all or a significant portion of its range." The ESA defines "threatened species" as "any species which is likely to become an endangered species within a foreseeable future throughout all or a significant portion of its range." The ESA does not define "extinction," but by standard definition, "extinct" means "no longer existing."

The ESA replaced and expanded on regulations introduced by the Endangered Species Preservation Act (1966) and the Endangered Species Conservation Act (1969). Among its many notable provisions, the ESA includes detailed procedures that government agencies must follow in order to list a species as endangered or threatened. The law also allows individual citizens to request listing for at-risk species, although the process for doing so is complicated. Earthjustice, an environmental law organization, notes a significant point about listing: "Unlike other parts of the Endangered Species Act, the listing of a threatened or endangered species is based solely on science, not on economics or other factors." This stipulation about listing was part of a 1982 amendment to the ESA.

The ESA also established the government's responsibility to designate "critical habitat" and develop recovery plans for listed species. Recovery plans go beyond the goal of preventing extinction; they are designed to actively promote improvement of listed species and their habitats. "Critical habitat" is defined as specific geographical areas that have "physical or biological features . . . essential to the conservation of the [listed] species." The designation of critical habitat can be controversial if people have previously been accustomed to using the designated areas for their own purposes, without regulation. However, Congress addressed this potential conflict in a 1978 amendment. The ESA now states that before critical habitat can be officially designated, an economic analysis must be conducted to ensure that the potential benefits for a listed species outweigh the costs for people who have economic interests in the land.

The opening lines of the ESA declare that various forms of wildlife have become extinct in the United States "as a consequence of economic growth and development untempered by adequate concern and conservation." The ESA includes many provisions, including an economic hardship exemption, that try to balance the interests of wildlife and the economic interests of people. Despite this attempt to address economic concerns, the ESA continues to be challenged by various groups that prefer less governmental regulation and more opportunity for development and use of the land. In addition, the complex process required for listing an at-risk species often limits the effectiveness of the law; that is, listing sometimes takes so long that the species becomes extinct before federal protection can be secured.

Under the ESA, all species other than pest insects are eligible for protection. All federal agencies must comply with ESA regulations (although a 2004 amendment granted an exemption to the Department of Defense). All citizens can participate in the process of listing endangered or threatened species. The ESA was meant to be all-inclusive, a sweeping reform that would put conservation ideals into practice. Its effectiveness continues to be a matter of political debate, but the ESA succeeds in expressing a belief in the interconnectedness of all, one of the key ideas in animal rights philosophy.

FURTHER READING

Assault on Wildlife: The Endangered Species Act under Attack. Washington, DC: Defenders of Wildlife, 2001. http://www.defenders.org/sites/default/files/publications/assault_on _wildlife_the_endangered_species_act_under_attack.pdf.

Dickson, Barnabas, and Jon Hutton. *Endangered Species Threatened Convention: The Past, Present and Future of CITES, the Convention on International Trade in Endangered Species of Wild Fauna and Flora.* Hoboken, NJ: Taylor and Francis, 2013.

"DOD Exemption a Sad Day for America." World Wildlife Fund, November 12, 2003. http://www.worldwildlife.org/press-releases/dod-exemption-a-sad-day-for-america.

Doub, J. Peyton. *The Endangered Species Act: History, Implementation, Successes, and Controversies.* Boca Raton, FL: CRC Press, 2012.

"Endangered Species Act—A History of the Endangered Species Act of 1973: 1978 ESA Amendment." U.S. Fish & Wildlife Services. http://www.fws.gov/endangered/laws -policies/esa-1978.html.

"Endangered Species Act—A History of the Endangered Species Act of 1973: 1982 ESA Amendment." U.S. Fish & Wildlife Services. http://www.fws.gov/endangered/laws -policies/esa-1982.html.

"Endangered Species Act—A History of the Endangered Species Act of 1973: 2004 ESA Amendment." U.S. Fish & Wildlife Services. http://www.fws.gov/endangered/laws -policies/esa-2004.html.

"ESA Basics: 40 Years of Conserving Endangered Species." U.S. Fish & Wildlife Services, January 2013. http://www.fws.gov/ENDANGERED/esa-library/pdf/ESA_basics.pdf.

Goble, Dale D., J. Michael Scott, and Frank W. Davis, eds. *The Endangered Species Act at Thirty: Renewing the Conservation Promise.* Washington, DC: Island Press, 2006.

Matsumoto, Sarah, Cara Pike, Tom Turner, and Ray Wan. *Citizens' Guide to the Endangered Species Act*. San Francisco: Earthjustice, 2003. http://earthjustice.org/sites/default/files/library/reports/Citizens_Guide_ESA.pdf.

"Threatened and Endangered Species." Humane Society of the United States, accessed December 11, 2014. http://www.humanesociety.org/issues/endangered_species/.

"CONSIDER THAT PROCEDURES THAT CAUSE PAIN OR DISTRESS IN HUMAN BEINGS MAY CAUSE PAIN OR DISTRESS IN OTHER ANIMALS"

- **Document:** *U.S. Government Principles for the Utilization and Care of Vertebrate Animals Used in Testing, Research, and Training,* a document developed by the Interagency Research Animal Committee.
- **Date:** 1985.
- **Where:** Washington, D.C.
- **Significance:** These principles became "the foundation for humane care and use of laboratory animals" for all research carried out or sponsored by government agencies and institutions in the United States.

DOCUMENT

The development of knowledge necessary for the improvement of the health and well-being of humans as well as other animals requires in vivo experimentation with a wide variety of animal species. Whenever U.S. Government agencies develop requirements for testing, research, or training procedures involving the use of vertebrate animals, the following principles shall be considered; and whenever these agencies actually perform or sponsor such procedures, the responsible Institutional Official shall ensure that these principles are adhered to:

I. The transportation, care, and use of animals should be in accordance with the Animal Welfare Act (7 U.S.C. 2131 et. seq.) and other applicable Federal laws, guidelines, and policies.

II. Procedures involving animals should be designed and performed with due consideration of their relevance to human or animal health, the advancement of knowledge, or the good of society.

III. The animals selected for a procedure should be of an appropriate species and quality and the minimum number required to obtain valid results. Methods such as mathematical models, computer simulation, and in vitro biological systems should be considered.

IV. Proper use of animals, including the avoidance or minimization of discomfort, distress, and pain when consistent with sound scientific practices, is imperative. Unless the contrary is established, investigators should consider that procedures that cause pain or distress in human beings may cause pain or distress in other animals.

V. Procedures with animals that may cause more than momentary or slight pain or distress should be performed with appropriate sedation, analgesia,

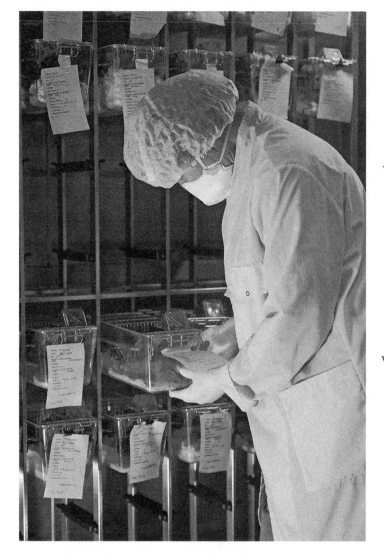

A scientist examines a mouse in an experimental lab. In 1985, the Interagency Research Animal Committee of the U.S. Public Health Service created nine principles for the Utilization and Care of Vertebrate Animals Used in Testing, Research, and Training. The principles were established to ensure the humane treatment of animals used in a research environment. (RDS/Wellcome Trust Photographic Library)

or anesthesia. Surgical or other painful procedures should not be performed on unanesthetized animals paralyzed by chemical agents.

VI. Animals that would otherwise suffer severe or chronic pain or distress that cannot be relieved should be painlessly killed at the end of the procedure or, if appropriate, during the procedure.

VII. The living conditions of animals should be appropriate for their species and contribute to their health and comfort. Normally, the housing, feeding, and care of all animals used for biomedical purposes must be directed by a veterinarian or other scientist trained and experienced in the proper care, handling, and use of the species being maintained or studied. In any case, veterinary care shall be provided as indicated.

VIII. Investigators and other personnel shall be appropriately qualified and experienced for conducting procedures on living animals. Adequate arrangements shall be made for their in-service training, including the proper and humane care and use of laboratory animals.

IX. Where exceptions are required in relation to the provisions of these Principles, the decisions should not rest with the investigators directly concerned but should be made, with due regard to Principle II, by an appropriate review group such as an institutional animal care and use committee. Such exceptions should not be made solely for the purposes of teaching or demonstration.

Source: Guide for the Care and Use of Laboratory Animals. Prepared by the National Research Council. Published in the Federal Register, May 20, 1985, vol. 50, no. 97, by the Office of Science and Technology Policy.

ANALYSIS

There are nine principles that the U.S. Public Health Service (PHS), a division of the U.S. Department of Health and Human Services, implemented that provide a foundation for the treatment, care, and use of laboratory animals in the United

States. The Interagency Research Animal Committee developed these principles and they were adopted by the Office of Science and Technology Policy in 1985.

The principles are based on a reference book called the *Guide for the Care and Use of Laboratory Animals* that was created by the Institute for Laboratory Animal Research and the National Academy of Sciences. Professionals use the guide as a reference for caring for animals in a research and testing environment. The guide makes it clear that these animals must be treated in a humane way. It provides explicit standards and responsibilities that researchers, veterinarians, and other professionals who deal with animals on a continuous basis should follow. According to the National Institutes of Health (NIH) Web site, examples of responsibilities include "monitoring animal care and use, provisions for veterinary care, training for personnel, and the establishment of an appropriate occupational health and safety program." The standards also "encompass the animal environment, animal husbandry and management, veterinary care, and design and construction of animal facilities."

The AWA, the principle federal law protecting animals, was amended in 1985 to include protection for animals being used in laboratory experiments and other research projects. According to the NIH Web site, this amendment to the AWA was "considered a watershed for laboratory animal welfare because for the first time the AWA clarified humane care, minimization of pain and distress, consideration of alternatives, institutional animal care and use committees, psychological well-being of primates, and exercise for dogs." This act came at a time when more and more people were becoming aware of animal testing and had concerns about how this testing was being implemented. Researchers must comply with these principles and governmental agencies such as the USDA, Food and Drug Administration (FDA), and NIH work together to ensure that compliance takes place.

The NIH clarifies the definition of animal as "any live, vertebrate animal used or intended for use in research, research training, experimentation, or biological testing or for related purposes." Birds, mice, and rats are excluded from this definition. Along with following the nine principles, compliance with the AWA is necessary for any public or private research institution, business, or agency receiving support from the PHS Policy, as well as following any state, local, or federal regulations that are in place concerning animals. These principles also apply to research institutions all over the world that receive any funds or support from the PHS.

To ensure that compliance is taking place, the PHS requires written reassurance to the Office of Laboratory Animal Welfare (OLAW) that the nine principles are being followed, all requirements of the AWA are being met, and the facilities and equipment being used are up to standard. An outline on how the particular agency or institution will care for and use the animals is also required. Approval or disapproval is given by OLAW and once approval is granted, it is given for a specified period of time, typically five years or less. If an institution is rejected, it can try again after making any necessary changes. Finally, once approval has been granted, the institution or agency is periodically monitored along the way to ensure that compliance is being maintained.

The nine principles for the *Utilization and Care of Vertebrate Animals Used in Testing, Research, and Training* were created to ensure that animals being used for laboratory testing and research are treated as decently and as humanely as possible. Several agencies are intimately involved in ensuring that these principles are being met, along with all requirements that are part of the Animal Welfare Act. These principles provide a clear definition for all research institutions on how animals should be treated and cared for.

FURTHER READING

Bayne, Kathryn, and Patricia V. Turner, eds. *Laboratory Animal Welfare*. Bethesda, MD: National Institutes of Health, 1985.

Committee for the Update of the Guide for the Care and Use of Laboratory Animals. *Guide for the Care and Use of Laboratory Animals*. Washington, DC: National Academies Press, 2010.

"Grants & Funding: Documents Relevant to the PHS Policy." National Institutes of Health, accessed December 11, 2014. http://grants.nih.gov/grants/olaw/tutorial/relevant.htm.

"PAIN AND DISTRESS MUST BE MINIMIZED IN EXPERIMENTAL PROCEDURES"

- **Document:** Improved Standards for Laboratory Animals Act.
- **Date:** Enacted on December 23, 1985.
- **Where:** Washington, D.C.
- **Significance:** This law addresses continued concerns surrounding pain and suffering with laboratory animals.

DOCUMENT

Summary: Also called "The Improved Standards for Laboratory Animals Act" and enacted December 23, 1985, this section clarifies what is meant by "humane care" by mentioning specifics such as sanitation, housing, and ventilation. It directs the Secretary of Agriculture to establish regulations to provide exercise for dogs and an adequate physical environment to promote the psychological well-being of non-human primates. It specifies that pain and distress must be minimized in experimental procedures and that alternatives to such procedures be considered by the principle investigator. It also defines practices that are considered to be painful. No animal can be used in more than one major operative experiment with recovery (exceptions are listed). The establishment of the Institutional Animal Care and Use Committee (IACUC) is introduced with a description of its roles, composition, and responsibilities to APHIS. Also included is the formation of an information service at the National Agricultural Library to assist those regulated by the act in prevention of unintended duplication of research, employee training, searching for ways to reduce or replace animal use, and to provide information on how to decrease pain and distress. The final section explains the penalties for release of trade secrets by regulators and the regulated community.

DEC. 23, 1985
FOOD SECURITY ACT OF 1985
TITLE XVII-RELATED AND MISCELLANEOUS MATTERS

Note: Brackets, [ ], indicate notes found in the corresponding margin of the hardcopy document.

SUBTITLE F — ANIMAL WELFARE

FINDINGS

SEC. 1751.[*7 USC 2131 note.*] For the purposes of this subtitle, the Congress finds that—

[*Research and development.*] (1) the use of animals is instrumental in certain research and education for advancing knowledge of cures and treatment for diseases and injuries which afflict both humans and animals;

(2) methods of testing that do not use animals are being and continue to be developed which are faster, less expensive, and more accurate than traditional animal experiments for some purposes and further opportunities exist for the development of these methods of testing;

(3) measures which eliminate or minimize the unnecessary duplication of experiments on animals can result in more productive use of Federal funds; and

(4) measures which help meet the public concern for laboratory animal care and treatment are important in assuring that research will continue to progress.

STANDARDS AND CERTIFICATION PROCESS

SEC. 1752. (a) Section 13 of the Animal Welfare Act (7 U.S.C. 2143) is amended by—

(1) redesignating subsections (b) through (d) as subsections (f) through (h) respectively; and

(2) striking out the first two sentences of subsection (a) and inserting in lieu thereof the following new sentences: "(1) The Secretary shall promulgate standards to govern the humane handling, care, treatment, and transportation of animals by dealers, research facilities, and exhibitors.

"(2) The standards described in paragraph (1) shall include minimum requirements—

"(A) for handling, housing, feeding, watering, sanitation, ventilation, shelter from extremes of weather and temperatures, adequate veterinary care, and separation by species where the Secretary finds necessary for humane handling, care, or treatment of animals; and

"(B) for exercise of dogs, as determined by an attending veterinarian in accordance with general standards promulgated by the Secretary, and for a physical environment adequate to promote the psychological well-being of primates.

"(3) In addition to the requirements under paragraph (2), the standards described in paragraph (1) shall, with respect to animals in research facilities, include requirements—

"(A) for animal care, treatment, and practices in experimental procedures to ensure that animal pain and distress are minimized, including adequate veterinary care with the appropriate use of anesthetic, analgesic, tranquilizing drugs, or euthanasia;

"(B) that the principal investigator considers alternatives to any procedure likely to produce pain to or distress in an experimental animal;

"(C) in any practice which could cause pain to animals—

"(i) that a doctor of veterinary medicine is consulted in the planning of such procedures;

"(ii) for the use of tranquilizers, analgesics, and anesthetics;

"(iii) for pre-surgical and post-surgical care by laboratory workers, in accordance with established veterinary medical and nursing procedures;

"(iv) against the use of paralytics without anesthesia, and

"(v) that the withholding of tranquilizers, anesthesia, analgesia, or euthanasia when scientifically necessary shall continue for only the necessary period of time;

[*Prohibition.*] "(D) that no animal is used in more than one major operative experiment from which it is allowed to recover except in cases of—

"(i) scientific necessity; or

"(ii) other special circumstances as determined by the Secretary; and

"(E) that exceptions to such standards may be made only when specified by research protocol and that any such exception shall be detailed and explained in a report outlined under paragraph (7) and filed with the Institutional Animal Care Committee."

[*7 USC 2143.*] (b) Section 13(a) of such Act is further amended—

(1) by designating the third and fourth sentences as paragraph (4);

(2) by designating the fifth sentence as paragraph (5); and

(3) by striking out the last sentence and inserting in lieu thereof the following:

[*Prohibition.*] "(6)(A) Nothing in this Act—

"(i) except as provided in paragraphs (7) of this subsection, shall be construed as authorizing the Secretary to promulgate rules, regulations, or orders with regard to the design, outlines, or guidelines of actual research or experimentation by a research facility as determined by such research facility;

[*Regulations.*] "(ii) except as provided subparagraphs (A) and (C) (ii) through (v) of paragraph (3) and paragraph (7) of this subsection, shall be construed as authorizing the Secretary to promulgate rules, regulations, or orders with regard to the performance of actual research or experimentation by a research facility as determined by such research facility; and

[*Research and development.*] "(iii) shall authorize the Secretary, during inspection, to interrupt the conduct of actual research or experimentation.

[*Prohibition.*] "(B) No rule, regulation, order, or part of this Act shall be construed to require a research facility to disclose publicly or to the Institutional Animal Committee during its inspection, trade secrets or commercial or financial information which is privileged or confidential.

[*Research and development.*] "(7)(A) The Secretary shall require each research facility to show upon inspection, and to report at least annually, that the provisions of this Act are being followed and that professionally acceptable standards governing the care, treatment, and use of animals are being followed by the research facility during actual research or experimentation.

"(B) In complying with subparagraph (A), such research facilities shall provide—

"(i) information on procedures likely to produce pain or distress in any animal and assurances demonstrating that the principal investigator considered alternatives to those procedures;

"(ii) assurances satisfactory to the Secretary that such facility is adhering to the standards described in this section; and "(iii) an explanation for any deviation from the standards promulgated under this section.

[*Prohibition.*] "(8) Paragraph (1) shall not prohibit any State (or a political subdivision of such State) from promulgating standards in addition to those standards promulgated by the Secretary under paragraph (1)."

[*Ante, p.1645*] (c) Section 13 of such Act is further amended by inserting after subsection (a) the following new subsections:

"(b)(1) The Secretary shall require that each research facility establish at least one Committee. Each Committee shall be appointed by the chief executive officer of each such research facility and shall be composed of not fewer than three members. Such members shall possess sufficient ability to assess animal care, treatment, and practices in experimental research as determined by the needs of the research facility and shall represent society's concerns regarding the welfare of animal subjects used at such facility. Of the members of the Committee—

"(A) at least one member shall be a doctor of veterinary medicine;

"(B) at least one member—

[*Prohibitions.*] "(i) shall not be affiliated in any way with such facility other than as a member of the Committee;

"(ii) shall not be a member of the immediate family of a person who is affiliated with such facility; and

"(iii) is intended to provide representation for general community interests in the proper care and treatment of animals; and

"(C) in those cases where the Committee consists of more than three members, not more than three members shall be from the same administrative unit of such facility.

"(2) A quorum shall be required for all formal actions of the Committee, including inspections under paragraph (3).

"(3) The Committee shall inspect at least semiannually all animal study areas and animal facilities of such research facility and review as part of the inspection—

"(A) practices involving pain to animals, and

"(B) the condition of animals,

to ensure compliance with the provisions of this Act to minimize pain and distress to animals. Exceptions to the requirement of inspection of such study areas may be made by the Secretary if animals are studied in their natural environment and the study area is prohibitive to easy access.

[*Reports.*] "(4)(A) The Committee shall file an inspection certification report of each inspection at the research facility. Such report shall—

"(i) be signed by a majority of the Committee members involved in the inspection;

[*Research and development.*] "(ii) include reports of any violation of the standards promulgated, or assurances required, by the Secretary, including any deficient conditions of animal care or treatment, any deviations of research practices from originally approved proposals that adversely affect animal welfare, any notification to the facility regarding such conditions, and any corrections made thereafter;

"(iii) include any minority views of the Committee; and

"(iv) include any other information pertinent to the activities of the Committee.

[*Report.*] "(B) Such report shall remain on file for at least three years at the research facility and shall be available for inspection by the Animal and Plant Health Inspection Service and any funding Federal agency.

"(C) In order to give the research facility an opportunity to correct any deficiencies or deviations discovered by reason of paragraph (3), The Committee shall notify the administrative representative of the research facility of any deficiencies or deviations from the provisions of this Act. If, after notification and an opportunity for correction, such deficiencies or deviations remain uncorrected, the Committee shall notify (in writing) the Animal and Plant Health Inspection Service and the funding Federal agency of such deficiencies or deviations.

[*Records. Reports.*] "(5) The inspection results shall be available to Department of Agriculture inspectors for review during inspections. Department of Agriculture inspectors shall forward any Committee inspection records which include reports of uncorrected deficiencies or deviations to the Animal and Plant Health Inspection Service and any funding Federal agency of the project with respect to which such uncorrected deficiencies and deviations occurred.

"(c) In the case of Federal research facilities, a Federal Committee shall be established and shall have the same composition and responsibilities provided in subsection (b), except that the Federal Committee shall report deficiencies or deviations to the head of the Federal agency conducting the research rather than to the Animal and Plant Health Inspection Service. The head of the Federal agency conducting the research shall be responsible for—

"(1) all corrective action to be taken at the facility; and

"(2) the granting of all exceptions to inspection protocol.

"(d) Each research facility shall provide for the training of scientists, animal technicians, and other personnel involved with animal care and treatment in such facility as required by the Secretary. Such training shall include instruction on—

"(1) the humane practice of animal maintenance and experimentation;

"(2) research or testing methods that minimize or eliminate the use of animals or limit animal pain or distress;

"(3) utilization of the information service at the National Agricultural Library, established under subsection (e); and

"(4) methods whereby deficiencies in animal care and treatment should be reported.

"(e) The Secretary shall establish an information service at the National Agricultural Library. Such service shall, in cooperation with the National Library of Medicine, provide information—

"(1) pertinent to employee training;

"(2) which could prevent unintended duplication of animal experimentation as determined by the needs of the research facility; and

"(3) on improved methods of animal experimentation, including methods which could—

"(A) reduce or replace animal use; and

"(B) minimize pain and distress to animals, such as anesthetic and analgesic procedures.

[*Research and development.*] "(f) In any case in which a Federal agency funding a research project determines that conditions of animal care, treatment, or practice in a particular project have not been in compliance with standards promulgated under this Act, despite notification by the Secretary or such Federal agency to the research facility and an opportunity for correction, such agency shall suspend or revoke Federal support for the project. Any research facility losing Federal support as a result of actions taken under the preceding sentence shall have the right of appeal as provided in sections 701 through 706 of title 5, United States Code."

INSPECTIONS

SEC. 1753. Section 16(a) of the Animal Welfare Act (7 U.S.C. 2146(a) is amended by inserting after the first sentence the following: "The Secretary shall inspect each research facility at least once each year and, in the case of deficiencies or deviations from the standards promulgated under this Act, shall conduct such follow-up inspections as may be necessary until all deficiencies or deviations from such standards are corrected."

PENALTY FOR RELEASE OF TRADE SECRETS

[*7 USC 2157*] SEC. 1754. The Animal Welfare Act (7 U.S.C. 2131-2156) is amended by adding at the end thereof the following section:

"Sec. 27. (a) It shall be unlawful for any member of an Institutional Animal Committee to release any confidential information of the research facility including information that concerns or relates to—

"(1) the trade secrets, processes, operations, style of work, or apparatus; or

"(2) the identity, confidential statistical data, amount or source of any income, profits, losses, or expenditures, of the research facility.

"(b) It shall be unlawful for any member of such Committee—

"(1) to use or attempt to use to his advantages; or

"(2) to reveal to any other person, any information which is entitled to protection as confidential information under subsection (a).

"(c) A violation of subsection (a) or (b) is punishable by—

"(1) removal from such Committee; and

"(2)(A) a fine of not more than $1,000 and imprisonment of not more than a year; or

"(B) if such violation is willful, a fine of not more than $10,000 and imprisonment of not more than three years.

"(d) Any person, including any research facility, injured in its business or property by reason of a violation of this section may recover all actual and consequential damages sustained by such person and the cost of the suit including a reasonable attorney's fee.

[*Prohibition.*] "(e) Nothing in this section shall be construed to affect any other rights of a person injured in its business or property by reason of a violation of this section. Subsection (d) shall not be construed to limit the exercise of any such rights arising out of or relating to a violation of subsections (a) and (b)."

INCREASED PENALTIES FOR VIOLATION OF THE ACT

SEC. 1755. (a) Subsection (b) of section 19 of the Animal Welfare Act (7 U.S.C. 2149 (b)) is amended—

(1) in the first sentence by striking out "$1,000 for each such violation" and inserting in lieu thereof "$2,500 for each such violation"; and

(2) in the sixth sentence by striking out "$500 for each offense" and inserting in lieu thereof "$1,500 for each offense."

(b) Subsection (d) of such section is amended by striking out "$1,000" and inserting in lieu thereof "$2,500."

DEFINITIONS

SEC. 1756. (a) Section 2 of the Animal Welfare Act (7 U.S.C. 2132) is amended by—

(1) striking out "and" after the semicolon in subsection (i);

(2) striking out the period at the end of subsection (j) and inserting in lieu thereof a semicolon; and

(3) adding after subsection (j) the following new subsections:

[*Animals.*] "(k) The term 'Federal agency' means an Executive agency as such term is defined in section 105 of title 5, United States Code, and with respect to any research facility means the agency from which the research facility receives a Federal award for the conduct of research, experimentation, or testing, involving the use of animals;

[*Research and development. Grant. Loan. Contract.*] "(l) The term 'Federal award for the conduct of research experimentation, or testing, involving the use of animals' means any mechanism (including a grant, award, loan, contract, or cooperative agreement) under which Federal funds are provided to support the conduct of such research.

"(m) The term "quorum" means a majority of the Committee members;

[*Ante, p. 1647.*] "(n) The term 'Committee' means the Institutional Animal Committee established under section 13(b); and

[*Research and development.*] "(o) The term 'Federal research facility' means each department, agency, or instrumentality of the United States which uses live animals for research or experimentation."

[*7 USC 2131 note.*] (B) For purposes of this Act, the term "animal" shall have the same meaning as defined in section 2(g) of the Animal Welfare Act (7 U.S.C. 2132(g).

CONSULTATION WITH THE SECRETARY OF HEALTH AND HUMAN SERVICES

[*Regulations.*] SEC. 1757. Section 15(a) of the Animal Welfare Act (7 U.S.C. 2145(a) is amended by adding after the first sentence the following: "The Secretary shall consult with the Secretary of Health and Human Services prior to issuance of regulations."

TECHNICAL AMENDMENT

SEC. 1758. Section 14 of the Animal Welfare Act (7 U.S.C. 2144) is amended by changing "section 13" to "sections 13 (a), (f), (g), and (h)" wherever it appears.

EFFECTIVE DATE

[*7 USC 2131 note.*] SEC. 1759. This subtitle shall take effect 1 year after the date of the enactment of this Act.

Source: "Improved Standards for Laboratory Animals Act." U.S. Department of Agriculture, National Agricultural Library, December 23, 1985. http://awic.nal. usda.gov/public-law-99-198-food-security-act-1985-subtitle-f-animal-welfare.

ANALYSIS

In 1966, in response to heightened public awareness of animal cruelty, Congress enacted Public Law 89-544, more commonly known as the AWA. This law was the first in the United States to deal with the welfare of warm-blooded animals bought, sold, transported, exhibited, or used in experiments. The USDA is responsible for enforcing the law, including the licensing, monitoring, and inspecting of animal dealers and other businesses that handle specific animals frequently adopted as pets or used in research [defined as "live dogs, cats, monkeys (nonhuman primates), guinea pigs, hamsters, and rabbits"]. According to President Lyndon B. Johnson, the intent of the law is to put an end to abuses and provide humane standards of care in procuring and handling animals. However, in comments made during the signing of the bill, Johnson averred that "the bill does not authorize any sort of interference with actual research or experimentation."

The law was amended several times in the 1970s. However, it wasn't until the 1980s that some of the most substantial changes were made.

In 1981, Alex Pacheco, a student at George Washington University and founding member of People for the Ethical Treatment of Animals (PETA), posed as a research student and gained an internship with the Institute for Behavioral Research (IBR), with the aim of documenting the conditions of animals held in U.S. research labs. While there, he worked with and helped lead studies on 17 primates that were living in deplorable conditions and subjected to horrific tests. Pacheco documented and photographed the "psychological suffering, lack of cage space, and critical sanitation problems" and was even able to bring in outside experts, who signed affidavits confirming that the studies on the primates were unethical. After Pacheco filed his findings with the police, legal charges were filed against IBR and its lead scientist, Dr. Edward Taub.

According to the mandates of the AWA, the USDA's APHIS had visited IBR prior to Pacheco's involvement and had reported no violations. As a result, Taub was eventually vindicated on all counts. However, the publicity of the case and the information provided by Pacheco led many to realize that the AWA needed to be beefed up.

In October 1981, congressional hearings were convened regarding the care, use, and treatment of laboratory animals. These hearings, conducted by U.S. senator Bob Dole (R-Kansas) and U.S. representative George Brown (D-California), lasted throughout the early 1980s. Their findings built support for the Improved Standards for Laboratory Animals Act, which was enacted on December 23, 1985, as an amendment to the AWA.

While acknowledging the importance of animal research for "advancing knowledge of cures and treatment for diseases and injuries," the amendments emphasize the importance of looking for alternatives to animal testing and of strengthening the standards of care to minimize the pain and distress experienced by laboratory animals. The legislation provides a more specific definition of *humane* handling, care, and treatment; increases enforcement of the AWA (including increased penalties for violations); and mandates that those who care for and use such animals must have the proper training. It also established the Animal Welfare Information Center, a national service that provides information on alternatives to animal research, as well as on ways to reduce unintended duplication of experiments. Another stipulation is that a single animal may not be used for multiple surgeries from which it is allowed to recover (known as "survival" surgery).

The amendments also take into consideration the psychological well-being of laboratory animals, establishing regulations for regular exercise for dogs and for the provision of adequate physical environments for nonhuman primates. Each institution that uses laboratory animals must establish an IACUC, which must include a veterinarian and an unaffiliated person from the community. Each IACUC is responsible for inspecting animal laboratories two times a year and alerting the USDA to any violations.

The legislation addresses many of the issues of concern. However, it also has exceptions to the rules. For example, regarding the prohibition of "survival" surgery, the amendment states, "except in cases of scientific necessity . . . or other special circumstances as determined by the Secretary [of Agriculture]." Although some critics state that the amendments have not gone far enough and provide too many loopholes, many supporters state that the legislation is a step in the right direction. According to Wayne Pacelle, president of the Humane Society of the United States, "if animal suffering was relieved even to a small extent, then a good purpose was served."

FURTHER READING

"Animal Welfare Act." American Anti-Vivisection Society, accessed December 31, 2014. http://aavs.org/animals-science/laws/federal-regulations/.

"Animal Welfare Act." National Association for Biomedical Research. http://www.nabr.org/biomedical-research/oversight/animal-welfare-act/.

Animal Welfare Institute: Working for the Passage of Animal Welfare Laws Since 1951. Washington, DC: Animal Welfare Institute, n.d. https://awionline.org/sites/default/files/products/awi_legislative_brochure_pdf.pdf.

Brown, George E., Jr. "30 Years of the Animal Welfare Act." *Animal Welfare Information Center Newsletter* 8, no. 1 (Spring 1997). http://www.nal.usda.gov/awic/newsletters/v8n1/8n1brown.htm.

Curnutt, Jordan. *Animals and the Law: A Sourcebook.* Santa Barbara, CA: ABC-CLIO, 2001.

Francione, Gary L. *Rain Without Thunder: The Ideology of the Animal Rights Movement.* Philadelphia: Temple University Press, 1996.

"Grants & Funding: Documents Relevant to the PHS Policy." National Institutes of Health, Office of Extramural Research, accessed December 11, 2014. http://grants.nih.gov/grants/olaw/tutorial/relevant.htm.

Pacheco, Alex, and Anna Francione. "The Silver Spring Monkeys," in *In Defense of Animals.* Edited by Peter Singer. New York: Basil Blackwell, 1985, pp. 135–47.

"The Silver Spring Monkeys: The Case That Launched PETA." People for the Ethical Protection of Animals, accessed December 11, 2014. http://www.peta.org/issues/animals-used-for-experimentation/silver-spring-monkeys/.

Silverman, Jerald, Mark A. Suckow, and Sreekant Murthy, eds. *The IACUC Handbook,* 3rd ed. Boca Raton, FL: CRC Press, 2014.

"WHY WORRY ABOUT THEIR LONELINESS, THEIR PAIN, THEIR DEATH?"

- **Document:** "The Case for Animal Rights," an excerpt from an essay by philosophy professor emeritus Tom Regan on the issue of animal rights, from Peter Singer's book *In Defense of Animals*.
- **Date:** 1985.
- **Where:** New York City.
- **Significance:** Animal rights activist Tom Regan asserts that animal pain and suffering at the hands of humans is based on a mistaken—and deplorable—viewpoint that animals exist to serve human beings. This criticism has become one of the pillars of the animal rights movement, and Regan's articulation of it has become one of the best-known works in the movement's history.

DOCUMENT

I regard myself as an advocate of animal rights—as a part of the animal rights movement. That movement, as I conceive it, is committed to a number of goals, including:

- the total abolition of the use of animals in science;
- the total dissolution of commercial animal agriculture;
- the total elimination of commercial and sport hunting and trapping.

There are, I know, people who profess to believe in animal rights but do not avow these goals. Factory farming, they say, is wrong—it violates animals' rights—but traditional animal agriculture is all right. Toxicity tests of cosmetics on animals violates their rights, but important medical research—cancer research, for example—does not. The clubbing of baby seals is abhorrent, but not the harvesting of adult seals. I used to think I understood this reasoning. Not anymore. You don't change unjust institutions by tidying them up.

What's wrong—fundamentally wrong—with the way animals are treated isn't the details that vary from case to case. It's the whole system. The forlornness of the veal calf is pathetic, heart wrenching; the pulsing pain of the chimp with electrodes planted deep in her brain is repulsive; the slow, tortuous death of the raccoon caught in the leg-hold trap is agonizing. But what is wrong isn't the pain, isn't the suffering, isn't the deprivation. These compound what's wrong. Sometimes—often—they make it much, much worse. But they are not the fundamental wrong.

The fundamental wrong is the system that allows us to view animals as *our resources*, here for *us*—to be eaten, or surgically manipulated, or exploited for sport or money. Once we accept this view of animals—as our resources—the rest is as predictable as it is regrettable. Why worry about their loneliness, their pain, their death? Since animals exist for us, to benefit us in one way or another, what harms them really doesn't matter—or matters only if it starts to bother us, makes us feel a trifle uneasy when we eat our veal escalope, for example. So, yes, let us get veal calves out of solitary confinement, give them more space, a little straw, a few companions. But let us keep our veal escalope.

But a little straw, more space and a few companions won't eliminate—won't even touch—the basic wrong that attaches to our viewing and treating these animals as our resources. A veal calf killed to be eaten after living in close confinement is viewed and treated in this way: but so, too, is another who is raised (as they say) "more humanely." To right the wrong of our treatment of farm animals requires more than making rearing methods "more humane"; it requires the total dissolution of commercial animal agriculture.

How we do this, whether we do it or, as in the case of animals in science, whether and how we abolish their use—these are to a large extent political questions. People must change their beliefs before they change their habits. Enough people, especially those elected to public office, must believe in change—must want it—before we will have laws that protect the rights of animals. This process of change is very complicated, very demanding, very exhausting, calling for the efforts of many hands in education, publicity, political organization and activity, down to the licking of envelopes and stamps. As a trained and practising philosopher, the sort of contribution I can make is limited but, I like to think, important. The currency of philosophy is ideas—their meaning and rational foundation—not the nuts and bolts of the legislative process, say, or the mechanics of community organization. That's what I have been exploring over the past ten years or so in my essays and talks and, most recently, in my book, *The Case for Animal Rights*. I believe the major conclusions I reach in the book are true because they are supported by the weight of the best arguments. I believe the idea of animal rights has reason, not just emotion, on its side.

Source: Regan, Tom. "The Case for Animal Rights," in *In Defense of Animals*. Edited by Peter Singer. New York: Basil Blackwell, 1985, pp. 14–15.

ANALYSIS

Tom Regan, a professor of philosophy, wrote this passage more than 2,000 years after Aristotle wrote "Animals Are Created for the Sake of Men." Like Albert Schweitzer (see excerpt from *Civilisation and Ethics*), Regan disagrees with Aristotle—and with anyone who believes that nonhuman animals are resources for human beings to use. Furthermore, Regan believes that improving the treatment or living conditions of animals used for farming or science, or reducing the suffering of hunted or trapped animals, "won't even touch . . . the basic wrong" of viewing those animals as resources.

Regan's perspective highlights the difference between advocating for animal welfare and advocating for animal rights. Regan is a staunch advocate for animal rights.

He believes the life of a nonhuman animal matters to that animal, just as the life of a human being matters to that human being (compare Schweitzer's "will to live" concept in the excerpt from *Civilisation and Ethics*). According to Regan, nonhuman animals have inherent value and therefore have a right to be treated with respect, just as human beings do. For that reason, human beings have a moral obligation not to treat animals in ways that human beings would not want to be treated. For example, a moral person would not carry out a dangerous experiment on another human being; therefore, people should not carry out dangerous experiments (or experiments of any kind) on animals either. For Regan, the goal of animal welfare advocates—improving or reforming conditions for animals while allowing those animals to be used for human benefit—remains morally unacceptable.

In the selected passage, Regan suggests that passing laws to make conditions "more humane" for animals might make people feel better but will not change the animals' fate, whether they are in laboratories, on farms, or in traps. In another essay titled "The Myth of 'Humane' Treatment," Regan goes into more detail on this point. He describes the low standards for "humane care" set by the Animal Welfare Act and explains how the public is lulled by the knowledge that official inspections are being carried out—inspections that merely enforce the low standards of the legislation. Regan supports his assertions with disturbing examples of how animals are treated in research laboratories that operate in accordance with the law.

Regan and co-author Gary Francione made an even stronger statement against animal welfare advocacy in an article written for *The Animals' Agenda* in 1992. In that essay, they claimed that "the enactment of animal welfare measures actually impedes the achievement of animal rights." They explained their position as follows:

> Under the [animal welfare] framework, only people have rights enforceable by law. Animals are regarded as the *property* of humans. . . . When we confront a situation in which human and nonhuman interests conflict, we should attempt to balance those interests, but, under the animal welfare framework, we balance two very dissimilar interests: the interest of the nonhuman animal, who is regarded as property . . ., against the interest of the human rightholder. And the animal is almost always bound to lose. . . . (Regan and Francione, 1992).

In other words, according to Regan and Francione, as long as nonhuman animals are considered to be property (objects without rights), human beings will exercise their right to use that property as they wish. Under such circumstances, the interests of "property" (nonhuman animals) will rarely outweigh the interests of people who believe that human beings are the only animal species with rights. In this scenario, the continued exploitation of animals is inevitable.

Throughout the selected passage, there is a tone of impatience or frustration. Regan creates this effect through his choice of words and his use of repetition. For example, in the first paragraph, Regan lists "total abolition," "total dissolution," and "total elimination" of animal uses/abuses as goals of the animal rights movement. Strictly speaking, the word *total* is unnecessary, because the other terms—

abolition, *dissolution*, and *elimination*—imply a complete, absolute end. But Regan makes this strong opening statement in order to emphasize his belief that compromise and halfway measures are unacceptable in the fight for animal rights.

Although Regan includes some emotion in this passage, he is primarily a philosopher, and he is known for using clear and careful reasoning to make his case for animal rights. (For another example, see the excerpt from Regan's "Philosophy of Animal Rights.") The excerpt is taken from Regan's *The Case for Animal Rights*, one of the earliest books on the subject of rights for nonhumans. The book was important to the animal rights movement because Regan's rational approach drew interest from other thinkers and people previously outside the movement. His ideas inspired serious discussion and thought and brought more respect to the cause of animal rights. *The Case for Animal Rights* was nominated for a Pulitzer Prize, and it remains an authoritative text on the philosophy of the animal rights movement. Regan continues to play a significant role in the movement during the twenty-first century.

FURTHER READING

"The ALF Credo and Guidelines." Animal Liberation Front.com. http://www. animalliberationfront.com/ALFront/alf_credo.htm.

Cohen, Carl, and Tom Regan. *The Animal Rights Debate*. Lanham, MD: Rowman and Littlefield, 2001.

Jonsson, Patrik. "Tracing an Animal-Rights Philosophy." *Christian Science Monitor*, October 9, 2001. http://www.csmonitor.com/2001/1009/p14s1-leca.html.

Panaman, Roger, "Philosophers Three," *How to Do Animal Rights* (blog). April 2008. http:// www.animalethics.org.uk/i-ch6-10-regan-ryder-singer.html.

Regan, Tom. *Animal Rights, Human Wrongs: An Introduction to Moral Philosophy*. Lanham, MD: Rowman and Littlefield, 2003.

Regan, Tom. "Animal Rights 101," *Tom Regan Rights & Writes* (blog). 2014. http:// tomregan.info/essays/animal-rights-101/.

Regan, Tom. *The Case for Animal Rights*. Updated edition. Berkeley: University of California Press, 2010.

Regan, Tom. *Empty Cages: Facing the Challenge of Animal Rights*. Lanham, MD: Rowman & Littlefield, 2004.

Regan, Tom. "Animal Rights & the Myth of 'Humane Treatment.' " *Tom Regan Rights & Writes* (blog). n.d. http://tomregan.info/essays/animal-rights-the-myth-of-humane-treatment/.

Regan, Tom, Gary Francione, and Ingrid Newkirk. "Point/Counterpoint—Point: A Movement's Means Create Its Ends / Counterpoint: Total Victory, Like Checkmate, Cannot Be Achieved in One Move." *The Animals' Agenda*, January/February 1992, pp. 40–43. http://arzonetranscripts.files.wordpress.com/2011/06/point_counterpoint -regan_francione_newkirk.pdf.

Steiner, Gary. "Ask the Prof: The Differences Between Singer, Regan, and Francione." *The Abolitionist: Animal Ethics Magazine*, February 14, 2012. http://theabolitionist .info/article/ask-the-prof-the-differences-between-singer-regan-and-francione/.

"IT'S NOT THE KILLING OF THE ANIMALS THAT IS THE CHIEF ISSUE HERE, BUT RATHER THE UNSPEAKABLE QUALITY OF THE LIVES THEY ARE FORCED TO LIVE"

- **Document:** Introduction to John Robbins's best-selling book *Diet for a New America.*
- **Date:** 1987.
- **Where:** Walpole, New Hampshire.
- **Significance:** Best-selling author Robbins talks about the "deplorable conditions" in which animals live and how this affects food processing and, ultimately, human health.

DOCUMENT

I was born in the heart of the Great American Food Machine. From childhood on, it was expected that I would someday take over and run what has become the world's largest ice cream company—Baskin-Robbins. Year after year I was groomed and prepared for the task, given an opportunity to live the Great American Dream on a scale very few people can ever hope to attain. The ice cream cone shaped pool in the backyard of the house in which I lived was a symbol of the success awaiting me.

But when the time came to decide, I said thank you very much, I appreciate the kind offer, but "No!" I had to say no, because something else was calling me, and no matter how hard I tried, I could not ignore it.

There is a sweeter and deeper dream than the one I turned down. It is the dream of a society in which all beings share because it is founded on a reverence for life. A dream of a society at peace with its conscience because it respects and lives in harmony with all life forms. A dream of a people living in accord with the laws of Creation, cherishing and caring for the natural environment, conserving nature instead of destroying it. A dream of a society that is truly healthy, practicing a wise and compassionate stewardship of a balanced ecosystem.

This is not my dream alone. It is really the dream of all human beings who feel the plight of the Earth as their own, and sense our obligation to respect and protect the world in which we live. To some degree, all of us share in this dream. Yet few of us are satisfied that we are doing all that is needed to make it happen.

Almost none of us is aware of just how powerfully our eating habits affect the possibility of this dream becoming a reality. We do not realize that one way or the other, how we eat has a tremendous impact. *Diet for a New America* is the first book to show in full detail the nature of this impact, not only on our own health, but in addition on the vigor of our society, the health of our world, and the well-being of its creatures. As it turns out, we have cause to be grateful, for *what's best for us personally is also best for the other life forms and for the life support systems on which we all depend.*

The more I have uncovered about the dark side of the Great American Food Machine, the more appropriate it has felt to have declined the opportunity to be part of it. And the more urgent it has seemed that people be made aware of the profound and far-reaching consequences of their eating habits.

Diet for a New America exposes the explosive truths behind the food on America's plates. These are truths the purveyors of the Great American Food Machine don't want you to know, for in many cases they are not pretty truths. But if exposing them makes America healthier, the world a kinder and more life-sustaining place, then so be it.

Increasingly in the last few decades, the animals raised for meat, dairy products, and eggs in the United States have been subjected to ever more deplorable conditions. Merely to keep the poor creatures alive under these circumstances, even more chemicals have had to be used, and increasingly, hormones, pesticides, antibiotics, and countless other chemicals and drugs end up in foods derived from animals. The more unnaturally today's livestock are raised, the more chemical residues end up in our food.

But that's just the half of it. The suffering these animals undergo has become so extreme that to partake of food from these creatures is to partake unknowingly of the abject misery that has been their lives. Millions upon millions of Americans are merrily eating away, unaware of the pain and disease they are taking into their bodies with every bite. We are ingesting nightmares for breakfast, lunch, and dinner.

Diet for a New America reveals the effects on your health, on your consciousness, and on the quality of life on earth that comes from eating the products of an obscenely inhumane system of food production. You don't have to forego animal products to derive great benefit from this book. You don't have to be a vegetarian to be concerned about your health, and to want your life to be a statement of compassion. *It's not the killing of the animals that is the chief issue here, but rather the unspeakable quality of the lives they are forced to live.*

The purveyors of the Great American Food Machine don't want you to know how the animals have lived whose flesh, milk and eggs end up in your body. They also don't want you to know the health consequences of consuming the products of such a system, nor do they want you to know its environmental impact. Because they know only too well that if word got out the resultant public outcry would shake the foundations of their industry.

But I want you to know. I'm letting the cat out of the bag. I don't care about their profits. I care about your health, your well-being, and the welfare of our planet and all its creatures.

Eating should be a pleasure. It should be a celebration and a communion with life. The information in this book will provide you access to a whole new sense of pleasure in eating—a pleasure all the deeper for being at no one's expense, a pleasure all the more wonderful for being productive of radiant health.

Exciting things have been learned in the last few decades regarding health and food choices. There have at last been enormous breakthroughs in the science of human nutrition, and for the first time now we are receiving irrefutable scientific evidence of how different eating patterns affect health. We've always known that it was best to eat a "balanced diet," but now we are finding out just what a balanced diet really is, and it's not at all what we had thought. Thousands of impeccably conducted modern research studies now reveal that the traditional assumptions regarding our need for meats, dairy products and eggs have been in error. *In fact it is an excess of these very foods, which had once been thought to be the foundations of good eating habits, that is responsible for the epidemics of heart disease, cancer, osteoporosis, and many other diseases of our time.*

Diet for a New America is the first book to reveal the latest findings of nutritional research in a language anyone can understand, and at the same time document these findings so you can rest assured of their legitimacy. It takes into account the marvelous and undeniable fact that you are a unique person, with your own special tastes, needs, and biochemical individuality. It does not sell you short by presenting rigid rules you have to follow obsessively. On the contrary, the goal is for you to be truly healthy and happy in every dimension of your being, and to be free from any kind of compulsion. *Diet for a New America* contains no dogmatic list of shoulds and shouldn'ts, but instead gives you information that will help you select and enjoy foods that day by day will make you healthier and happier. It shows you how to protect yourself against heart attacks, cancer, osteoporosis, diabetes, strokes, and the other scourges of our time. It shows you how to keep your body free from cholesterol, saturated fat, artificial hormones, antibiotic-resistant bacteria, pesticides, and the countless other disease-producing agents found all too often in many of today's foods. It shows you how you can enjoy eating food that leaves your mind and heart clear and unpolluted.

As Americans we are indeed privileged to have the option of selecting the optimum diet. But for most of the world, the struggle is a far different one; it is survival itself. *Diet for a New America* shows you how your food choices can be of tremendous benefit, not only to your own life, but to the less fortunate of the world as well. No self-deprivation is called for, but simply the understanding that the healthiest, tastiest, and most nourishing way to eat is also the most economical, most compassionate, and least polluting. Heeding this message is without doubt one of the most practical, economical and potent things you can do today to heal, not only your own life, but also the ecosystem on which all life depends. You benefit, the rest of humankind benefits, the animals benefit, and so do the forests and the rivers and the soil and the air and the oceans.

There is enormous suffering today that stems from people feeling isolated and alienated from nature. *Diet for a New America* is a statement of our inter-existence with all forms of life, and provides a means to experience the profound healing powers of our inter-connectedness. You'll learn how to care for your health and to improve the quality of your life. *You'll see that the very eating habits that can do so much to give you strength and health are exactly the same ones that can significantly reduce the needless suffering in the world, and do much to preserve our ecosystem.* And you'll discover the profound liberation that comes from bringing your eating habits into harmony with life's deepest ecological basis. You will become increasingly sensitive, and increasingly able to live and act as an agent of world spiritual awakening.

Few of us are aware that the act of eating can be a powerful statement of commitment to our own well-being, and at the very same time to the creation of a healthier habitat. In *Diet for a New America* you will learn how your spoon and fork can be tools with which to enjoy life to the fullest, while making it possible that life, itself, might continue. In fact, you will discover that your health, happiness, and the future of life on earth are rarely so much in your own hands as when you sit down to eat.

When I declined to be a top cog in the Great American Food Machine, and turned down the opportunity to live the American Dream, it was because I knew there was a deeper dream. I did it because I knew that with all the reasons that each of us has to despair and become cynical, there still beats in our common heart our deepest prayer for a better life and a more loving world. The book you hold in your hands is a key that will enable you to be an instrument of this prayer.

John Robbins
Summer, 1987

Source: Robbins, John. "Introduction." In *Diet for a New America*. Walpole, NH: Stillpoint Publishing, 1987, pp. xiii–xvii.

ANALYSIS

Published in 1987, *Diet for a New America* was one of the works that helped elevate nutrition, healthy eating, organic food, and the morality and impact of individual food consumption choices to a new level of public interest. The author, John Robbins, presented a revolutionary idea: What people choose to eat matters, not just to them but to the entire planet and all the living beings on it. Going beyond the philosophy and legislation that helped build the animal rights movement, Robbins offered to show people what they could do, every day, to improve their lives and the lives of other species. For Robbins, food choices represent a statement about human commitment to compassion and well-being—for all.

Like other authors who support animal rights, Robbins believes human beings have an "obligation to respect and protect the world in which we live." He bases his belief on "a reverence for life," the same phrase used several decades earlier by Albert Schweitzer. However, in the selected passage, Robbins puts a great deal of emphasis on human health, asserting that the poor treatment of farm animals can affect the health of people who eat those animals or their products (such as milk or eggs). His main concern seems to be animal welfare, rather than animal rights. For example, while discussing the "deplorable conditions" endured by animals raised for food, Robbins states the following: "It's not the killing of animals that is the chief issue here, but rather the unspeakable quality of the lives they are forced to live." But despite these words, Robbins is, in fact, a strong advocate for animal rights. His focus on inhumane conditions is intended to lead readers from an interest in their own health to bigger decisions about the ethics of eating factory-farmed animals.

Robbins wrote this passage as an introduction to his first book, so he presents his vision of "a new America" in general terms: It is "a dream of a people living in accord with the laws of Creation." Robbins then supports this idealistic statement by packing subsequent chapters with statistics and scientific data to support the author's views. Still, Robbins stresses that his book "contains no dogmatic list of shoulds and shouldn'ts." He is careful to avoid being judgmental, because he does not believe moral judgments or self-righteousness will help win support for animal rights.

In a 1997 interview, Robbins expressed this inclusive attitude again: "We've really got to clean up our environment, and if someone is motivated to do that because they like to eat fish, and want their fish to be clean, I see that person as an ally, not an enemy in the greater environmental struggle" (*VegSource*, 1997). Robbins's message of acceptance and encouragement for anyone willing to take small steps that will further the animal rights cause has remained consistent into the twenty-first century.

Diet for a New America was a best-selling book, but not all reviewers were impressed with Robbins's message of interconnectedness. In 1992, after Robbins's second book (*May All Be Fed*) was published, a review in the *New York Times* offered this criticism: "Mr. Robbins's message is not always clear. In his books, better nutrition and a cleaner environment flow from animal rights. In person and in videos, Mr. Robbins appears to have reversed the order: if people had healthier diets and cared more about their environment, animals would be treated more humanely" (Burros, 1992). Quoted within this review is another critique of Robbins's approach: "What's being missed is an opportunity to support a strong position for reduced meat consumption from a nutrition and environmental perspective without the other baggage [i.e., animal rights]. By putting all of the issues together [Robbins] makes it harder for a broad group of people to support the issues" (Burros, 1992). Despite these criticisms, Robbins is still considered one of the most influential voices in the animal rights movement, and *Diet for a New America* remains one of the movement's most influential works. A twenty-fifth-anniversary edition of *Diet for a New America* was published in 2012.

FURTHER READING

Burros, Marian. "Eating Well." *New York Times*, December 2, 1992. http://www.nytimes .com/1992/12/02/garden/eating-well.html?pagewanted=all&src=pm.

DeSilver, Drew. "John Robbins: Ice Cream Heir Turns Vegetarian Voice." *Vegetarian Times*, July 1988: 48–49.

Gianni, Kevin. "Can the Whole World Be Vegan with John Robbins: The Renegade Health Show Episode #623." *Renegade Health* (blog). July 29, 2010. http://renegadehealth .com/blog/2010/07/29/can-the-whole-world-be-vegan-with-john-robbins.

Kirschner, Andrew. "An Interview with John Robbins." *Kirschner's Korner* (blog). http:// kirschnerskorner.wordpress.com/2012/08/15/the-scoop-on-john-robbins/.

Robbins, John. *The Food Revolution: How Your Diet Can Help Save Your Life and Our World.* Berkeley, CA: Conari Press, 2001.

Robbins, John. "A Question about the Amish." *Food Revolution Network* (blog). May 24, 2014. http://foodrevolution.org/blog/a-question-about-the-amish/.

Robbins, John. In *Why We Love Dogs, Eat Pigs and Wear Cows: An Introduction to Carnism.* Melanie Joy. San Francisco: Conari Press, 2010.

Robbins, John. "John Robbins on Being a 'Pure' Vegan." VegSource, October 6, 1997. http://www.vegsource.com/articles/robbins_pure.htm.

Robbins, John. *Voices of the Food Revolution: You Can Heal Your Body and Your World with Food!* San Francisco: Conari Press, 2013.

Robbins, John. "Why I Went Vegetarian." *John Robbins.info*, accessed December 11, 2014. http://johnrobbins.info/videos/why-i-went-vegetarian/.

"WHEN AN INJUSTICE IS ABSOLUTE, ONE MUST OPPOSE IT ABSOLUTELY"

- **Document:** *The Philosophy of Animal Rights* by Tom Regan.
- **Date:** 1989.
- **Where:** United States.
- **Significance:** *The Philosophy of Animal Rights* is a seminal text in the animal rights movement. This passage from the work, written by philosopher and animal rights advocate Tom Regan, presents philosophical reasons in favor of the rights of animals and provides detailed rebuttals to common objections raised to animal rights.

DOCUMENT

The other animals humans eat, use in science, hunt, trap, and exploit in a variety of ways, have a life of their own that is of importance to them apart from their utility to us. They are not only in the world, they are aware of it. What happens to them matters to them. Each has a life that fares better or worse for the one whose life it is.

That life includes a variety of biological, individual, and social needs. The satisfaction of these needs is a source of pleasure, their frustration or abuse, a source of pain. In these fundamental ways, the nonhuman animals in labs and on farms, for example, are the same as human beings. And so it is that the ethics of our dealings with them, and with one another, must acknowledge the same fundamental moral principles.

At its deepest level, human ethics is based on the independent value of the individual: The moral worth of any one human being is not to be measured by how useful that person is in advancing the interest of other human beings. To treat human beings in ways that do not honor their independent value is to violate that most basic of human rights: the right of each person to be treated with respect.

The philosophy of animal rights demands only that logic be respected. For any argument that plausibly explains the independent value of human beings implies that other animals have this same value, and have it equally. And any argument that plausibly explains the right of humans to be treated with respect, also implies that these other animals have this same right, and have it equally, too.

It is true, therefore, that women do not exist to serve men, blacks to serve whites, the poor to serve the rich, or the weak to serve the strong. The philosophy of animal rights not only accepts these truths, it insists upon and justifies them.

But this philosophy goes further. By insisting upon and justifying the independent value and rights of other animals, it gives scientifically informed and morally impartial reasons for denying that these animals exist to serve us.

10 Reasons FOR Animal Rights and Their Explanation	10 Reasons AGAINST Animal Rights and Their Replies
1. Rational	1. Equating animals and humans
2. Scientific	2. Rights: human vs. animals
3. Unprejudiced	3. Vegetables vs. animals
4. Just	4. Where to draw the line
5. Compassionate	5. Experience pain
6. Unselfish	6. Animals respecting our rights
7. Individually fulfilling	7. Dominion over other animals
8. Socially progressive	8. Immortal souls
9. Environmentally wise	9. Animal overabundance
10. Peace-loving	10. Other problems

Once this truth is acknowledged, it is easy to understand why the philosophy of animal rights is uncompromising in its response to each and every injustice other animals are made to suffer.

It is not larger, cleaner cages that justice demands in the case of animals used in science, for example, but empty cages: not "traditional" animal agriculture, but a complete end to all commerce in the flesh of dead animals; not "more humane" hunting and trapping, but the total eradication of these barbarous practices.

For when an injustice is absolute, one must oppose it absolutely. It was not "reformed" slavery that justice demanded, not "reformed" child labor, not "reformed" subjugation of women. In each of these cases, abolition was the only moral answer. Merely to reform injustice is to prolong injustice.

The philosophy of animal rights demands this same answer—abolition—in response to the unjust exploitation of other animals. It is not the details of unjust exploitation that must be changed. It is the unjust exploitation itself that must be ended, whether on the farm, in the lab, or among the wild, for example. The philosophy of animal rights asks for nothing more, but neither will it be satisfied with anything less.

10 Reasons FOR Animal Rights and Their Explanation

1. **The philosophy of animal rights is rational.**

   Explanation: It is not rational to discriminate arbitrarily. And discrimination against nonhuman animals is arbitrary. It is wrong to treat weaker human beings, especially those who are lacking in normal human intelligence, as "tools" or "renewable resources" or "models" or "commodities." It cannot be right, therefore, to treat other animals as if they were "tools," "models" and the like, if their psychology is as rich as (or richer than) these humans. To think otherwise is irrational.

   "To describe an animal as a physico-chemical system of extreme complexity is no doubt perfectly correct, except that it misses out on the 'animalness' of the animal."—E. F. Schumacher

2. **The philosophy of animal rights is scientific.**

   Explanation: The philosophy of animal rights is respectful of our best science in general and evolutionary biology in particular. The latter teaches that, in Darwin's words, humans differ from many other animals "in degree," not "in kind."

Questions of line drawing to one side, it is obvious that the animals used in laboratories, raised for food, and hunted for pleasure or trapped for profit, for example, are our psychological kin. This is no fantasy, this is fact, proven by our best science.

"There is no fundamental difference between humans and the higher mammals in their mental faculties."—Charles Darwin

3. **The philosophy of animal rights is unprejudiced.**
   Explanation: Racists are people who think that the members of their race are superior to the members of other races simply because the former belong to their (the "superior") race. Sexists believe that the members of their sex are superior to the members of the opposite sex simply because the former belong to their (the "superior") sex. Both racism and sexism are paradigms of unsupportable bigotry. There is no "superior" or "inferior" sex or race. Racial and sexual differences are biological, not moral, differences.

   The same is true of speciesism—the view that members of the species Homo sapiens are superior to members of every other species simply because human beings belong to one's own (the "superior") species. For there is no "superior" species. To think otherwise is to be no less prejudiced than racists or sexists.

   "If you can justify killing to eat meat, you can justify the conditions of the ghetto. I cannot justify either one."—Dick Gregory

4. **The philosophy of animal rights is just.**
   Explanation: Justice is the highest principle of ethics. We are not to commit or permit injustice so that good may come, not to violate the rights of the few so that the many might benefit. Slavery allowed this. Child labor allowed this. Most examples of social injustice allow this. But not the philosophy of animal rights, whose highest principle is that of justice: No one has a right to benefit as a result of violating another's rights, whether that "other" is a human being or some other animal.

   "The reasons for legal intervention in favor of children apply not less strongly to the case of those unfortunate slaves—the (other) animals."—John Stuart Mill

5. **The philosophy of animal rights is compassionate.**
   Explanation: A full human life demands feelings of empathy and sympathy—in a word, compassion—for the victims of injustice—whether the victims are humans or other animals. The philosophy of animal rights calls for, and its acceptance fosters the growth of, the virtue of compassion. This philosophy is, in Lincoln's words, "the way of a whole human being."

   "Compassion in action may be the glorious possibility that could protect our crowded, polluted planet. . . ."—Victoria Moran

6. **The philosophy of animal rights is unselfish.**

   Explanation: The philosophy of animal rights demands a commitment to serve those who are weak and vulnerable—those who, whether they are humans or other animals, lack the ability to speak for or defend themselves, and who are in need of protection against human greed and callousness. This philosophy requires this commitment, not because it is in our self-interest to give it, but because it is right to do so. This philosophy therefore calls for, and its acceptance fosters the growth of, unselfish service.

   "We need a moral philosophy in which the concept of love, so rarely mentioned now by philosophers, can once again be made central."—Iris Murdoch

7. **The philosophy of animal rights is individually fulfilling.**

   Explanation: All the great traditions in ethics, both secular and religious, emphasize the importance of four things: knowledge, justice, compassion, and autonomy. The philosophy of animal rights is no exception. This philosophy teaches that our choices should be based on knowledge, should be expressive of compassion and justice, and should be freely made. It is not easy to achieve these virtues, or to control the human inclinations toward greed and indifference. But a whole human life is impossible without them. The philosophy of animal rights both calls for, and its acceptance fosters the growth of, individual self-fulfillment.

   "Humaneness is not a dead external precept, but a living impulse from within; not self-sacrifice, but self-fulfillment."—Henry Salt

8. **The philosophy of animal rights is socially progressive.**

   Explanation: The greatest impediment to the flourishing of human society is the exploitation of other animals at human hands. This is true in the case of unhealthy diets, of the habitual reliance on the "whole animal model" in science, and of the many other forms animal exploitation takes. And it is no less true of education and advertising, for example, which help deaden the human psyche to the demands of reason, impartiality, compassion, and justice. In all these ways (and more), nations remain profoundly backward because they fail to serve the true interests of their citizens.

   "The greatness of a nation and its moral progress can be measured by the way its animals are treated."—Mahatma Gandhi

9. **The philosophy of animal rights is environmentally wise.**

   Explanation: The major cause of environmental degradation, including the greenhouse effect, water pollution, and the loss both of arable land and top soil, for example, can be traced to the exploitation of animals. This same pattern exists throughout the broad range of environmental problems, from acid rain and ocean dumping of toxic wastes, to air pollution and the destruction of natural habitat. In all these cases, to act to protect the affected animals (who are, after all, the first to suffer and die from these environmental ills), is to act to protect the earth.

"Until we establish a felt sense of kinship between our own species and those fellow mortals who share with us the sun and shadow of life on this agonized planet, there is no hope for other species, there is no hope for the environment, and there is no hope for ourselves."—Jon Wynne-Tyson

10. **The philosophy of animal rights is peace-loving.**

    Explanation: The fundamental demand of the philosophy of animal rights is to treat humans and other animals with respect. To do this requires that we not harm anyone just so that we ourselves or others might benefit. This philosophy therefore is totally opposed to military aggression. It is a philosophy of peace. But it is a philosophy that extends the demand for peace beyond the boundaries of our species. For there is a war being waged, every day, against countless millions of nonhuman animals. To stand truly for peace is to stand firmly against speciesism. It is wishful thinking to believe that there can be "peace in the world" if we fail to bring peace to our dealings with other animals.

"If by some miracle in all our struggle the earth is spared from nuclear holocaust, only justice to every living thing will save humankind."—Alice Walker

10 Reasons AGAINST Animal Rights and Their Replies.

1. **You are equating animals and humans, when, in fact, humans and animals differ greatly.**

   Reply: We are not saying that humans and other animals are equal in every way. For example, we are not saying that dogs and cats can do calculus, or that pigs and cows enjoy poetry. What we are saying is that, like humans, many other animals are psychological beings, with an experiential welfare of their own. In this sense, we and they are the same. In this sense, therefore, despite our many differences, we and they are equal.

"All the arguments to prove man's superiority cannot shatter this hard fact: in suffering, the animals are our equals."—Peter Singer

2. **You are saying that every human and every other animal has the same rights, which is absurd. Chickens cannot have the right to vote, nor can pigs have a right to higher education.**

   Reply: We are not saying that humans and other animals always have the same rights. Not even all human beings have the same rights. For example, people with serious mental disadvantages do not have a right to higher education. What we are saying is that these and other humans share a basic moral right with other animals—namely, the right to be treated with respect.

"It is the fate of every truth to be an object of ridicule when it is first acclaimed."—Albert Schweitzer

3. **If animals have rights, then so do vegetables, which is absurd.**

   Reply: Many animals are like us: they have a psychological welfare of their own. Like us, therefore, these animals have a right to be treated with respect.

On the other hand, we have no reason, and certainly no scientific one, to believe that carrots and tomatoes, for example, bring a psychological presence to the world. Like all other vegetables, carrots and tomatoes lack anything resembling a brain or central nervous system. Because they are deficient in these respects, there is no reason to think of vegetables as psychological beings, with the capacity to experience pleasure and pain, for example. It is for these reasons that one can rationally affirm rights in the case of animals and deny them in the case of vegetables.

"The case for animal rights depends only on the need for sentiency."—Andrew Linzey

4. **Where do you draw the line? If primates and rodents have rights, then so do slugs and amoebas, which is absurd.**
   Reply: It often is not easy to know exactly where to "draw the line." For example, we cannot say exactly how old someone must be to be old, or how tall someone must be to be tall. However, we can say, with certainty, that someone who is eighty-eight is old, and that another person who is 7'1" is tall. Similarly, we cannot say exactly where to draw the line when it comes to those animals who have a psychology. But we can say with absolute certainty that, wherever one draws the line on scientific grounds, primates and rodents are on one side of it (the psychological side), whereas slugs and amoebas are on the other—which does not mean that we may destroy them unthinkingly.

"In the relations of humans with the animals, with the flowers, with all the objects of creation, there is a whole great ethic scarcely seen as yet."—Victor Hugo

5. **But surely there are some animals who can experience pain but lack a unified psychological identity. Since these animals do not have a right to be treated with respect, the philosophy of animal rights implies that we can treat them in any way we choose.**
   Reply: It is true that some animals, like shrimp and clams, may be capable of experiencing pain yet lack most other psychological capacities. If this is true, then they will lack some of the rights that other animals possess. However, there can be no moral justification for causing anyone pain, if it is unnecessary to do so. And since it is not necessary that humans eat shrimp, clams, and similar animals, or utilize them in other ways, there can be no moral justification for causing them the pain that invariably accompanies such use.

"The question is not, 'Can they reason?' nor 'Can they talk?' but 'Can they suffer?' "—Jeremy Bentham

6. **Animals don't respect our rights. Therefore, humans have no obligation to respect their rights either.**
   Reply: There are many situations in which an individual who has rights is unable to respect the rights of others. This is true of infants, young children,

and mentally enfeebled and deranged human beings. In their case we do not say that it is perfectly all right to treat them disrespectfully because they do not honor our rights. On the contrary, we recognize that we have a duty to treat them with respect, even though they have no duty to treat us in the same way.

What is true of cases involving infants, children, and the other humans mentioned, is no less true of cases involving other animals, Granted, these animals do not have a duty to respect our rights. But this does not erase or diminish our obligation to respect theirs.

"The time will come when people such as I will look upon the murder of (other) animals as they now look upon the murder of human beings."—Leonardo Da Vinci

7. **God gave humans dominion over other animals. This is why we can do anything to them that we wish, including eat them.**
   Reply: Not all religions represent humans as having "dominion" over other animals, and even among those that do, the notion of "dominion" should be understood as unselfish guardianship, not selfish power. Humans are to be as loving toward all of creation as God was in creating it. If we loved the animals today in the way humans loved them in the Garden of Eden, we would not eat them. Those who respect the rights of animals are embarked on a journey back to Eden—a journey back to a proper love for God's creation.

   "And God said, Behold, I have given you every herb bearing seed, which is upon the face of all the earth, and every tree, in which is the fruit of a tree yielding seed; to you it shall be for meat."—Genesis 1:29

8. **Only humans have immortal souls. This gives us the right to treat the other animals as we wish.**
   Reply: Many religions teach that all animals, not just humans, have immortal souls. However, even if only humans are immortal, this would only prove that we live forever whereas other animals do not. And this fact (if it is a fact) would increase, not decrease, our obligation to insure that this—the only life other animals have—be as long and as good as possible.

   "There is no religion without love, and people may talk as much as they like about their religion, but if it does not teach them to be good and kind to other animals as well as humans, it is all a sham."—Anna Sewell

9. **If we respect the rights of animals, and do not eat or exploit them in other ways, then what are we supposed to do with all of them? In a very short time they will be running through our streets and homes.**
   Reply: Somewhere between 4–5 billion animals are raised and slaughtered for food every year, just in the United States. The reason for this astonishingly high number is simple: there are consumers who eat very large amounts of animal flesh. The supply of animals meets the demand of buyers.

When the philosophy of animal rights triumphs, however, and people become vegetarians, we need not fear that there will be billions of cows and pigs grazing in the middle of our cities or in our living rooms. Once the financial incentive for raising billions of these animals evaporates, there simply will not be millions of these animals. And the same reasoning applies in other cases—in the case of animals bred for research, for example. When the philosophy of animal rights prevails, and this use of these animals cease[s], then the financial incentive for breeding millions of them will cease, too.

"The worst sin toward our fellow creatures is not to hate them, but to be indifferent to them. That is the essence of inhumanity."—George Bernard Shaw

10. **Even if other animals do have moral rights and should be protected, there are more important things that need our attention—world hunger and child abuse, for example, apartheid, drugs, violence to women, and the plight of the homeless. After we take care of these problems, then we can worry about animals' rights.**

    Reply: The animal rights movement stands as part of, not apart from, the human rights movement. The same philosophy that insists upon and defends the rights of nonhuman animals also insists upon and defends the rights of human beings.

    At a practical level, moreover, the choice thoughtful people face is not between helping humans or helping other animals. One can do both. People do not need to eat animals in order to help the homeless, for example, any more than they need to use cosmetics that have been tested on animals in order to help children. In fact, people who do respect the rights of nonhuman animals, by not eating them, will be healthier, in which case they actually will be able to help human beings even more.

    "I am in favor of animal rights as well as human rights. That is the way of a whole human being."—Abraham Lincoln

Source: Regan, Tom. "The Philosophy of Animal Rights." Culture and Animals Foundation, 1989. http://www.cultureandanimals.org/pop1.html. Used by permission of Tom Regan.

ANALYSIS

In the selected passage, philosopher and animal rights activist Tom Regan lays out the fundamental reasons why the philosophy of animal rights deserves support from human beings. He also provides a point-by-point defense against common objections to the animal rights cause. Published after Regan's *The Case for Animal Rights*, an almost 500-page book, "The Philosophy of Animal Rights" offers a brief overview of animal rights philosophy. According to supporters, Regan's essay utilizes rational arguments to demonstrate that the concept of animal rights is not an extreme idea, but rather, a logical part of the same thinking that supports human rights and social progress.

The structure of this passage—featuring 10 points "for" animal rights and 10 points "against"—is clear and practical, designed to reach and persuade a broad audience. The way Regan presented his ideas helped the animal rights movement gain many supporters. It also helped supporters explain and defend their position to those who questioned animal rights philosophy. Regan hoped that by clearly and rationally expressing his ideas, he could help people understand why animal rights advocates are uncompromising in their beliefs. As he explains in his introduction to the 10-point lists, "When an injustice is absolute, one must oppose it absolutely."

Regan's first 10-point list illustrates that animal rights philosophy is based on principles and ideals that all moral human beings support, such as justice, compassion, and unselfishness. In Regan's view, animals have moral worth and therefore moral rights. By "moral worth," he means that animals have an inherent value that has nothing to do with their usefulness (or lack of usefulness) to human beings. By "moral rights," Regan means certain basic, universal rights, such as the right not to be enslaved, or more broadly, the right to be treated with respect. In this sense, human beings and nonhuman animals are the same, and therefore both groups deserve respect and equally moral treatment.

As he builds his case, Regan aligns the animal rights cause with accepted progressive causes that were once controversial, such as the women's movement for gender equality and the civil rights movement. However, he does this indirectly. For example, he states that "women do not exist to serve men, blacks to serve whites, the poor to serve the rich, or the weak to serve the strong." Regan is highlighting social beliefs that evolved—beliefs that *needed* to evolve so that women, minorities, and other disadvantaged people could receive their due rights and respect.

Throughout the selected passage, Regan continues to link animal rights and human rights, trying to help his readers understand the logic and moral principles of animal rights philosophy. For example, in point 3 in favor of animal rights ("The philosophy of animal rights is unprejudiced"), Regan shows that "speciesism"—a person's belief that human beings are superior to other species—is a prejudice, like racism or sexism. And in point 10 supporting animal rights, Regan implicitly connects animal rights with another once-controversial cause, the peace (or anti-war) movement that began in the United States in the 1960s. This is in direct contrast to those who espouse more destructive methods of releasing animals, such as the group known as the Animal Liberation Front. The ALF has forthrightly stated that it views criminal activity—especially destruction of property belonging to businesses and other enterprises that exploit, harm, and kill animals—as a legitimate and necessary tool in reducing animal suffering.

Regan's references to human rights issues reflect the historical context of this passage, which was published about a decade after the women's movement and about two decades after the civil rights movement and the peace movement in the United States. In 1992, in an article in the *Animals' Agenda*, Regan and co-author Gary

Francione made a more explicit statement about the animal rights–human rights connection: "The philosophy of animal rights views the systematic exploitation of animals as a symptom of a society that tolerates the systematic exploitation of 'the other,' including those human 'others' who lack the economic and other means to resist oppression. Thus, the philosophy of animals rights necessarily calls for human, not only animal, liberation."

Like Regan's "The Case for Animal Rights," "The Philosophy of Animal Rights" focuses on the ideas behind animal rights philosophy, not details such as legislative actions undertaken on behalf of nonhuman animals. As Regan stated in "The Case for Animal Rights," "All that philosophy can do, and all I have attempted, is to offer a vision of what our deeds should aim at. And the why. But not the how." Regan's goal is to help change commonly held beliefs that conflict with moral principles, with the hope that changing people's beliefs will lead to changes in their behavior toward nonhuman animals.

FURTHER READING

Cohen, Carl, and Tom Regan. *The Animal Rights Debate*. Lanham, MD: Rowman & Littlefield, 2001.

Hile, Kevin. *Animal Rights (Point/Counterpoint)*. Philadelphia: Chelsea House, 2004.

"Professor Tom Regan Interview." ARZone: A Record of Rational Discourse, May 21, 2011. http://arzonetranscripts.wordpress.com/2011/05/20/professor-tom-regan-interview/.

Regan, Tom. *Animal Rights, Human Wrongs: An Introduction to Moral Philosophy*. Lanham, MD: Rowman & Littlefield, 2003.

Regan, Tom. "The Case for Animal Rights," in *In Defense of Animals*. Edited by Peter Singer. New York: Basil Blackwell, 1985, pp. 13–26.

Regan, Tom. *Empty Cages: Facing the Challenge of Animal Rights*. Lanham, MD: Rowman & Littlefield, 2003.

Regan, Tom, Gary Francione, and Ingrid Newkirk. "Point/Counterpoint—Point: A Movement's Means Create Its Ends / Counterpoint: Total Victory, Like Checkmate, Cannot Be Achieved in One Move." *The Animals' Agenda*, January/February 1992, pp. 40–43. http://arzonetranscripts.files.wordpress.com/2011/06/point_counterpoint-regan_francione_newkirk.pdf.

Singer, Peter. *Animal Liberation: The Definitive Classic of the Animal Movement*. Updated edition. New York: HarperCollins, 2009.

"Tom Regan on Rights." *Animal Ethics* (blog), July 14, 2012. http://animalethics.blogspot.com/2012/07/tom-regan-on-rights_14.html.

Williams, Erin E., and Margo DeMello. *Why Animals Matter: The Case for Animal Protection*. Amherst, NY: Prometheus Books, 2007.

"DOLPHINS . . . ARE FREQUENTLY KILLED IN THE COURSE OF TUNA FISHING OPERATIONS"

- **Document:** The Dolphin Protection Consumer Information Act of 1990.
- **Date:** November 28, 1990.
- **Where:** Washington, D.C.
- **Significance:** This law established standards for labeling canned tuna and ensuring that methods used to catch tuna did not harm dolphins.

DOCUMENT

(a) **Short title**

This section may be cited as the "Dolphin Protection Consumer Information Act."

(b) **Findings**

The Congress finds that—

(1) dolphins and other marine mammals are frequently killed in the course of tuna fishing operations in the eastern tropical Pacific Ocean and high seas driftnet fishing in other parts of the world;

(2) it is the policy of the United States to support a worldwide ban on high seas driftnet fishing, in part because of the harmful effects that such driftnets have on marine mammals, including dolphins; and

(3) consumers would like to know if the tuna they purchase is falsely labeled as to the effect of the harvesting of the tuna on dolphins.

(c) **Definitions**

For purposes of this section—

(1) the terms "driftnet" and "driftnet fishing" have the meanings given those terms in section 4003 of the Driftnet Impact Monitoring, Assessment, and Control Act of 1987 (16 U.S.C. 1822 note);

(2) the term "eastern tropical Pacific Ocean" means the area of the Pacific Ocean bounded by 40 degrees north latitude, 40 degrees south latitude, 160 degrees west longitude, and the western coastlines of North, Central, and South America;

(3) the term "label" means a display of written, printed, or graphic matter on or affixed to the immediate container of any article;

(4) the term "Secretary" means the Secretary of Commerce; and

(5) the term "tuna product" means a food item which contains tuna and which has been processed for retail sale, except perishable sandwiches, salads, or other products with a shelf life of less than 3 days.

(d) **Labeling standard**

(1) It is a violation of section 45 of title 15 for any producer, importer, exporter, distributor, or seller of any tuna product that is exported from or offered for sale in the United States to include on the label of that product the term "dolphin safe" or any other term or symbol that falsely claims or suggests that the tuna contained in the product were harvested using a method of fishing that is not harmful to dolphins if the product contains tuna harvested—

(A) on the high seas by a vessel engaged in driftnet fishing;

(B) outside the eastern tropical Pacific Ocean by a vessel using purse seine nets—

(i) in a fishery in which the Secretary has determined that a regular and significant association occurs between dolphins and tuna (similar to the association between dolphins and tuna in the eastern tropical Pacific Ocean), unless such product is accompanied by a written statement, executed by the captain of the vessel and an observer participating in a national or international program acceptable to the Secretary, certifying that no purse seine net was intentionally deployed on or used to encircle dolphins during the particular voyage on which the tuna were caught and no dolphins were killed or seriously injured in the sets in which the tuna were caught; or

(ii) in any other fishery (other than a fishery described in subparagraph (D)) unless the product is accompanied by a written statement executed by the captain of the vessel certifying that no purse seine net was intentionally deployed on or used to encircle dolphins during the particular voyage on which the tuna was harvested;

(C) in the eastern tropical Pacific Ocean by a vessel using a purse seine net unless the tuna meet the requirements for being considered dolphin safe under paragraph (2); or

(D) by a vessel in a fishery other than one described in subparagraph (A), (B), or (C) that is identified by the Secretary as having a regular and significant mortality or serious injury of dolphins, unless such product is accompanied by a written statement executed by the captain of the vessel and an observer participating in a national or international program acceptable to the Secretary that no dolphins were killed or seriously injured in the sets or other gear deployments in which the tuna were caught, provided that the Secretary determines that such an observer statement is necessary.

(2) For purposes of paragraph (1)(C), a tuna product that contains tuna harvested in the eastern tropical Pacific Ocean by a vessel using purse seine nets is dolphin safe if—

(A) the vessel is of a type and size that the Secretary has determined, consistent with the International Dolphin Conservation Program, is not capable of deploying its purse seine nets on or to encircle dolphins; or

(B)

(i) the product is accompanied by a written statement executed by the captain providing the certification required under subsection (h) of this section;

(ii) the product is accompanied by a written statement executed by—

(I) the Secretary or the Secretary's designee;

(II) a representative of the Inter-American Tropical Tuna Commission; or

(III) an authorized representative of a participating nation whose national program meets the requirements of the International Dolphin Conservation Program, which states that there was an observer approved by the International Dolphin Conservation Program on board the vessel during the entire trip and that such observer provided the certification required under subsection (h) of this section; and

(iii) the statements referred to in clauses (i) and (ii) are endorsed in writing by each exporter, importer, and processor of the product; and

(C) the written statements and endorsements referred to in subparagraph (B) comply with regulations promulgated by the Secretary which provide for the verification of tuna products as dolphin safe.

(3)

(A) The Secretary of Commerce shall develop an official mark that may be used to label tuna products as dolphin safe in accordance with this Act.

(B) A tuna product that bears the dolphin safe mark developed under subparagraph (A) shall not bear any other label or mark that refers to dolphins, porpoises, or marine mammals.

(C) It is a violation of section 45 of title 15 to label a tuna product with any label or mark that refers to dolphins, porpoises, or marine mammals other than the mark developed under subparagraph (A) unless—

(i) no dolphins were killed or seriously injured in the sets or other gear deployments in which the tuna were caught;

(ii) the label is supported by a tracking and verification program which is comparable in effectiveness to the program established under subsection (f) of this section; and

(iii) the label complies with all applicable labeling, marketing, and advertising laws and regulations of the Federal Trade Commission, including any guidelines for environmental labeling.

(D) If the Secretary determines that the use of a label referred to in subparagraph (C) is substantially undermining the conservation goals of the International Dolphin Conservation Program, the Secretary shall report that determination to the United States Senate Committee on Commerce, Science, and Transportation and the United States House of Representatives Committees on Resources and on Commerce, along with recommendations to correct such problems.

(E) It is a violation of section 45 of title 15 willingly and knowingly to use a label referred to in subparagraph (C) in a campaign or effort to mislead or deceive consumers about the level of protection afforded dolphins under the International Dolphin Conservation Program.

(e) **Enforcement**

Any person who knowingly and willfully makes a statement or endorsement described in subsection (d)(2)(B) of this section that is false is liable for a civil penalty of not to exceed $100,000 assessed in an action brought in any appropriate district court of the United States on behalf of the Secretary.

(f) **Regulations**

The Secretary, in consultation with the Secretary of the Treasury, shall issue regulations to implement this Act, including regulations to establish a domestic tracking and verification program that provides for the effective tracking of tuna labeled under subsection (d) of this section. In the development of these regulations, the Secretary shall establish appropriate procedures for ensuring the confidentiality of proprietary information the submission of which is voluntary or mandatory. The regulations shall address each of the following items:

(1) The use of weight calculation for purposes of tracking tuna caught, landed, processed, and exported.

(2) Additional measures to enhance current observer coverage, including the establishment of criteria for training, and for improving monitoring and reporting capabilities and procedures.

(3) The designation of well location, procedures for sealing holds, procedures for monitoring and certifying both above and below deck, or through equally effective methods, the tracking and verification of tuna labeled under subsection (d) of this section.

(4) The reporting, receipt, and database storage of radio and facsimile transmittals from fishing vessels containing information related to the tracking and verification of tuna, and the definition of set.

(5) The shore-based verification and tracking throughout the fishing, transshipment, and canning process by means of Inter-American Tropical Tuna Commission trip records or otherwise.

(6) The use of periodic audits and spot checks for caught, landed, and processed tuna products labeled in accordance with subsection (d) of this section.

(7) The provision of timely access to data required under this subsection by the Secretary from harvesting nations to undertake the actions required in paragraph (6) of this paragraph.

The Secretary may make such adjustments as may be appropriate to the regulations promulgated under this subsection to implement an international tracking and verification program that meets or exceeds the minimum requirements established by the Secretary under this subsection.

(g) **Secretarial findings**

(1) Between March 1, 1999, and March 31, 1999, the Secretary shall, on the basis of the research conducted before March 1, 1999, under section 1414a (a) of this title, information obtained under the International Dolphin Conservation Program, and any other relevant information, make an initial finding regarding whether the intentional deployment on or encirclement of dolphins with purse seine nets is having a significant adverse impact on any depleted dolphin stock in the eastern tropical Pacific Ocean. The initial finding shall be published immediately in the Federal Register and shall become effective upon a subsequent date determined by the Secretary.

(2) Between July 1, 2001, and December 31, 2002, the Secretary shall, on the basis of the completed study conducted under section 1414a (a) of this title, information obtained under the International Dolphin Conservation Program, and any other relevant information, make a finding regarding whether the intentional deployment on or encirclement of dolphins with purse seine nets is having a significant adverse impact on any depleted dolphin stock in the eastern tropical Pacific Ocean. The finding shall be published immediately in the Federal Register and shall become effective upon a subsequent date determined by the Secretary.

(h) **Certification by captain and observer**

(1) Unless otherwise required by paragraph (2), the certification by the captain under subsection (d)(2)(B)(i) of this section and the certification provided by the

observer as specified in subsection (d)(2)(B)(ii) of this section shall be that no dolphins were killed or seriously injured during the sets in which the tuna were caught.

(2) The certification by the captain under subsection (d)(2)(B)(i) of this section and the certification provided by the observer as specified under subsection (d)(2)(B)(ii) of this section shall be that no tuna were caught on the trip in which such tuna were harvested using a purse seine net intentionally deployed on or to encircle dolphins, and that no dolphins were killed or seriously injured during the sets in which the tuna were caught, if the tuna were caught on a trip commencing—

(A) before the effective date of the initial finding by the Secretary under subsection (g)(1) of this section;

(B) after the effective date of such initial finding and before the effective date of the finding of the Secretary under subsection (g)(2) of this section, where the initial finding is that the intentional deployment on or encirclement of dolphins is having a significant adverse impact on any depleted dolphin stock; or

(C) after the effective date of the finding under subsection (g)(2) of this section, where such finding is that the intentional deployment on or encirclement of dolphins is having a significant adverse impact on any such depleted stock.

Source: Public Law 101-627, November 28, 1990 (104 Stat. 4465).

ANALYSIS

The tuna industry has enjoyed huge success for more than 100 years. In 1903, Albert Halfhil, a canner in Southern California, discovered that tuna, once considered a "nuisance" fish caught during sardine hauls, "tasted delicious when steam cooked." He canned the albacore tuna and sold 700 cases his first year. Over the course of the next 50 years, his idea evolved into a booming industry led by the United States, which emerged as the world's largest producer of canned tuna.

Tuna became so popular, however, that as early as the 1940s, anxieties were being expressed about overfishing. In response to these concerns, the United States and Costa Rica signed the Convention for the Establishment of an Inter-American Tropical Tuna Commission (IATTC). One of the main duties of the commission is to investigate the status of not only yellowfin and skipjack tuna but also the "other kinds of fish taken by tuna fishing vessels." The commission established a monitoring area known as the Eastern Tropical Pacific (ETP), an eight-million-square-mile region of the Pacific that reaches from northern California down to the southern end of Chile and out to Hawaii. This region produces nearly 30 percent of the world's yellowfin tuna and is home to approximately 10 million dolphins.

In 1959 the U.S. tuna fishing industry began using purse seine nets to catch schools of fish. The purse seine is so named because it has a cable threaded through the bottom that closes like a huge drawstring purse as the net is pulled onto the boat. It was well known that yellowfin tuna often swim beneath pods of dolphins. Therefore, the boats would encircle pods of dolphins with the nets, knowing that they would be able to catch the tuna swimming below. Another method was to set out drift nets, fine nets that can stretch for as far as 60 kilometers and that catch everything in their path. Unfortunately, these practices took a heavy toll on dolphin populations—as many as six million by some estimates—over the next 35 years.

In the late 1980s a video made the rounds of the news, showing dolphins thrashing in the nets of a tuna boat. The resulting public outcry quickly led three major canneries to announce in April 1990 that they would no longer buy tuna caught by encircling dolphins with seine purses. On November 28 of that same year, the U.S. Congress enacted the Dolphin Protection Consumer Information Act (DPCIA), authored by U.S. representative Barbara Boxer (D-CA). This act is part of the Marine Mammal Protection Act of 1972, which prohibits the hunting, killing, capturing, or harassing of marine mammals. The United States had also been a supporter of a worldwide ban on driftnet fishing.

The main purpose of the DPCIA was to mandate a labeling standard and seal to notify consumers that the tuna being sold was caught in a manner that was "safe" for dolphins and to establish a system of monitoring tuna fishing operations. "Dolphin safe" tuna means that the fish were not caught by a vessel using driftnet fishing or purse seine nets in the ETP and that no dolphins were killed or seriously injured during the capture of the tuna being sold. Fines of up to $100,000 were established for falsely claiming that a product was dolphin safe. To enforce the law, provisions were included mandating that each vessel of a certain capacity (400 short tons) have an IATTC-approved observer onboard on every fishing trip in the ETP.

The law, in conjunction with the IATTC, has made the ETP one of the most monitored fishing regions in the world. The data collected by IATTC observers and others has evolved into one of the most comprehensive databases on marine life. The IATTC reported that in 1993, just three years after the act was signed, the international fleet in the ETP had released more than 99 percent of captured dolphins without harm (although about 3500 dolphins were still killed that year from tuna harvesting operations). However, the new fishing practices established in response to the law were capturing smaller, sexually immature tuna that had not yet reproduced. Scientists have cautioned that this could lead to significant declines in wild yellowfish tuna populations. In addition, although canned tuna is labeled "dolphin safe," this does not mean other species, including sharks, sea turtles, rays, and other fish, are not killed or harmed in the nets. Thus, even as the mortality rate for dolphins plummeted, new concerns were raised about the depletion of other marine animals as a result of tuna fishing. This has led to a contentious debate among the fishing industry, various nation members of the IATTC (most notably Mexico and the United States), and even different environmental groups about how to regulate the industry in such a way as to preserve species and still maintain the financial viability of the industry.

FURTHER READING

"Boxer Calls on U.S. Trade Representative to 'Vigorously Defend' U.S. Dolphin-Safe Tuna Label." U.S. Senator Barbara Boxer, July 6, 2011. https://www.boxer.senate.gov/en/press/releases/070611b.cfm.

Carpenter, Betsy. "What Price Dolphin?" *U.S. News & World Report*, June 13, 1994.

"Digest of Federal Resource Laws of Interest to the U.S. Fish and Wildlife Service: Dolphin Protection Consumer Information Act." U.S. Fish & Wildlife Service, Congressional and Legislative Affairs, accessed December 12, 2014. http://www.fws.gov/laws/lawsdigest/dolphin.html.

"Dolphin Safe." Greener Choices: Consumers Reports, accessed December 12, 2014. http://www.greenerchoices.org/eco-labels/label.cfm?LabelID=98.

Gastman, Alexander. "Dolphin Protection Consumer Information Act, United States." Encyclopedia of Earth, accessed December 12, 2014. http://www.eoearth.org/view/article/151770/.

"IATTC—International Dolphin Conservation Program (IDCP)." Inter-American Tropical Tuna Commission, accessed December 12, 2014. http://www.iattc.org/IDCPENG.htm.

"Marine Mammal Protection Act (MMPA)." NOAA Fisheries, accessed December 12, 2014. http://www.nmfs.noaa.gov/pr/laws/mmpa/.

Miyake, Makoto, Patrice Guillotreau, Chin-Hwa Sun, and Gaku Ishimura. "Recent developments in the tuna industry: stocks, fisheries, management, processing, trade and markets." FAO Fisheries and Aquaculture Technical Paper. No. 543. Rome, FAO, 2010.

O'Barry, Richard. *Beyond the Dolphin Smile*. Chapel Hill, NC: Algonquin Books of Chapel Hill, 1988.

Ogilvie, David. "So What's Wrong with Fish?" MESA: Marine Education Society of Australasia, accessed December 12, 2014. http://www.mesa.edu.au/seaweek2010/fishing02.asp.

Platt, Teresa. "A Tuna Tale: Managing a Fishery to Increase Positives, Reduce Negatives." *Trumpet Call*, April 1996. http://www.maninnature.com/Fisheries/tuna1b.html.

Scott, Michael. "The Tuna-Dolphin Controversy." *Whalewatcher* 30, no. 1 (August 1998): 16–30.

"Wild-Caught Seafood—Tuna: Overview." World Wildlife Fund, accessed December 12, 2014. http://www.worldwildlife.org/industries/tuna.

"PLACE ... THE PROTECTION OF ... HUMAN RIGHTS SOMEWHAT ABOVE OR AT LEAST ON AN EQUAL FOOTING WITH WOLVES, BEARS, [AND] SALMON"

- **Document:** Statement of Robert Sears, Idaho Cattle Association, a livestock industry group opposed to wolf recovery efforts in Idaho, Montana, and Wyoming, at *Introducing Gray Wolves in Yellowstone and Idaho*, a hearing before the House Committee on Resources.
- **Date:** January 26, 1995.
- **Where:** Washington, D.C.
- **Significance:** In the early 1990s, Interior Department officials in the Clinton administration approved a plan to reintroduce gray wolves into the Rocky Mountains, where they had been extirpated decades earlier by farmers and livestock owners who viewed them as a vicious predator that threatened their livelihoods. Specifically, the wolf recovery scheme spearheaded by the U.S. Fish and Wildlife Service (USFS) proposed to release captured gray wolves from Canada into Yellowstone National Park and the remote valleys of central Idaho's Frank Church–River of No Return Wilderness. The legal authority for this initiative came from the ESA. The USFS plan, however, triggered angry rebukes from rural landowners in the regions surrounding these public lands, as well as from their elected representatives in Washington, D.C., and the state capitols of Wyoming and Idaho. Conservative Republicans opposed to the reintroduction plan quickly convened congressional hearings in Washington in an effort to scuttle the reintroduction. One of the private citizens who spoke out against the wolf recovery effort was Robert Sears, representing the Idaho Cattle Association.

DOCUMENT

I appreciate the opportunity to appear here. I represent not only the Idaho Cattle Association but the Idaho Wool Growers Association as I testify before this Committee today.

It is apparent to anyone who lives in the more remote areas of our western States that cattle and sheepmen have a distinct fear of having wolves, bears, and other predators in direct proximity to their livestock. This has been the case since the dawn of recorded history. One needs but to recall the biblical records of the lives of Cain, David, and the Good Shepherd, and others as examples of the constant vigil these individuals keep over their livestock and of the need to slay the predators that threaten the herds and the flocks. By the way, our 3,000,000 animal herd of sheep of a few years back has now dwindled to 225,000 partly because of Government action, partly because of imported lamb, and partly because of coyotes, and we certainly don't need wolves to add to the reduction of those numbers.

With this in mind, I assure you that the herdsmen and shepherds of today are no less concerned than their counterparts throughout recorded history with the thought of having these vicious predators nearby while the cattle and sheep they depend upon for their livelihood graze on the meadows and hillsides.

Today's herdsmen and shepherds trying to survive in the modern world on lands that were passed down to them for several generations by ancestors who, through the years of effort, succeeded in eliminating what was recognized as a significant threat to their livelihood, that being the wolves and the bears, are now faced with the prospect of having those same predators reintroduced to the land by that referred-to menace, the wolf in sheep's clothing. This menace, of course, was represented by the Federal Fish and Wildlife Service under the direction of the Secretary of the Interior . . . [who are] justifiably suspect by those I represent.

Nevertheless, some cattle and sheep owners in Idaho, against their better judgment, perplexed and bewildered by the burning desire of preservationists and conservationist groups from the east to return these animals to their backyards, agreed to serve on the congressionally-appointed Wolf Management Committee to develop a plan whereby a nonessential experimental population of wolves could be reintroduced into the Frank Church Wilderness Area of central Idaho.

This committee produced such a plan and presented it, I believe, to this Committee, where it was pigeonholed because of opposition of some of the environmental groups and never acted upon. Subsequently the Fish and Wildlife Service prepared an environmental impact statement on which numerous comments were submitted by our members and others presenting the essentials of the original management plan that included the right to protect their livestock and not only their livestock but their guard dogs and their herd dogs and those animals with which they are closely associated, many of them more importantly than the loss of a cow or a sheep and their pets from being attacked by these vicious predators, making the agency responsible for their actions, namely the reintroduction and for the subsequent financial losses incurred by the owners of those domestic animals. Most of these reasonable safeguards were ignored in the final wolf recovery environmental impact statement, making it impossible for reasonable and prudent livestock producers to support the process. One avenue for obtaining this protection did, however, still exist, the opportunity to participate in developing a State wolf management plan that could be adopted by the State by the Fish and Wildlife Service, allowing the Idaho Department of Fish and Game to provide the management of the reintroduced, nonessential, experimental population of wolves.

Once again, livestock producer representatives worked with others to develop a plan that provided for a growing population of wolves in central Idaho and reasonable assurance of the right to protect one's domestic animals and provide for just compensation for actual animal losses. These essential elements of the plan were rejected by the U.S. Fish and Wildlife Service along with one other very critical element of the plan, which is the statutory right of the Idaho State Legislature to

A gray wolf, one of a once abundant species that is now endangered, howls in the woods. In the early 1990s, two sides battled over U.S. Interior Department plans to reintroduce gray wolves into a wide area from Canada down into Yellowstone National Park. Proponents favored this as a way of boosting the gray wolf population; opponents—many of whom were farmers and livestock owners—viewed the wolves as vicious predators who could threaten other animals. The program was carried out, but opposition continued into the twenty-first century. (Corel).

maintain control over the actions of the Idaho Fish and Game Department in managing these wolves.

We have been assured by the U.S. Fish and Wildlife Service that the wolves will be retained under the nonessential experimental status. However, as I speak, the Sierra Club and others have lawsuits in Federal courts calling for elimination of this status. The U.S. Fish and Wildlife Service then assures us that should this happen they will remove the wolves from the area. However, since one wolf was killed by the dart process and the gathering process, it is entirely probable that a subsequent lawsuit by animal rights groups would keep U.S. Fish and Wildlife Service from keeping this promise.

The bottom line is that every elected official in the State of Idaho Capitol Building, 75 percent of the members of our Idaho legislature, and the entire Idaho congressional delegation requested that Interior Secretary Babbitt halt his plans to transport wolves into central Idaho until such time as the . . . legitimate concerns of our citizens could be properly dealt with in a workable wolf management plan. I do not know if the letters requesting this action reached the Secretary before he left Washington for Yellowstone Park where he personally participated in the first release of wolves in that location. I would like to give him the benefit of the doubt in regard to those first four wolves that came into central Idaho. Perhaps he was unaware of the concerns of our citizens and our legislature. However, I cannot extend the same doubt to the apparent disregard for those express concerns in subsequent releases of 11 more wolves several days later.

This is not the first time the Secretary has shown his apparent lack of concern for the wishes of our State's elected officials. He has been a party to a number of such actions in the past two years, including total disregard of the wishes of our recently retired governor and former Secretary of Interior Cecil Andrus relative to a new Air Force training range also supported by ranchers who graze livestock in the area.

We would ask Congress to intercede in this matter and prohibit the Secretary and U.S. Fish and Wildlife Service from any further reintroduction of wolves in the State of Idaho and to further instruct him to negotiate in good faith with the State of Idaho in the development of a realistic, workable management plan or, as an alternative, get the wolves out of our backyard. Not to do so is tantamount to inviting international terrorist groups to bring small detachments of trainees into the area, allowing them to practice their activities on the unsuspecting local communities and then prohibiting the locals from protecting themselves from these killers. Such actions are unconscionable.

We would further request that Congress take timely action to proceed on reauthorization of the Endangered Species Act, therein providing some much needed safeguards that recognize the right of human beings to exist in the presence of other species in this land and place reasonable priorities for the protection of their human rights somewhat above or at least on an equal footing with wolves, bears, salmon, and the now infamous Bruneau Hotspring Snail, also an Idaho resident.

The taxpayer burden on this reintroduction has, we believe, been seriously underestimated. The net economic value to the central Idaho area reported in the EIS at $8.4 million is ludicrous. Mr. Bangs, the U.S. Fish and Wildlife Service project chairman for the EIS, has with a straight face told me that this estimate is based largely upon anticipated tourist expenditures from those drawn to the area in anticipation of seeing a wolf. Can you honestly believe that tourists are going to buy $8.4 million worth of T-shirts, sculptures, and photo prints of wolves in central Idaho? This is one of the most ridiculous examples of bureaucratic hoodwinking I have ever heard.

Please consider the private property rights of Idahoans and the rights of Idaho State Government in managing the affairs within its border. Halt this activity until proper safeguards can be worked out and put into place, or halt it permanently.

I thank you for your consideration.

Source: Statement of Robert Sears, Idaho Cattle Association, in *Introducing Gray Wolves in Yellowstone and Idaho: Oversight Hearing Before the Committee on Resources, House of Representatives,* 104th Congress, 1st session, on federal efforts to introduce Canadian gray wolves into Yellowstone National Park and the central Idaho wilderness, January 26, 1995. Washington, DC: Government Printing Office, 1995, pp. 58–60.

ANALYSIS

Sears's testimony touched on many of the pillars of opposition to the wolf recovery plan. It raised the specter of economically devastating livestock losses, excoriated federal authorities for running roughshod over the clearly stated desire of Idaho residents to remain "wolf-free," and asserted that the Endangered Species Act was being applied in ways that put the "rights" of animals on an even plane with those of humans—or even above those of humans.

Despite implacable opposition from Republicans, industry groups, and private landowners—opposition that frequently took the form of legal challenges to the recovery plan—the wolf reintroduction campaign ultimately went forward. In 2011 the USFS reported that wolf reintroduction efforts in Idaho, Montana, and Wyoming had all been successful, producing about 1,650 wolves and nearly

250 packs across the three states. Anger about the presence of these wolves is still palpable among some residents of these states, but several major policy changes that have been implemented since the initial release of transplanted wolves in 1995–1997 have diminished the overall level of hostility. These include livestock indemnity measures to compensate livestock owners for losses attributable to wolves, vaguely worded state laws that permit shooting of "pest" wolves, the aerial shooting of wolves linked to livestock depredation by U.S. wildlife agents, and a clunky and litigation-heavy, but ultimately successful, transfer of wolf management responsibilities to state-level wildlife agencies after the gray wolf was delisted from endangered species status. Limited hunting of wolves is now permitted in all three states, but all three states have crafted wolf management plans that they say will maintain sustainable, viable wolf populations within their borders.

Interior Department officials and environmental groups alike have promised to closely scrutinize adherence to the official plans to ensure that they are not distorted or otherwise sabotaged by wolf-extermination advocates that still wield political influence in Idaho, Montana, and Wyoming. In the spring of 2014, for instance, wildlife conservation organizations threatened legal action after Idaho Governor Butch Otter signed a wolf "depredation" bill that they claimed would massacre the state's wolf population. "This is not about hunting," said Jamie Rappaport Clark, a former U.S. Fish and Wildlife Service director turned president of Defenders of Wildlife. "This is an issue of extermination as fast as they can" (Barker, 2014). Idaho wildlife officials responded by insisting that they are committed to maintaining a sustainable wolf population in the state, but critics pointed out that since the state took over management of its wolf population, the wolf population in Idaho has dropped to less than 500 from a high of 850. As of the spring of 2014, the USFS has declined to intervene, but agency officials have emphasized that "should wolf numbers drop below [150 animals living wild in Idaho], the [USFS] can re-list either or both populations of the gray wolf under the Endangered Species Act and re-assume responsibility for wolf management," said one USFS official (Barker, 2014).

FURTHER READING

Barker, Rocky. "Otter Signs Bill Creating New Wolf Control Board." *Idaho Statesman*, March 27, 2014. http://www.idahostatesman.com/2014/03/27/3103860/otter-signs -bill-creating-new.html.

Mech, L. David. "The Challenge of Wolf Recovery: An Ongoing Dilemma for State Managers." *Wildlife Society News*, March 22, 2013. http://news.wildlife.org/featured/ the-challenge-of-wolf-recovery/.

Nie, Martin A. *Beyond Wolves: The Politics of Wolf Recovery and Management.* Minneapolis: University of Minnesota Press, 2003.

Ring, Ray. "The Gospel According to Ron Gillett." *High Country News*, May 12, 2008, http://www.hcn.org/issues/370/17691.

"HOW DO WE DETERMINE THE COST OF REMOVING ONE NOTE FROM A MOZART SYMPHONY?"

- **Document:** Statement of Renée Askins, executive director of the Wolf Fund, a pro-wolf reintroduction group, at *Introducing Gray Wolves in Yellowstone and Idaho*, a hearing before the House Committee on Resources.

- **Date:** January 26, 1995.

- **Where:** Washington, D.C.

- **Significance:** After the ESA was signed into law in 1973, it became the single most important legal tool available to conservationists devoted to protecting wild species and habitat. During the 1980s and 1990s, though, property and states' rights advocates, energy and timber interests, and supporters of other economic development bitterly criticized the ESA for "locking up" valuable land and accused ESA supporters of placing a higher priority on the welfare of endangered plants and animals than on human communities and families. Battles over the ESA became especially fierce in western states, where resource-extraction industries had traditionally exerted enormous influence over local economies and attitudes. The confrontation over the ESA between the environmentalist/wilderness conservation/animal rights camp and the pro-development coalition reached a boiling point of sorts in the mid-1990s, when the U.S. Fish and Wildlife Service unveiled an ESA-based plan to reintroduce endangered gray wolves into Yellowstone National Park and central Idaho's Frank Church–River of No Return Wilderness Area. In both of these places, the wolf population had been exterminated decades before by ranchers, farmers, and bounty hunters. This plan unleashed a tsunami of protests that were heard all the way across the country in Washington, D.C. Conservative Republicans quickly arranged for hearings on the wolf reintroduction plan in the GOP-led House Committee on Resources. The Republicans lined up a wide range of witnesses opposed to the reintroduction, but Democratic supporters of the USFS wolf recovery scheme were able to schedule witnesses as well. One supporter of the wolf reintroduction plan who testified at the hearing was Renée Askins, founder of a grassroots organization called the Wolf Fund that was devoted to seeing wolves reintroduced to parts of the West where they had been eradicated.

DOCUMENT

If I were a rancher I probably would not want wolves returned to the West. If I had significant numbers of sheep or cattle killed each year by predators I would dread and fight the addition of another predator. If I faced the conditions that ranchers face in the West—falling stock prices, rising taxes, prolonged drought, and a nation that is eating less and less beef and wearing more and more synchilla—I would not want to add wolves to my woes. If I were a rancher in Montana, Idaho, or Wyoming in 1995, watching my neighbors give up and my way of life fade away, I would be afraid. If everything I believed in and worked for and prayed for was disappearing, I would be afraid and I would be angry. I would want to blame something, to fight something, even kill something because Westerners are not, on the whole, a helpless lot.

Ranchers can't change the weather, or make people eat beef or wear wool, the tax thing is hopeless, but they can fight to stop those wolves, they could even kill those wolves. Ranchers know, and the people in this room know, that the wolves aren't the cause of western woes or the changes that are causing those woes, any more than the rooster crowing is the cause for the sun rising.

Almost every rancher I know in the West right now is afraid and angry. I have lived in the West for fifteen years. I spent a good part of two of those years on the road talking to people in rural Wyoming, Montana, and Idaho, mostly ranchers, mostly about wolves. When you talk to ranchers (the ones on the ground, the ones running stock, not lobbying organizations) they say, "You know it's not the wolves we're worried about, it's what the wolves represent. It's not what they'll do, it's what they mean." Wolves mean changes. Wolves mean challenges to the old way of doing things. Wolves mean loss of control.

Ranchers deserve our compassion and our concern. Whether the threat of wolves is perceived or actual, their fear and anger are real. I honor that. It is my job, however, as a scientist and an advocate to distinguish the fact from the fiction, and the purpose from the perceived. It is the job of the members of this committee, as representatives of a democratic public, to create laws and, in creating them, inform your decision-making with the most accurate information, and it is Secretary [Bruce] Babbitt's job to implement and enforce those laws.

Democracy must be more than laws expressing exemplary ideals. . . . It is through our participation and our representation that we are rendered accountable to the ideas of our legislation. It is easy to pass visionary laws; it is often difficult to live by their mandates.

When Congress passed The Endangered Species Act it expressed the nation's willingness to sacrifice some economic advantage for the protection and restoration of species. The creation of Yellowstone National Park expressed our desire to preserve our natural heritage. The Wilderness Act expressed our commitment to wild places and their wild inhabitants. All were recognized, by the world, as visionary legislation. Now we face the difficult task of living up to our visions.

To possess a fine recipe is one thing, to prepare a fine meal requires more—some thought and effort and care. The Endangered Species Act is like a fine recipe, but it needs to be enacted to be meaningful to America. The northern Rocky Mountain wolf was classified as an Endangered Species in 1973. This classification required the return of wolves to Yellowstone. The wolves are not yet running free in Yellowstone, and—so far—our legislation has proved unequal to its mission. After twenty years of stalling and sabotage by special interest groups, Jefferson's original vision of democracy, laws made of the people, by the people, and for the people is itself endangered.

The Endangered Species Act was passed by an overwhelming majority in Congress in 1973 and it enjoyed tremendous support among the general public. Our laws, however, are only as good as our ability to live up to them. Americans want clean air, clean water, wild places, wild creatures, and are willing to sacrifice to have those things, but because of pressure from special interest groups, usually industry-driven special interests, our laws are not always observed, and what Americans sought to protect is bartered away in nickels and dimes . . . one acre at a time, one species at a time. . . .

The wolf is a prime victim of industry's "barter" methods. For over twenty years special interests have undermined national law by intentionally dragging out the legal process of wolf recovery and driving up the costs. Ironically, the wolf issue has recently been depicted as a "hurried and autocratic" effort by the federal government, forced upon the states of Wyoming, Idaho, and Montana, that has ignored the concerns and interest of the local public. The foundation of this plan was forged under the Reagan and Bush administrations with an emphasis on deriving a solution from the West, rather than imposing one on the West. In 1991 Wyoming GOP Senators Malcolm Wallop and Alan Simpson, working with former U.S. Fish and Wildlife Service Director John Turner (who was also a former Republican state senator and a third generation western rancher), established a wolf management committee bringing together federal and state agencies, conservationists and ranchers to find a solution that carried out the law and considered people. Their work provided the foundation for today's plan, a hard won, middle of the road position.

Assertions have also been made that the states have not been involved, and that the public, particularly the ranchers, have not had the opportunity to comment. This is simply untrue. Since 1973, when the wolf was placed on the Endangered Species list, the livestock industry has participated on the Wolf Recovery Team in the production of two wolf recovery plans. Four volumes (1,314 pages) of research on the economic, biological and social impact of wolf reintroduction were produced principally to respond to their concerns. (More research had been done on wolves than on any animal that lives here!) Ranchers and hunters were represented on the Wolf Management Committee, and participated extensively at hearing associated with the Committee.

Ranchers, hunters, and representatives from the state government also participated extensively in the two-year EIS [environmental impact statement] process. . . . Opponents of wolf recovery have participated in this planning process every step of the way, and their concerns have indeed been addressed, although not necessarily acceded to, in both the EIS and the Rulemaking.

Additionally, the Game and Fish Departments of all three states have already been paid $7,000 a year to participate in the planning and implementation of the EIS and each state received $30,000 in 1993 to develop their wolf management plans. Objections have been raised about the U.S. Fish and Wildlife Service proceeding with reintroduction before state plans are in place. The time frame of the reintroduction has been known for several years [and] the preparation and completion of these plans is of course the responsibility of the state game and fish departments and not the federal government.

Opponents of this project have also asserted that residents in the region are opposed to this, but numerous regional surveys have shown majorities of the residents in Wyoming, Montana, and Idaho support the presence of wolves. A 1991 survey in Wyoming, commissioned by the Wyoming Game and Fish Department (which at the time was on record against reintroduction) indicated that Wyoming residents favored reintroduction by a margin of 44% to 34.5%.... Bath and Phillips (1990) and Bath (1991)... found that 43.7% of Montanans, 48.5% of Wyomingites and 56% of Idahoans favored wolf reintroduction into Yellowstone National Park. 40.3% of Montanans, 34.5% of Wyomingites, and 27% of Idahoans were opposed. No opinion on wolf reintroduction was held by 16% of Montanans, 17% of Wyomingites and 17% of Idahoans.... National surveys indicate an overwhelming majority of the national public support Yellowstone wolf reintroduction.

Reintroduction opponents claim that wolves will devastate the livestock industry in the West, and yet all the science, the studies, the experts, and the facts show that wolves kill less than 1/10 of 1 percent of the livestock available to them....

According to the *Bozeman Chronicle*, even if federal specialists have wildly underestimated the number of cows and sheep that wolves would kill in the Yellowstone and Central Idaho areas, the total would be much smaller than the number that die each year in the state of Montana alone because of storms, dogs, and ovine ineptitude. In fact, the number of wolf-caused sheep deaths would have to be almost 30 times higher than predicted before it would match the number of Montana sheep that died in 1993 because they rolled over onto their backs and were unable to get up and starved....

Opponents claim that reintroducing wolves is a waste of taxpayer dollars. Let's take a closer look at the projected 6.7 million dollars it would take to reintroduce wolves. One man's "cost" is another man's "income," as we have learned with defense spending cuts. Whatever money is spent on wolf reintroduction largely flows into the regional economy, as will money for the ongoing management of a recovered population. The cost of not doing anything, that is, allowing natural recolonization to occur, would be higher due to the prolonged time it would take for natural recovery to occur and due to the increased restrictions that accompany the presence of a fully endangered species.

It is projected that wolf reintroduction will cost approximately $900,000 a year. Of those costs the federal government anticipates earmarking approximately $100,000 to $150,000/year for each of the three states or a total of $300,000 to $450,000/year to support state involvement in management of wolves. Because wolf management is not a full time proposition the equipment (trucks, snowmobiles, telemetry receivers, etc.), salaries, etc. would most likely be used for other projects as well....

Let's also take a look at the expenditure of 6.7 million dollars in relationship to other expenditures. For the first 17 years of the Endangered Species Act (1973–1990), the federal government spent a total of approximately $700 million to implement the Act, including land acquisition and grants to the states. The appropriation to the Fish and Wildlife Service for implementing the Act in 1992 was $35.7 million. By comparison, a single mile of interstate highway costs, on average, $39 million. For less than the price of a mile of four-lane highway, the U.S. Fish and Wildlife Service ran its entire endangered species program nationwide for a year. To say that we cannot afford to protect endangered species is absurd.

Here is another way to look at it. The significant number of timber sales on the national forests of this country have lost money. By subsidizing timber sales we over harvested our national forests and, in many places, ruined opportunities for sustainable forests. Every year we—the taxpayers—subsidize the logging of federal forests at the rate of over $250 million. At this rate, the total costs of the entire 18 years of Endangered Species Act could be recovered in a little more than 2 years if below-cost timber sales were eliminated. Applied to wolf reintroduction: we could recover the entire cost of wolf recovery ($12.7 million) by eliminating below-cost timber sales on public lands for nineteen days. . . . Can we afford to reintroduce wolves? Relative to other federal projects, it's a bargain.

Let's take a look at one direct subsidy ranchers receive. (I am a supporter of controlling wolves that kill livestock, and the funding that is allocated in the FEIS budget for ADC.) Taxpayers pay approximately 36 million a year to support Animal Damage Control which clearly benefits just a few special interests. . . .

The livestock industry has successfully transferred one of their most basic operational costs to the general public—prevention of predator losses. If you raise Christmas trees, part of the cost, and risk of doing business is losing a few to gypsy moths and ice storms; inherent in the cost of ranching, particularly on public lands, should be the cost and risk of losing livestock to predators. Instead, every year 36 million tax dollars go to kill native wildlife on our public lands so that private industry can make a profit. We shouldn't bar wolves from Yellowstone because of the possibility that a livestock depredation might occur anymore than we should close highways because a cow could get hit by a motorist.

The livestock industry has been very effective in promoting the concept that having wolves in Yellowstone is some sort of environmental luxury, some romantic nonsense that only urbanites and rich easterners advocate, at the costs of the poor beleaguered western livestock industry. Having wolves in Yellowstone is not a luxury but a right, a right of the people in the Yellowstone region and the people of this nation who own Yellowstone and the public lands surrounding it. We should not have to pay for clean air or water . . . nor should we believe that they are somehow a luxury. In a similar manner, we have a right to a full complement of wildlife on our public lands, particularly in our national parks. We should not have to accept a degraded environment—such as one devoid of predators and other native wildlife—nor should we have to pay the operational expenses of any industry whose profit interests conflict with our right to a healthy environment. Clean air, clean water, and a healthy environment are a right and no one should be allowed to degrade them, especially if they are making a profit as a result.

Wolves are missing from the Yellowstone region because we eliminated them. They didn't disappear in response to a loss of prey or the lack of habitat; they didn't die out in response to a natural disease or catastrophic event; we didn't just remove wolves that killed livestock. We systematically, intentionally, consciously killed every wolf we could find. And we found them all. Yellowstone has been without wolves for sixty years. We came to accept the absence of wolves as normal. That is the tragedy. Wolves were an integral part of the Yellowstone ecosystem for thousands of years. We made a grave error in exterminating them and their current absence is an ecologically perverse and abnormal situation.

Opponents falsely assume that because there are no wolves, there should be no wolves, and over the last two decades they have very effectively framed the wolf recovery arguments around that assumption. In fact, they have promoted the idea that the return of wolves is somehow radical or extreme. The costs to the general public of not having wolves have virtually been eclipsed by the livestock industry's cry of economic loss or burden. In the West we now live in a "wolf-free" environment. Or is it "wolf-deprived"? Who has gained and who has lost? How do we assign a value to the importance of a predator in an ecosystem? How do we determine the cost of removing one note from a Mozart symphony or one brush stroke from a Rembrandt? How do we quantify the loss to the millions of people who have visited Yellowstone and never had the opportunity to experience the wild, hair-raising chill of a wolf howl or see the real drama of life enacted as elk or antelope streak across sage plains pursued by the predator responsible for their swiftness and agility. Who should be compensating whom?

Because of the passion and the emotion and the politics it is very easy to try to diminish this debate to one of black or white. Opponents of reintroduction want to use wolves as the proverbial "line in the sand" that divides the old West from the new. They want us to see this issue as a distillation of all Endangered Species conflicts, as simply a question of "either/or": Don't touch a tree vs. clear-cut all trees; no wolves vs. fully protected, untouchable wolves; unrestricted grazing vs. no grazing. But these issues, like wolves, come in many different shades.

Both sides have tried to use the wolf as a principle weapon in what I call the crush and conquer warfare. Both sides have used exaggerated rhetoric to alarm and frighten constituents. The tragedy is that while the crush and conquer armies fight their wars, the rest of America stands by, confused, uncertain, and unaware that something they care about might be at stake. I believe this "us against them" rhetoric is simply a construct to enable not the war on the West, but the war from the West. There is no us against them, it is us against us. We are all in it together. Chief Seattle said,

> If all the beasts were gone, we would die from a great loneliness of spirit, for whatever happens to the beast, happens to us. All things are connected. Whatever befalls the earth, befalls the children of the earth.

We have to give up this notion of who is winning and who is losing—we need to return to the things that we care about—the trees, the range, the wildlife, our livelihood, our families, our homes. The real issue is one of making room—for there is still a little room in the West—for hunters, for environmentalists, for ranchers, and for wolves.

Source: Statement of Renée Askins, Executive Director, Wolf Fund. *Introducing Gray Wolves in Yellowstone and Idaho: Oversight Hearing Before the Committee on Resources, House of Representatives,* 104th Congress, 1st session, on federal efforts to introduce Canadian gray wolves into Yellowstone National Park and the central Idaho wilderness, January 26, 1995. Washington, DC: U.S. Government Printing Office, 1995, pp. 109–114.

ANALYSIS

In her appearance before the Committee on Resources, Askins appeared to make a conscious decision not to place her primary focus on the welfare or rights of gray wolves. Instead, she spent most of her time discussing the human side of the equation. She empathized with ranchers and other natural resource-dependent people living in the West—although she also insisted that their hostility to wolf reintroduction was largely based on ignorance of the animals' true economic impact and a general feeling of helplessness in the face of larger economic and cultural changes in the West. Askins also returned again and again to the idea that reintroducing wolves to ecosystems in Wyoming, Montana, and Idaho amounted to an opportunity to rectify a wrong that had made our own existence a more impoverished one. To be sure, she spoke of how the "current absence" of wolves from Yellowstone was "ecologically perverse." But she expounded at greater length on how returning wolves to Yellowstone and other wild parts of the West was a right of all Americans, including "millions . . . who have visited Yellowstone and never had the opportunity to experience the wild, hair-raising chill of a wolf howl."

Askins and other wolf-reintroduction proponents ultimately prevailed in this battle, despite staunch opposition from congressional Republicans and a slew of lawsuits that aimed to derail the plan. Forty-one wolves from Canada and northern Montana were released into Yellowstone from 1995 to 1997, while another 35 wolves were reintroduced in the central Idaho wilderness in 1996–1996. Since that time, gray wolves have been delisted from endangered species status in Idaho, Wyoming, and Montana after years of legal jousting between proponents and critics of wolf restoration in the West. Wolves in all three states are now managed by state wildlife agencies, albeit under close monitoring by the U.S. Fish and Wildlife Service to ensure that their populations remain healthy and viable. In 2011 the USFS estimated that the Northern Rocky Mountain district, which includes areas of Idaho, Montana, and Wyoming, contained about 1,650 wolves and nearly 250 packs.

Opposition to the presence of the wolves remains strong in many rural communities in these states. However, researchers indicate that their economic impact on the livestock industry has been modest, and that their presence has been beneficial to regional ecosystems (by reducing high elk populations that were degrading area rivers, for example).

FURTHER READING

Barker, Rocky. "Idaho Seeks Middle Ground on Wolf Control." *Idaho Statesman*, March 1, 2014. http://www.idahostatesman.com/2014/03/01/3055651/idaho-seeks-middle-ground-on-wolf.html.

Government Accountability Office (GAO). *Endangered Species: Time and Costs Required to Recover Species Are Largely Unknown*. Washington, DC: GAO, 2006. http://www.gao .gov/assets/100/94110.pdf.

Musiani, Marco, Luigi Boitani, and Paul Paquet, eds. *A New Era for Wolves and People*. Calgary, AB: University of Calgary Press, 2009.

Williams, Ted. "Living with Wolves." *Audubon*, November–December 2000.

"Wolf Restoration." Yellowstone National Park, accessed December 12, 2014. http://www .nps.gov/yell/naturescience/wolfrest.htm.

"TO ELIMINATE THE WASTEFUL AND UNSPORTSMANLIKE PRACTICE OF SHARK FINNING"

- **Documents:** The Shark Finning Prohibition Act and President Bill Clinton's comments following his signing of the bill.
- **Date:** The law was enacted on December 21, 2000, and President Clinton made his comments on December 26, 2000.
- **Where:** Washington, D.C.
- **Significance:** This law made it unlawful for fishing operations to possess a shark fin without it being attached to the carcass of the shark. It was designed to reduce "shark finning," a practice wherein fishing vessels at sea harvest the fins of captured sharks—easily the most commercially valuable part of sharks because of the fins' popularity in Asian culinary dishes and folk cures—and discard the maimed shark to die.

DOCUMENT

An Act

To amend the Magnuson-Stevens Fishery Conservation and Management Act to eliminate the wasteful and unsportsmanlike practice of shark finning.

Be it enacted by the Senate and House of Representatives of the United States of America in Congress assembled,

SECTION 1. SHORT TITLE.

This Act may be cited as the 'Shark Finning Prohibition Act'.

SEC. 2. PURPOSE.

The purpose of this Act is to eliminate shark-finning by addressing the problem comprehensively at both the national and international levels.

SEC. 3. PROHIBITION ON REMOVING SHARK FIN AND DISCARDING SHARK CARCASS AT SEA.

Section 307(1) of the Magnuson-Stevens Fishery Conservation and Management Act (16 U.S.C. 1857(1)) is amended—

(1) by striking 'or' after the semicolon in subparagraph (N);

(2) by striking 'section 302(j)(7)(A).' in subparagraph (O) and inserting 'section 302(j)(7)(A); or'; and

(3) by adding at the end the following:

'(P)(i) to remove any of the fins of a shark (including the tail) and discard the carcass of the shark at sea;

'(ii) to have custody, control, or possession of any such fin aboard a fishing vessel without the corresponding carcass; or

'(iii) to land any such fin without the corresponding carcass.

For purposes of subparagraph (P) there is a rebuttable presumption that any shark fins landed from a fishing vessel or found on board a fishing vessel were taken, held, or landed in violation of subparagraph (P) if the total weight of shark fins landed or found on board exceeds 5 percent of the total weight of shark carcasses landed or found on board.'

SEC. 4. REGULATIONS.

No later than 180 days after the date of the enactment of this Act, the Secretary of Commerce shall promulgate regulations implementing the provisions of section 3076(1)(P) of the Magnuson-Stevens Fishery Conservation and Management Act (16 U.S.C. 1857(1)(P)), as added by section 3 of this Act.

SEC. 5. INTERNATIONAL NEGOTIATIONS.

The Secretary of Commerce, acting through the Secretary of State, shall—

(1) initiate discussions as soon as possible for the purpose of developing bilateral or multilateral agreements with other nations for the prohibition on shark-finning;

(2) initiate discussions as soon as possible with all foreign governments which are engaged in, or which have persons or companies engaged in shark-finning, for the purposes of—

(A) collecting information on the nature and extent of shark-finning by such persons and the landing or transshipment of shark fins through foreign ports; and

(B) entering into bilateral and multilateral treaties with such countries to protect such species;

(3) seek agreements calling for an international ban on shark-finning and other fishing practices adversely affecting these species through the United Nations, the Food and Agriculture Organization's Committee on Fisheries, and appropriate regional fishery management bodies;

(4) initiate the amendment of any existing international treaty for the protection and conservation of species of sharks to which the United States is a party in order to make such treaty consistent with the purposes and policies of this section;

(5) urge other governments involved in fishing for or importation of shark or shark products to fulfill their obligations to collect biological data, such as stock abundance and by-catch levels, as well as trade data, on shark species as called for in the 1995 Resolution on Cooperation with FAO with Regard to study on the Status of Sharks and By-Catch of Shark Species; and

(6) urge other governments to prepare and submit their respective National Plan of Action for the Conservation and Management of Sharks to the 2001 session of the FAO Committee on Fisheries, as set forth in the International Plan of Action for the Conservation and Management of Sharks.

SEC. 6. REPORT TO CONGRESS.

The Secretary of Commerce, in consultation with the Secretary of State, shall provide to Congress, by not later than 1 year after the date of the enactment of this Act, and every year thereafter, a report which—

(1) includes a list that identifies nations whose vessels conduct shark-finning and details the extent of the international trade in shark fins, including estimates of value and information on harvesting of shark fins, and landings or transshipment of shark fins through foreign ports;

(2) describes the efforts taken to carry out this Act, and evaluates the progress of those efforts;

(3) sets forth a plan of action to adopt international measures for the conservation of sharks; and

(4) includes recommendations for measures to ensure that United States actions are consistent with national, international, and regional obligations relating to shark populations, including those listed under the Convention on International Trade in Endangered Species of Wild Flora and Fauna.

SEC. 7. RESEARCH.

The Secretary of Commerce, subject to the availability of appropriations authorized by section 10, shall establish a research program for Pacific and Atlantic sharks to engage in the following data collection and research:

(1) The collection of data to support stock assessments of shark populations subject to incidental or directed harvesting by commercial vessels, giving priority to species according to vulnerability of the species to fishing gear and fishing mortality, and its population status.

(2) Research to identify fishing gear and practices that prevent or minimize incidental catch of sharks in commercial and recreational fishing.

(3) Research on fishing methods that will ensure maximum likelihood of survival of captured sharks after release.

(4) Research on methods for releasing sharks from fishing gear that minimize risk of injury to fishing vessel operators and crews.

(5) Research on methods to maximize the utilization of, and funding to develop the market for, sharks not taken in violation of a fishing management plan approved under section 303 or section 307(1)(P) of the Magnuson-Stevens Fishery Conservation and Management Act (16 U.S.C. 1853, 1857(1)(P)).

(6) Research on the nature and extent of the harvest of sharks and shark fins by foreign fleets and the international trade in shark fins and other shark products.

SEC. 8. WESTERN PACIFIC LONGLINE FISHERIES COOPERATIVE RESEARCH PROGRAM.

The National Marine Fisheries Service, in consultation with the Western Pacific Fisheries Management Council, shall initiate a cooperative research program with the commercial longlining industry to carry out activities consistent with this Act, including research described in section 7 of this Act. The service may initiate such shark cooperative research programs upon the request of any other fishery management council.

SEC. 9. SHARK-FINNING DEFINED.

In this Act, the term 'shark-finning' means the taking of a shark, removing the fin or fins (whether or not including the tail) of a shark, and returning the remainder of the shark to the sea.

SEC. 10. AUTHORIZATION OF APPROPRIATIONS.

There are authorized to be appropriated to the Secretary of Commerce for fiscal years 2001 through 2005 such sums as are necessary to carry out this Act.

Speaker of the House of Representatives.
Vice President of the United States and
President of the Senate.

Source: Public Law 106-557. U.S. Government Printing Office. Washington, DC. December 21, 2000.

DOCUMENT

I have signed H.R. 5461, the "Shark Finning Prohibition Act." Shark-finning is the taking of a shark, removing the fin, and returning the carcass to the sea. This legislation prohibits shark-finning in all U.S. waters; provides for initiation of international negotiations to prohibit shark-finning; and authorizes research to conserve shark populations.

The Administration has actively supported the prohibition of shark-finning because of the harmful impact on sharks and shark populations. The practice has been administratively banned in the Atlantic Ocean, the Gulf of Mexico, and the Caribbean Sea. H.R. 5461 will establish the ban in law and extend it to the Pacific Ocean.

The United States has been a leading proponent of international shark conservation at the United Nations Food and Agriculture Organization and has advocated prohibiting wasteful fishing practices, including shark finning. We have also demonstrated considerable leadership in other international fora to conserve sharks and ban shark-finning. In the Eastern Pacific, the United States has been active in the Inter-American Tropical Tuna Commission in dealing effectively with issues such as shark management on the high seas. And the United States has been participating, along with thirty other countries, in the High-Level Multilateral Conferences for the Conservation and Management of Highly Migratory Species in the Western and Central Pacific. Finally, the United States plans to continue in its efforts at the International Commission for the Conservation of Atlantic Tunas to obtain a proposal that would ban shark-finning, as well as implement a variety of conservation measures.

Only through international cooperation can effective management be ensured for sharks, especially on the high seas. The United States will intensify efforts to convince other countries to join in prohibiting shark finning, consistent with the goals of H.R. 5461.

I note, however, that two provisions of the bill raise constitutional concerns. Because the Constitution vests the conduct of foreign affairs with the President, Congress may not dictate the executive branch's negotiations with foreign governments (section 5). Because the Constitution preserves to the President the authority to decide whether and when the executive branch should recommend new legislation, Congress may not require the President or his subordinates to present such recommendations (section 6). I therefore direct executive branch officials to carry out these provisions in a manner that is consistent with the President's constitutional responsibilities.

Source: Clinton, William J. "Statement on Signing the Shark Finning Prohibition Act," December 26, 2000. *Public Papers of the Presidents: William J. Clinton, 2000, Book 3.* Washington DC: Government Printing Office, p. 2782.

ANALYSIS

Sharks have roamed the world's oceans for more than 400 million years. Since the 1960s, however, the planet's shark population has been under assault by a combination of overfishing, pollution, and habitat destruction. As concerns about shark conservation mounted, the United States imposed an administrative ban on shark finning that applied to the Atlantic Ocean, the Gulf of Mexico, and the Caribbean Sea. However, this ban did not include the Pacific Ocean and was not a legal act. Then, in December 2000, during his final days in office, President Bill Clinton signed into law the Shark Finning Prohibition Act as an amendment to the Magnuson-Stevens Fishery Conservation and Management Act. The purpose of the act was to "eliminate the wasteful and unsportsmanlike practice of shark finning" at both the national and international levels and extend existing U.S. bans to include the Pacific Ocean.

The act prohibits anyone under U.S. jurisdiction from engaging in shark finning, possessing shark fins on a fishing vessel without carcasses, or landing shark fins without carcasses. In addition, it includes a rebuttable presumption that a vessel or fishery is in violation of the act if the total weight of shark fins on the vessel or landed exceeds 5 percent of the total weight of shark carcasses.

Although the United States cannot enforce its laws on other nations, this act stipulates that the U.S. secretary of commerce should, among other things, initiate discussions with other nations to develop multilateral agreements on the prohibition of shark finning and other fishing practices that have an adverse effect on sharks. The secretary of commerce is also given the responsibility of helping to establish research programs to study the conservation of shark populations, fishing practices that minimize incidental catching of sharks, and the incidence of shark finning by foreign fleets.

The Shark Finning Prohibition Act was the first step in the United States toward prohibiting the practice of shark finning. However, in one of the first court cases related to the act, a loophole was found that allowed vessels to transport or land fins, as long as the sharks were not finned on that vessel. In addition, other loopholes prevented enforcement of the act. Thus, the practice of shark finning continued mostly unabated until the Shark Conservation Act of 2011, which stipulates that all federally managed sharks be brought to port with their fins naturally attached.

Neither the Shark Finning Prohibition Act nor the Shark Conservation Act, however, extend their provisions beyond waters in U.S. jurisdiction. In many other parts of the world, meaningful restrictions on shark finning still do not exist, even as commercial demand for the fins remains stubbornly high in China and other parts of Asia, where they are seen as a delicacy and a key ingredient in traditional medicines.

In Chinese culture, shark fin soup has traditionally been served at special occasions such as royal banquets and weddings to signify wealth, sophistication, and prestige. In recent decades, China's dramatic economic expansion has triggered a corresponding rise in the demand for fins, which can now fetch up to US$500 per pound. In light of this strong economic incentive to engage in shark finning, the carnage wreaked on numerous shark species has been considerable. It has also revealed the limitations of the Shark Finning Prohibition Act and other laws that only govern waters under U.S. jurisdiction. In 2013, in fact, researchers at Dalhousie University announced that according to their comprehensive study of the issue, about 100 million sharks worldwide are being killed annually for their fins. The report even stressed that the 100 million number was a conservative estimate, and that the real total could be almost three times that. The scientists also concluded that between 6.4 percent and 7.9 percent of all species of shark are being killed annually. "There's a staggering number of sharks being caught every year and the number is way too high considering the biology of species," says Dalhousie biologist Boris Worm, the lead researcher on the study (quoted in Stone, 2013).

A common misconception is that shark populations are virtually inexhaustible, especially as they have no natural predator and are thus at the top of the oceanic food chain. However, with their slow growth and low reproductive rates, they are not able to reproduce even remotely fast enough to keep up with their current mortality rate. Scientists warn that this sharp decline in shark numbers also can cause a ripple effect in oceanic ecosystems, leading to unknown and irreversible effects on all other species in the ocean.

In light of multiple alarming reports of unsustainable levels of shark harvesting, conservation organizations and national governments alike have demanded more decisive action from CITES. In 2013 CITES officials announced that it was placing five species of shark—including three hammerhead species—under special protection. This move, which extended significant international legal protection to the listed species, was widely applauded in the environmental community, but shark advocates say that CITES should extend protections to many other shark species as well.

FURTHER READING

"Big Gains Made in Shark Conservation, but Extinction Still Possible." *AlterNet.* January 7, 2011. http://www.alternet.org/story/149442/big_gains_made_in_shark_conservation, _but_extinction_still_possible.

Crawford, Dean. *Shark*. London: Reaktion, 2008.

Ellis, Richard. *Shark: A Visual History*. Guilford, UK: Globe Pequot Press, 2012.

Evans, Michael. "Shark Fin Soup Sales Plunge in China." *Aljazeera*. April 10, 2014. http://www.aljazeera.com/indepth/features/2014/04/shark-fin-soup-sales-plunge-china-20144913514600433.html.

Fairclough, Caty. "Shark Finning: Sharks Turned Prey." *Ocean Portal*. Smithsonian National Museum of Natural History. http://ocean.si.edu/ocean-news/shark-finning-sharks-turned-prey.

National Marine Fisheries Service. "2005 Report to Congress Pursuant to the Shark Finning Prohibition Act of 2000." U.S. Department of Commerce, National Oceanic and Atmospheric Administration. http://www.nmfs.noaa.gov/by_catch/Shark%20Finning%20Report.pdf.

Owen, David. *Shark: In Peril in the Sea*. Crows Nest, NSW: Allen & Unwin, 2009.

"Shark Conservation Act." Animal Welfare Institute, accessed December 12, 2014. https://awionline.org/content/shark-conservation-act.

Stone, Dan. "100 Million Sharks Killed Every Year, Study Shows on Eve of International Conference on Shark Protection." *National Geographic: Newswatch*, March 1, 2013. http://newswatch.nationalgeographic.com/2013/03/01/100-million-sharks-killed-every-year-study-shows-on-eve-of-international-conference-on-shark-protection/.

"EXOTIC CATS IN CAPTIVITY SHOULD BE ABLE TO LIVE HUMANELY AND HEALTHFULLY"

- **Document:** Comments from U.S. senators Jim Jeffords (I-Vermont) and John Ensign (R-Nevada) in support of the proposed Captive Wildlife Safety Act.
- **Date:** January 30, 2003.
- **Where:** Washington, D.C.
- **Significance:** This bill, which was passed by Congress and signed into law by President George W. Bush on December 19, 2003, prohibited the interstate transport of exotic lions, tigers, and the like for private ownership as pets.

DOCUMENT

Mr. [Jim] JEFFORDS: Mr. President, I rise today to introduce the Captive Wildlife Safety Act, a firm commitment to protect public safety and the welfare of wild cats that are increasingly being kept as pets. I am joined by Senator Ensign of Nevada, Senator [Ron] Wyden of Oregon (D), and Senator [Carl] Levin of Michigan (D) as original co-sponsors of this legislation.

This bill amends the Lacy Act Amendment of 1981 to bar the interstate and foreign commerce of carnivorous wild cats, including lions, tigers, leopards, cheetahs, and cougars. The legislation would not ban all private ownership of these prohibited species, but would outlaw the commerce of these animals for use as pets.

Current figures estimate that there are more than 5,000 tigers in captivity in the United States. In fact, there are more tigers in captivity in the United States than there are in native habitats throughout the range in Asia. While some tigers are kept in zoos, most of these animals are kept as pets, living in cages behind someone's house, in a State that does not restrict private ownership of dangerous animals.

Tigers are not the only animals sought as exotic pets. Today there are more than 1,000 web sites that specialize in the trade of lions, cougars, and leopards to promote them as domestic pets.

Untrained owners are not capable of meeting the needs of these animals. Local veterinarians, animal shelters, and local governments are ill equipped to meet the challenge of providing for their proper care. If they are to be kept in captivity, these animals must be cared for by trained professionals who can meet their behavioral, nutrition, and physical needs.

People who live near these animals are also in real danger. These cats are large and powerful animals, capable of injuring or killing innocent people. There are countless stories of many unfortunate and unnecessary incidents where dangerous exotic cats have endangered public safety. Last year in Lexington, TX, a three-year-old boy was killed by his stepfather's pet tiger. In Loxahatchee, FL, a 58 year-old woman was bitten on the head by a 750 pound Siberian-Bengal Tiger being kept as a pet, and in Quitman, AR, four 600 to 800 pound tigers escaped from a "private safari." Parents living nearby sat in their front yards with high-powered rifles, guarding their children at play, frightened that the wild tigers might attack them.

This is a balanced approach that preserves the rights of those already regulated by the Department of Agriculture under the Animal Welfare Act such as circuses, zoos, and research facilities. This Act specifically targets unregulated and untrained individuals who are maintaining these wild cats as exotic pets.

The Captive Wildlife Safety Act represents an emerging consensus on the need for comprehensive federal legislation to regulate what animals can be kept as pets. The United States Department of Agriculture states, "Large wild and exotic cats such as lions, tigers, cougars, and leopards are dangerous animals... Because of these animals' potential to kill or severely injure both people and other animals, an untrained person should not keep them as pets. Doing so poses serious risks to family, friends, neighbors, and the general public. Even an animal that can be friendly and lovable can be very dangerous."

The American Veterinary Medical Association also "strongly opposes the keeping of wild carnivore species of animals as pets and believes that all commercial traffic of these animals for such purpose should be prohibited."

This bill preserves those local regulations already in existence. Full bans are already in place in 12 States and partial bans have been enacted in 7 States. I sincerely hope that grassroots organizations continue to encourage State and local governments to ban the private ownership of exotic cats.

Former world heavyweight boxing champion Mike Tyson leaves a gym with his pet tiger in October 1995. The Captive Wildlife Safety Act, which became law on January 30, 2003, banned the interstate transport of exotic animals, such as tigers, lions, and jaguars, for personal ownership because of the potential danger to people who come into contact with them. (AP Photo/Lennox McLendon).

The Captive Wildlife Safety Act is supported by the Association of Zoos and Aquariums, the Humane Society of the United States, the Funds for Animals, and the International Fund for Animal Welfare.

No one should be endangered by those who cannot properly keep these animals. Exotic cats in captivity should be able to live humanely and healthfully....

Mr. ENSIGN:... During my days as a practicing veterinarian, I saw firsthand exotic animals being mistreated by owners who were ill-prepared to care for them. All too often, large cats are put in cages that are too small to accommodate their growing needs. Owners often buy a young tiger or cat, paying more attention to their cuddly exterior rather than the overwhelming responsibility that comes along with raising an animal that will grow into a large, wild, predator.

In my home State of Nevada, there is a burgeoning population of exotic animals being kept as pets. I have been contacted by animal control centers throughout the State that are called to aid in situations where a wild tiger or lion has escaped and run amok. In these situations, not only are the owners and the animal control professionals in danger, so too are children and other neighbors who may be in the wrong place at the wrong time. These animals' instinct is to attack, and they will do so, if given the opportunity. That is why only highly trained individuals who have the know-how and the resources should be able to own exotic animals.

In fact, I am informed that officials in Nye County in my home State, are working to pass a county ordinance that would ban the ownership of exotic animals because of the threat they pose to public safety. We have the support and backing of the Humane Society of the United States, the American Veterinary Medical Association, and the American Zoo and Aquarium Association.

This legislation protects the public, but also ensures that the animals receive the best care possible from certified and trained owners. I look forward to having the overwhelming support of my colleagues in the Senate.

Source: Statements of Senators Jeffords and Ensign. *Congressional Record-Senate*, January 30, 2003, S1833. http://www.justice.gov/jmd/ls/legislative_histories/pl108-191/cr-s1833-34-2003.pdf.

ANALYSIS

According to Wild Animal World, a company that provides exotic animals for parties, the company offers "quality animals, combined with well-seasoned trainers, [to give] you the most entertaining, diverse, and hands-on show in South Florida!" Unfortunately, in at least two instances, it was the animals that had the "hands-on" experience. In 2001 a Wild Animal World leopard attacked a child at a company picnic. Five years later, at a birthday party for Goya Foods president Francisco Unanue's son, a four-year-old girl suffered severe cuts to her head and had her ear partially severed by a 62-pound cougar that was brought in to entertain the children.

These are just two of nearly 400 incidents since 1990 in which big cats have injured or killed humans in the United States. Although some of these incidents occurred at facilities accredited by the Association of Zoos and Aquariums, those with the highest risk of fatal attacks or injuries took place in unaccredited locations ranging from private homes to roadside "zoos." For many years, acquiring big cats for personal ownership was a relatively easy task across much of the country. Prior to 2013, only 21 states had a ban on private ownership of exotic animals, including nondomesticated cats, wolves, bears, reptiles, and nonhuman primates. The remaining states allowed varying levels of ownership of exotic animals provided the owners possessed the stipulated paperwork (generally a license, permit, or veterinary certificate). Most of these animals are bred in the United States, in large part because commercially importing endangered species has been restricted since the 1970s. However, even in states that ban ownership of wild animals, the existing laws are often not enforced. And some people who perceive ownership of a powerful wild animal as a symbol of power or prestige are perfectly willing to turn to the black market to own one.

Big cats can be found for sale online and in newspaper and magazine advertisements. At one time, self-described wildlife sanctuaries would breed and sell cubs, in addition to providing shelter. A tiger cub can be purchased for as little as $400. These little cubs are cute and playful; however, they soon grow to more than 500 pounds, thanks to their diet of up to 15 pounds of raw meat a day. When this happens, many owners become overwhelmed by their new pets and either fail to provide for the animal's needs or are simply financially or physically unable to do so. These animals are often kept in cramped cages full of filth and become malnourished. According to the U.S. Humane Society, captive big cats often suffer from high levels of stress and serious physical ailments, including "shrunken hearts, shortened tendons, club feet, kidney ailments, malformed backbones, deformed faces, and contorted necks" (Humane Society, 2013).

Some proponents of exotic animal ownership proclaim that they should not be persecuted because of the actions of "bad pet owners." They have urged reforms that would regulate the care of such animals rather than impose an outright ban of ownership. When confronted with the number of people injured or killed by big cats and other exotic animals, these proponents aver that it is nowhere near the number of people attacked by dogs. However, a 2003 article in the journal *Zoo Biology* determined that after adjusting for the greater number of privately owned dogs than privately owned big cats, the latter are anywhere from 360 to 720 times more likely to be involved in a fatal attack against a human.

In the early 2000s, this contentious issue led a group of animal advocates to put together a federal legislative campaign that would combat the trade in big cats used as pets. Actress and animal rights activist Tippi Hedren and Wayne Pacelle, senior vice president of the U.S. Humane Society, coauthored the Captive Wildlife Safety Act (CWSA) and worked together to bring it before Congress. During her five-minute testimony before Congress in June 2003, Hedren described about 15 attacks involving big cats, as well as information about the inhumane treatment of such animals by nonaccredited owners. Exotic cat owners who opposed the restrictions tried to derail the bill. According to Zuzana Kukol, cofounder of Responsible Exotic Animal Ownership, "Placing bans on wild animal ownership will only increase the population of illegal exotics. . . . Bans do not work. We've seen this with alcohol and prostitution." Their protests did not sway Congress, however. The legislation passed unanimously in both the House and the Senate in the fall of 2003, and Bush signed the bill into law on December 19, 2003.

The law, an amendment to the Lacey Act Amendments of 1981, prohibits the interstate transport of exotic cats for private ownership as pets. The law applies to lions, tigers, leopards, snow leopards, clouded leopards, jaguars, cheetahs, and cougars, as well as any subspecies or hybrid combination of these species. According to the CWSA, it is illegal to sell, purchase, receive, or acquire these cats across state lines. However, the act does not make it illegal to own a big cat, as this is mandated by state laws. According to U.S. senator Jim Jeffords (I-Vermont), the act preserved the rights of those regulated by the USDA, such as circuses, zoos, and research facilities, while making it much more difficult for untrained people to acquire big cats as pets.

Animal welfare groups describe the Captive Wildlife Safety Act as an intermediate step on the road toward a federal ban on the private ownership of exotic animals. They say that while the CWSA helped contain the problem, it did not eradicate it altogether—an assessment supported by continued occasional stories on maulings and deaths from privately owned big cats. In fact, the International Fund for Animal Welfare (IFAW) estimates that 10,000 lions, tigers, and other big cats are being kept as pets or as roadside attractions across the United States—and that there are now more privately owned tigers in the United States than exist in all of the wild.

In May 2013, U.S. representative Howard "Buck" McKeon (R-California), who had helped introduce the CWSA in the House back in 2003, presented the Big Cats and Public Safety Protection Act. This proposed act would extend the CWSA to prohibit breeding or possessing any prohibited wildlife species. The bill was introduced to the Senate by U.S. senator Richard Blumenthal (D-Connecticut) and is supported by a range of organizations, including the IFAW, the Humane Society of the United States, and the World Wildlife Fund. Even the USDA has stated, "Because of these animals' potential to kill or severely injure both people and other animals, an untrained person should not keep them as pets. . . . Even an animal that can be friendly and lovable can be very dangerous." The Big Cats and Public Safety Protection Act did not come up for a vote in 2013, but supporters of a ban on private big cat ownership vow to continue lobbying on behalf of the measure.

FURTHER READING

"Captive Wildlife Safety Act." Feline Conservation Federation, accessed December 12, 2014. http://www.felineconservation.org/legislative_information/captive_wildlife _safety_act.htm.

Eustace, Chantal. "Actress Fights to Protect Big Cats." *Vancouver Sun*, May 21, 2008. http:// www2.canada.com/vancouversun/news/westcoastnews/story.html?id=d60d036a-34e4 -4f84-9c44-ee9d000d63b6&p=1.

"Girl Mauled by a Captive Cougar at a Children's Birthday Party." *Herald Tribune*, December 8, 2006. http://www.heraldtribune.com/article/20061208/BREAKING/61208009.

Handwerk, Brian. "Big Cats Kept as Pets across U.S., Despite Risk." *National Geographic*, October 9, 2003. http://news.nationalgeographic.com/news/2002/08/0816_020816 _EXPLcats.html.

Humane Society. "Dangerous Exotic Pets: Big Cats." Humane Society of the United States. May 24, 2013. http://www.humanesociety.org/issues/exotic_pets/facts/dangerous -exotic-pets-big-cats.html?credit=web_id85539248.

International Fund for Animal Welfare. "Big Cats and Public Safety Protection Act." IFAW.org, 2013. http://www.ifaw.org/sites/default/files/BigCatsPublicSafety_0.pdf.

Nyhus, P. J., R. L. Tilson, and J. L. Tomlinson. "Dangerous Animals in Captivity: Ex Situ Tiger Conflict and Implications for Private Ownership of Exotic Animals." *Zoo Biology*, 22 (2003): 573–586.

Pacelle, Wayne. "The Captive Wildlife Safety Act." Shambala, accessed December 12, 2014. http://www.shambala.org/education_capsafetyact.htm.

Slater, Lauren. "Wild Obsession: The Perilous Attraction of Owning Exotic Pets." *National Geographic*, April 2014. http://ngm.nationalgeographic.com/2014/04/exotic-pets/slater-text.

"Summary of State Laws Relating to Private Possession of Exotic Animals." Born Free USA, accessed December 12, 2014. http://www.bornfreeusa.org/b4a2_exotic_animals_summary.php.

"Wild Animal World, Inc." Wild Animal World, Inc., accessed December 12, 2014. http://www.wildanimalworld.net/.

4

ANIMAL RIGHTS CAMPAIGNS
ELICIT PRAISE
AND CONDEMNATION

"PETA'S EFFORTS HAVE CROSSED THE LINE OF FREE SPEECH AND FIRST AMENDMENT PROTECTION"

- **Document:** Statement of Jonathan Blum, senior vice president of public affairs at Yum! Brands, at *Animal Rights: Activism vs. Criminality*, a hearing before the U.S. Senate Committee on the Judiciary.
- **Date:** May 18, 2004.
- **Where:** Washington, D.C.
- **Significance:** From the 1980s through the early twenty-first century, animal rights activism acquired a considerably more combative and even radical tone. Led by organizations like People for the Ethical Treatment of Animals (PETA), which crafted animal rights campaigns for maximum shock value and media exposure, corporations and industries engaged in activities that injured or killed animals for food, clothing, or research purposes felt intensifying pressure to change their practices and policies. Most of these "corporate campaigns" by PETA and other animal rights groups complemented the more traditional campaigns decided to convince consumers to embrace vegetarianism or reject products made by harvesting fur or other animal parts.

  Some corporations and industry groups responded to these offensives by altering their business operations. But others, like the KFC restaurant chain, adopted a more defiant stance. When accused by PETA of tolerating or even condoning massive and cruel animal rights abuses by its leading suppliers of chickens, KFC defended its animal welfare record. It also counterattacked, accusing PETA of a pattern of intimidation that amounted to psychological terrorism. The primary points of emphasis in this counterattack can be found in this congressional testimony from Jonathan Blum, a senior vice president of public affairs at YUM! Brands Inc., KFC's parent company.

DOCUMENT

Good morning. My name is Jonathan Blum. I'm Senior Vice President of Public Affairs at Yum! Brands. We're the world's largest restaurant company, with about 33,000 restaurants around the globe—we own Taco Bell, Kentucky Fried Chicken, Pizza Hut, Long John Silver's, and A&W All-American Foods. We operate in about 102 countries and have revenues of $8.4 billion, with system sales exceeding $24 billion since the majority of our system is franchised.

I'm here today to talk with you about a "corporate campaign" that's been waged against KFC for about three years by an organization called People for Ethical Treatment of Animals, or PETA.

What I'd like to do is outline for you how PETA's efforts have crossed the line of free speech and first amendment protection, to what we consider to be invasion of privacy and harassment of our executives and their families, our neighbors, and others in our community.

In my view, PETA's campaign has been nothing short of what I'd call "corporate terrorism." I hope that by the time I'm done testifying, you'll agree, and perhaps we can do something about this since PETA has waged similar corporate campaigns against a number of our competitors, including McDonald's, Wendy's, Burger King, and Applebees, just to name a few.

As background, PETA has attempted to pressure our company into forcing our suppliers to make changes to their processing methods. They want our suppliers to use a method of gas killing of chickens rather than humane processing techniques that have been perfected for years.

What PETA ultimately wants is a vegetarian or vegan world. No consumption of meat, no poultry, no pork, no fish, no leather goods, and no dairy products.

Not very likely in our society.

To be clear, KFC does not own any farms or processing facilities. We buy our chickens from the same trusted companies you do when you buy chicken in the supermarket—companies like Tyson, Pilgrim's Pride, and Goldkist, among others. KFC buys about 5% of all the chicken in the United States.

Rather than calling on the farms or processing companies to consider the changes PETA recommends, PETA has focused its attention on KFC. They have attempted to disrupt our supply chain and pressure KFC to force our suppliers to make the changes PETA seeks.

Changes that are impractical, unnecessary, unproven and very costly. In fact, it is our estimate that these changes, if implemented, would cost our company over $50 million.

Our suppliers have told us they will not implement these changes—they'd rather not provide us with chicken than make the changes PETA demands. Of course, that would make PETA very happy, as it would be a step toward a vegetarian world.

First, let me assure that we have fully studied this matter, and we believe our suppliers are acting responsibly in the area of animal welfare.

In fact, we established an animal welfare advisory council, comprised of many of the world's leading experts in this area, and they concur with our analysis.

We audit our suppliers throughout the year to be sure they are following our guidelines, and each of them has signed an agreement with us that they will honor our strict supplier code of conduct.

And we took an industry leadership position by working with our association to adopt animal welfare guidelines for poultry farm[s].

So we're comfortable with our current actions.

When we resisted making the changes PETA demanded, they began to escalate their campaign and moved from rhetoric and dialogue, to harassment and threats.

They've enlisted the help of a number of celebrities, from Paul McCartney and Pamela Anderson, to Russell Simmons, Richard Pryor, Dick Gregory, and Bea Arthur.

They've spread misinformation in the press, and have lied about facts that simply don't exist. They've placed billboards on highway across the country doing the same, and disparaging our brand.

They've picketed at our headquarters, in front of our restaurants and those of our franchises, legally handing out leaflets and flyers, and have attempted to gain access to our business meetings.

They've placed a proxy statement before our shareholders, attempting to cause us to change our course of business.

We're perfectly fine with PETA exercising their First Amendment [rights], and acting within their legal rights.

We're strong supporters of free speech and shareholders' rights, and we're glad we live in a country that protects these activities.

We are also fine with communication to us in a normal business manner, contacting us at work or through normal business channels.

But PETA has stepped over the line of protected free speech, and has resorted to pressure through intimidation, harassment, and invasion of privacy.

Let me also say this is no warm and fuzzy, garden variety animal protection group. This is not the ASPCA.

PETA's Bruce Friedrich has admitted under oath in a court of law recently that he has told his supporters at a rally that all fast food restaurants should be bombed or exploded, and he would say "hallelujah" to anyone who perpetrated these crimes.

Let me give you a few examples of what Mr. Friedrich and others have done to KFC, and why several of us have 24-hour a day, 7-day a week police protection around the clock at our homes during frequent periods throughout the year.

I'm sure you can imagine that is a horrible way to raise our children, and puts a strain on our relationships with our family and neighbors—just the thing PETA is hoping for through their psychological intimidation.

Last year, a leader of PETA in Germany was prosecuted for throwing actors' blood-paint and feathers on our chairman and CEO at a public event. PETA then publicized this activity by sending the photo to the news media in a means of embarrassing our CEO. He was accompanied on this trip by members of his family, who were horrified by the behavior.

Additionally, PETA has published on their website the home addresses of several of our executives, including our CEO and me, and has encouraged their 700,000 members to write us regularly and frequently at our homes. Every day letters are sent to our homes from PETA members around the world, imploring us to stop killing chickens.

PETA hired a photographer to use a long-distance telephoto lens to secretly take our photos. When caught, the photographer said these photos were to be used on billboards and in ads showing the faces of quote-unquote chicken killers.

PETA has gone door to door in our neighborhoods handing out packets of misinformation to our neighbors, telling them we are chicken killers and inhumane. They're trying to make us uncomfortable in our community and with friends and neighbors. . . .

On Halloween Eve, PETA came into our neighborhoods dressed in a chicken outfit, and handed out trick or treats to our neighbors' children. Instead of candy, PETA gave these little kids videotapes of chickens being slaughtered and the packets of misinformation previously mentioned. Imagine the horror on these kids faces as they went home and played these new videos.

PETA's Friedrich sent me an e-mail threatening me by telling me "I shouldn't sleep easy at night."

PETA has made nasty phone calls and sent letters to the homes of our board of directors.

They found our CEO's mother in Kansas, and called her on the phone, then followed up with a letter to her. They similarly contacted the president of KFC's parents, and our CEO's sister on her cell phone.

PETA has gone to the church where several of our executives attend, and have disrupted services and marched in front with banners and slogans that are less than flattering. . . . .

On Christmas Eve, PETA's Friedrich and his wife dressed as Santa and an elf, drove onto our CEO's property, disrupting his holiday and scaring his 9-year-old nephew by leaving a bag of coal and videotape of chickens being slaughtered. When they were forced off the property by the police, they proceeded to my home just a few minutes away.

They trespassed on my property, and fortunately my family and I were out of town. But the police cited the Friedrichs for criminal trespass, and last week they were convicted by a jury in criminal court.

I could go on and on about PETA's campaign of corporate terrorism. This goes beyond free speech. It's pure intimidation, and frankly, it has only served to strengthen our resolve. We won't capitulate to PETA's demands, or deal with corporate terrorists.

You might say that any individual action I've just mentioned isn't enough to even be concerned about. And we'd agree.

But when you string all these actions together, along with dozens of others over a three-year period, and recognizing that they all have been designed to attack us personally, not corporately, hopefully you'd agree that enough is enough.

We should tell PETA and others that this type of corporate terrorism won't be tolerated. I'm sure the majority of PETA's 700,000 members have no idea of the types of personal intimidation their leadership has resorted to. The members are probably good folks who love animals. But PETA's leadership act like an animal-worshipping cult, intimidating anyone who doesn't agree with their philosophy.

You can do something about this by making it a criminal act for any animal rights activist to personally harass or intimidate an executive, or cause a business disruption in the way PETA has done to us. Let's not wait until someone gets hurt physically. Surely the perpetration of continued and repeated psychological infliction is enough to classify this as a crime.

I'd also . . . urge Congress to consider eliminating PETA's tax free status, as they benefit from the tax laws designed to help not-for-profit organizations. Their corporate terrorist activities do not warrant this benefit.

Source: Statement of Jonathan Blum. *Animal Rights: Activism vs. Criminality. Hearing Before the Committee on the Judiciary, United States Senate, 108th Congress, 2nd Session,* May 18, 2004. Washington, DC: U.S. Government Printing Office, 2005, pp. 34–38.

ANALYSIS

Later in the day, some elements of Blum's testimony were denounced as untruthful by PETA spokesperson Lisa Lange. But in the months and years that followed, Blum and other KFC and YUM! executives continued to condemn PETA's tactics as harassment that should not be protected by First Amendment free speech guarantees.

PETA continued to campaign against the operating practices of KFC and its principal chicken suppliers, and in Canada, at least, their relentless criticism paid off. In 2008 KFC Canada, which operates independently from its American counterparts, agreed to make sweeping changes to its operations to address PETA concerns about living conditions and inhumane slaughtering methods. In the United States, however, KFC and its suppliers refused to make any concessions to animal rights activists.

PETA's public relations campaign against KFC is ongoing, and it has almost certainly convinced some American consumers to boycott the chain. PETA has not derailed KFC's operations, however. To the contrary, as of 2014 approximately 18,000 KFC outlets were operating in 115 countries and territories around the world. YUM! Brands, Inc., meanwhile, ranks as the world's largest restaurant company in terms of system units with nearly 37,000 outlets in more than 110 countries and territories. Jonathan Blum remains a top executive with the company as well. In March 2012 he was named chief public affairs officer and global nutrition officer (while still holding his title of senior vice president) at YUM! Brands.

FURTHER READING

"Animal Welfare," YUM! Brands, accessed December 13, 2014. http://www.yumcsr.com/food/animal-welfare.asp.

McNeil, Donald G., Jr. "KFC Supplier Accused of Animal Cruelty." *New York Times*, July 20, 2004. http://www.nytimes.com/2004/07/20/business/kfc-supplier-accused-of-animal-cruelty.html.

"PETA to Drop Its Lawsuit against KFC," *Entrepreneur*, September 12, 2003. http://www.entrepreneur.com/article/64216.

Smith, Wesley J. *A Rat Is a Pig Is a Dog Is a Boy: The Human Cost of the Animal Rights Movement.* New York: Encounter Books, 2010.

"PETA HAS A CAMPAIGN TO REFORM TRULY HEINOUS FORMS OF CRUELTY SUPPORTED BY KFC"

- **Document:** Statement of Lisa Lange, vice president of communications for PETA, at *Animal Rights: Activism vs. Criminality*, a hearing before the U.S. Senate Committee on the Judiciary.
- **Date:** May 18, 2004.
- **Where:** Washington, D.C.
- **Significance:** Since its founding in 1980 by animal rights activists Ingrid Newkirk and Alex Pacheco, PETA has become one of the most visible animal rights organizations around the world. Known for its confrontational style, undercover investigations, and media-savvy use of public demonstrations and sympathetic celebrities, PETA has jumped to the forefront of the animal rights and welfare crusade in the United States. In the process, however, the organization became a symbol of extreme animal rights fanaticism to various sectors of the meat industry, fur farmers, and organizations and businesses that utilize animals for research, entertainment, and other purposes. In this excerpted congressional testimony, a PETA spokesperson offers a rebuttal to claims of illegal harassment leveled against the group by an executive for KFC, the fast-food chain that became a target of PETA demonstrations in the early 2000s. In doing so, the spokesperson offers insights into the group's philosophy and provocative style of activism.

DOCUMENT

My name is Lisa Lange. I am the Vice President of Communications for PETA, People for the Ethical Treatment of Animals.

The testimony of Jonathan Blum, public affairs director for KFC's parent company (Yum!), before this Committee on May 18, 2004, is a lesson in how today, the fast-food and other industries, including the tobacco, alcohol, and lumber industries, are unashamedly distorting the truth in order to protect their interests at the expense of democracy and American freedoms, as well as how KFC and others in those industries are trying to take advantage of fears of real terrorism to improperly insulate themselves against public criticism and protest regarding their practices.

PETA has a campaign to reform truly heinous forms of cruelty supported by KFC. For the first two years of our campaign, it consisted solely of patiently writing letters to KFC to seek meetings and to persuade KFC to see the worth of adopting options like humane controlled-atmosphere killing and mechanized gathering, which would greatly reduce the fear and pain of birds who are still shackled and often scalded alive, subjected to broken and painfully bruised wings and legs from rough handling, and more.

A supporter of People for the Ethical Treatment of Animals (PETA) demonstrates in New York City in May 1993 by wearing red paint and leghold traps to protest a fur fashion show. PETA is well known for its dramatic and highly visible displays in support of the animal rights movement. (Hulton Archive/Getty Images)

This campaign has always been carried out through the peaceful, legal exercise of our right to free speech and in no other way. Mr. Blum and the executives he speaks for know this and know that any statement to the contrary is deliberately false.

It may be uncomfortable for KFC's executives and their families to hear what we have to say about their cruel practices, to read our placards, to know that we have introduced ourselves to their neighbors and often engaged these good people in discussion, and to find that we have delivered our petitions to their doors, called their relatives to ask for assistance, pled our case to their associates, and, in the case of several of our members and staff, given up Christmas Day with our own families to appeal peacefully to KFC executives at their place or worship, but these activities are all protected by the First Amendment. Nonetheless, KFC has made a choice to deceive the public, the consumer, and, now, the United States Senate about the nature of our campaign, and we intend to defend and continue to exercise our rights to state our opinions and to stick up for animals who cannot defend themselves.

Every discussion and interaction between PETA and KFC has, on our part, been polite and respectful of the laws of this land. In one case, and one case alone, PETA's Bruce Friedrich, whose comments and position were deliberately mischaracterized in Mr. Blum's testimony, was cited, along with Dr. Alka Chandna, and charged with minor offenses. Contrary to Mr. Blum's statement to the Senate, all charges were dismissed against Dr. Chandna, and she is preparing to sue the police officers who acted in KFC's interest rather than to protect the public's constitutional rights. These arrests were improper and will be shown to be so (for instance, the arresting officer admitted under oath that he would not have issued any citations if the people had not been with PETA). Both Dr. Chandna and Mr. Friedrich, who were dressed as an elf and as Santa Claus, respectively, were cited after pulling into Mr. Blum's driveway to deliver, as pre-announced, a gift of a small bag of coal. They had been in touch with the police and had had a police escort for approximately 1 mile before being blocked into the driveway as they exited their vehicle.

If peacefully approaching a front door is now a criminal act, someone had better advise the Jehovah's Witnesses and the Girl Scouts who sell cookies in their neighborhoods that they are in danger of going to jail. Mr. Friedrich was found guilty—we believe wrongly—of a fineable offense only, not a crime, as defined by Kentucky law. Although he received just a $24 fine, which he paid, he is appealing that conviction on principle. No one has, at any time, interrupted or attempted to interrupt any church service or even approached the entrance to a church. The peaceful assembly that Mr. Blum deliberately mischaracterized was held on a public sidewalk and involved holding signs appealing for mercy on Christmas Day for the chickens needlessly suffering because of KFC's failure to make basic reforms in its suppliers' catching, housing, and killing methods.

Nor is it true that anyone from PETA has, on any occasion, made any threats or intimidating or even rude remarks to anyone at KFC. . . . Furthermore, contrary to Mr. Blum's testimony . . . no videos showing bloody footage or videos of any sort have been given to children in KFC executives' neighborhoods at Halloween or at any other time. Some videos, clearly marked with their content, i.e., "KFC Cruelty," have been handed to parents. . . .

I am attaching the full text of the e-mail message sent to Mr. Blum and other then-executives at KFC that contains the words "I hope you can't sleep at night," to which Mr. Blum referred. Contrary to Mr. Blum's testimony—in which he actually changes the words used by Mr. Friedrich, yet still attributes them as a direct quote—the e-mail message is not a threat, but an invitation to attend a news conference that PETA was holding in Louisville to announce, ironically, the lawsuit PETA filed to stop KFC from making false statements to the public. . . .

PETA has repeatedly attempted to negotiate with KFC, to meet with its officials, and to engage in productive dialogue . . . and we have written letters and made telephone calls pointing out that, as much as PETA would like a vegetarian world, our campaign to reform KFC only concerns—and will be satisfied by the abatement of—the most egregious of the horrific and remediable abuses inflicted on the 750 million birds KFC acquires from suppliers and slaughterers on contract.

Mr. Blum refers to other fast-food companies, namely Burger King, McDonald's, and Wendy's. PETA did campaign to reform those companies, and reforms were indeed made. McDonald's always states that the reforms had nothing to do with PETA, although we think that they did, but the only important point is that reforms were made and animal suffering reduced. Again, in every campaign, we made extensive efforts to meet with the corporations involved. And when the companies agreed to make reforms, far from continuing the campaign, which Mr. Blum says that PETA will do even when KFC implements our suggestions, PETA immediately withdrew all criticism of these corporations and, indeed, has praised and supported—even advertised—these corporations' reform publicly and on its Web sites. In the case of Burger King, since that corporation introduced a veggie burger, which is now on sale alongside its meat fare, PETA has gone to great lengths to promote that burger and praise the company. . . .

KFC's willingness to mislead the Congress is certainly consistent with the company's past examples of public dishonesty. In fact, PETA had to file a lawsuit last year after KFC refused requests to remove false claims about the care of chickens from its Web site and its consumer-information line scripts. Despite Mr. Blum's public denunciation of PETA and the lawsuit through the media, KFC did not even *attempt* to defend its deceptive practices. Instead, the company avoided further legal proceedings by making sweeping changes to its Web site and consumer-information line scripts. . . .

The changes that PETA has asked KFC to make are not, as Mr. Blum characterized them, "impractical, unnecessary, [and] unproven." While installing the machinery to facilitate speedy yet more humane handling and killing practices would indeed require an initial outlay of several million dollars, these reforms will pay for themselves within the first few years by reducing the amount of meat that is bruised and unusable. . . . Both overseas and in the United States, our recommended changes not only have the endorsement of animal-welfare experts within the industry, but are being implemented by other chicken providers and would afford the hundreds of millions of animals KFC contracts with suppliers to raise and kill a great deal of relief from unimaginable physical suffering and fear.

And contrary to Mr. Blum's assertions, KFC's own "animal welfare" committee members have agreed with PETA that the reforms we suggest are achievable and desirable. Indeed, two previous members of the four-person KFC committee resigned over KFC's failure to implement the committee's recommendations regarding animal welfare, only to be replaced by persons handpicked by KFC for their apparent interest in maintaining the status quo and retaining the archaic slaughtering and handling systems KFC uses. . . .

KFC and its executives would be criminally prosecuted for doing to dogs, cats, or horses what they are doing to equally sentient chickens. KFC and its executives have now added to their abuse of chickens an attempt to abuse the system that allows all Americans to speak freely and to peacefully protest wrongdoing—and PETA's efforts have been uniformly peaceful. As President John F. Kennedy said, "Those who make peaceful change impossible make violent revolution inevitable." While PETA has been the peaceful, if colorful and forceful, voice of those who wish to bring some humane consideration into modern factory farming and mass animal-slaughtering, KFC is attempting to create the very frustrations that would compel other factions of any movement to rise up against the impossibility of properly seeking change.

Source: Statement of Lisa Lange. Animal Rights: Activism vs. Criminality. Hearing before the Committee on the Judiciary, United States Senate, 108th Congress,

2nd Session, May 18, 2004. Washington, DC: U.S. Government Printing Office, 2005, pp. 78–86.

ANALYSIS

Lange's testimony showcases not only the sense of moral urgency and righteousness that drives PETA campaigns, but also the highly dramatic and confrontational actions the organization often employs in service to the animal rights cause. Indeed, PETA's campaigns, which continue to focus on animal suffering and mistreatment in factory farms, the clothing industry, laboratory research, and the entertainment industry, remain predicated on the idea that the best way to force change in business practices is by bombarding target companies with adverse publicity. Over the years, however, even some observers sympathetic to the PETA cause have taken issue with their methods, criticizing them as counterproductive to efforts to arouse public opinion against animal abuses.

The 2004 *Animal Rights: Activism vs. Criminality* hearings did not alter the pro-industry tide of the early 2000s, however. Instead, the hearings—and the pro-industry sympathies of the Bush administration and GOP-controlled Congress —gave additional momentum to KFC and other "animal enterprise" corporations pushing for new legislation to restrict the range of legal protest actions available to animal rights activists, expand the definition of "terrorism" against corporate business practices, and increase punishments for violations. Their persistent lobbying helped pave the way for the passage of the Animal Enterprise Terrorism Act (AETA) of 2006.

That 2006 law did not end the battle between PETA and KFC, however. Their clash, which was on such vivid display at the *Animal Rights: Activism vs. Criminality* hearing, continued unabated. The animal rights organization has maintained a Kentucky Fried Cruelty campaign, first launched in 2003, to shine a spotlight on alleged animal mistreatment by KFC and its suppliers. This campaign has taken an array of forms, including the development of a Kentucky Fried Cruelty Web site (kentuckyfriedcruelty.com), purchases of stock in Yum! Brands, KFC's parent company, for the purpose of introducing shareholder resolutions to "eliminate the worst abuses its chickens suffer," and an estimated 12,000 protest actions outside individual KFC restaurants. For its part, executives with KFC and Yum! Brands continue to maintain that their production processes place a high priority on animal welfare. Otherwise, they have largely adopted a policy of ignoring PETA protest actions across the United States.

The lone break in hostilities between PETA and KFC occurred in Canada in 2008. That year, executives with KFC Canada, which operates separately from KFC establishments in the United States, announced plans to buy dramatically greater quantities of chicken from suppliers who use gas to kill their chickens. This method of slaughter is regarded by PETA as the most painless and humane method available to suppliers. KFC Canada also announced the addition of a vegetarian alternative to their chicken dishes to its menus and a phase-out of some growth hormones and other drugs. In return for these and various other operating changes, PETA agreed to end its Kentucky Fried Cruelty campaign in Canada.

FURTHER READING

Beam, Alex. "The PETA Enthusiast: There's a Fearless Zeal in Using Extremism to Defend the Furred and Finny," *Boston Globe*, July 11, 2013. http://www.bostonglobe.com/opinion/2013/07/10/undying-love-peta/cjgZNoamm2zvm9yG6cI5uL/story.html.

Canadian Press. "Feathers Settle in PETA, KFC Canada Battle," CBC News, June 2, 2008. http://www.cbc.ca/news/feathers-settle-in-peta-kfc-canada-battle-1.769518.

Crisan, Hannah. "PETA: How the Messenger Kills the Message." *Commonplace*, Winter 2009. http://www.mhlearningsolutions.com/commonplace/index.php?q=node/3798.

Hawthorne, Mark. *Striking at the Root: A Practical Guide to Animal Activism.* Washington, DC: Changemakers, 2007.

"History and Resources." KentuckyFriedCruelty.com, n.d. http://www.kentuckyfriedcruelty.com/h-history.asp.

"THE ANIMAL LIBERATION FRONT AND THE EARTH LIBERATION FRONT HAVE BECOME THE MOST ACTIVE CRIMINAL EXTREMIST ELEMENTS IN THE UNITED STATES"

- **Document:** Transcript of the testimony by Federal Bureau of Investigation (FBI) deputy assistant director John E. Lewis before the U.S. Senate Judiciary Committee concerning animal rights terrorism.
- **Date:** May 18, 2004.
- **Where:** Washington, D.C.
- **Significance:** The FBI deputy assistant director provides numerous examples of extreme behavior displayed by animal rights groups who espouse violence in support of their cause. He emphasizes that "the FBI has made the prevention and investigation of animal rights extremists/ eco-terrorism matters a domestic terrorism investigative priority."

DOCUMENT

Good morning Chairman [Orrin] Hatch, and members of the Committee, I am pleased to have this opportunity to appear before you and discuss the threat posed by animal rights extremists and eco-terrorists in this country, as well as the measures being taken by the FBI and our law enforcement partners to address this threat, and some of the difficulties faced by law enforcement in addressing this crime problem.

As you know, the FBI divides the terrorist threat facing the United States into two broad categories, international and domestic. International terrorism involves violent acts that occur beyond our national boundaries and are a violation of the criminal laws of the United States or similar acts of violence committed by individuals or groups under some form of foreign direction occurring within the jurisdiction of the United States.

Domestic terrorism involves acts of violence that are a violation of the criminal laws of the United States or any state, committed by individuals or groups without any foreign direction, and appear to be intended to intimidate or coerce a civilian population, or influence the policy of a government by intimidation or coercion, and occur primarily within the territorial jurisdiction of the United States.

During the past decade we have witnessed dramatic changes in the nature of the domestic terrorist threat. In the 1990s, right-wing extremism overtook left-wing terrorism as the most dangerous domestic terrorist threat to the United States. During the past several years, however, special interest extremism, as characterized by the Animal Liberation Front (ALF), the Earth Liberation Front (ELF), and related extremists, has emerged as a serious domestic terrorist threat. Special interest terrorism differs from traditional right-wing and left-wing terrorism in that extremist special interest groups seek to resolve specific issues, rather than effect widespread political change. Such extremists conduct acts of politically motivated violence to force segments of society, including the general public, to change attitudes about issues considered important to the extremists' causes. Generally, extremist groups engage in much activity that is protected by constitutional guarantees of free speech and assembly. Law enforcement only becomes involved when the volatile talk of these groups transgresses into unlawful action. The FBI estimates that the ALF/ELF and related groups have committed more than 1,100 criminal acts in the United States since 1976, resulting in damages conservatively estimated at approximately $110 million.

The ALF, established in Great Britain in the mid-1970s, is a loosely organized extremist movement committed to ending the abuse and exploitation of animals. The American branch of the ALF began its operations in the late 1970s. Individuals become members of the ALF not by filing paperwork or paying dues, but simply by engaging in "direct action" against companies or individuals who, in their view, utilize animals for research or economic gain, or do some manner of business with those companies or individuals. "Direct action" generally occurs in the form of criminal activity designed to cause economic loss or to destroy the victims' company operations or property. The extremists' efforts have broadened to include a multinational campaign of harassment, intimidation and coercion against animal testing companies and any companies or individuals doing business with those targeted companies. Huntingdon Life Sciences (HLS) is one such company. The "secondary" or "tertiary" targeting of companies which have business or financial relationships with the target company typically takes the form of fanatical harassment of employees and interference with normal business operations, under the threat of escalating tactics or even violence. The harassment is designed to inflict increasing economic damage until the company is forced to cancel its contracts or business relationship with the original target. Internationally, the best example of this trend involves Great Britain's Stop Huntingdon Animal Cruelty (SHAC) organization, a more organized sub-group within the extremist animal rights movement. SHAC has targeted the animal testing company HLS and any companies with which HLS conducts business. While the SHAC organization attempts to portray itself as an information service or even a media outlet, it is closely aligned with the ALF and its pattern of criminal activities—many of which are taken against companies and individuals selected as targets by SHAC and posted on SHAC's Internet website.

Investigation of SHAC-related criminal activity has revealed a pattern of vandalism, arsons, animal releases, harassing telephone calls, threats and attempts to disrupt business activities of not only HLS, but of all companies doing business with HLS. Among others, these companies include Bank of America, Marsh USA, Deloitte and Touche, and HLS investors, such as Stephens, Inc., which completely terminated their business relationships with HLS as a result of SHAC activities. Examples of SHAC activities include publishing on its website as a regular feature "Targets of the Week" for followers to target with harassing telephone calls and e-mails in order to discourage that company or individual from doing business with HLS.

In recent years, the Animal Liberation Front and the Earth Liberation Front have become the most active criminal extremist elements in the United States. Despite the destructive aspects of ALF and ELF's operations, their stated operational philosophy discourages acts that harm "any animal, human and nonhuman." In general, the animal rights and environmental extremist movements have adhered to this mandate. Beginning in 2002, however, this operational philosophy has been overshadowed by an escalation in violent rhetoric and tactics, particularly within the animal rights movement. Individuals within the movement have discussed actively targeting food producers, biomedical researchers, and even law enforcement with physical harm. But even more disturbing is the recent employment of improvised explosive devices against consumer product testing companies, accompanied by threats of more, larger bombings and even potential assassinations of researchers, corporate officers and employees.

The escalation in violent rhetoric is best demonstrated by language that was included in the communiqués claiming responsibility for the detonation of improvised explosive devices in 2003 at two separate northern California companies, which were targeted as a result of their business links to HLS. Following two pipe bomb blasts at the Chiron Life Sciences Center in Emeryville, California on August 28, 2003, an anonymous claim of responsibility was issued which included the statement: "This is the endgame for the animal killers and if you choose to stand with them you will be dealt with accordingly. There will be no quarter given, no half measures taken. You might be able to protect your buildings, but can

Tattoos cover the legs of an animal rights extremist/ecoterrorist who attended a national tour of such groups as the Animal Liberation Front and Earth Liberation Front, who were suspected of committing violent acts. FBI deputy assistant director John E. Lewis testified before a Senate committee investigating animal rights terrorism in May 2004. (AP Photo/Fred Hayes)

you protect the homes of every employee?" Just four weeks later, following the explosion of another improvised explosive device wrapped in nails at the headquarters of Shaklee, Incorporated in Pleasanton, California on September 26, 2003, another sinister claim of responsibility was issued via anonymous communiqué by the previously unknown "Revolutionary Cells of the Animal Liberation Brigade." This claim was even more explicit in its threats: "We gave all of the customers the chance, the choice, to withdraw their business from HLS (Huntingdon Life Sciences). Now you will all reap what you have sown. All customers and their families are considered legitimate targets.... You never know when your house, your car even, might go boom.... Or maybe it will be a shot in the dark.... We will now be doubling the size of every device we make. Today it is 10 pounds, tomorrow 20 ... until your buildings are nothing more than rubble. It is time for this war to truly have two sides. No more will all the killing be done by the oppressors, now the oppressed will strike back." It should be noted that the FBI Joint Terrorism Task Force in San Francisco has identified and charged known activist Daniel Andreas San Diego, who is currently a fugitive from justice, in connection with these bombings. While no deaths or injuries have resulted from this threat or the blasts at Chiron and Shaklee, it demonstrates a new willingness on the part of some in the movement to abandon the traditional and publicly stated code of nonviolence in favor of more confrontational and aggressive tactics designed to threaten and intimidate legitimate companies into abandoning entire projects or contracts.

Despite these ominous trends, by far the most destructive practice of the ALF/ELF to date is arson. The ALF/ELF extremists consistently use improvised incendiary devices equipped with crude but effective timing mechanisms. These incendiary devices are often constructed based upon instructions found on the ALF/ELF websites. The ALF/ELF criminal incidents often involve pre-activity surveillance and well-planned operations. Activists are believed to engage in significant intelligence gathering against potential targets, including the review of industry/trade publications and other open source information, photographic/video surveillance of potential targets, obtaining proprietary or confidential information about intended victim companies through theft or from sympathetic insiders, and posting details about potential targets on the Internet for other extremists to use as they see fit.

In addition to the upswing in violent rhetoric and tactics observed from animal rights extremists in recent years, new trends have emerged in the eco-terrorist movement. These trends include a greater frequency of attacks in more populated areas, as seen in Southern California, Michigan and elsewhere, and the increased targeting of Sport Utility Vehicles (SUVs) and new construction of homes or commercial properties in previously undeveloped areas by extremists combating what they describe as "urban sprawl." Eco-terrorists have adopted these new targets due to their perceived negative environmental impact. Recent examples of this targeting include the August 1, 2003 arson of a large condominium complex under construction near La Jolla, California, which resulted in an estimated $50 million in property damages; the August 22, 2003 arson and vandalism of over 120 SUVs in West Covina, California; and the arson of two new homes under construction near Ann Arbor, Michigan in March 2003. It is believed these trends will persist, as extremists within the environmental movement continue to fight what they perceive as greater encroachment of human society on the natural world.

The FBI has developed a strong response to the threats posed by domestic and international terrorism. Between fiscal years 1993 and 2003, the number of special agents dedicated to the FBI's counterterrorism programs more than doubled. In recent years, the FBI has strengthened its counterterrorism program to enhance its abilities to carry out these objectives.

Cooperation among law enforcement agencies at all levels represents an important component of a comprehensive response to terrorism. This cooperation assumes its most tangible operational form in the Joint Terrorism Task Forces (JTTFs) that are established in FBI field divisions across the nation. These task forces are particularly well-suited to respond to terrorism because they combine the national and international investigative resources of the FBI with the expertise of other federal law enforcement and local law enforcement agencies. The FBI currently has

84 JTTFs nationwide, one in each of the 56 Field Offices, and 28 additional annexes. By integrating the investigative abilities of the FBI, other federal law enforcement and local law enforcement agencies, these task forces represent an effective response to the threats posed to U.S. communities by domestic and international terrorists.

The FBI and our law enforcement partners have made a number of arrests of individuals alleged to have perpetrated acts of animal rights extremism or eco-terrorism. Some recent arrests include eco-terror fugitive Michael James Scarpitti and accused ELF arsonist William Cottrell. Scarpitti, commonly known by his "forest name" of Tre' Arrow, was arrested by Canadian law enforcement authorities on March 13, 2004 in British Columbia. Scarpitti had been a fugitive since August 2002, when he was indicted for his role in two separate ELF-related arsons that occurred in the Portland, Oregon area in 2001. William Cottrell was arrested by the FBI's Los Angeles Division on March 9, 2004, and indicted by a federal grand jury on March 16, 2004 for the role he played in a series of arsons and vandalisms of more than 120 sport utility vehicles that occurred on August 22, 2003 in West Covina, California. Those crimes resulted in more than $2.5 million in damages.

Between December 8, 2003 and January 12, 2004, three members of an ELF cell in Richmond, Virginia entered guilty pleas to federal arson and conspiracy charges, following their arrests by the FBI Richmond Division and local authorities. Adam Blackwell, Aaron Linas and John Wade admitted to conducting a series of arson and property destruction attacks in 2002 and 2003 against sport utility vehicles, fast food restaurants, construction vehicles and construction sites in the Richmond area, which they later claimed were committed on behalf of the ELF. In addition, the FBI Richmond Division, working in concert with the Henrico County Police Department, successfully identified, disrupted and prevented another arson plot targeting SUVs by a second, independent ELF cell in February 2004. The four members of this alleged cell, all juveniles, are currently awaiting trial on federal and state charges.

In February 2001, teenagers Jared McIntyre, Matthew Rammelkamp, and George Mashkow all pleaded guilty, as adults, to Title 18 U.S.C. 844(i), arson, and 844(n), arson conspiracy. These charges pertained to a series of arsons and attempted arsons of new home construction sites in Long Island, NY, which according to McIntyre were committed in sympathy of the ELF movement. An adult, Connor Cash, was also arrested on February 15, 2001, and charged under federal statutes for his role in these crimes. Cash is currently on trial in federal court for charges of providing material support to terrorism. The New York Joint Terrorism Task Force played a significant role in the arrest and prosecution of these individuals.

Despite these recent successes, however, FBI investigative efforts to target these movements for identification, prevention and disruption have been hampered by a lack of applicable federal criminal statutes, particularly when attempting to address an organized, multi-state campaign of intimidation, property damage, threats and coercion designed to interfere with legitimate interstate commerce, as exhibited by the SHAC organization. While it is a relatively simple matter to prosecute extremists who are identified as responsible for committing arsons or utilizing explosive devices, using existing federal statutes, it is often difficult if not impossible to address a campaign of low-level (but nevertheless organized and multi-national) criminal activity like that of SHAC in federal court.

In order to address the overall problem presented by SHAC, and to prevent it from engaging in actions intending to shut down a legitimate business enterprise, the FBI initiated a coordinated investigative approach beginning in 2001. Investigative and prosecutive strategies were explored among the many FBI offices that had experienced SHAC activity, the corresponding United States Attorneys' Offices, FBIHQ, and the Department of Justice. Of course, the use of the existing Animal Enterprise Terrorism (AET) statute was explored. This statute, set forth in Title 18 U.S.C., Section 43, provides a framework for the prosecution of individuals involved in animal rights extremism. In practice, however, the statute does not reach many of the criminal activities engaged in by SHAC in furtherance of its overall objective of shutting down HLS.

As written, the AET statute prohibits traveling in commerce for the purpose of causing physical disruption to an animal enterprise, or causing physical disruption by intentionally stealing, damaging or causing the loss of property used by an animal enterprise, and as a result, causing economic loss exceeding $10,000. An animal enterprise includes commercial or academic entities that use animals for food or fiber production, research, or testing, as well as zoos, circuses and other lawful animal competitive events. Violators can be fined or imprisoned for not more than three years, with enhanced penalties if death or serious bodily injury result.

While some ALF activities have involved direct actions covered by this statute, such as animal releases at mink farms, the activities of SHAC generally fall outside the scope of the AET statute. In fact, SHAC members are typically quite conversant in the elements of the federal statute and appear to engage in conduct that, while criminal (such as trespassing, vandalism or other property damage), would not result in a significant, particularly federal, prosecution. However, given SHAC's pattern of harassing and oftentimes criminal conduct, and its stated goal of shutting down a company engaged in interstate as well as foreign commerce, other statutory options were explored at the federal level in order to address this conduct. Ultimately, prosecution under the Hobbs Act (Title 18 U.S.C., Section 1951) was the agreed upon strategy.

The theory advanced to support a Hobbs Act prosecution was that the subjects were (and continue to be) engaged in an international extortion scheme against companies engaged in, or doing business with companies engaged in, animal-based research. In furtherance of this scheme of extortion, the victims are subjected to criminal acts such as vandalism, arson, property damage, harassment and physical attacks, or the fear of such attacks, until they discontinue their animal-based research or their association with or investment in companies such as HLS, engaged in animal-based research.

However, as a result of the Supreme Court's 2003 decision in *Scheidler v. National Organization for Women*, the use of the Hobbs Act in prosecuting SHAC was removed as an option. In the *Scheidler* decision, the Supreme Court held that, while activists may be found to illegally interfere with, disrupt or even deprive victims of the free exercise of their property rights or their right to conduct business, this activity does not constitute extortion as defined under the Hobbs Act unless the activists seek to obtain or convert the victims' property for their own use.

Currently, more than 34 FBI field offices have over 190 pending investigations associated with ALF/ELF activities. Extremist movements such as the ALF and the

ELF present unique challenges. There is little, if any, known hierarchal structure to such entities. The animal rights extremist and eco-terrorism movements are unlike traditional criminal enterprises that are often structured and organized. They exhibit remarkable levels of security awareness when engaged in criminal activity, and are typically very knowledgeable of law enforcement techniques and the limitations imposed on law enforcement.

The FBI's commitment to address the threat can be seen in the proactive approach that we have taken regarding the dissemination of information. Intelligence Information Reports (IIRs) are used as a vehicle for delivering FBI intelligence information to members of the Intelligence, Policy and Law Enforcement Communities. Since its establishment in March 2003, the Domestic Collection, Evaluation and Dissemination Unit has issued 20 IIRs to the field relating specifically to animal rights/eco-terrorism activity.

The commitment to addressing the threat posed by animal rights extremists and eco-terrorism movements can also be demonstrated by the FBI's proactive information campaign. This campaign has included ongoing liaison with federal, state, and local law enforcement and prosecutors, relevant trade associations and targeted companies and industries. The FBI has established a National Task Force and Intelligence Center at FBIHQ to coordinate this information campaign, and develop and implement a nationwide, strategic investigative approach to addressing the animal rights/eco-terrorism threat in the United States. The FBI has also conducted liaison and cooperated in investigations with foreign law enforcement agencies regarding animal rights extremist/eco-terrorism matters.

In conclusion, the FBI has made the prevention and investigation of animal rights extremists/eco-terrorism matters a domestic terrorism investigative priority. The FBI and all of our federal, state and local law enforcement partners will continue to strive to address the difficult and unique challenges posed by animal rights extremists and eco-terrorists. Despite the continued focus on international terrorism, we in the FBI remain fully cognizant of the full range of threats that confront the United States.

Chairman Hatch and members of the committee, this concludes my prepared remarks. I would like to express appreciation for your concentration on these important issues and I look forward to responding to any questions you may have.

Source: Lewis, John E. "Testimony." Federal Bureau of Investigation. May 18, 2004. http://www.fbi.gov/news/testimony/animal-rights-extremism-and-ecoterrorism.

ANALYSIS

After the attacks of 9/11, the U.S. government developed joint task forces so that various government and law enforcement agencies could pool their resources to track, monitor, and prevent terrorist activities. A common misconception is that these task forces focus solely on international threats or acts, such as those perpetrated by Al Qaeda. However, another significant threat is domestic terrorism, which the U.S. Department of Justice defines as "the unlawful use of *force or violence*, committed by a group(s) ... to *intimidate or coerce* a government, the civilian population, or any segment thereof, in furtherance of *political or social objectives.*" Frequently cited sources of such domestic terrorism include far right-wing anti-government activists and hate groups such as the Ku Klux Klan. But law enforcement and national security agencies have also identified left-wing groups that use acts or threats of violence to combat environmental or animal rights abuses as domestic terrorism threats as well.

On May 18, 2004, FBI deputy assistant director John E. Lewis testified before the U.S. Senate Judiciary Committee about animal rights and environmental terrorism. During his testimony, he focused on the potential dangers of such extremists, the measures being taken to address the threat, and the difficulties faced by the FBI and other law enforcement agencies in combating illegal acts perpetrated by radical activists in the animal rights and environmental movements.

In most instances, ecoterrorist and animal rights extremist groups consist of loosely organized individuals or cells. These groups do not have membership requirements or dues. Instead, to be a member, people must simply take "direct action" against an organization or person that uses animals for research or against anyone who does business with such organizations. This loose affiliation of people makes it particularly difficult to track or investigate.

Two of the most prevalent organizations are the Animal Liberation Front (ALF) and the Earth Liberation Front (ELF). From 1976 until the early 2000s, these two groups committed more than 1,000 criminal acts, resulting in more than $100 million in damages. Although no person has been killed by these activities, critics warned that the potential for serious injury or death is significant.

At first, the "direct action" of these organizations involved criminal activity that caused economic hardships for victim organizations and operations. The ALF and ELF stated that they discourage any act that would harm or endanger "any animal," whether human or nonhuman. The most common tactics employed by these groups tended to be arson, vandalism, and harassment.

The early 2000s, however, saw a dramatic escalation in violence committed by animal rights activists. It started with an increase in violent rhetoric, with individuals threatening organizations with actual bodily harm. Then, in 2003, environmental activist Daniel Andreas San Diego allegedly set off two separate pipe bombs in protest against enterprises engaged in what San Diego considered abusive treatment of animals. The first was detonated at Chiron Corp., a biotechnology company in Emeryville, California; the second bomb exploded at Shaklee Corp., a Pleasanton, California, firm that makes health, beauty, and household products. One of the bombs was wrapped in nails to act as shrapnel with the sole purpose of inflicting bodily harm to anyone within the blast zone. Although no one was injured, the attacks led the FBI to warn that any institution or individual involved in biomedical research is a potential target of future attacks. In April 2009 San Diego became the first domestic environmentalist to appear on the FBI's most wanted list.

In addition, the rhetoric intensified, with threats of larger bombs or even assassination attempts. Soon after the Shaklee attack, an anonymous letter stated, "It is time for this war to truly have two sides. No more will all the killing be done by the oppressors; now the oppressed will strike back."

In addition to the rare but potentially devastating pipe bombs, the ELF and ALF urge members to use arson to damage the property of victim organizations. Individuals can even follow instructions from the ALF and ELF Web sites to create incendiary devices. These arson attacks have resulted in millions of dollars of damage, though, again, no one has been killed by the attacks as of mid-2014.

Since the early 2000s the FBI has more than doubled the number of agents assigned to counterterrorism programs. These agents work with other law enforcement personnel in Joint Terrorism Task Forces (JTTFs) across the nation. According to Lewis, these JTTFs have been effective in responding to the threats posed by domestic terrorists such as animal rights extremists, including ELF arsonist William Cottrell and ecoterrorist Michael James Scarpitti.

However, Lewis expresses deep concern that the more low-level acts perpetrated by ecoterrorists are difficult to prosecute. He argues that although the Animal Enterprise Terrorism (AET) statute establishes a system for prosecuting those involved in animal rights extremism, it does not sufficiently prosecute many of their activities, such as trespassing, vandalism, and harassment. A more promising legal avenue seemed to be the Hobbs Act, which prohibits extortion by force, violence, or fear. However, in 2003, the U.S. Supreme Court held in *Scheidler v. National Organization for Women* that extremists who "illegally interfere with, disrupt, or even deprive victims of the free exercise of their property rights" are not in violation of the Hobbs Act unless they aim to convert the property for their own use.

The FBI continues to devise ways to investigate animal rights extremists and ecoterrorists. Its main tool is communication with national and international law enforcement agencies, targeted organizations, prosecutors, and the public at large. At the National Task Force and Intelligence Center, information on domestic terrorist activities and groups is coordinated, examined, and disseminated to others in order to develop a nationwide strategy for addressing the extremists. Lewis avers that the FBI has made the investigation of animal rights extremists/ecoterrorism matters "a domestic terrorism investigative priority."

FURTHER READING

"Animal Rights Extremism." National Association for Biomedical Research. http://www .nabr.org/animal-rights-extremism/.

Best, Steven, and Anthony J. Nocella. *The Animal Liberation Front: A Political and Philosophical Analysis.* New York: Lantern Books, 2011.

"Ecoterrorism: Extremism in the Animal Rights and Environmentalist Movements." *Anti-Defamation League,* accessed December 13, 2014. http://archive.adl.org/learn/ext_us/ ecoterrorism.html.

Fimrite, Peter. "$50,000 Reward in Chiron Probe; FBI Seeking Fresh Tips on Blast Suspect." *SFGate,* December 5, 2003. http://www.sfgate.com/bayarea/article/50-000-reward-in -Chiron-probe-FBI-seeking-2510197.php.

Greenquist, Brittany. "An Animal Rights Extremist Is America's Most Wanted Terrorist." *RYOT News + Action,* accessed December 13, 2014. http://www.ryot.org/animal -rights-extremist-americas-most-wanted-terrorist/600713.

Liddick, Don. *Eco-Terrorism: Radical Environmental and Animal Liberation Movements.* Westport, CT: Praeger, 2006.

Mackey, Robert. "F.B.I. Calls Animal Rights Activist 'Terrorist.'" *The Lede* (blog). April 23, 2009. http://thelede.blogs.nytimes.com/2009/04/23/fbi-calls-animal-rights-activist -terrorist/?_php=true&_type=blogs&_r=0.

Newkirk, Ingrid. *Free the Animals: The Amazing True Story of the Animal Liberation Front.* New York: Lantern Books, 2000.

Pickering, Leslie James. *The Earth Liberation Front, 1997–2002.* 2nd ed. Portland, OR: Arissa Media Group, 2007.

Rosebraugh, Craig. *Burning Rage of a Dying Planet: Speaking for the Earth Liberation Front.* New York: Lantern Books, 2004.

Smith, Wesley J. *A Rat Is a Pig Is a Dog Is a Boy: The Human Cost of the Animal Rights Movement.* New York: Encounter Books, 2010.

Strand, Rod, and Patti Strand. *The Hijacking of a Humane Movement.* Wilsonville, OR: Doral, 1993.

Young, Peter. *The Animal Liberation Front: Complete U.S. Diary of Actions: The First 30 Years.* U.S.: Voice of the Voiceless Communications, 2010.

"THE ANIMAL LIBERATION MOVEMENT IS A LOOSELY-ASSOCIATED COLLECTION OF CELLS OF PEOPLE WHO INTENTIONALLY VIOLATE THE LAW IN ORDER TO FREE ANIMALS FROM CAPTIVITY AND THE HORRORS OF EXPLOITATION"

- **Document:** This document is a summary of both the animal liberation movement (ALM) and ALF from the ALF itself.
- **Date:** Undated.
- **Where:** England.
- **Significance:** This document, a summary of the ALM's history and philosophy from one of its best-known organizations, provides insights into the actions that the more extreme members of the animal rights movement are willing to take to defend animals from "abuse" or death at the hands of humans.

DOCUMENT

The Animal Liberation Movement (ALM) consists of small autonomous groups of people all over the world who carry out direct action according to certain guidelines. The ALM evolved from the Animal Liberation Front (ALF), which in turn grew out of the hunt saboteur movement in England in the 1970s.

The Animal Liberation Movement is a loosely-associated collection of cells of people who intentionally violate the law in order to free animals from captivity and the horrors of exploitation. As activists in one cell do not know activists in another cell, their non-hierarchical structure and anonymity prevents legal authorities from breaking up the organization. Animal Liberation activists break into any building or compound—be it a fur farm or university laboratory—in order to release and/or rescue animals. They also destroy property in order to prevent further harm done to animals and to weaken exploitation industries economically. Their actions have damaged many operations, shut down others, and prevented still others from ever forming for fear of attack. They may also utilize intimidation to prevent further animal abuse and murder.

The men and women of the Animal Liberation Movement pattern themselves after the freedom fighters in Nazi Germany who liberated war prisoners and Holocaust victims and destroyed equipment—such as weapons, railways, and gas ovens that the Nazis used to torture and kill their victims. Other comparisons would include the Apartheid movement, led by Nelson Mandela, who used and supported violence in the fight for liberation in South Africa, and the current struggle by Palestinians against their Israeli oppressors.

Similarly, by providing veterinary care and homes for many of the animals they liberate, a comparison can be made to the US Underground Railroad movement, which helped fugitive human slaves reach free states and Canada in the 1800s. Whereas corporate society, the state, and mass media brand the liberationists as terrorists, the ALM has important similarities with some of the great freedom fighters of the past two centuries, and is akin to contemporary peace and justice movements in its quest to end bloodshed and violence toward life and to win justice for other species.

On the grounds that animals have basic rights, animal liberationists repudiate the argument that scientists or industries can own any animal as their property. Simply stated, animals have the right to life, liberty, and the pursuit of happiness, all of which contradict the property status that is often literally burnt into their flesh. Even if animal "research" assists human beings in some way, and there are significant doubts that it does, that is no more guarantee of legitimacy than if the data came from experimenting on non-consenting human beings, for the rights of an animal trump utilitarian appeals to human benefit.

The blanket privileging of human over animal interests is simply speciesism, a prejudicial and discriminatory belief system as ethically flawed and philosophically unfounded as sexism or racism, but far more murderous and consequential in its implications. Thus, the ALM holds that animals are freed, not stolen, from fur farms or laboratories, and that when one destroys the inanimate property of animal exploiters, one is merely leveling what was wrongfully used to violate the rights of living beings.

The ALM believes that there is a higher law than that created by and for the corporate-state complex, a moral law that transcends the corrupt and biased statues of the US political system. When the law is wrong, the right thing to do is to break it. This is often how moral progress is made in history, from defiance of American slavery and Hitler's anti-Semitism to sit-ins at "whites only" lunch counters in Alabama.

As the Animal Liberation Movement continues to operate and grow, it will inspire and incorporate numerous other direct action and animal liberation efforts. These range from groups such as the Justice Department and the Animal Rights Militia, who unlike the ALF defend and use violent tactics (such as personnel bombs delivered through the mail) to Compassion Over Killing and Mercy For Animals who break into factory farms to free animals in cages but eschew tactics of property destruction.

History of the Animal Liberation Movement

In 1970s England, animal activists turned from legal tactics of hunt disruption to illegal tactics of sabotage when they grew weary of being assaulted and jailed and sought more effective strategy. A hunt saboteur's group known as the Band of Mercy broadened the focus to target other animal exploitation industries such as vivisection and began to use arson as a potent tool of property destruction. Two of its leaders were arrested in 1974 and released a year later. One, Cliff Goodman, turned snitch and left the movement; the other, Ronnie Lee, deepened his convictions and in 1976 began a new militant group that he called the Animal Liberation Front which would forever change the face of direct action struggle.

Taking shape in the mid-1990s, the numerous anti-vivisection struggles provoking controversy in England can be seen as a second wave of direct action, following the first wave that began in the 1960s with the actions of hunt saboteur groups. The new struggles often overlap with the ALF, but they are also independent of it. Whereas the ALF is an underground movement pursuing illegal tactics such as property destruction, the second wave of direct action is an aboveground presence that disavows the use of sabotage or violence and uses strictly legal forms of pressure.

The second wave of direct action began with attacks on vivisection suppliers. In September 1996, activists began a campaign against Consort Kennels, a dog breeder for vivisection labs. After months of applying intense pressure, they closed the kennel in July 1997 and adopted 200 beagles to loving homes. In September 1997, fresh on the heels of this victory, activists began a campaign against Hillgrove Farm, a vivisection cat breeding operation. The same tactics proved effective and Hillgrove closed in August 1999. Over 800 cats were rescued and re-homed.

From these struggles, the group Stop Huntingdon Animal Cruelty (SHAC) emerged in the late 1990s and quickly became a major force in the UK and US. SHAC's sole focus is to bring down one of the world's worst animal testing laboratories, Huntingdon Life Sciences (HLS). SHAC has pioneered hard-hitting direct action techniques that include jamming email, phone, and fax systems, demonstrations at the homes of targeted individuals, and relentless pressure on secondary companies that provide any services for HLS, be it insurance or laundry cleaning. While SHAC Inc. is an aboveground legal protest movement, the "SHAC movement" resorts to illegal tactics such as property destruction to exert added pressure on HLS and its clients.

Inspired by SHAC's success in weakening HLS and driving its stock prices down, numerous other direct action anti-vivisection groups have sprouted up in England. One such group, SPEAK, has been crucial in shutting down plans to build new animal research facilities at Cambridge University and Oxford University in 2004. Similarly, since 1999, the Save the Newchurch Guinea Pigs (SNGP) movement has been waging a relentless battle to pressure the Chris and John Hall family to close their guinea pig breeding farm in the Staffordshire village of Newchurch.

The ALF had migrated to the U.S. in the early 1980s and is now an international movement in over twenty countries. Learning from other liberation movements from around the world, animal liberation activists have now begun to utilize a wider range of tactics shown to be effective, including the use of force to stop perpetrators of massive violence against non-human animals.

Thus, contemporary direct action movements for animal liberation are diverse, powerful, and effective, and they are growing in sophistication and strength. In Britain, animal liberation movements now threaten the viability of the multibillion dollar vivisection and pharmaceutical industry and therefore pose a serious economic threat. In response to the growing strength of the animal liberation movement on an international level, legal authorities such as the British Home Office and the Federal Bureau of Investigation are taking increasingly strong and repressive measures against it.

Animal liberation will end when animal exploitation ends. Meanwhile, the animal liberation movement is the most active and dynamic justice movement of our time. It is vital, therefore, that we monitor and understand it.

Animal Liberation Guidelines

To liberate animals from places of abuse, i.e., laboratories, factory farms, fur farms, etc., and place them in good homes where they may live out their natural lives, free from suffering.

To inflict economic damage to those who profit from the misery and exploitation of animals.

To reveal the horror and atrocities committed against animals behind locked doors, by performing nonviolent direct actions and liberations.

To hold those who are responsible and complicitous in the abuse, torture and death accountable for the terrorism they commit against innocent, sentient non-human animals.

Any group of people who are vegetarians or vegans and who carry out actions according to these guidelines have the right to regard themselves as part of the Animal Liberation Movement.

These groups, called cells, range from one individual to many individuals working closely together. Activists in one cell do not know the underground activists in another because they choose to remain anonymous.

Since there is not a central organization or membership guide to underground Animal Liberation cells, people are driven only by their own personal conscience or cell decisions to carry out illegal actions. These cells are non-hierarchical in their structure, which allows for only those people involved directly in the action to control their own destiny.

Since there isn't a way to contact any of these individuals (their identity is not known to anyone in the above ground movement), the use of communiqués is one way the underground communicates with the above ground movement. Communiqués can be sent directly to anyone including the press, underground support groups, aboveground animal rights groups, etc.

Because the individuals who engage in underground actions cannot reveal their identities to anyone, a North American Animal Liberation Press Office has been created to try to answer some of the questions as to why these actions may have been carried out, and to place the actions in a historical and philosophical context. Since we do not engage in illegal activities ourselves, we do not know the details of these actions, but we can try to the best of our ability to give you a better understanding of why a particular action may have been carried out.

Source: "History of the Animal Liberation Front." Animal Liberation Front, accessed December 13, 2014. http://www.animalliberationfront.com/ALFront/Premise_History/ALF_History.htm.

ANALYSIS

The history of direct action in terms of animal rights activism dates back to the 1950s, when the League against Cruel Sports stepped up its 30-year effort to ban fox, stag, otter, and hare hunting in the United Kingdom. The league used a variety of tactics in an attempt to prevent cruelty to animals during the hunt. For example, it investigated hunts and published alleged evidence of the cruelty involved in these activities. It also purchased tracts of land and created sanctuaries for hunted animals.

In 1963, John Prestige, a journalist in the United Kingdom, published the story of a pregnant doe that was torn to pieces by hunting dogs after being chased into the center of a village. Prestige decided that the League was not doing enough to stop the cruelty of animal hunts, so in December of that year, he formed the Hunt Saboteurs Association (HSA), which used nonviolent, legal direct action to sabotage hunts. Examples of such actions included covering fox and hare scent trails with essential oils to keep the hounds from being able to track the animals, blowing hunting horns to confuse packs of dogs long enough for their quarry to escape, and using voice calls to distract and confuse hounds and hunters.

Nearly 10 years later, HSA members Ronnie Lee and Cliff Goodman formed a more radical splinter group called the Band of Mercy. This group's aim was to prevent the hunts from even occurring—for example, by slashing the tires of hunt trucks so they could not get to their destination. The early efforts, which were often illegal, were so successful in preventing hunts that the Band of Mercy expanded its purpose and became much more daring in its tactics. In 1973, it learned of a vivisection facility (surgery conducted on living animals for experimental purposes) being built by Hoechst Pharmaceuticals. The activists used the same logic applied to the hunt: if they could prevent the building's construction, they would keep animals from being injured. On November 10, they set the building on fire, causing £26,000 of damage (which today would be nearly £275,000, or almost $500,000). Six days later they set another fire in the same facility to destroy the rest of it. These were the first acts of arson in the attempt to prevent cruelty to animals, but they were definitely not the last.

In August 1974, after two years of successful attacks, Lee and Goodman were arrested and sentenced to three years in prison. After 12 months, they were both paroled. By this time, Lee had become even more militant and soon renamed the Band of Mercy as the Animal Liberation Front. He and 30 new and existing members started a movement that would change the direct action struggle, eventually leading to what is known as the ALM.

The ALM is an underground movement that uses legal and illegal tactics to prevent cruelty to animals. There are no dues or membership requirements. Meetings are not held, and activists often work in isolation from one another. Instead, a variety of autonomous groups from around the world take direct action, often in violation of the law, to release animals from research facilities, cause financial loss to research facilities and those who support them, or destroy the property of such facilities. These groups include the ALF, the more violent Animal Rights Militia (an organization that often delivers mail bombs to vivisection facilities), and Mercy for Animals (an organization that goes undercover to document and publicize cruelty to farm animals).

ALM activists liken themselves to freedom fighters of the past, such as those who fought to liberate war prisoners and Holocaust victims during World War II and destroyed weapons, railways, and even gas ovens. But rather than liberating people, they are liberating tortured and abused animals. They claim that putting human rights above those of animals is speciesism, similar to the racism fought against during the civil rights movement.

The ALF posts a list of guidelines that reflect its philosophy of monitoring and understanding what it calls "the most active and dynamic justice movement of our time." According to the ALF, it follows a nonviolent campaign, in which activists take "all precautions not to harm any animal (human or otherwise)" during the liberation of animals from places of abuse. The ALF also states in its final guideline that it does not perform illegal activities. However, this statement seems in direct contrast to the Web site's description of the ALF as "an underground movement pursuing illegal tactics such as property destruction." In either case, the organization does not condemn other ALM activists who do perform actions that may result in the injury or death of other humans. In fact, in its final guideline, the ALF avers that whenever possible, it will do its best to communicate why other groups may have performed illegal activities, which essentially shows that it approves of any action taken to free animals and destroy organizations that do them harm.

Since its beginnings, the ALM has evolved into a highly effective movement that poses serious threats to the vivisection and pharmaceutical industries. According to the National Association of Biomedical Research, "Criminal activities by the extremists of these groups . . . pose the gravest threat to the biomedical research industry." Due to the ALM's structure of loosely affiliated cells of people working in isolation, law enforcement agencies around the world have a difficult time tracking their activities and prosecuting instances of harassment and vandalism, which often eventually escalate into more serious destruction of property. In fact, in 2009, the FBI added an animal rights activist to its Most Wanted Terrorists list for the alleged bombing of two research facilities in 2003.

FURTHER READING

"The ALF Credo and Guidelines." Animal Liberation Front. http://www.animal liberationfront.com/ALFront/alf_credo.htm.

"Animal Rights Extremism." National Association for Biomedical Research. http://www .nabr.org/animal-rights-extremism/.

"Animal Rights Militia (ARM)." TRAC: Terrorism Research & Analysis Consortium, accessed December 13, 2014. http://www.trackingterrorism.org/group/animal-rights -militia-arm.

Best, Steven, and Anthony J. Nocella. *The Animal Liberation Front: A Political and Philosophical Analysis*. New York: Lantern Books, 2011.

Best, Steven, and Anthony J. Nocella. *Terrorists or Freedom Fighters?: Reflections on the Liberation of Animals*. New York: Lantern Books, 2004.

"The Hunt Saboteurs." *ALiberation*, accessed December 13, 2014. http://aliberation .vegaplanet.org/hunt.sabs.php.

"League against Cruel Sports." *League against Cruel Sports*, accessed December 13, 2014. http://www.league.org.uk/.

Merchant, Brian. "Dangerous Environmental Terrorist/Animal Rights Eco Extremist on
    FBI's Most Wanted List." *Treehugger*, April 24, 2009. http://www.treehugger.com/
    corporate-responsibility/dangerous-environmental-terroristanimal-rights-eco-extremist
    -on-fbis-most-wanted-list.html.
Newkirk, Ingrid. *Free the Animals: The Amazing True Story of the Animal Liberation Front.*
    New York: Lantern Books, 2000.
"Profile: Hunt Saboteurs Association." History Commons, accessed December 13, 2014.
    http://www.historycommons.org/entity.jsp?entity=hunt_saboteurs_association_1.
Smith, Wesley J. *A Rat Is a Pig Is a Dog Is a Boy: The Human Cost of the Animal Rights
    Movement.* New York: Encounter Books, 2010.
"SHAC Ends: We Made History . . . The Future Is Ours." Stop Huntingdon Animal Cruelty,
    accessed December 13, 2014. http://www.shac.net/.
Strand, Rod, and Patti Strand. *The Hijacking of a Humane Movement.* Wilsonville, OR:
    Doral, 1993.
Young, Peter. *The Animal Liberation Front: Complete U.S. Diary of Actions: The First 30 Years.*
    U.S.: Voice of the Voiceless Communications, 2010.

"ZOOS ... MUST CONTINUALLY MAKE ADJUSTMENTS TO HAVE A MEANINGFUL ROLE IN MODERN SOCIETY"

- **Document:** *Animal Care and Management at the National Zoo: Final Report*, which was produced by a committee of experts from the National Academies' Board on Agriculture and Natural Resources and Institute for Laboratory Animal Research.
- **Date:** 2005.
- **Where:** Washington, D.C.
- **Significance:** This report was produced by the Committee on the Review of the Smithsonian Institution's National Zoological Park in response to a series of animal injuries and deaths at the Smithsonian's National Zoo in Washington, D.C., one of the flagship zoos in the entire United States. The panel of experts responsible for the study were critical of the zoo's management, asserting that they found "a longstanding failure of staff to abide by National Zoo policy and procedures. In some cases these failures endanger the safety of the animal collection."

DOCUMENT

After a series of publicized animal deaths at the Smithsonian Institution's National Zoological Park (National Zoo) in early 2003, Congress asked the National Academies to carry out a fast-track, science-based assessment of the quality and effectiveness of animal management and care at the National Zoo's Rock Creek Park facility in downtown Washington DC and Conservation Research Center (CRC) in Front Royal, Virginia. Congress specifically requested that the Academies' report be in two parts: an interim report to be completed within 6 months of the beginning of committee deliberations and a final report. The committee's interim report, released on February 25, 2004, focused on problems in need of immediate attention in the areas of animal care and management, recordkeeping, pest control, and strategic planning. This final report examines whether the institution is responding adequately to concerns raised in the interim report and addresses other aspects of its task, such as strategic planning, human resources, training, and occupational health and safety.

The National Zoo has been through a year of substantial upheaval as it attempts to reverse a decade-long decline in facilities, animal collection, and quality of animal programs. Over the last 12 months, the committee interviewed all levels of zoo staff, examined copious documentation and internal correspondence, received input from concerned members of the public and zoo community, and spent many hours observing operations at the zoo. The committee was presented with persuasive evidence that the zoo has many strengths, including the quality of its science programs and the dedication of its staff. The committee commends the staff of the zoo for the time, energy, and personal commitment that have resulted in an enormous number of positive changes in a short amount of time and thanks the staff for their efforts in fulfilling the committee's requests for documents, which required a substantial amount of staff time.

It is apparent to the committee that the zoo's deterioration evident in the fall of 2003 was the result of long-standing, systemic problems at the highest levels of the zoo's operations. Lack of overall vision, inatttentiveness to American Zoo and Aquarium Association (AZA) and internal evaluations, and laxity in observing federal laws by the management of the zoo and Smithsonian Institution allowed for a system-wide breakdown in communications and responsibilities. This resulted in more than a decade of decline in almost every aspect of zoo operation, until a groundswell of change began in 2000. While some initial efforts at change may have faltered, continued efforts for change have gained momentum. The staff of the National Zoo must be applauded for their efforts that have resulted in noticeable improvement of zoo operations over the past year. Over the last 6 months, they have reorganized their preventive-medicine and nutrition programs and made substantial strides in developing an electronic keeper record system, centralizing their commissary, and establishing performance measures for all levels of the organization that are monitored by senior management. The committee encourages the staff of the National Zoo to continue in a positive direction towards regaining the National Zoo's preeminence in the zoo community.

A rhinoceros sleeps near a barred window. The National Zoo in Washington, D.C., came under scrutiny after a number of animals died between 2000 and 2004. A committee formed at the request of Congress found multiple problems and provided many recommendations for improvement. (Lisa F. Young/Dreamstime.com)

However, several problems need attention if positive changes to ensure animal health and welfare are to continue. These problems include immediate needs identified in the interim report as well as the recommendations made in this final report. Most pressing of these recommendations is the establishment of rigorous animal-care staff training as well as a climate of accountability and personal responsibility. Of equal importance are the completion of renovation or construction of animal facilities and the development of a complete and comprehensive strategic plan.

Other recommendations that must be addressed are the establishment of clear standards of professional behavior at all levels; filling the head positions in the clinical nutrition and pathology departments with highly qualified individuals; and following through on efforts currently underway, such as establishing a comprehensive integrated pest management (IPM) effort, developing electronic recordkeeping systems, and completing and documenting diet evaluations. For the zoo to regain its preeminence in the zoo community, the leadership of the Smithsonian Institution and the zoo must ensure that resources and support continue to flow into the zoo so that it can address these major obstacles. . . .

Collections of wild and exotic animals have been maintained in menageries by the powerful and wealthy since the time of the pharaohs. However, the first known public collection of caged animals to be constructed in a park-like setting was in Vienna, Austria; it was inaugurated in 1752 and opened to the general public in 1779. The term *zoo* originated later, probably in the middle of the 19th century, as an abbreviation for the name of the Zoological Garden in Regent's Park, London. That zoo, which opened in 1828, and the earlier one created at Versailles, near Paris, around the beginning of the 18th century were intended as scientific laboratories for studying live animals. But, like similar zoos established later throughout urban Europe and North America, those institutions quickly became places of entertainment and relaxation for working people. The National Zoological Park (National Zoo) in Washington is a good example. Created in 1889 by an act of Congress, the National Zoo became part of the Smithsonian Institution in 1890. Its original mission was "the advancement of science and the instruction and recreation of the people." The National Zoo quickly became a crowd pleaser, attracting large numbers of visitors from the local populace.

The popularity of zoos continues today. In 2000, over 134 million people visited zoos, aquariums, and wildlife parks accredited by the American Zoo and Aquarium Association (AZA)—more than the combined attendance at professional baseball, football, and basketball events. The popularity of zoos is both a challenge to and a dilemma for modern zoo staffs, which must balance the entertainment value of the zoological park with other equally important and demanding zoo missions. Much has been written about the modern zoo and about how zoos are evolving to keep pace with public tastes, to deal with thorny ethical issues, and to establish and define their roles in conservation, education, and research. The nation's outstanding zoos have transformed themselves over the last 30 years in response to a variety of external pressures and emerging viewpoints. The number of species in a zoo's collection no longer rates it as excellent or poor. Instead, it is how the exhibits are designed, how the animals are managed, the quality of the educational and scientific programs, and, most recently, the efforts to conserve species that determine the quality of an institution. Whether a zoo is successful in achieving and maintaining excellence by reforming its infrastructure and mission depends not only on the financial resources available to it but on focused and dedicated leadership and staff, short- and long-term vision and strategic planning, and organizational structure.

No longer can zoological parks be mere repositories of caged animals organized primarily for public viewing and for observation by a few resident staff scientists. Three related movements appear to have caused zoos to reinvent themselves in the last half century. First, beginning as early as the 1930s at such places as the Bronx Zoo, curators and the educated public became concerned about the physical and psychological well-being of captive animals and about the needs of many of the animals for more space and more hospitable, natural surroundings. What started as a small movement at a few top zoos to improve the lives of the animals has become all but a requirement at accredited institutions and has been limited less by a reluctance to change than by the availability of funds and space. Space is a particular problem at urban zoos, where a new or renovated exhibit can occupy several acres in a compact park setting.

Second, there is an increasing aversion to collecting animals from the wild. Not only has such a practice become expensive and politically charged, it has generally been perceived as counter to the conservation ideal except when a species was hovering on the brink of extinction and needing protection from ultimate destruction or when there was a need to broaden the genetic diversity of a captive species. Nearly 90% of the mammals and 70% of the birds in a modern zoo collection are now bred in captivity under careful management schemes that seek to avoid inbreeding—a commendable improvement over past practice but one that can lead to surplus animals unless properly controlled.

Third, it is recognized that species are becoming extinct at rates unprecedented since the end of the Cretaceous geologic period 65 million years ago, when the dinosaurs disappeared from the earth. The primary cause of this emerging tragedy is human activity with its accompanying destruction and fragmentation of habitat. The concept of the "zoo ark" emerged as a way for zoos to rescue endangered species and possibly to reintroduce them into the wild. Perhaps more important, zoos have positioned themselves, with the support of their members and visitors, as centers for conservation of wildlife.

Each of these ideals—exhibits that cater to animal well-being and public education, captive breeding programs, and survival of species in their natural habitats— has become an essential aspect of the mission of most world-class zoos.

Thus, zoos continue to be popular places of entertainment but must continually make adjustments to have a meaningful role in modern society. At their best, they are organizations dedicated to conservation, education, and science, and they exhibit an array of species to reflect these ideals. At their worst, they are shameless indulgences. Exhibits in a world-class zoo are designed in a manner that is sensitive to the physical and psychologic needs of their animals. The best zoos employ expert veterinarians, pathologists, nutritionists, and other professionals dedicated to the animals they care for and to wildlife conservation. They are institutions of education and learning, providing both on-site and outside training opportunities for their staff and using state-of-the-art electronic communication to assist these efforts.

Modern zoos have become responsive to the unprecedented declines in wildlife population and habitat destruction by promoting captive breeding programs, interinstitutional cooperation, and off-site conservation. Increasingly, they have to be concerned with their public image in the mass media, with raising funds, and with promoting cooperative interactions with other zoos to live up to their core missions. As a result of those activities and responsibilities, zoos have become complex structures that place great demands on leadership and on communication among management, staff, and the general public.

Source: Committee on the Review of the Smithsonian Institution's National Zoological Park. *Animal Care and Management at the National Zoo: Final Report.* Washington, DC: National Academies Press, 2005, pp. 1–2, 11–12.

ANALYSIS

The Committee on the Review of the Smithsonian Institution's National Zoological Park was established in response to a formal request from the U.S. Congress, which has oversight authority over the Smithsonian Institution and the National Zoo. Congress called for the study after the deaths of several animals at the zoo from 2000 to 2004, including the deaths of two Grevy's zebras from cold weather exposure, two red pandas from ingesting rat poison, and a female lion from misdiagnosis of a common medical condition.

The excerpts above provide a brief summary of the problems found during the committee's investigation of National Zoo operations, as well as a historical overview of the evolving mission of zoos—including their importance in wildlife conservation and public education efforts. And while it praised zoo staff for their dedication, it warned that without significant operational reforms and infrastructure upgrades, the National Zoo would be unable to live up to its education and conservation responsibilities.

In the midst of the Committee's investigation, National Zoo director Lucy Spelman, who had come under heavy scrutiny for her management of the zoo facilities and staff, announced her resignation. After the Committee released its findings, the zoo made significant progress in implementing the administrative and animal welfare changes urged in the report. By the close of the decade, it appeared to many that the National Zoo had put the allegations of veterinary malpractice, indifferent animal care, and systemic mismanagement behind it.

In 2013, however, new questions about the zoo were raised after a spate of highly publicized animal escapes, injuries, and deaths. Critics blamed everyone from the zoo's management for cramming too many animals into exhibit spaces to Congress for cutting funding to the zoo (the National Zoo does not charge admission, so it is wholly dependent on Congress to keep its doors open). "The lesser-known species, the less charismatic species aren't getting the attention that they clearly need," charged Cathy Liss, president of the Animal Welfare Institute (Lawrence, 2013). Zoo spokespeople responded that they are making operational changes to fix problems despite diminishing financial support, and they pointed out that in 2013 the park was again accredited by the AZA after what the zoo called "an extensive and rigorous review."

FURTHER READING

Attkisson, Sharyl. "Are There Animal Care Problems at the National Zoo?" CBS News online, December 10, 2013. http://www.cbsnews.com/news/are-there-animal-care -problems-at-national-zoo/.

Barker, Karlyn. "5 Animal Deaths Renew Criticism of Care at Zoo." *Washington Post*, June 29, 2005. http://www.washingtonpost.com/wp-dyn/content/article/2005/06/28/ AR2005062801674.html.

Grimaldi, James V., and Karlyn Barker. "Spelman to Quit Zoo Post," *Washington Post*, February 25, 2004. http://www.washingtonpost.com/wp-dyn/articles/A4949-2004 Feb25.html?referrer%3Demail.

Hancocks, David. *A Different Nature: The Paradoxical World of Zoos and Their Uncertain Future*. Berkeley: University of California Press, 2001.

Kelly, J.D. "Effective Conservation in the Twenty-First Century: The Need to Be More than a Zoo." *International Zoo Yearbook* 35 (2004), pp. 1–14.

Lawrence, Chris. "Report Shows Animal Care 'Severely Lacking' at Smithsonian National Zoo." CNN PoliticalTicker blog, December 13, 2013. http://politicalticker.blogs.cnn .com/2013/12/13/report-shows-animal-care-severely-lacking-at-smithsonian-national -zoo/.

Smithsonian National Zoological Park Web site, accessed December 13, 2014. http:// nationalzoo.si.edu/default.cfm.

"[T]HEY APPEARED AT HOMES WITH A TRUCK THAT HAD A VIDEO MONITOR ON IT DISPLAYING IMAGES OF ANIMALS IN CAGES, AND THEY SHOUTED WITH BULLHORNS OBSCENITIES AND DEFAMATORY STATEMENTS"

- **Documents:** The first document is a transcript of testimony given before Congress by University of Wisconsin physiology professor Michele Basso in support of the Animal Enterprise Terrorism Act. The second document is a fact sheet of the act.
- **Date:** Basso testified before Congress on May 23, 2006; the act was signed into law on November 27, 2006.
- **Where:** Washington, D.C.
- **Significance:** A scientist working with laboratory animals in an attempt to treat Parkinson's disease provides examples of animal rights activists' extreme behavior and testifies in favor of the Animal Enterprise Terrorism Act, which makes vandalism of animal research laboratories a federal crime.

DOCUMENT

Testimony of Michele Basso, Ph.D., Assistant Professor, Department of Physiology, University of Wisconsin

Thank you, Mr. Chairman, Ranking Member Scott, and other Congresspersons for the invitation to speak to you about my experiences.

I am an assistant professor of physiology at the University of Wisconsin. I am also an affiliate of the Wisconsin Regional Primate Center because of my work with nonhuman primates, and our goal is to try to understand the brain mechanisms of Parkinson's disease, which, as you know, is a debilitating disorder of movement.

We work together very closely with neurologists and neurosurgeons who develop state-of-the-art techniques for treating Parkinson's disease, and our goal is to understand how these techniques work and how to improve them in order to increase the quality of life for patients who suffer from movement disorders such as Parkinson's disease.

My experience with animal rights activity began about 3 years or so ago. And two organizations at the University of Wisconsin tried to purchase property immediately adjacent to two of the primate centers located on campus, the Harlow Lab and the Wisconsin Regional Primate Center. They rented it with an option to purchase, and their mission or their goal, stated goal, was to establish a holocaust museum for the monkeys that were killed in the research programs going on at the Primate Center.

The second thing was these two groups also started a meeting on campus monthly called Primate Vivisection, A to Z, where they talk about—or try to engage investigators to discuss animal research and also the use of animals in research. Because of the chancellor at the university's commitment to free speech, of course, these programs continue on campus, and they use university facilities.

Now, I first heard of these activists, the same groups, with respect to a protest that took place at the University of Wisconsin, and with targeting members of the University of Wisconsin at their homes. I was among eight of the faculty members and the academic staff who were targeted. Although they went to the wrong home— they didn't have my correct address—what they did was they appeared at homes with a truck that had a video monitor on it displaying images of animals in cages, and they shouted with bullhorns obscenities and defamatory statements about the persons in the home, went and rang the doorbell and ran away and various activity like that— activities such as that. They also handed out fliers with my photograph and contact information, as well as sort of defamatory statements regarding me and my research.

So in response to this—I was very nervous and concerned about my safety, so I tried to protect myself in two ways. The first was I removed my name from the Internet sites where you can go to the tax assessor's office and find out the property that a person owns by typing in their name. So I removed that from the Website. And the second thing I did was to hire an attorney to quit-claim deed my house into another name so that if someone were to go to the tax assessor's office, they would not be able to find out where I lived or my home address.

But within 2 months' time—less than 2 months, I started to receive magazine subscriptions. First they came slowly, but then they came rather aggressively. I have over 50-plus magazine subscriptions and various paraphernalia. I also received various books, the titles of which are things like fatal—"Oh, What a Slaughter," "Fatal Burn," "Predator," "The Perfect Orgasm," things like this. At the same time, I received two phone calls, voice messages, anonymous voice messages, through a messaging service that said something to the effect of, Hello, Michele, we know you're a monkey killer, and you can't get away from us. We hope you enjoy the magazines that you are receiving. And you will never get away, even though you tried to change the name on your house, things like that. So there were at least two of those messages.

So I guess I can't stress the critical impact that this has had on me and my ability to do my work. And I know that a number of my colleagues across the country experience similar targeting as well as more violent and aggressive—one colleague has had their house windows broken and their yards destroyed in California, for example.

So it's critical, also, to point out that the work that I do is subject to very strict regulations and oversight, and we have at least five animal care and use committees on campus that regulate what we do. And we also abide by the 3R principles for research: We reduce, refine or replace our animal models whenever possible. And when we are doing that already, we are required to justify why we don't do it even more. So working on animals, we believe, is a privilege, and one that we don't take lightly.

So I would like to just thank all of you for considering this important legislation and hearing my testimony. Thank you.

Source: Hearing before the Subcommittee on Crime, Terrorism, and Homeland Security of the Committee on the Judiciary, House of Representatives, 109th Congress, 2nd Session on H.R. 4239. Washington, DC: U.S. Government Printing Office, May 23, 2006. http://www.gpo.gov/fdsys/pkg/CHRG-109hhrg27742/html/CHRG-109hhrg27742.htm.

DOCUMENT

Animal Enterprise Terrorism Act Fact Sheet

- Amends the Animal Enterprise Protection Act of 1992 to give the Department of Justice better tools to respond to recent trends in the animal rights terrorism movement.
- Broadens the definition of animal enterprise to include commercial and academic enterprises that use or sell animals or animal products.
- Addresses the "tertiary targeting" system used by animal rights terrorists by prohibiting the intentional damaging of property of a person or entity having a connection to an animal enterprise. Previously, only the animal enterprise itself was covered by the AEPA of 1992.
- Increases penalties for intentionally causing a person bodily injury or intentionally placing a person in reasonable fear of death or bodily injury.
- Includes penalties based on the amount of economic damage, which does not include lawful boycotts.
- Allows for restitution for the cost of repeating an experiment.
- First Amendment activity is expressly excluded from coverage under the AETA's Rules of Construction.

Source: "Animal Enterprise Terrorism Act: Fact Sheet." 109th Congress, November 27, 2006.

ANALYSIS

In 1992 the Animal Enterprise Protection Act (AEPA) was signed into law. It was supported by many well-funded industries, including biomedical and agribusiness. Lobbyists for these industries stated that the existing laws were not sufficient to prevent costly vandalism and other illegal attacks being perpetrated by animal rights extremists against research facilities and farming enterprises. The passage of AEPA, however, failed to quell the unrest from animal rights activists. To the contrary, radical groups and individuals embraced sabotage of commercial facilities and high-pressure tactics against individual executives and researchers as legitimate weapons in their crusade throughout the 1990s and early 2000s.

Outrage at the tactics employed by radical animal rights groups spurred demands for new legislation that would squarely address their "terrorism" once and for all. One of those who testified in favor of a proposed Animal Enterprise Terrorism Act was Michele Basso, an assistant professor of physiology at the University of Wisconsin (UW). In a statement before Congress on May 23, 2006, Basso documented her experiences with animal rights activists to show her support for the proposed bill.

Basso decried the actions of two organizations on the UW campus. In the first instance, the Primate Freedom Project, headed by founder Rick Bogle, signed a contract to purchase property located within walking distance of two UW primate research facilities. According to Bogle, his group's purpose in purchasing the building was to establish the nation's first animal rights exhibition hall, or what Basso refers to as a "holocaust museum for the monkeys killed in the research programs." In the second instance, the Primate Freedom Project, in conjunction with the Madison Coalition for Animal Rights, presents a series of talks titled "Primate Vivisection, A to Z," where they claim to "provide a window into the hidden world of publicly funded primate experimentation occurring on the UW, Madison campus." Basso asserted that both of these initiatives provided an unfair and distorted depiction of the operations of the primate research facilities at UW.

In addition, Basso described her personal experiences with the activists. According to her testimony, the activist groups targeted Basso and eight other faculty members with various forms of harassment, ranging from shouting obscenities and defamatory statements outside their homes to juvenile schoolyard pranks such as ringing their doorbells and running away. Basso stated that the activists also passed out fliers with each person's photograph and contact information and statements about their alleged practices within the primate research laboratory. According to Basso, she tried various methods to avoid the harassment, but all to no avail. At least in her instance, the activists did not break any laws; their harassment was simply aggravating, allegedly having a severe impact on Basso and her ability to do her work.

Basso's aim in testifying before the Subcommittee on Crime, Terrorism, and Homeland Security was to encourage passage of the AETA, which was also supported by such groups as the Animal Enterprise Protection Coalition (membership of which includes such organizations as Pfizer, Wyeth, and GlaxoSmithKline), the American Legislative Exchange Council, and the Center for Consumer Freedom. The AETA enjoyed bipartisan support in Congress, and on November 27, 2006, President George W. Bush signed the bill into law.

Whereas the AEPA had been a mere one page long, with scant specifics on prosecution and sentencing, the AETA goes into much more detail. Even so, both sides of the animal rights argument have complained that the new law still features too much vague language subject to considerable interpretation.

FURTHER READING

"Animal Enterprise Terrorism Act." National Agricultural Library, United States Department of Agriculture, accessed December 13, 2014. http://www.nal.usda.gov/awic/legislat/pl102346.htm.

"The Animal Enterprise Terrorism Act (AETA)." Center for Constitutional Rights, accessed December 13, 2014. http://ccrjustice.org/learn-more/faqs/factsheet%3A-animal-enterprise-terrorism-act-%28aeta%29.

"Animal Enterprise Terrorism Act (AETA)." Civil Liberties Defense Center, accessed December 13, 2014. http://cldc.org/organizing-resources/animal-enterprise-terrorism -act-aeta/.

Conn, P. Michael, and James V. Parker. *The Animal Research War*. New York: Palgrave Macmillan, 2008.

"A Critical Look at Primate Experimentation at the University of Wisconsin." Primate Vivisection A to Z, accessed December 13, 2014. http://www.madisonmonkeys.com/ 01.17%20atoz%20release.pdf.

Del Gandhi, Jason, and Anthony J. Nocella. *The Terrorization of Dissent: Corporate Repression, Legal Corruption, and the Animal Enterprise Terrorism Act*. New York: Lantern Books, 2014.

Headman, Lynn. "Primate Center Hits Legal Snag." *Badger Herald*, November 28, 2006. http://badgerherald.com/news/2006/11/28/primate-center-hits/#.U6TcO6iSJco.

"National Animal Interest Alliance." Source Watch, accessed December 12, 2014. http:// www.sourcewatch.org/index.php?title=National_Animal_Interest_Alliance.

Potter, Will. "Analysis of the Animal Enterprise Terrorism Act (AETA)." Green Is the New Red, accessed December 13, 2014. http://www.greenisthenewred.com/blog/ aeta-analysis-109th/.

"Text of the Animal Enterprise Terrorism Act." Govtrack.us. November 27, 2006. https:// www.govtrack.us/congress/bills/109/s3880/text.

Ziff, Deborah. "UW-Madison Suspends Researcher over Animal Welfare Problems." *Wisconsin State Journal*, March 19, 2010. http://host.madison.com/news/local/ education/university/uw-madison-suspends-researcher-over-animal-welfare-problems/ article_2df54462-32eb-11df-98ea-001cc4c002e0.html.

"THIS LEGISLATION WILL ... FORCE AMERICANS TO DECIDE IF SPEAKING UP FOR ANIMALS IS WORTH THE RISK OF BEING LABELED A 'TERRORIST'"

- **Document:** Statement of journalist Will Potter at a special House legislative hearing on H.R. 4239, the "Animal Enterprise Terrorism Act."
- **Date:** May 23, 2006.
- **Where:** Washington, D.C.
- **Significance:** The bill that became the Animal Enterprise Terrorism Act was crafted in response to the illegal and widely publicized activities of radical animal rights groups such as ALF and Stop Huntingdon Animal Cruelty (SHAC). These groups engaged in property destruction and other criminal acts to interfere with the operations and commercial activities of businesses and research facilities that, according to the activists, were killing or mistreating animals for profit. Proponents of the AETA said that the legislation would give law enforcement an important new tool in combating "animal rights extremists" and "eco-terrorists." But opponents asserted that it would not stop groups like ALF, which was already engaging in illegal acts punishable by law. They charged that the main impact—in part due to vague language in the bill—would be to suppress free speech, criminalize peaceful acts of protest, and silence whistleblowers who publicized embarrassing information about the workings of the livestock industry or animal research. One of these critics was Will Potter, an environmental journalist who testified before Congress on his concerns about AETA.

DOCUMENT

I am honored to be invited to discuss civil liberties concerns raised by H.R. 4239, the Animal Enterprise Terrorism Act.

I should be clear from the outset, though. I am not a lawyer. I'm not a First Amendment scholar. And I'm not a spokesperson for the animal rights movement, or underground groups.

I'm here because of my freelance reporting. I have written for publications including *The Chicago Tribune*, *The Dallas Morning News*, and *Legal Affairs*. And since 2000, I have closely followed the animal rights and environmental movements, and the corporate-led backlash against them. I've documented an increasingly disturbing trend of "terrorist" rhetoric, sweeping legislation, grand jury witch hunts, blacklists, and FBI harassment reminiscent of tactics used against Americans during the Red Scare. The Animal Enterprise Terrorism Act is a continuation of that trend.

The bill is ostensibly a response to illegal actions committed by underground activists in the name of animal rights. Business groups have lobbied for this legislation for years. And Department of Justice officials have said they need help prosecuting these crimes.

At the same time, they have been patting themselves on the back for arresting so-called "eco-terrorists." Just this weekend, four individuals were indicted for the 1998 fire at a Vail ski resort.

Earlier this year, the government rounded up over a dozen environmental activists in the Northwest for property crimes. And on top of that, six animal activists were convicted in March of "animal enterprise terrorism" and other charges.

If committee members want law enforcement to focus resources on the animal rights and environmental movements, that's already being done. The government has been able to make arrests and convictions using existing laws.

This legislation will not help solve crimes. It will, however, risk painting legal activity and non-violent civil disobedience with the same broad brush as illegal activists. It takes the administration's "you're either with us or against us" mentality of the War on Terrorism and applies it to activists.

This legislation criminalizes any activity against an animal enterprise, or any company connected to an animal enterprise, that causes "economic damage." That includes the replacement costs of lost or damaged property or records, the costs of repeating an interrupted or invalidated experiment, and "the loss of profits."

That clause, "loss of profits," would sweep in not only property crimes, but legal activity like protests, boycotts, investigations, media campaigning, and whistle-blowing. It would also include campaigns of non-violent civil disobedience, like blocking entrances to a laboratory where controversial animal testing is taking place.

Those aren't acts of terrorism. They are effective activism. Businesses exist to make money, and if activists want to change a business practice, they must make that practice unprofitable. That principle guided the grape boycotts of the United Farm Workers, the lunch-counter civil disobedience of civil rights activists, and the divestment campaigns of anti-apartheid groups.

Those tactics all hurt profits. And those tactics, if directed at an animal enterprise, would all be considered "terrorism" under this bill. In fact, those three examples would probably receive stiffer penalties, because they caused "significant" or "major" economic damage or disruption. In other words, the more successful that activists are, the greater terrorist threat they become under this bill.

It is my understanding at the time of drafting this testimony that proposed changes might exclude "expressive conduct (including peaceful picketing or other peaceful demonstration) protected from legal prohibition by the First Amendment." It is a positive, yet incremental, first step to include peaceful picketing. However, the bill does not specifically exclude other activity like boycotts, whistleblowing, undercover investigation, and non-violent civil disobedience.

Furthermore, the inclusion of "trespassing" in damaging and disruptive activity puts undercover investigators and whistleblowers further at risk. Undercover video and photography undoubtedly impact profits. They have also led to prosecutions, animal welfare reforms, and a more informed democratic process on these issues.

Exceptions are made in the bill for disruption or damage "that results from lawful public, governmental, or business reaction to the disclosure of information about an animal enterprise." But this is no safeguard. For instance, undercover investigators and whistleblowers may cause financial loss for a company beyond the losses related to third party reactions. Companies may argue that salaries for undercover investigators, increased internal security, and extensive employee background checks are added costs of doing business because of activists. In short, this exemption seems to pose more questions than it answers.

You probably have noted that I have not focused on the clauses of this legislation dealing with significant bodily injury or death caused by activists. Those provisions are each problematic, but they are also, in some ways, non-issues. It's unlikely that even illegal, underground activists like the Animal Liberation Front would be impacted. Their actions, such as releasing mink from fur farms, spray-painting buildings, and arson, have not claimed a single human life.

This legislation will impact all animal activists, even if they never enter the courtroom. It will add to the chilling effect that already exists because of "eco-terrorism" rhetoric by corporations, lawmakers, and law enforcement. Through my interviews with grassroots animal rights activists, national organizations, and their attorneys, I have heard widespread fears that the word "terrorist" could one day be turned against them, even though they use legal tactics.

They point to full-page anonymous ads in both *The New York Times* and *The Washington Post* this month, labeling animal rights activists "terrorists." The ads promote a website, www.nysehostage.com, that says "anti-business activists" like the Teamsters, Communication Workers of America and Greenpeace could be the next "eco-terrorists." Media campaigns by the Center for Consumer Freedom and other industry groups have used similar rhetoric to smear legal activist groups.

Activists also feel that the government is disproportionately focusing resources and attention on the animal rights and environmental movements. They cite reporting by *Congressional Quarterly* that showed the Department of Homeland Security does not list right-wing terrorists on a list of national security threats.

Those groups have been responsible for the Oklahoma City bombing, the Olympic Park bombing in Atlanta, violence against doctors, and admittedly creating weapons of mass destruction, but animal rights activists still top the domestic terrorist list.

This legislation will add to this fear and distrust, and will force Americans to decide if speaking up for animals is worth the risk of being labeled a "terrorist," either in the media or the courtroom. That's not a choice anyone should have to make.

Animal rights activists have been among the first victims of this terrorist scaremongering, but if it continues they will not be the last. Changes in the Supreme Court seem to have revitalized the anti-abortion movement, which, unlike the animal rights movement, has a documented history of bloodshed. But there's also a potential for backlash if upcoming elections alter the balance of power in Washington. Some anti-abortion organizations, like the Thomas More Society, have already raised concerns that this legislation could become a model for labeling other activists as terrorists.

All Americans should be concerned about this trend, regardless of how they feel about animal rights. The word terrorism should not be batted around against the enemy of the hour, to push a partisan political agenda. Public fears of terrorism since the tragedy of September 11th should not be exploited for political points. I urge you to reject this legislation in its entirety, and ensure that limited anti-terrorism resources are not spent targeting non-violent activism.

Source: Statement of Will Potter, Legislative Hearing on H.R. 4239, the "Animal Enterprise Terrorism Act." House Committee on the Judiciary, Subcommittee on Crime, Terrorism, and Homeland Security, May 23, 2006. Washington, DC: Government Printing Office, 2006, pp. 21–24. http://www.gpo.gov/fdsys/pkg/CHRG-109hhrg27742/html/CHRG-109hhrg27742.htm.

ANALYSIS

According to Potter and other critics who testified at the hearing, the AETA amounted to nothing more than a cynical, manipulative scheme by agricultural interests and the pharmaceutical industry, and their political allies, to use post-9/11 security fears to protect corporate profits from embarrassing revelations about inhumane practices. They say that by essentially criminalizing any actions that cause economic harm to an animal enterprise, the law casts a shadow over all sorts of First Amendment–based activism. The whole *point* of picket lines, boycotts, and other peaceful forms of protest against businesses, they say, is to convince the public that the company in question does not deserve their patronage.

The civil liberties concerns raised by Potter and other opponents of AETA failed to derail the legislation, however. The final version of the Animal Enterprise Terrorism Act was passed by unanimous consent in the U.S. Senate on September 29, 2006. The Senate version, identical in most respects to H.R. 4239, passed the House on November 13 and was signed into law by President George W. Bush on November 27.

AETA has been used infrequently by prosecutors since its passage—a fact that some animal rights advocates attribute to its "chilling effect" on free speech. Legal challenges to the law on constitutional grounds have been filed, but none have as yet been upheld or otherwise shaken its foundations. Since 2006, meanwhile, several states have passed or are considering so-called "ag-gag" laws that criminalize undercover journalism or whistleblowing activities that expose animal abuses in slaughterhouses and concentrated animal feeding operations (CAFOs), also known as factory farms. Animal rights advocates contend that AETA and newer "ag-gag" measures are all part of an industrial "green scare" campaign. "Neither the AETA nor ag-gag laws are aimed at protecting businesses from illegal radical activism," declared Rachel Meeropol of the Center for Constitutional Rights, which has been at the forefront of legal challenges to AETA. "Existing law already punishes vandalism, harassment, and fraud. Rather, these laws aim to protect animal industries from radical *ideas*. Animal rights activists want to fundamentally change the way we view animals: to get us to see animals not as food, textiles, test tubes, or performers, but as individuals with lives worth living" (Meeropol, 2014).

FURTHER READING

Lovitz, Dara. *Muzzling a Movement: The Effects of Anti-Terrorism Law, Money, and Politics on Animal Activism*. New York: Lantern Books, 2010.

Meeropol, Rachel. "Activists Are Fighting to Speak. Are You Willing to Listen?" *Huffington Post*, March 3, 2014. http://www.huffingtonpost.com/the-center-for-constitutional -rights/activists-are-fighting-to_b_4716986.html.

Sheppard, Kate. "Are Animal Rights Activists Terrorists?" *Mother Jones*, December 21, 2011. www.motherjones.com/environment/2011/12/are-animal-rights-activists -terrorists.

Smith, Wesley J. *A Rat Is a Pig Is a Dog Is a Boy: The Human Cost of the Animal Rights Movement*. New York: Encounter Books, 2012.

"IN THIS SPECTACLE, DOGS AND ROOSTERS ARE OFTEN DRUGGED TO MAKE THEM HYPER-AGGRESSIVE AND FORCED TO KEEP FIGHTING EVEN AFTER SUFFERING SEVERE INJURIES"

- **Document:** Comments made by U.S. senator Patrick Leahy (D-VT) in favor of passage of the Animal Fighting Prohibition Enforcement Act.
- **Date:** April 10, 2007.
- **Where:** Washington, D.C.
- **Significance:** The Animal Fighting Prohibition Enforcement Act, which received strong bipartisan support in the wake of revelations that star quarterback Michael Vick of the NFL's Atlanta Falcons was deeply involved in pit bull fighting operations, amended the Animal Welfare Act to strengthen prohibitions against animal fighting.

DOCUMENT

ANIMAL FIGHTING PROHIBITION ENFORCEMENT ACT OF 2007

The PRESIDING OFFICER. The clerk will report the bill by title. The legislative clerk read as follows:

A bill (H.R. 137) to amend Title 18 United States Code to strengthen prohibitions against animal fighting, and for other purposes.

There being no objection, the Senate proceeded to consider the bill.

Mr. LEAHY. Mr. President, this bill has broad bipartisan support with more than 300 co-sponsors in the House. The companion Senate bill is S. 261. The lead Senate sponsor is Senator CANTWELL. There are 30 Senate cosponsors. The Senate Judiciary Committee considered and voted to report the bill favorably on March 8, 2007, and the Senate bill is on the Senate Business Calendar. The legislation in similar forms has passed one or both Houses of Congress several times. The bill also has strong endorsements ranging from the American Veterinary Medical Association to the poultry industry to hundreds of law enforcement groups nationwide. The bill has been endorsed by the United States Department of Agriculture, the Humane Society of the United States, and numerous other animal rights and law enforcement groups, including more than 400 police departments.

This bill contains a clarifying amendment like the one we adopted in the Senate Judiciary Committee to ensure that it does not affect legitimate hunting activities.

Animal fighting is cruel. In this spectacle, dogs and roosters are often drugged to make them hyper-aggressive and forced to keep fighting even after suffering severe injuries. The animals are enclosed in a pit that they cannot escape, and often are killed during the fights.

Animal fighting also spawns other criminal conduct, and endangers public safety. Animal fighting is often associated with illegal gambling, narcotics trafficking, public corruption, and gang activity. Cockfighting has been identified as a pathway for the spread of bird flu, and banning animal fighting is an important step to protect against this pandemic.

Federal anti-animal fighting legislation is already on the books, but this new law brings penalties for animal fighting more in line with other penalties for animal cruelty and creates new tools for law enforcement to enforce these laws nationwide. Those engaged in animal fighting ventures must know that this crime is serious and will be punished as a felony.

Source: "Animal Fighting Prohibition Enforcement Act of 2007." Congressional Record, Vol 153 No 57, Tuesday April 10, 2007, p S4317. http://www.gpo.gov/fdsys/pkg/CREC-2007-04-10/html/CREC-2007-04-10-pt1-PgS4317-2.htm.

ANALYSIS

In 2007 dogfighting was dragged from the deepest shadows of American culture and into the public spotlight when investigators arrested—and later convicted—NFL quarterback Michael Vick for operating a dogfighting ring on his property. Dogfighting is considered one of the most serious forms of animal cruelty and abuse because it causes great suffering for the animals involved. Many animal welfare advocates also voice concern about children and adults who are exposed to this violence and become desensitized to it.

In response to the sickening accounts of dogfighting that accompanied the Vick scandal, Congress crafted the Animal Fighting Prohibition Enforcement Act, which was signed into law by President George W. Bush on May 3, 2007. The bill amends the Animal Welfare Act by prohibiting the "sale, purchase, transportation, or delivery of dogs and other animals in interstate or foreign commerce where the animals will be used for fighting." It also prohibits the "sale, purchase, transportation, or delivery in interstate or foreign commerce of any knife, gaff, or other sharp instrument used in a bird-fighting venture." The law effectively strengthens prohibitions against animal fighting in all 50 states. It established such activity as a felony punishable by a term of up to three years in prison and a fine of $250,000.

The original Senate bill was introduced by U.S. senators Maria Cantwell (D-Washington), John Ensign (R-Nevada), Arlen Specter (R-Pennsylvania), and Dianne Feinstein (D-California). A public statement written by U.S. senator Patrick Leahy (D-Vermont), chairman of the Senate Judiciary Committee, in favor of the act, was given on April 10, 2007. Leahy has been heavily involved in animal rights issues at the government level.

Animal welfare advocates applauded this bill because it provides law enforcement officials with new tools to go after and dismantle illegal dogfighting and cockfighting groups throughout the country. Currently, dogfighting is illegal in all 50 states and cockfighting became illegal in all 50 states when Louisiana became the last state to ban the sport. Many groups have endorsed this legislation, including the majority of the animal humane organizations, the U.S. Department of Agriculture, the American Veterinary Medical Association, the National Chicken Council, the National Sheriffs' Association, and numerous law enforcement agencies across the country.

Despite the federal ban on dogfighting and cockfighting, the underground animal fighting industry continues to thrive. Determined to stamp out this practice, Leahy and other legislators passed another animal fighting law in 2014. This law, referred to as the Animal Fighting Spectator Prohibition Act, further amends the Animal Welfare Act by making it a federal felony for any person to knowingly attend an animal fighting event. It also prohibits people from bringing a minor to one of these events and makes this a separate offense with stricter penalties. This law is considered an upgrade to the Animal Fighting Prohibition Enforcement Act. It provides additional means for law enforcement officers to stop organized dogfighting and cockfighting by specifically targeting the spectators that provide financial support for these illegal events.

The Animal Fighting Spectator Prohibition Act had the support of both the House and the Senate and was introduced into law as part of the Farm Bill in February 2014. This became the fourth time the federal law on animal fighting has been upgraded.

FURTHER READING

"H.R. 137—Animal Fighting Prohibition Enforcement Act of 2007." Congress.gov. https://beta.congress.gov/bill/110th-congress/house-bill/137.

Laufer, Peter. *No Animals Were Harmed: The Controversial Line between Entertainment and Abuse.* Guilford, CT: Lyons Press, 2012.

"S. 261 Animal Fighting Prohibition Enforcement Act." Born Free USA, accessed December 13, 2014. http://www.bornfreeusa.org/legislation.php?p=1060&more=1.

"ANIMAL RESEARCH HAS PLAYED A VITAL ROLE IN VIRTUALLY EVERY MEDICAL ADVANCE OF THE LAST CENTURY FOR BOTH HUMAN AND ANIMAL HEALTH"

- **Document:** Testimony before the U.S. House of Representatives' Committee on Agriculture's Subcommittee on Livestock, Dairy, and Poultry from Steven L. Leary, assistant vice chancellor of veterinary affairs at Washington University in St. Louis, on behalf of the National Association for Biomedical Research.
- **Date:** May 8, 2007.
- **Where:** Washington, D.C.
- **Significance:** Leary speaks of the benefits of using animals for medical research in order to benefit the health of livestock and other animals as well as the well-being of humans.

DOCUMENT

Mr. LEARY. Thank you for allowing me to testify today and for conducting this hearing on animal welfare. By the way, Mr. Chairman, I was born and raised in Des Moines and graduated from Iowa State. It is nice to see you here.

I am testifying today on behalf of the National Association for Biomedical Research. NABR is the only national nonprofit organization dedicated solely to advocating sound public policy that recognizes the vital role of humane animal use in biomedical research, higher education and product safety testing. Founded in 1979, NABR provides the unified voice for the scientific community on legislative and regulatory matters affecting laboratory animal research. NABR's membership is comprised of more than 300 public and private universities, medical and veterinary schools, teaching hospitals, voluntary health agencies, professional societies, pharmaceutical and biotechnology companies and other animal research–related firms.

Animal research has played a vital role in virtually every medical advance of the last century for both human and animal health. Ample proof of the success of animal research can be found in the vast body of Nobel Prize–winning work in physiology and medicine where 68 awardees since 1901 have relied at least in part on animal research. Thanks to animal research, many diseases that once killed millions of people every year are either treatable or have been eradicated all together. Six of the discoveries related to cancer using animals were recognized with the Nobel Prize, among them bone marrow transplantation, cloning of the first gene and the discovery that a normal cell could have latent cancer genes. Animal research for animal health has also resulted in many remarkable life-saving and life-extending treatments for animals. Pacemakers, artificial joints, organ transplants and vaccines contribute to longer, happier and healthier lives for animals. Through research with animals, sciences are learning more every day.

Key findings from a recent national public opinion survey on animal research found overwhelming support. In fact, 81 percent agree with medical and scientific research using laboratory animals if they believe it will help alleviate suffering from a serious disease. Animal research is still a requirement.

Research on animals is in many cases an obligation that prevents humans from being used as medical guinea pigs. The Declaration of Helsinki states that medical research on human subjects should be based on accurately performed laboratory and animal experimentation. Responsible regulation is a very important component of oversight to instill public confidence in animal research. Congress already has provided the mechanism for assurances of proper care and treatment of laboratory animals with the 1966 enactment of the Animal Welfare Act and multiple subsequent amendments. For example, the 1985 amendments require the establishment of the Institutional Animal Care and Use Committee, or IACUC. The IACUC, which is taken very seriously by each research institution, is an internal committee that is charged with reviewing, approving and monitoring research protocols. IACUC approval for a proposed research project must be acquired before any government funds can be secured and any animals used.

Many institutions have gone above and beyond what is required of them by the law. Ninety-nine of the top 100 NIH awardee institutions have voluntarily sought accreditation with the Association for Assessment and Accreditation of Laboratory Animal Care.

In addition, a number of non-animal procedures and tests have been developed to supplement animal research. Computer modeling and in vitro testing serve as valuable adjuncts to basic animal research but there is still no replacement for animal research.

In conclusion, we are all challenged with that delicate balance of ensuring the public trust and the highest standard of care for laboratory animals with a regulatory mandate that still allows the freedom of inquiry so important to medical discovery. We who are directly involved with animal research share this challenge and concern. In fact, it is that very concern which has drawn many of us to choose careers in veterinary medicine or medical research. We too have family members who contract diseases. We too have pets that become ill. For these reasons, we are dedicated to finding ways to cure both human and animal ailments. In the words of the esteemed Dr. Michael E. DeBakey, chancellor emeritus of the Baylor College of Medicine and director of the DeBakey Heart Center: "These scientists, veterinarians, physicians, surgeons and others who do research in animal labs are as much concerned about the care of the animals as anyone can be. Their respect for the dignity of life and compassion for the sick and disabled in fact is what motivated them to search for ways of relieving the pain and suffering caused by diseases."

Thank you, Mr. Chairman and members of the subcommittee again for this opportunity to testify.

Source: Statement of Steven L. Leary, DVM, to the Review of the Welfare of Animals in Agriculture Hearing Before the Subcommittee on Livestock, Dairy, and Poultry of the Committee on Agriculture, House of Representatives, May 8, 2007. 110th Congress, 1st Session. Washington DC: Government Printing Office, 2008, p 20. http://www.gpo.gov/fdsys/pkg/CHRG-110hhrg39809/pdf/CHRG -110hhrg39809.pdf

ANALYSIS

The National Association for Biomedical Research (NABR) was established in 1979 as the only nonprofit organization with the professed goal of protecting the practice of animal testing in scientific, academic, and medical institutions. The organization claims that the use of animal subjects to test new drugs, procedures, technologies, and practices is an integral and as-of-yet indispensable component of the contemporary research process. Unless or until scientific research advances make such testing unnecessary, the NABR asserts that responsible research on animals is the only viable way to administer, assess, and refine new and potentially dangerous processes, practices, and treatments in an applied, nontheoretical environment.

NABR is principally an advocacy group, representing over 300 hundred institutions that depend on the practice of animal testing for some or all of their studies. It also advises its members on the ethical and humane treatment of research animals as a means of ensuring that the practice can continue without being eroded by animal-rights groups.

In the short speech above, the U.S. House of Representatives' Committee on Agriculture's Subcommittee on Livestock, Dairy, and Poultry heard from one of the leading voices in the field of animal research. Leary, who at the time of his testimony had over 20 years of experience directing laboratory animal medicine training programs, echoes the organization's position that animal testing is a vital part of the modern research process, providing the only way to refine medical developments without having to use human subjects. He claims that the people and institutions responsible for animal testing "are as much concerned about the care of the animals as anyone can be," because their "respect for the dignity of life and compassion for the sick and disabled in fact is what motivated them to search for ways of relieving the pain and suffering caused by diseases." He also points out that animal research has produced great strides in veterinary medicine, thus improving the quality of life for millions of animals.

The hearing at which Leary's testimony was delivered had been called as part of the process of drafting the Food, Conservation, and Energy Act of 2008 (also known as the 2008 Farm Bill), the comprehensive law that determines the agriculture and food policy of the United States. The United States Farm Bill is a piece of legislation, renewed every five years, by which the U.S. government determines the conditions of agricultural and food policy. This omnibus bill covers a broad range of topics, including conservation, food safety and practice, international trade, food and nutrition programs, and marketing.

A subcommittee of the Department of Agriculture called the hearing to inform the legislators responsible for creating the act about the state of animal welfare, in both agricultural and academic contexts. Other people asked to speak during the hearings disagreed with Leary, requesting that the bill include provisions to further restrict or regulate the use of animals as research subjects. However, they were unsuccessful, as the final version of the law made no changes to its predecessor, the Farm Security and Rural Investment Act of 2002, in that respect.

FURTHER READING

Norwood, F. Bailey, and Jayson L. Lusk. *Compassion, by the Pound: The Economics of Farm Welfare*. New York: Oxford University Press, 2011.

Pond, Wilson G., Fuller Warren Bazer, and Bernard E. Rollin. *Animal Welfare in Animal Agriculture: Husbandry, Stewardship and Sustainability in Animal Production*. Boca Raton, FL: CRC Press, 2012.

"Subcommittee on Livestock, Dairy, and Poultry Forwards Farm Bill Recommendations to House Agriculture Committee." May 24, 2007. House Committee on Agriculture. https://agriculture.house.gov/press-release/subcommittee-livestock-dairy-and-poultry -forwards-farm-bill-recommendations-house.

"Subcommittee Reviews the Welfare of Animals in Agriculture." May 8, 2007. House Committee on Agriculture. http://agriculture.house.gov/press-release/subcommittee -reviews-welfare-animals-agriculture.

"PRODUCTION AGRICULTURE HAS NOT AND WILL NEVER BE GIVEN THE CREDIT IT IS DUE BY ANIMAL RIGHTS ACTIVISTS AND THAT WE TOO CARE ABOUT THE WELFARE OF OUR ANIMALS"

- **Document:** This document is testimony in front of the Subcommittee of Livestock, Dairy, and Poultry of the House of Representatives, from Charlie Stenholm, Democratic representative of the 17th District of Texas and member of the House Committee on Agriculture.
- **Date:** May 8, 2007.
- **Where:** Washington, D.C.
- **Significance:** Stenholm speaks in favor of the animal agriculture industries and harshly criticizes the "antics" of several animal rights groups as counterproductive and damaging to American farming families and industries that are the economic lifeblood of rural communities.

DOCUMENT

Mr. STENHOLM. Thank you, Mr. Chairman, Ranking Member Hayes, members of the committee. I appreciate very much the opportunity to testify here today on behalf of all animal agriculture. If you eat or wear clothes, you are affected by agriculture. The industry remains an important part of the United States economy. According to USDA, animal products account for the majority, 51 percent, of the value of U.S. agricultural products, exceeding $100 billion per year.

I am sure many of you went to zoos as a child or will bring your children or grandchildren to one this summer. Caregivers at zoos nationwide care about the welfare of their animals. Many of you probably remember the first time you saw a circus and may attend one when it comes here. The Ringling Brothers Barnum and Bailey Center for Elephant Conservation has one of the most successful breeding programs for endangered Asian elephants outside of Southeast Asia. They care about the welfare of their animals. Just like these groups of animal owners, production agriculture has not and will never be given the credit it is due by animal rights activists and that we too care about the welfare of our animals.

There is one thing though that everyone you will hear from today agrees on. All animals should be treated humanely from birth until death. Now, what you will not hear is an agreement on the facts. Everyone is entitled to their opinions but not everyone is entitled to their interpretation of the facts. You will hear testimony today from several livestock producer associations and they all care about the same thing: ensuring the health and well-being of their animals is their number one priority.

The livestock industry has worked hard both from a legislative standpoint through this committee and through industry guidelines to improve animal welfare conditions. Animal agriculture constantly works to accept new technologies and science and apply them to industry, investing millions of dollars every year to ensure the wellness of their livestock. Producers recognize the need to maintain animal welfare regulations for the safety and nutrition of their livestock, for the conservation of the environment and for the profitability of their operations. But those regulations should be based on sound science from veterinary professionals that best understand animals, working together with legitimate animal use industries.

While the livestock industry has a long history of supporting animal welfare, many activist groups such as PETA, the Humane Society of the United States, and Farm Sanctuary have used falsehoods and scare tactics to push their hidden agendas of fundraising and systematically abolishing all use of animals including production agriculture, zoos, circuses and sporting events. These groups campaign for animal rights, which is not synonymous with animal welfare, using half truths or complete deception. These groups also fail to mention the millions of dollars in fundraising and assets that drive their misguided goals. The Humane Society has accumulated $113 million in assets, has a budget 3 times the size of PETA's, and according to the ActivistCash website, has more than enough funding to finance animal shelters in all 50 States. Yet it only operates one animal sanctuary, Black Beauty Ranch in Texas, which is at full capacity. Now, you will hear later that they are doing more, and that is great, we commend them for it, but they haven't to this point. According to the *Wall Street Journal*, two off-shoots of Humane Society spent $3.4 million on Congressional elections and ballot initiatives, which is more than Exxon Mobil Corporation spent and there is an ongoing investigation by the Louisiana Attorney General to determine if the $30 million the Humane Society fundraised during the Hurricane Katrina crisis has been handled appropriately.

Now, these activist groups use the platform of animal rights to advocate for regulations so strict they will put animal agriculture out of business, which is their real goal. A video recently circulated to Members of Conservation and a video produced by the Humane Society make numerous false claims against the livestock industry. For example, the video suggests that horses are inhumanely transported on double-deck trailers on their way to slaughter, and if a horse does arrive in one of those trailers, the processing facility would not accept it. They say that we are still doing it. It has been against the law since 1995. In addition, numerous truck drivers invested in new trailers at a tremendous investment on their part to comply with the law and agriculture has stepped up once again to improve animal welfare conditions.

Another example of misleading rhetoric by animal rights activists involves the process of captive bolt euthanasia. The previously mentioned videos claim that captive bolt is not humane. Interestingly, however, the 2000 report of the AVMA's panel on euthanasia specifically approves the use of captive bolt as a humane technique of euthanasia for horses. It is also an approved method of euthanasia for pork, cattle and lamb. The captive bolt method meets specific humane requirements set forth by AVMA's panel on euthanasia, USDA and, interestingly, the Humane Society of the United States statement on euthanasia because it results in instantaneous brain death and is generally agreed to be the most humane method of euthanasia for livestock. Watching the end of life for any living creature is not a pleasant experience, even when performed in the most humane manner. However, these groups continue to use human emotion and sensationalism to prey on the public's sensitivity in order to reach their goal of abolishing animal agriculture.

Unfortunately, we all know mistakes happen and laws are broken. We cannot say that any form of euthanasia is perfect. I will not try to convince you or anyone else otherwise. But when these unfortunate incidents occur, appropriate action should be taken. We should not get in the habit of creating arbitrary, uninformed and emotionally based regulations on an industry whose livelihood depends on the health and well-being of its animals. We should not tie the hands of researchers and investors that continually seek improvements in animal welfare practices and we should not tie the hands of producers who work night and day to ensure the quality of life of their livestock so they can provide this country and others with the most abundant, safest, and the most affordable food supply.

In conclusion, Mr. Chairman, professional experts such as AVMA, the American Association of Equine Practitioners and USDA should not have their expertise continue to be questioned by animal rights activists who line their own pockets with donations secured by exploiting and distorting the issues. These groups throw sensationalistic and often staged photos in the faces of those who do not understand it including your fellow Members of Congress not on this committee. What they do not do is use their millions of dollars in fundraising to build animal shelters and provide research for new technologies and procedures or provide truthful information to consumers about animal agriculture industry. Emotions run high and with continued antics by activist groups, the ultimate outcome will be devastating. If animal rights activist groups continue to be successful like we have seen in recent months with the closing of U.S. horse processing facilities, abandonment of animals will increase, animal welfare will decline, honest and legal businesses will close, America's trade balance will worsen, jobs will disappear, family heritage and livelihood will be stolen and the best interest in the welfare of animals will be lost.

As the Agriculture Committee, it is your job and responsibility to keep science and best management practices at the forefront of your decisions when developing legislation. Emotional, feel-good policy is not reasonable for the agricultural industry. As a committee, you are tasked with providing the type of environment for your agricultural constituents and your other constituents, the 99.3 percent of your constituents who enjoy the food that is produced by the .07 percent that in fact are the producers.

Thank you, Mr. Chairman.

Source: Statement of Hon. Charlie Stenholm to the Review of the Welfare of Animals in Agriculture Hearing Before the Subcommittee on Livestock, Dairy, and Poultry of the Committee on Agriculture, House of Representatives, May 8, 2007. 110th Congress, 1st Session. Washington DC: Government Printing Office, 2008, pp. 4–7. http://www.gpo.gov/fdsys/pkg/CHRG-110hhrg39809/pdf/CHRG-110hhrg39809.pdf.

ANALYSIS

Democrat Charles Stenholm served in the U.S. Congress from 1979 to 2004 as the representative for the state of Texas's 17th District, where agricultural interests were an important part of his constituency. During his entire 25 years on Capitol Hill, Stenholm sat on the House Committee on Agriculture, which is responsible for deliberating on agrarian matters, often settling disputes and proposing bills for consideration that fall under the subheading of husbandry. After a Republican redistricting scheme forced him into a heavily Republican district, Stenholm lost his seat in Congress in the 2004 elections. He subsequently began lobbying for various agricultural interests, including three foreign-owned horse slaughtering plants in the United States. As a third-party participant, Stenholm's interests coincided with those of animal agriculture groups, and his testimony is evidence of that interest.

The above hearing took place in response to proposed legislation for the 2008 Farm Bill. The Farm Bill is an omnibus bill that serves to define terms of agriculture, conservation, trade, research, and other components that comprise the proposed legislature for the following five to six years. By the time Stenholm testified in 2007, however, the Farm Bill had also been touched by the issue of animal rights.

In his statement before his former colleagues, Stenholm argues in favor of the rights of animal agriculture groups, explicitly stating that it is in their best interests to maintain the health and welfare of their livestock. As a consequence, he asserts, federal legislation should work in favor of their interests in order to facilitate prosperity and economic growth. Stenholm also emphasizes that the animal agriculture industry comprises 51 percent of the total U.S. agricultural industry, and that the impact of these companies on the economic welfare of American farming and rural communities is immense. He bluntly warns against regulations that would "tie the hands of producers who work night and day to ensure the quality of life of their livestock so they can provide this country and others with the most abundant, safest, and the most affordable food supply."

Stenholm further insists that the campaigns carried out on the part of major activist groups is not in the best interests of the animals, as it purports to be. He claims that their hidden agenda is to deliver a mortal blow to the agricultural industry. Their intentions include implementing "regulations so strict they will put animal agriculture out of business," and "line their own pockets with donations secured by exploiting and distorting the issues." By distorting facts, animal rights initiatives are able to draw on the public's sensitivity to practices like captive bolt euthanasia, which is actually a humane form of euthanasia, according to Stenholm.

Stenholm's testimony exhibits the multifaceted position of agricultural industry proponents in their campaign against animal rights groups. Evidence from the statement suggests a role reversal on the part of animal rights groups and animal agriculture groups. While animal activists are often painted as the facilitators of animal welfare, Stenholm suggests that the animal agriculture industry cares more about the welfare of their animals, as the level of their care affects production. Meanwhile, he argues that animal rights groups are out to do more damage than good by destroying the agricultural industry's income gleaned through animal production.

FURTHER READING

Barnett, Mike. "Charlie Stenholm Garners AFBF's Highest Honor." Texas Farm Bureau. January 19, 2007. http://www.texasfarmbureau.org/newsmanager/templates/TexasAg. aspx?articleid=1321&zoneid=34.

Cheeke, Peter R. *Contemporary Issues in Animal Agriculture*. 3rd ed. Upper Saddle River, NJ: Prentice Hall, 2004.

House Committee on Agriculture, accessed December 13, 2014. http://agriculture.house. gov/.

U.S. House of Representatives, House Committee on Agriculture. "2008 Farm Bill Livestock Title: Supporting Livestock and Poultry Producers." May 10, 2008. http:// agriculture.house.gov/sites/republicans.agriculture.house.gov/files/documents/ title11factsheet.pdf.

"IF OUR FOOD IS SO SAFE, WHY ARE WE SO UNHEALTHY?"

- **Document:** Testimony before the U.S. House Committee on Agriculture, Subcommittee on Livestock, Dairy, and Poultry from Gene Baur, president of the Farm Sanctuary, an organization that is "committed to ending cruelty to farm animals and promoting compassionate vegan living through rescue, education, and advocacy efforts."
- **Date:** May 18, 2007.
- **Where:** Washington, D.C.
- **Significance:** Baur implores Congress to fix existing laws and regulations that, in his words, have failed "to require basic humane consideration for farm animals." He urges changes that would "eliminate the cruelest farming practices" and "bring agricultural practices more into line with societal values."

DOCUMENT

Dear Mr. Chairman and members of the subcommittee, thank you for accepting these comments, which are being submitted for the record in response to statements that were made at the May 8th, 2007 subcommittee hearing regarding farm animal welfare.

At the outset I must respectfully disagree with the opinion expressed at the hearing that individuals in the animal farming industry are best suited to determine appropriate guidelines for the humane treatment of farm animals. Voluntary "humane" standards that have been developed by producer groups are grossly inadequate and demonstrate this point. Agribusiness, like other business, is driven largely by the desire to make a profit, a priority that tends to limit perspective and undermine the ability to objectively assess whether particular farming practices are humane. Rather than critically examining its practices, agribusiness proponents have tended to create rationalizations and "scientific" studies to justify the use of cruel and unnatural farming systems.

During his May 8th testimony, Charles Stenholm defended the veal industry practice of denying calves solid food and fiber. Citing industry sources, he asserted that "it is typically to not give calves fiber because it is not healthy for a calf's developing digestive system." In fact, in a more normal environment (i.e., on pasture), calves start nibbling on grass and obtaining dietary fiber at just a few days old. This brings about the natural, healthy development of their digestive systems. In veal production, denying calves solid food prevents the development of their digestive system. While there may be research to show that veal calves who have been restricted to an all liquid diet can experience digestive ailments when they are suddenly given fiber (e.g. hay), such findings should not be used to justify the veal industry's unhealthy and unnatural feeding regimen wherein calves are denied solid food.

The animal farming industry has developed various questionable practices that have come to be accepted as "normal," and it has tended to defend such practices, sometimes [through] narrowly focused "science." Some veal industry proponents have even said that it's healthier for calves if they are removed from their mothers immediately at birth. While this attitude may serve a certain production oriented mindset, and while it may be possible to cite science to make the point, it does not comport with thousands of years of biological history, and it is rejected by most people who believe that it's better for calves to nurse and be raised with their mothers.

During her testimony, Dr. Gail Golab of the American Veterinary Medical Association (AVMA) mentioned the importance of assessing agricultural systems holistically, and there seemed to be a general acceptance of this concept. However, contrary to this approach, industrial farming proponents tend to look at things in isolated terms and to cite limited "facts" to justify particular practices.

At the hearing, a pork industry representative was asked about sow productivity and responded that sows today are much more productive, and wean more piglets now than in the past. She implied that confining sows in crates helped ensure a better piglet survivability rates and that crating sows makes it less likely that they will lay on and crush their young. She failed to explain that it is common for up to 15% of piglets to die before weaning and for about half of these deaths to occur when piglets are crushed by the sow. Ironically, millions of piglets are crushed by sows in crates every year while industrialized pig farming proponents argue that these crates protect piglets from crushing.

Contrary to the notion that sows need to be confined to protect their piglets, thousands of years of biological history as well as common sense suggests that mother sows instinctively know how to raise their young. When given the chance, sows build nests, and raise their young cooperatively in groups with other sows.

On today's mass production animal farms, cruel procedures are sometimes promoted as a way to improve animal welfare because they minimize problems that are caused by cruel conditions. For example, parts of chickens and turkey beaks are cut off to prevent injuries that could result when birds who are crowded in stressful, inhuman conditions resort to pecking each other. Rather than taking off parts of the birds' beaks, providing an environment that allows normal behaviors and social interactions could help prevent the problem in the first place. But providing animals with more natural environments is generally not considered because it is assumed to be cost prohibitive.

Among the most pervasive underlying justifications for subjecting animals to inhumane, industrialized farming conditions is the notion that such production systems are necessary to produce large quantities of cheap food. But while the price paid at the retail counter for mass produced animal foods may appear low, there are numerous externalized costs of production (e.g. environmental degradation and pollution; resource depletion; destruction of rural communities; human health risks; ethical issues). Our cheap food can actually be very costly.

Producing animal foods requires vastly more land and water resources than producing plant foods, and industrial animal farming is notorious for polluting the environment. Concerns about greenhouse gasses and global warming have garnered the public's attention in recent years, and according to a 2006 report by the United Nations entitled "Livestock's Long Shadow," one of the greatest contributors to this problem is livestock production.

Ironically, while farmers often consider themselves to be staunchly independent, they are also the beneficiaries of billions of dollars of government support. In some cases the assistance is in the form of direct subsidies and payments, but it can also be in the form of tax breaks and preferential access to water and other valuable resources. Some agriculturalists even joke about "farming the government."

There is now a burgeoning societal interest in food production along with increasing opposition to cruel and irresponsible factory farming practices. I strongly urge members of this subcommittee and all members of Congress to examine these matters carefully in the coming months during consideration of the Farm Bill.

We should provide incentives for sustainable, community based farming systems, and discourage the mass production of cheap, unhealthy food that is produced in an inhumane and irresponsible manner. We should critically examine the assumption that our current farming system efficiently produces cheap food, and we should question the often stated belief that the U.S. has the world's safest food supply. If our food is so safe, why are we so unhealthy?

In our current food and farming system, we have seen the emergence and spread of virulent, sometimes fatal, pathogens, like *E. coli* 0157:H7. And, we are also beginning to discover other new diseases. Crowding animals in stressful, unhealthy conditions exacerbates the development and spread of disease while the routine use of antibiotics has contributed to the development of antibiotic resistant bacteria, which are becoming increasingly difficult to combat.

Sick and diseased animals are commonly slaughtered and used for human food in the U.S., contrary to what most citizens believe. Farm Sanctuary petitioned the USDA to eliminate diseased animals from the human food supply in 1998, but our petition was denied, and the USDA explicitly stated that diseased animals could be used for human food. In their March 25, 1999, letter, the USDA said: "The FMIA [i.e. Federal Meat Inspection Act], FSIS [i.e. Food Safety Inspection Service] regulations, and past practices clearly provide for the slaughter and processing of diseased animals for human food."

The USDA even recommends that diseased animals be slaughtered for human food. Regarding to cattle with Johne's diseases, a chronic diarrhea condition in cattle that some people believe may be linked to Crohn's disease in humans, the U.S.D.A. advises, "Culture-positive cattle should be sent to slaughter or rendering." Farm Sanctuary has rescued chickens infected with avian influence from slaughter. Ironically, they were only tested and found to have the disease because they were removed from the slaughterhouse. Otherwise, they would have been slaughtered and consumed without being tested for avian influenza. . . .

In addition to marketing animals with various pathogens and diseases, our industrialized food production system promotes unhealthy eating habits and contributes to the growing prevalence of obesity, diabetes, and other serious health problems in the United States. Officials for the Centers for Disease Control say that Americans do not eat well and advises that improved nutrition can help lower people's risk for heart disease, stroke, some cancers, diabetes, and osteoporosis. And, the Surgeon General has warned that our overweight population and obesity are among our most pressing health challenges, causing hundreds of thousands of human deaths and costing more than 100 billion dollars per year. We should be eating more whole foods, including fruits, vegetables, legumes, and grains, and we should be eating less meat, milk, and eggs. . . .

Numerous athletes and fitness experts have excelled on a vegetarian diet, including Jack La Lanne, an American fitness icon who remains active today in his 90s. It is unfair and inaccurate to malign vegetarian and vegan lifestyles as unhealthy. Dr. T. Colin Campbell, a Cornell University professor and author of *The China Study*, has conducted extensive research on health and diet. Campbell has linked diets rich in animal foods to chronic health problems, and found plant based diets to be healthier.

In closing, I want to touch on what I said at the May 8th hearing. Specifically, while Farm Sanctuary encourages people to consider a vegan lifestyle, we recognize that each person must make their own decision on the matter. But, it's also important for people to make informed decisions, and whether individuals decide to eat animals or not, it is apparent that practices currently employed in production agriculture are repugnant to most citizens.

The law currently fails to require basic humane consideration for farm animals. At the very least, laws should be enacted to eliminate the cruelest farming practices (e.g. veal crates, battery cages, gestation crates, foie gras production) and to bring agricultural practices more into line with societal values. Thank you.

Source: Supplemental Comments by Gene Bauer to the Review of the Welfare of Animals in Agriculture Hearing Before the Subcommittee on Livestock, Dairy, and Poultry of the Committee on Agriculture, House of Representatives, May 8, 2007. 110th Congress, 1st Session. Washington DC: Government Printing Office, 2008, pp. 304–307. http://www.gpo.gov/fdsys/pkg/CHRG-110hhrg39809/pdf/CHRG -110hhrg39809.pdf.

ANALYSIS

The United States Farm Bill is a piece of legislation, renewed every five years, by which the U.S. government determines the conditions of agricultural and food policy. This omnibus bill covers a broad range of topics including conservation, food safety and practice, international trade, food and nutrition programs, and marketing. The 2007 congressional hearing from which the above statement was taken occurred in preparation for the 2008 version of that bill, officially known as the Food, Conservation and Energy Act of 2008. Baur's testimony specifically responded to statements made several days earlier, at a May 8 subcommittee hearing regarding farm animal welfare.

The Farm Sanctuary, which was founded in 1986 by Baur and his team, is an animal sanctuary foundation whose programs rescue farm animals from conditions of factory farming and promotes farming practices deemed more "humane."

The organization's mission statement is "To protect farm animals from cruelty, inspire change in the way society views and treats farm animals, and promote compassionate vegan living." Much of the Farm Sanctuary's work involves the dissemination of information regarding humane practices of animal husbandry. Baur's congressional presentation drew heavily from foundational principles of the organization.

During the May 8 hearings, committee members had stated that "individuals in the animal farming industry are best suited to determine appropriate guidelines for the humane treatment of farm animals." Baur countered by highlighting alleged misconduct on the part of farm industry executives, citing incidents of animal abuse, health violations, and industry guidelines that he considered "grossly inadequate." Baur attributed these practices to internal biases that promoted efficient production conditions over healthy ones: "agribusiness, like other business, is driven largely by the desire to make a profit, a priority that tends to limit perspective and undermine the ability to objectively assess whether particular farming practices are humane."

Baur also referenced data that undermined the prevalent notion that factory farming allowed for inexpensive production of food. Specifically, he charged that other externalized expenses borne by the wider society—"environmental degradation and pollution; resource depletion; destruction of rural communities; human health risks; ethical issues"—rivaled or even exceeded the monetary savings for industry.

Baur also critically explored the use of diseased animals in the production of meat, revealing that USDA regulations allowed for the use of diseased livestock in the production of human food. He also asserted that, while the use of antibiotics in factory farming operations had increased in order to curb the spread of disease, they had also "contributed to the development of antibiotic resistant bacteria, which are becoming increasingly difficult to combat." While scientific evidence was cited in the May 8 hearing that suggested that conditions of factory farms were up to par, Baur argued that this purportedly "scientific" evidence was decidedly biased and too limited in scope.

The final version of the Food, Conservation and Energy Act of 2008 included provisions that promoted the organic production of foods and instituted industry-wide regulations. However, Farm Sanctuary and other animal rights organizations were unable to convince Congress to force changes in animal welfare regulations in the animal agriculture industry.

FURTHER READING

Baur, Gene. *Farm Sanctuary: Changing Hearts and Minds about Animals and Foods*. New York: Simon & Schuster, 2008.

Brown, Jenny. *The Lucky Ones: My Passionate Fight for Farm Animals*. New York: Avery, 2012.

"Explanation of the Federal Animal Welfare Act." National Anti-Vivisection Society, accessed December 13, 2014. http://www.navs.org/legal/animal-welfare-act.

Farm Sanctuary. *Life Behind Bars: An Introduction to Factory Farming*. Watkins Glen, NY: Farm Sanctuary, 2002.

Kirby, David. *Animal Factory: The Looming Threat of Industrial Pig, Dairy, and Poultry Farms to Humans and the Environment*. New York: St. Martin's Press, 2010.

"THE TWO COMPONENTS OF SCIENTIFIC IDEOLOGY ... CREATED A FORMIDABLE BARRIER TO THE AWARENESS OF THE ETHICAL ISSUES INHERENT IN ANIMAL RESEARCH"

- **Document:** "Animal Research: A Moral Science," by Bernard E. Rollin, a bioethicist and professor of philosophy, animal sciences, and biomedical sciences at Colorado State University.
- **Date:** June 2007.
- **Where:** Heidelberg, Germany.
- **Significance:** Rollin demonstrates how scientific ideologies have inhibited the moral discussion regarding animal use in research. He uses moral theory to explain shortcomings in the treatment of research animals and explains how conditions should be improved.

DOCUMENT

Animal Research: A Moral Science. Talking Point on the Use of Animals in Scientific Research

Historically, the scientific community—at least in the USA—did not perceive the use of animals in research as an ethical issue. Anyone who raised questions about the way animals were kept and treated during experiments ran the risk of being stigmatized as an anti-vivisectionist; a misanthrope preferring animals to people; or an ingrate who did not value the contributions of biomedical science to human health and well-being. I received a full barrage of such charges when I drafted and promoted what eventually became two US federal laws to protect laboratory animals: the 1985 Health Research Extension Act and an "Animal Welfare" amendment to the 1985 Food Security Act. Indeed, a reviewer of my book *Animal Rights and Human Morality* (Rollin, 1981)—in which I argue for elevating the moral status of animals and codifying that status into law for laboratory animals—wrote that I "exonerate the Nazis" by comparing the killing of animals for science with the Holocaust, and that the book gives "a false cloak of morality" to attacks on research laboratories (Visscher, 1982).

To be fair, anti-vivisectionists were not much more sophisticated at the time— conceptually or morally. The day after I received the published review, abolitionists criticized the book, castigating me for accepting the reality of science, and scolding me for proposing regulations that would result in short-term improvements for animals, thereby retarding the complete abolition of animal research.

My own experience of being vilified as "anti-science" by the scientific community has been reflected in societal debates on animal research. Although abolitionists argue that using animals in biomedical research produces no benefits for humans, the scientific community has adopted an equally extreme position. The Foundation for Biomedical Research—a non-profit organization in Washington, DC, USA—produced a film in 1984 entitled *Will I Be All Right, Doctor?*. The query in the title is uttered by a frightened child before undergoing surgery; the physician's response is that he will be all right if anti-vivisectionist extremists let scientists get on with their animal testing. When I attended the premiere of the film at the annual meeting of the American Association for Laboratory Animal Science in 1984, before a putatively friendly audience of laboratory animal veterinarians, the only comment came from an attendee who said that he was ashamed to be associated with something pitched lower than the worst anti-vivisectionist propaganda.

Such extreme responses to the anti-vivisection movement date back to the famed physiologist Walter Cannon in the early twentieth century. A background note to a collection of Cannon's writings from 1905 to 1928, produced by the American Philosophical Society, states that "the most vocal defenders of vivisection often argued against all forms of outside interference in medical education and research. They opposed not only the abolition of the use of animals, but even its regulation, maintaining that any concession on their part would lead to dire consequences for medical science" (Cannon, 2000). Little changed after Cannon's writings and before the passage of the US federal laws in 1985. In the decade between 1975 and 1985, I searched scientific journals for reasoned defences of invasive research on animals and found none. What I did find were variations on the theme orchestrated in the film described above. How can we explain this blind spot in what is an otherwise sophisticated and informed community?

In various publications, I have described what I call scientific ideology: a set of basic, uncriticized assumptions about twentieth-century science (Rollin, 2006). In general, ideologies operate in many different areas: religious, political, sociological, economic and ethnic. Therefore, it is not surprising that an ideology about science would emerge—after all, science has been the dominant method of generating knowledge in Western societies since the Renaissance. The ideology underlying modern—post-medieval—science has grown and evolved along with science itself. An important component of that ideology is a strong positivistic tendency, which is still dominant today, to believe that true science must be based on experience only, because the tribunal of experience is the objective, universal judge of what really happens in the world.

If one asks most working scientists what separates science from religion, speculative metaphysics or shamanistic worldviews, they would reply without hesitation that it is an emphasis on validating claims through experience, observation or experiment. This component of scientific ideology can be traced back to Isaac Newton, who proclaimed that he did not feign hypotheses (*hypotheses non fingo*) but operated directly from experience. The fact that Newton operated with non-observable ideas such as gravity or, more generally, action at a distance and absolute space and time, did not stop him from issuing an ideological proclamation that one should not do so.

This insistence on experience as the foundation for scientific research persists today, where it reaches its most philosophical articulation in the reductionistic movement known as logical positivism, which was designed to exclude the unverifiable from science. A classic and profound example of this attitude is Albert Einstein's rejection of Newton's concepts of absolute space and time on the grounds that such talk was not testable. Other targets of positivists' criticisms are Henri-Louis Bergson's hypothesis of a life force (*élan vital*) as separating the living from the non-living, and the embryologist Hans Driesch's postulation of "entelechies" to explain regeneration in starfish.

Although logical positivism took many subtly different and varied forms, the message, as received by working scientists and passed on to students including myself, was that proper science should not tolerate unverifiable statements. This was strengthened further by the British philosopher and logical positivist Sir Alfred Jules Ayer's vastly popular and aggressively polemical book *Language, Truth, and Logic* (Ayer, 1946); it was first published in 1936 and has remained in print ever since. Easy to read and highly critical of wool-gathering, speculative metaphysics and other "soft" and ungrounded ways of knowing, the book was long used in introductory philosophy courses and, in many cases, represented the only contact with philosophy that aspiring young scientists—or even senior scientists—had.

Be that as it may, the positivist demand for empirical verification of all meaningful claims became a mainstay of scientific ideology from the time of Einstein to the present day. Through it, one could in good conscience dismiss religious or metaphysical claims or other speculative assertions not merely as false and irrelevant to science, but in fact as meaningless. Only what could be verified or falsified empirically was meaningful.

What does all this have to do with ethics? Quite a bit, as it turns out. The philosopher Ludwig Wittgenstein, who greatly influenced the logical positivists, once remarked that, if you took an inventory of all the facts in the universe, you would not find that killing is wrong (Wittgenstein, 1965). You cannot, in principle, test the proposition that killing is wrong—it can be neither verified nor falsified. Consequently, in Wittgenstein's view, ethical judgements are meaningless. From this, it was concluded that ethics—and all judgements regarding values rather than facts—are not part of the scientific universe. The slogan that I learned in my science courses in the 1960s, and which is still taught in too many places, is that science is value-free in general, and ethics-free in particular.

This denial of the relevance of ethics to science was taught both explicitly and implicitly. The widely used Keeton and Gould textbook on biological science—in what one of my colleagues calls the "throat-clearing introduction", where the authors pay lip service to the scientific method and provide a bit of history and other "soft" issues before getting down to biological details—declares that "science cannot make value judgments [or] moral judgments" (Keeton & Gould, 1986). In the same vein, Sylvia Mader's textbook *Biology* asserts that "science does not make ethical or moral decisions" (Mader, 1987). The bottom line is that science might provide society with the facts relevant to making moral decisions, but it steers clear of any ethical debate.

That is not, however, the whole story. Positivist thinkers also felt compelled to explain why intelligent people feel inclined to make moral judgements. They argued that when people make assertions such as "killing is wrong", they are only expressing revulsion. "Killing is wrong" really expresses "Killing, yuck!" rather than describing a particular state of affairs. Therefore, a debate over the alleged morality of capital punishment expresses revulsion or approval, and any debate we can engender is really about factual questions such as whether capital punishment acts as a deterrent against murder.

It is therefore not surprising that when scientists are drawn into discussions of ethical issues, they are as emotional as their opponents. The scientific ideology dictates that these issues are nothing but emotional; therefore, the idea of rational ethics is an oxymoron, and he who generates the most effective emotional response "wins". This explains *Will I Be All Right, Doctor?*.

An ethical issue is one that challenges us to apply our concepts of right, wrong, good and bad to a new situation. Before the 1970s, US society had a very limited ethic for animal treatment—it prohibited deliberate, sadistic, overt, purposeless cruelty to animals. Under this definition, no regularly accepted use of animals in agriculture or research that was deemed "to minister to some of the necessities of man" (Colorado Supreme Court, 1896) could be prosecuted, no matter how much pain and suffering it caused. The cruelty ethic and the ensuing laws existed primarily to flush out sadists and psychopaths, who are known to begin inflicting pain and suffering on animals before "graduating" to people. It is not surprising then, that with "cruelty" being the only ethical tool available, opponents of animal research labelled researchers as cruel. Researchers, in turn, chafed at being grouped with psychopaths and were further alienated from approaching their critics rationally.

During the 1970s and 1980s, a growing amount of literature in moral philosophy finally provided a rational approach to the ethics of animal treatment. The first such book was Peter Singer's *Animal Liberation* (1975), followed by my book *Animal Rights and Human Morality* (Rollin, 1981), Tom Regan's *The Case for Animal Rights* (1983), and Steve Sapontzis' *Morals, Reason, and Animals* (1987). These books all discuss animal research from the point of view of moral theory, and argue for a higher moral status for animals. In particular, I pointed out that excluding animals from our moral machinery or concepts could not be justified logically for two reasons.

First, there is no morally relevant difference between humans and animals that justifies excluding animals from what I call "the moral arena" or the full "scope of moral concern". Just as skin colour or gender cannot morally justify discrimination against humans, certain beliefs about animals—for example, that they lack a soul, are "inferior" to humans in power or evolution, and lack reason or language—cannot morally justify their exclusion.

Second, there are positive reasons for including animals in our "moral arena". Most notably, what we do to animals matters to them—as Charles Darwin pointed out, they feel not only pain, but also the full range of emotions that feature in our moral deliberations about humans: fear, loneliness, boredom, frustration, anxiety and so forth (Darwin, 1896). In addition, following Aristotle, I called attention to the nature or *telos* of an animal: the pigness of a pig; the dogness of a dog. Their *telos* can guide our ethical obligations to animals just as human nature guides us in establishing human rights.

When applied to animal research, this analysis has moral implications for invasive experiments. Our social ethic does not allow us to use humans invasively to advance our knowledge or cure human disease without their explicit and informed consent. General benefit does not surpass concern for the individual in Western democratic systems. Indeed, the US Bill of Rights forbids sacrificing the interests of individuals for the general good. Whether this logic would forbid the painless killing of animals for research is another open question, because it seems that animals do not have the cognitive abilities to value life for its own sake; however, applying our ethical machinery to hurting something—even an animal—against its will forces us to conclude that such behaviour is at least highly problematic.

At the very least, the arguments for including animals in the moral arena should give those engaged in invasive research reason to pause and think. The first issue that arises is what morally justifies hurting animals for human benefit—or even to benefit other animals—when we would not feel morally allowed to do so to humans, even though we have done so. The public decried Nazi medical experiments on concentration-camp inmates, even those that produced benefit, and equally condemned the US Tuskegee syphilis study during which doctors deliberately left African-American patients untreated to study the pathology of the disease. In response to the claim that humans can provide informed consent to participate in invasive experiments that benefit other humans, whereas animals cannot, Sapontzis has offered a very clever response: open the cages and we will know if they wish to participate.

Notwithstanding these arguments from philosophers and ethicists, little morally sound discussion has come from the research community. If one presses scientists for a response, it usually takes one of two forms: we are "superior" to animals and can do as we wish; or invasive animal research is justified because it produces more benefit to humans and/or animals than harm to the animals. With respect to the first response, what does superior mean? Does it mean more powerful? If we follow that position, the mugger or rapist is justified in victimizing the weak, which is what much of ethics is designed to prevent. Does it mean intellectually superior? Why should that be morally relevant? Does it mean morally superior? If so, victimizing a sentient organism hardly shows moral superiority.

The second common reply is tendered in terms of cost compared with benefit. Apart from the fact that our consensus social ethic does not accept hurting the minority for the benefit of the majority, this argument is open to a much more practical point: let us assume that invasive animal research is justified only by the benefit produced. It would then seem that the only morally justifiable research would be research that benefits humans and/or animals. But there is in fact a vast amount of research that has not been shown to benefit humans or animals: much behavioural research, weapons research or toxicity testing as a legal requirement are obvious examples, but basic research also often has no clear benefits. Someone might respond that we never know what benefits might emerge in the future, and appeal to serendipity. But if that were a legitimate point, we could not discriminate between funding research likely to produce benefits and that unlikely to do so; however, we do. If we appeal to unknown but possible benefits, we are literally forced to fund everything, which we do not. Even if we disregard the general point about the morality of invasive animal research, we are still left with the fact that much of animal research does not fit with the researchers' own moral justification for it. If one accepts the benefit argument by appealing to utilitarian principles, we are left with the conclusion that the only justifiable animal research is that which produces more benefit than harm—however this is measured.

But this is not all: another moral problem arises. Suppose we ignore both the cost–benefit criteria and the argument questioning the morality of all invasive animal research, which is of course what we do in practice. Would it not then be morally required to treat the animals in the best possible manner commensurate with their use in research? The demand that we do our best to meet their interests and needs, minimize their suffering as much as possible and respect their *telos* seems to be a requirement of common decency, particularly if we are using animals in a way that ignores the moral problems recounted thus far. Sadly, this is not the case.

When I helped to draft the 1985 federal laws for laboratory animals, I needed to know about the deficiencies in animal care to prove to US Congress the need for legislation, which was strongly opposed by much of the research community. What I found could easily be chronicled in a book, but I will restrict myself to two paradigmatic examples: pain control and housing.

Common sense would dictate that one of the worst things one can do to a research animal is to cause unrelieved pain. As animals do not understand sources of pain—particularly the sort of pain inflicted in experiments—they cannot rationalize that it will end soon, and their whole life becomes the pain. This insight has led veterinary pain specialists Ralph Kitchell and Michael Guinan (1989) to surmise that animal pain might be even worse than human pain; after all, humans have hope. Furthermore, pain is a source of stress, and can skew the results of experiments in numerous ways. Therefore, for both moral and scientific reasons, one would expect a crucial emphasis on pain control in painful experiments. If someone were conducting fracture research, for example, one would expect the liberal use of pre-emptive and post-surgical or post-traumatic analgesia—pain relief—because the pain is not the point of the experiment, and unmitigated pain actually impedes healing.

A central component of the 1985 legislation was to mandate control of pain in research animals. Although I knew anecdotally that pain control was essentially non-existent in research, Congress demanded that I prove it, as the vocal portion of the research community opposing the legislation proclaimed that pain was already being controlled—and they were a powerful political lobby. I did a literature search, and found only two papers on animal analgesia, and none on laboratory animal analgesia. Of the two papers, one said, in essence, that there should be pain control, whereas the other described, in one page, what very little was known. Fortunately, this convinced Congress to mandate the control of pain and distress. As I expected, the legislative mandate galvanized the research community, and a literature search today would uncover thousands of such articles.

In the same vein, many veterinarians, typically trained before the mid-1980s, still equate anaesthesia with chemical restraint or sedation. The first US textbooks of veterinary anaesthesia (Lumb 1963; Lumb & Jones, 1973) do not mention pain control as a reason for anaesthesia—instead, it is used to keep the animal still to prevent injury to it or the researcher—and do not mention analgesia at all.

Some of the neglect of pain in animals dates back to the historical roots of veterinary medicine as ancillary to agriculture, which was concerned only with the economic and productive role of the animal, not its comfort. A 1906 textbook of veterinary surgery bemoans the failure of veterinarians to use anaesthesia even for surgery, with the episodic exception of the canine practitioner, whose clients presumably valued their animals enough in non-economic terms to demand anaesthesia (Merillat, 1906).

In the end, the counter-intuitive denial of pain can again be traced back to scientific ideology. The same logic that barred talking about ethics similarly forbade talking about mental states. It was strengthened by the advent of behaviourism in the early twentieth century, which affirmed that, for psychology to become a real science, it needed to eschew discussions about or the study of mental states in humans or animals, and instead study only overt behaviour. This did not significantly affect moral treatment of humans, but certainly reinforced the legitimacy of ignoring pain in animals. The two components of scientific ideology—denial of ethics in science and denial of mental states—worked synergistically to the detriment of laboratory animals and created a formidable barrier to the awareness of the ethical issues inherent in animal research, and the recognition of the pain and distress sometimes created in the process.

As important as reducing the infliction of pain and suffering, which arises only sometimes in research, is the fact that all animals used in research have basic needs and interests, stemming from their biological and psychological natures. It is for this reason that the initial drafts of the 1985 legislation mandated housing and husbandry to meet the nature of all research animals. Unfortunately, this portion of the law was not passed, but it nonetheless created an awareness of 'environmental enrichment' that can only benefit the animals.

In my view, new legislation and, more importantly, the growing societal concern for animals that enabled these laws, have had salubrious consequences for the moral status of animals in research. For one thing, they vividly underscore the fact that society sees invasive animal research as a significant moral issue. For another, they sink the scientific ideology precluding ethical engagement by animal-research scientists. Finally, they have led to what I call the "reappropriation of common sense" with regard to the reality of animal suffering and the need for its control. One can be guardedly optimistic that animal research will evolve into what it should have been all along: a moral science.

FURTHER READING

Ayer, A. J. 1946. *Language, Truth, and Logic*. London, UK: V. Gollancz.

Cannon, W. B. 2000. Walter B. Cannon Papers, 1905–1928. Philadelphia: American Philosophical Society.

Colorado Supreme Court. 1896. *Waters v. The People*, 23 Colo 33. 46: 112–113.

Darwin, C. 1896. *The Expression of the Emotions in Man and Animals*. New York: D. Appleton.

Kitchell, R., and Guinan, M. 1989. "The Nature of Pain in Animals." In *The Experimental Animal in Biomedical Research*, Vol. I. Edited by B. E. Rollin and M. L. Kesel, 185–205. Boca Raton, FL: CRC.

Lumb, W. V. *Small Animal Anesthesia*. Philadelphia: Lea & Febiger, 1963.

Lumb, W. V., and Jones, E. W. *Veterinary Anesthesia*. Philadelphia: Lea & Febiger, 1973.

Mader, S. S. *Biology: Evolution, Diversity, and the Environment*. Dubuque, IA: W. C. Brown, 1987.

Merillat, L. A. 1906. *Principles of Veterinary Surgery*. Chicago: A. Eger.

Regan, T. 1983. *The Case for Animal Rights*. Berkeley: University of California Press.

Rollin, B. E. 1981. *Animal Rights and Human Morality*. Buffalo, NY: Prometheus Books.

Rollin, B. E. 2006. *Science and Ethics*. Cambridge, UK: Cambridge University Press.

Sapontzis, S. F. 1987. *Morals, Reason, and Animals*. Philadelphia: Temple University Press.

Singer, P. 1975. *Animal Liberation: A New Ethics for our Treatment of Animals*. New York: Random House.

Visscher, M. B. 1982. "Review of 'Animal Rights and Human Morality'." *New England Journal of Medicine* 306: 1303–1304.

Wittgenstein, L. 1965. "A Lecture on Ethics." *Philosophical Review* 74: 3–12.

Source: *EMBO Reports* 8, no. 6 (June 2007): 521–25. http://www.ncbi.nlm.nih.gov/pmc/articles/PMC2002540/.

ANALYSIS

Bernard E. Rollin is a current professor of biomedical science, philosophy, and animal science at Colorado State University; an American philosopher; and an author of a number of influential publications on animal rights and ethics. His most widely acknowledged book, *Animal Rights & Human Morality*, draws on moral theory as an application for animal rights, arguing that each animal's needs entitle it to an elevated moral standing that ensures a protection and promotion of its rights. Widely recognized as the "father of veterinary ethics," in 1985 Rollin began designing legislation that would define humane practices for animals in veterinary and scientific settings.

In the above essay, Rollin discussed the foundations for scientific research's deeply rooted ideologies. Modern scientific theory, he proposed, was built upon the back of a philosophical articulation called "logical positivism," which sought to separate science from anything unverifiable. Scientific study, then, could only be defined by verifiable testing, "because the tribunal of experience is the objective, universal judge of what really happens in the world." Thus, moral theory, which does not fall within the realm of experience, was excluded from the umbrella of scientific study.

Rollin argued, however, that moral theory could not be overlooked in regard to what was deemed "ethical treatment" of animals for scientific purposes. A turning point came in the 1980s, when positivistic theory was challenged by a new wave of informed literature and study that sought to reexamine animal rights with respect to moral theory. This literature included Peter Singer's *Animal Liberation*, Tom Regan's *The Case for Animal Rights* (1983), and Steve Sapontzis's *Morals, Reason, and Animals* (1987), as well as Rollin's own work.

Rollin undercut two commonly held scientific justifications for inhumane treatment of animals in research settings. One was that "we are 'superior' to animals and can do as we wish," while the other held that "invasive animal research is justified because it produces more benefit to humans and/or animals than harm to the animals." Rollin addressed the first by stating that any purported form of superiority as grounds for immoral animal research is unjustifiable on moral grounds, be it the physical, moral, or intellectual superiority of humans. "If we follow that position," he asserted, "the mugger or rapist is justified in victimizing the weak, which is what much of ethics is designed to prevent."

In response to the second frequently made claim, Rollin holds that the knowing sacrifice of the minority for the benefit of the majority is deemed immoral by the prevailing social ethic, and that animals, who are the minority, should share protection under this sentiment. On these grounds it would not be ethical to force animals to undergo torture and pain to which they cannot consent.

Further, there is evidence to suggest that the pain experienced by animals may rival, if not exceed, that of humans. Animals, according to veterinary pain specialists Ralph Kitchell and Michael Guinan (1989), lack a crucial element of the human experience that allows for pain to be tolerated: hope. This is an essential factor, according to Rollin: "As animals do not understand sources of pain—particularly the sort of pain inflicted in experiments—they cannot rationalize that it will end soon, and their whole life becomes the pain." Rollin pointed to this evidence as justification for a higher level of care requirement in scientific testing.

Rollin's research to this day continues to press for the morally humane use of animals in scientific testing. His advocacy has taken many forms, from pushing for increased use of anesthetics to relieve animal pain to improving daily living conditions in accordance with each individual animal's needs.

FURTHER READING

Pluhar, Evelyn B. *Beyond Prejudice: The Moral Significance of Human and Nonhuman Animals.* Durham, NC: Duke University Press, 1995.

Rollin, Bernard. *Animal Rights & Human Morality.* 3rd ed. Amherst, NY: Prometheus Books, 2006.

Rollin, Bernard E. "Author Interviews: Putting the Horse before Descartes." Temple University Press, accessed December 13, 2014. http://www.temple.edu/tempress/authors/1969_qa.html.

Rollin, Bernard. *Putting the Horse before Descartes.* Philadelphia: Temple University Press, 2011.

Rollin, Bernard. *Science and Ethics.* Cambridge; New York: Cambridge University Press, 2006.

"Student Animal Legal Defense Fund (SALDF): Dr. Bernard E. Rollin—Saturday Keynote, the Animal Law Conference at Lewis & Clark." Lewis & Clark Law School. July 12, 2011. http://law.lclark.edu/live/news/12574.

"PEACE, PHILLIPS, AND VICK EXECUTED APPROXIMATELY 8 DOGS THAT DID NOT PERFORM WELL IN 'TESTING' SESSIONS"

- **Documents:** These two documents are related to the criminal case filed against NFL quarterback Michael Vick following revelations of his involvement in a dogfighting ring. The first is an excerpt from the criminal indictment of Vick and other associates; the second is the text of the Animal Fighting Spectator Prohibition Act.
- **Date:** Indictment, July 2007; Animal Fighting Spectator Prohibition Act, July 11, 2011.
- **Where:** Washington, D.C.
- **Significance:** When star quarterback Michael Vick was arrested in 2007 and charged with a variety of crimes for his role in an illegal pit bull fighting ring, the case sparked a media frenzy that shone a bright light on the brutal and bloody "sport" of dogfighting. In the wake of Vick's arrest, indictment, and conviction, lawmakers rushed to satisfy the demand from animal welfare organizations and the general public for a crackdown on organized animal fighting ventures. One of the laws passed in this period was the Animal Fighting Spectator Prohibition Act.

DOCUMENT

INDICTMENT
JULY 2007 TERM—At Richmond, Virginia
COUNT ONE
(Conspiracy to Travel in Interstate Commerce in Aid of Unlawful Activities and to Sponsor a Dog in an Animal Fighting Venture)
THE GRAND JURY CHARGES THAT:

1. Beginning in or about early-2001 and continuing through on or about April 25, 2007, in the Eastern District of Virginia and elsewhere, defendants PURNELL A. PEACE, also known as "P-hunk" and "Funk," QUANIS L. PHILLIPS, also known as "Q," TONY TAYLOR, also known as "T," and MICHAEL VICK, also known as "Ookie," did knowingly and willfully combine, conspire, confederate and agree with each other, and with persons known and unknown to the Grand Jury, to commit the following offenses against the United States, to wit:

   a. traveling in interstate commerce and using the mail or any facility in interstate commerce with intent to commit any crime of violence to further any unlawful activity and to promote, manage, establish, carry on, and facilitate the promotion, management, establishment, and carrying on of an unlawful activity, to wit: a business enterprise involving gambling in violation of Virginia Code Annotated Sections 3.1-796.124(A)(2), 18.2-326, and 18.2-328, and thereafter performing and attempting to perform acts to commit any crime of violence to further any unlawful activity and to promote, manage, establish, and carry on, and to facilitate the promotion, management, establishment, and carrying on of the unlawful activity, in violation of Title 18, United States Code, Section 1952;

b. knowingly sponsoring and exhibiting an animal in an animal fighting venture, if any animal in the venture has moved in interstate commerce. in violation of Title 7, United States Code, Section 2156(a)(1); and

c. knowingly buying, transporting, delivering, and receiving for purposes of transportation, in interstate commerce, any dog for purposes of having the dog participate in an animal fighting venture, in violation of Title 7, United States Code, Section 2156(h).

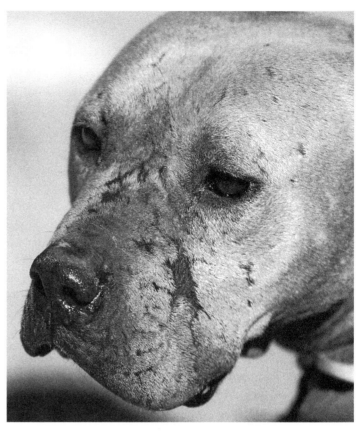

The scarred face of Lucas, a pit bull used in the Michael Vick illegal dogfighting operation, is shown at the Best Friends Animal Sanctuary in Utah in January 2009. Vick, a National Football League quarterback, brought much media attention to the case, which helped increase public awareness about dogfighting and animal cruelty in general. (AP Photo/Jae C. Hong)

MANNER AND MEANS OF THE CONSPIRACY

2. It was part of the conspiracy that the defendants and their co-conspirators would and did:

a. purchase and develop a parcel of property to serve as the main staging area for housing and training pit bulls involved in the animal fighting venture and for hosting dog fights,

b. establish a kennel name to represent the animal fighting venture in dog fighting competitions;

c. purchase pit bulls for use in dog fighting competitions;

d. train and breed pit bulls for participation in dog fighting competitions;

e. travel to other locations in interstate commerce to participate in dog fighting competitions;

f. sponsor and exhibit dogs in animal fighting competitions in interstate commerce involving dogs that have moved across state lines;

g. provide funding for the expenses associated with the ongoing animal fighting venture, including improvements on the property, dog food, medicine, travel expenses, and purse fees for dog fighting competitions; and

h. develop the animal fighting venture's pool of pit bulls by testing the fighting prowess of dogs within the venture, providing veterinary treatment for injured dogs slated to stay with the kennel, and destroying or otherwise disposing of dogs not selected to stay with the ongoing animal fighting venture.

OVERT ACTS

3. In furtherance of the conspiracy and to effect the objects thereof, at least one of the following overt acts, among others, was committed by the defendants and other conspirators in the Eastern District of Virginia and elsewhere:

2001–2002: Establishment of "Bad Newz Kennels" at 1915 Moonlight Road, Smithfield, Virginia:

4. At some point in or about early 2001, QUANIS L. PHILLIPS, also known as "Q," TONY TAYLOR, also known as "T," and MICHAEL VICK, also known as "Ookie," decided to start a venture aimed at sponsoring American Pit Bull Terriers in dog fighting competitions....

7. In or about 2001, the exact dates being unknown to the Grand Jury, PURNELL A. PEACE, also known as "P-Funk" and "Funk," PHILLIPS, TAYLOR, and VICK started acquiring pit bulls for the fighting operation from various locations inside and outside of Virginia, including the purchasing approximately 4 dogs from an individual in North Carolina, approximately 1 dog from an individual in New York, approximately 6 dogs and 6 puppies from an individual in Richmond, Virginia, and a female pit bull named "Jane" from an individual in Williamsburg, Virginia....

10. In or about early 2002, PEACE, PHILLIPS, TAYLOR, and VICK established a dog fighting business enterprise known as "Bad Newz Kennels." At one point, the defendants obtained shirts and headbands representing and promoting their affiliation with "Bad Newz Kennels."

11. Beginning in 2002 and continuing through at least 2005, the exact dates being unknown to the Grand Jury, "Bad Newz Kennels" members, aided and assisted by others known and unknown to the Grand Jury, continued to develop the 1915 Moonlight Road property for the ongoing dog fighting venture, including building: a fence to shield the rear portion of the compound from public view; multiple sheds used at various times to house training equipment, injured dogs, and organized fights; a house to be occupied by the defendants and others associated with maintaining the property; and kennels and buried car axles with chains for the pit bulls. The buried car axles allow the dog chains to pivot, allowing the pit bulls to avoid getting tangled in the chains.

2002: Execution of "Bad Newz Kennels" Pit Bulls that Performed Poorly in "Testing" Sessions:

12. In or about February 2002, PEACE and VICK "rolled" or "tested" some of their fighting dogs against other dogs owned by CW 1 and others in Virginia Beach,

Virginia. "Rolling" or "testing" a fighting dog means placing the dog in a short fighting match to determine how well the animal fights. One of the pit bulls sponsored by PEACE and VICK in this "testing" session did not fight very well.

13. In or about February 2002, PEACE executed the pit bull that did not perform well in the "testing" session by shooting it with a .22 caliber pistol....

2002: Fights Involving "Maniac," a Male Pit Bull Owned by an Individual from North Carolina, Versus Dogs Owned by "Bad Newz Kennels":

18. In or about the spring of 2002, PEACE, PHILLIPS, and TAYLOR traveled from Virginia to North Carolina with a male pit bull named "Seal" to participate in a dog light against a male pit bull named "Maniac," owned by an individual from North Carolina. The purse for the dog fight was established at approximately $500 per side, for a total of approximately $1,000.

19. In or about the spring of 2002, PEACE, PHILLIPS, and TAYLOR sponsored "Seal" in a dog fight against "Maniac."

20. In or about the spring of 2002, "Bad Newz Kennels," represented by PEACE, PHILLIPS, and TAYLOR, lost the purse when "Maniac" prevailed over "Seal"....

2003–2004: Fights Involving "Big Boy," a Male Pit Bull Owned by "Bad Newz Kennels," Versus Pit Bulls From South Carolina and New Jersey: ...

41. In or about late 2003, PEACE, PHILLIPS, TAYLOR, and VICK traveled from Atlanta, Georgia to South Carolina with a male pit bull named "Big Boy" to participate in a dog fight against a male pit bull owned by an individual from South Carolina unknown to the Grand Jury. The purse for the dog fight was established at approximately $3,600 per side, for a total of approximately $7,200.

42. In or about late 2003, PEACE, PHILLIPS, TAYLOR, and VICK sponsored "Big Boy" in a dog fight against the male pit bull from South Carolina.

43. In or about late 2003, "Bad Newz Kennels," represented by PEACE, PHILLIPS, TAYLOR, and VICK, won the purse when "Big Boy" prevailed over the male pit bull from South Carolina....

March 2003: Fights Involving Two Pit Bulls Owned by an Individual from North Carolina Versus Pit Bulls Owned by "Bad Newz Kennels":

47. In or about June 2002, Cooperating Witness Number 2 (C.W. #2) observed PEACE, VICK, and others unknown to the Grand Jury representing "Bad Newz Kennels" and "Hard Core Kennels" participate in two separate dog fights against "D.C. Kennels" at a location around Blackstone, Virginia. C.W. #2 approached an individual unknown to the Grand Jury after the fight to offer "Bad Newz Kennels" a future fight with two of his pit bulls, a 35 pound female pit bull and a 47 pound male pit bull.

48. In or about the late summer of 2002, an individual unknown to the Grand Jury from "Bad Newz Kennels" agreed to fight C.W. #2's pit bulls in or around March 2003.

49. In or about March of 2003, C.W. #2 traveled from North Carolina to a location near Blackstone, Virginia with his 35 pound female pit bull and a 47 pound male pit bull to participate in the dog fight matches against members of "Bad Newz Kennels."

50. In or about March of 2003, PEACE, VICK, and other individuals unknown to the Grand Jury sponsored a female pit bull in a dog fight against the 35 pound female pit bull owned by C.W. #2. The purse for the dog fight was established at approximately $13,000 per side, for a total of approximately $26,000.

51. In or about March of 2003, PEACE, VICK, and other individuals unknown to the Grand Jury sponsored a female pit bull in a fight against the 35 pound female pit bull owned by C.W. #2.

52. In or about March of 2003, "Bad Newz Kennels," represented by PEACE, VICK, and others unknown to the Grand Jury, lost the purse when the 35 pound female pit bull owned by C.W. #2 prevailed over the "Bad Newz Kennels" pit bull.

53. In or about March of 2003, PEACE, after consulting with VICK about the losing female pit bull's condition, executed the losing dog by wetting the dog down with water and electrocuting the animal.

54. In or about March of 2003, PEACE, VICK, and other individuals unknown to the Grand Jury sponsored a male pit bull in a dog fight against the 47 pound male pit bull owned by C.W. #2. The purse for the dog fight was established at approximately $10,000 per side, for a total of approximately $20,000.

55. In or about March of 2003, PEACE, VICK, and other individuals unknown to the Grand Jury sponsored a male pit bull in a fight against the 47 pound male pit bull owned by C.W. #2.

56. In or about March of 2003, "Bad Newz Kennels," represented by PEACE, VICK, and others unknown to the Grand Jury, lost the purse when the 47 pound male pit bull owned by C.W. #12 prevailed over the "Bad Newz Kennels" pit bull.

57. In or about March of 2003, VICK retrieved a book bag from a vehicle containing approximately $23,000 in cash. The cash was provided to C.W. #2 as payment for winning both dog fight matches....

Early 2007: "Bad Newz Kennels" Dog Fighting Operation Continues at 1915 Moonlight Road, Smithfield, Virginia:

81. In or about early 2007, the exact dates being unknown to the Grand Jury, PEACE, PHILLIPS, VICK, and others known and unknown to the Grand Jury continued operation of the animal fighting venture at 1915 Moonlight Road.

82. In or about April 2007, PEACE, PHILLIPS, VICK, and two others known and unknown to the Grand Jury "rolled" or "tested" additional "Bad Newz Kennels" dogs by putting the dogs through fighting sessions at 1915 Moonlight Road to determine which animals were good fighters.

83. In or about April 2007, PEACE, PHILLIPS, and VICK executed approximately 8 dogs that did not perform well in "testing" sessions at 1915 Moonlight Road by various methods, including hanging, drowning, and slamming at least one dog's body to the ground.

84. On or about April 25, 2007, PEACE, PHILLIPS, and VICK possessed various items associated with the continued operation of the dog fighting operation at 1915 Moonlight Road, including the sheds and kennels associated with housing the fighting dogs and hosting dog fights; approximately 54 American Pit Bull Terriers, some of which had scars and injuries appearing to be related to dog fighting; a "rape stand," a device in which a female dog who is too aggressive to submit to males for

breeding is strapped down with her head held in place by a restraint; a "break" or "parting" stick used to pry open fighting dogs' mouths during fights, treadmills and "slat mills" used to condition fighting dogs; and other items.

(In violation of Title 18, United States Code, Section 371).

Source: United States of America v. Purnell A. Peace, Quanis L. Phillips, Tony Taylor, Michael Vick, Defendants (2007). U.S. District Court for the Eastern District of Virginia, Richmond Division. http://aldf.org/downloads/vick_federal_indictment.pdf.

DOCUMENT

H.R. 2492—Animal Fighting Spectator Prohibition Act of 2011
(Introduced in House - IH)

HR 2492 IH

112th CONGRESS
1st Session
H.R. 2492

To prohibit attendance of an animal fighting venture, and for other purposes.

IN THE HOUSE OF REPRESENTATIVES
July 11, 2011

Mr. MARINO (for himself and Ms. SUTTON) introduced the following bill; which was referred to the Committee on Agriculture, and in addition to the Committee on the Judiciary, for a period to be subsequently determined by the Speaker, in each case for consideration of such provisions as fall within the jurisdiction of the committee concerned

A BILL

To prohibit attendance of an animal fighting venture, and for other purposes.

Be it enacted by the Senate and House of Representatives of the United States of America in Congress assembled,

SECTION 1. SHORT TITLE.

This Act may be cited as the "Animal Fighting Spectator Prohibition Act of 2011."

SEC. 2. PROHIBITION ON ATTENDING AN ANIMAL FIGHT OR CAUSING A MINOR TO ATTEND AN ANIMAL FIGHT.

Section 26 of the Animal Welfare Act (7 U.S.C. 2156) is amended—

(1) in subsection (a)—

(A) in the heading, by striking "Sponsoring or Exhibiting an Animal in" and inserting "Sponsoring or Exhibiting an Animal in, Attending, or Causing a Minor To Attend";

(B) in paragraph (1)—

    (i) in the heading, by striking "In General" and inserting "Sponsoring or Exhibiting"; and

    (ii) by striking "paragraph (2)" and inserting "paragraph (3)";

(C) by redesignating paragraph (2) as paragraph (3); and

(D) by inserting after paragraph (1) the following new paragraph:

(2) ATTENDING OR CAUSING A MINOR TO ATTEND—It shall be unlawful for any person to—

    (A) knowingly attend an animal fighting venture; or

    (B) cause a minor to attend an animal fighting venture; and

(2) in subsection (g), by adding at the end the following new paragraph:

(5) the term "minor" means a person under the age of 18 years old.

SEC. 3. ENFORCEMENT OF ANIMAL FIGHTING PROHIBITIONS.

Section 49 of title 18, United States Code, is amended—

    (1) by striking "Whoever" and inserting "(a) IN GENERAL—Whoever";

    (2) in subsection (a), as designated by paragraph (1) of this section, by striking "subsection (a)," and inserting "subsection (a)(1),"; and

    (3) by adding at the end the following new subsections:

"(b) Attending an Animal Fighting Venture—Whoever violates subsection (a)(2)(A) of section 26 of the Animal Welfare Act (7 U.S.C. 2156) shall be fined under this title, imprisoned for not more than 1 year, or both, for each violation.

"(c) Causing a Minor To Attend an Animal Fighting Venture—Whoever violates subsection (a)(2)(B) of section 26 (7 U.S.C. 2156) of the Animal Welfare Act shall be fined under this title, imprisoned for not more than 3 years, or both, for each violation."

Source: H.R. 2492, To Prohibit Attendance of an Animal Fighting Venture, and for Other Purposes. 112th Congress, 1st Session. Washington, DC: Government Publication Office, July 11, 2011. http://www.gpo.gov/fdsys/pkg/BILLS-112hr2492ih/html/BILLS-112hr2492ih.htm.

ANALYSIS

In late 2004, Michael Vick signed a $130 million contract extension with the Atlanta Falcons that made him the highest-paid player in the National Football League. By late 2007, he was in prison, having pled guilty to funding and participating in a dogfighting operation that violated federal laws. One year later, Vick and his codefendants each pled guilty to a felony charge of dogfighting in Virginia. Vick's celebrity status brought an unusual amount of media attention to the case, which raised significant public awareness about underground animal fighting practices.

The indictment against Vick and his associates in the dogfighting venture, known as Bad Newz Kennels, provides exhaustive detail on their illegal activities, including specific dogfights they organized, the dollar amounts gambled on each fight, and their execution of underperforming dogs. Key to the federal case was the fact that

Vick's dogfighting operation involved purchasing and transporting dogs from other states and conducting some of the dogfights in states outside of Virginia. Because Bad Newz Kennels operated across state lines, federal officials stepped in to investigate.

Federal authorities charged Vick with "conspiracy to travel in interstate commerce in aid of unlawful activities," which carries a stiffer maximum penalty than charges for violations of the Animal Welfare Act. After pleading guilty to the conspiracy charge, Vick faced up to five years in prison. At that time, though, the standard sentence for first-time offenders was 12 to 18 months, and prosecutors initially requested that sentence for Vick. Disregarding that recommendation, Judge Henry E. Hudson handed down a sentence of 23 months, citing the cruelty and callousness displayed by Vick and his associates at Bad Newz Kennels, as well as Vick's lies to federal agents about his part in the torture and killing of dogs. "You were instrumental in facilitating, putting together, organizing and funding this cruel and inhumane sporting activity," Hudson said. "While you have acknowledged guilt and apologized, I'm convinced it was not a momentary lapse of judgment on your part. You were a full partner" (quoted in Macur, 2007). Thus, while the main criminal charge focused on the commercial element of the dogfighting venture, the judge addressed the moral elements of the case (extreme cruelty, lying to federal agents) by imposing a longer-than-typical sentence.

When cases of dogfighting are uncovered, the dogs are seized by law enforcement officials. Often, the dogs are euthanized, either because of their injuries or because they are considered too aggressive to become companion animals. In the Michael Vick case, the Court appointed an expert to determine whether the dogs could be rehabilitated. Of the 49 dogs seized from Vick's property, 48 were saved; one was euthanized after displaying aggression toward people. The dogs received this second chance because of lobbying by some animal rights organizations and because Vick (under orders from the judge) paid almost $1 million for the dogs' ongoing care and rehabilitation. Media coverage of the case may have played a role in this court decision, since the court recognized that public sympathy for the dogs victimized by Vick and his cohorts might well translate into support for a course of action that at least offered the possibility of redemption for the dogs.

Surprisingly, though, not all animal rights organizations agreed with the effort to rehabilitate the dogs. The Humane Society of the United States (HSUS) and PETA both preferred that the dogs be euthanized. The American Society for the Prevention of Cruelty to Animals (ASPCA) and Best Friends Animal Society advocated saving the dogs and took part in their rehabilitation and placement. This fundamental disagreement, which existed before the Vick case, pivoted in large part on philosophical differences over the best way to utilize limited financial resources. Both PETA and the HSUS believed that the time and money could have been better spent helping large numbers of other animals that did not require extensive rehabilitation—and which did not, in their view, pose a potential danger to the public. The ASPCA and Best Friends subscribed to a more idealistic animal rights view and sought to carry it out in practice with Vick's dogs.

According to the ASPCA, the Michael Vick case "led to historic changes in the animal welfare field and the nation's perception of dog fighting. . . . Dog fighting is now banned throughout the United States and has gone from being a felony in forty-eight states to being a felony in all fifty states. Those convicted of federal animal fighting charges face up to three years in prison for each guilty count." One of the more recent changes related to the Vick case is presented in the second excerpt, the Animal Fighting Spectator Prohibition Act of 2011. This legislation is designed to deter adults and minors (people under the age of 18) from attending animal fights.

Notably, under the Animal Fighting Spectator Prohibition Act, the penalty for "causing a minor to attend an animal fighting venture" is greater than the penalty for adult attendance. With this approach, legislators hope to eliminate interest and participation in animal fighting by reducing future generations of spectators.

On July 19, 2011, roughly two years after his release from prison, Vick spoke on Capitol Hill in support of this new law. Vick also speaks regularly in support of HSUS. Vick's affiliation with that organization is controversial, as many people are skeptical of his motivations. However, the HSUS believes that by sharing his experience and expressing remorse for his actions, Vick can persuade young people and others to give up or avoid participating in all forms of animal fighting.

FURTHER READING

"Animal Fighting Case Study: Michael Vick." Animal Legal Defense Fund, accessed December 13, 2014. http://aldf.org/resources/laws-cases/animal-fighting-case-study-michael-vick/.

"Animal Fighting Facts." Animal Legal Defense Fund, accessed December 13, 2014. http://aldf.org/resources/laws-cases/animal-fighting-facts/.

"Apologetic Vick Gets 23-Month Sentence on Dogfighting Charges." *ESPN*. December 11, 2007. http://sports.espn.go.com/nfl/news/story?id=3148549.

Dashevskaya, Sonnet. "A Letter to PETA." Pit Bull Rescue Central, accessed December 13, 2014. http://pbrc.net/petbull/articles/petaletter.html.

"Dogfighting Fact Sheet." Humane Society of the United States. January 15, 2014. http://www.humanesociety.org/issues/dogfighting/facts/dogfighting_fact_sheet.html?credit=web_id100293785.

Gorant, Jim. *The Lost Dogs: Michael Vick's Dogs and Their Tale of Rescue and Redemption*. New York: Gotham Books, 2010.

"Historic Eight-State Dog Fighting Raid—July 2009." ASPCA, accessed December 13, 2014. http://www.aspca.org/fight-cruelty/field-investigations-and-response-team/blood-sports/historic-eight-state-dog-fighting-raid-july.

"The Investigation and Trial of Michael Vick—April 2007." ASPCA, accessed December 13, 2014. http://www.aspca.org/fight-cruelty/field-investigations-and-response-team/blood-sports/investigation-and-trial-michael-vick-april-2007.

Macur, Juliet. "Given Reprieve, N.F.L.'s Star's Dogs Find Kindness." *New York Times*, February 2, 2008.

Macur, Juliet. "Vick Receives 23 Months and a Lecture." *New York Times*, December 11, 2007.

"Michael Vick and the HSUS's Work to End Dogfighting." Humane Society of the United States. March 30, 2012. http://www.humanesociety.org/issues/dogfighting/qa/vick_faq.html.

Nockleby, April. "Support Tougher Dogfighting Laws for Criminals Like Michael Vick." Animal Legal Defense Fund. May 27, 2009. http://aldf.org/blog/support-tougher -dogfighting-laws-for-criminals-like-michael-vick/.

"Redskins Players Defend Falcon Quarterback's Dog Fighting Operation." *FOX News.* May 22, 2007. http://www.foxnews.com/story/2007/05/22/redskins-players-defend -falcons-quarterback-dog-fighting-operation/.

Rhoden, William C. "Vice Case Exposes Rift among Animal Rights Advocates." *New York Times*, March 12, 2008.

Ricaurte, Emma. "Son of Sam and Dog of Sam: Regulating Depictions of Animal Cruelty through the Use of Criminal Anti-Profit Statutes." *Animal Law* 16, no. 1 (January 13, 2010): 171–206. http://www.animallaw.info/journals/jo_pdf/lralvol16_p171.PDF.

Strouse, Kathy, and Dog Angel. *Badd Newz: The Untold Story of the Michael Vick Dog Fighting Case*. Charleston, SC: BookSurge, 2009.

Tischler, Joyce. "Obama Supports Michael Vick's Second Chance." Animal Legal Defense Fund, accessed December 13, 2014. http://aldf.org/blog/obama-supports-michael -vicks-second-chance/.

Vick, Michael. *Finally Free: An Autobiography*. Brentwood, TN: Worthy Publishing, 2011.

"Vick Apologizes, Asks for Forgiveness in Post-Plea Statement." *ESPN*. August 28, 2007. http://sports.espn.go.com/nfl/news/story?id=2993103.

"FOOD ANIMALS THAT ARE TREATED WELL AND PROVIDED WITH AT LEAST MINIMUM ACCOMMODATION OF THEIR NATURAL BEHAVIORS AND PHYSICAL NEEDS ARE HEALTHIER AND SAFER FOR HUMAN CONSUMPTION"

- **Document:** Excerpt entitled "Animal Welfare" from *Putting Meat on the Table*, published by the Pew Commission on Industrial Farm Animal Production.
- **Date:** 2008.
- **Where:** Washington, D.C.
- **Significance:** Pew's *Putting Meat on the Table* report sought to provide an authoritative overview on the effects of industrial farm animal production on public health, the environment, farm communities, and animal health. To that end, the organization assembled a commission to research and write the report that featured a diverse cross-section of individuals in such fields as business, government, education, and health care. The excerpt here focuses on animal welfare.

DOCUMENT

Impacts of Confinement on Animal Welfare

Today's concentrated animal production systems are dedicated to producing meat as cheaply as possible while achieving certain standards of taste, texture, and efficiency. Confinement systems are designed to produce animals of marketable weight in less time and with a lower incidence of some diseases. When the animals are confined indoors, discomfort due to weather is reduced. The downside is that animals are kept in more crowded conditions, are subject to a number of chronic and production-related diseases, and are unable to exhibit natural behaviors. In addition, the animals are often physically altered or restrained to prevent injury to themselves or IFAP [industrial farm animal production] workers.

Confinement animals are generally raised indoors and, in some cases (e.g., poultry, laying hens, hogs), the group size when raised indoors is larger than outdoors. In other cases (e.g., veal crates or gestation crates for sows), animals are separated and confined to spaces that provide for only minimal movement. The fundamental welfare concern is the ability of the animal to express natural behaviors—for example, having natural materials to walk or lie on, having enough floor space to move around with some freedom, and rooting (for hogs). Crates, battery cages, and other such systems fail to allow for even these minimal natural behaviors.

Other animal management practices that have been questioned include feeding and nutrition. For example, beef cattle finished in feedlots are typically fed grains rather than forage (grass, hay, and other roughage), even though their digestive systems are designed to metabolize forage diets. The result is that beef cattle put on weight faster, but they also often experience internal abscesses. Some laying hens still have their feed restricted at regular intervals in order to induce molting to encourage egg laying (although this practice is mostly phased out, according to United Egg Producers (UEP) standards).

Most animals are physically altered without pain relief when raised in concentrated, confined production systems (as well as in some more open systems), even though it is widely accepted that such alteration causes pain. For example, hogs have their tails docked to avoid tail biting by other hogs in close proximity. Laying hens and broilers have their toenails, spurs, and beaks clipped. Dairy cows may have their horns removed or their tails docked. The purpose of such alteration is to avoid injury to the animal, or to make it easier to handle, or to meet market demands on alteration, such as castration of bulls raised for beef, and so these practices are common throughout animal agriculture, not just in CAFOs [concentrated animal feeding operations] and IFAP.

The Five Freedoms

Contemporary concerns about the welfare of intensively farmed animals are generally considered to have originated with the 1964 publication of *Animal Machines* by Ruth Harrison of the United Kingdom. The book is widely regarded as having the same formative effect on the animal welfare movement as Rachel Carson's 1962 book, *Silent Spring*, had on the modern environmental movement. Harrison described what she called a "new type of farming . . . [with] animals living out their lives in darkness and immobility without the sight of the sun, of a generation of men who see in the animal they rear only its conversion to human food."

A year after Harrison's book was published, the Brambell Committee Report (1965) described criteria for the scientific investigation of farm animal welfare. The committee, made up of leading veterinarians, animal scientists, and biologists in the United Kingdom (UK), defined welfare as including both physical and mental well-being (Command Paper 2836). The report emphasized that the evaluation of animal welfare must include "scientific evidence available concerning the feelings of the animals that can be derived from their structure and functions and also from their behavior."

The emphasis on behavior and feelings was radical for its time (even in 2007, debate continues on this subject among animal scientists), but in 1997 the Farm Animal Welfare Council (FAWC), an independent advisory body established by the British government in 1979, adopted the principles of the Brambell report as the "Five Freedoms," which became the basis for guidelines and codes of practice for various organizations around the world. These five freedoms are described as follows:

The welfare of an animal includes its physical and mental state and we consider that good animal welfare implies both fitness and a sense of well-being. Any animal kept by man must, at least, be protected from unnecessary suffering. An animal's welfare, whether on farm, in transit, at market or at a place of slaughter, should be considered in terms of the *'five freedoms.'* These freedoms define ideal states rather than standards for acceptable welfare. They form a logical and comprehensive framework for analysis of welfare within any system together with the steps and compromises necessary to safeguard and improve welfare within the proper constraints of an effective livestock industry.

1. *Freedom from Hunger and Thirst*—by ready access to fresh water and a diet to maintain full health and vigor.
2. *Freedom from Discomfort*—by providing an appropriate environment including shelter and a comfortable resting area.
3. *Freedom from Pain, Injury or Disease*—by prevention or rapid diagnosis and treatment.
4. *Freedom to Express Normal Behavior*—by providing sufficient space, proper facilities, and company of the animals' own kind.
5. *Freedom from Fear and Distress*—by ensuring conditions and treatment that avoid mental suffering.

Source: (FAWC, 2007) at http://www.fawc.org.uk/freedoms.htm.

Animal husbandry methods designed to accommodate these five freedoms, particularly when it comes to housing characteristics, result in minimal cost to the consumer. More recently, scientists and advocates in the European Union have refined the five freedoms and further clarified the requirements for basic animal well-being. . . .

These criteria are intended to be taken in their entirety. Consequently, animals raised in conditions that meet the "Good Feeding" criteria but not the "Appropriate Behavior" criteria would not be considered to have good welfare. In the United States, the "Appropriate Behavior" criteria seem to be the hardest to satisfy and generally are not met for food animals. Fully implementing these criteria will require the education of both consumers and producers.

Voluntary Standards and Certification

Consumer concern for humane treatment of food-producing animals is growing and has prompted change in the industry. Retailers and restaurateurs are particularly sensitive to consumer concerns and have begun insisting on minimal animal welfare standards that they can report to their customers. Consolidation in the grocery and restaurant industries—10 grocery and 15 restaurant companies control the majority of sales in animal products—has brought those sectors the market power to demand change from their suppliers.

McDonald's and Wal-Mart are among those calling for at least minimal standards for animal well-being from their suppliers. McDonald's, for example, began auditing packing plants several years ago to ensure that cattle were handled and killed humanely according to the voluntary standards developed by the American Meat Institute [the group representing packing and food processing companies].

Later, McDonald's appointed an animal welfare committee of outside experts and established on-farm standards for their suppliers, beginning with laying hens. Other retailers, such as Whole Foods, adopted more stringent standards to accommodate the interests of their customer base. Their competitors quickly followed suit, and in 2000 the trade associations of supermarkets (the Food Marketing Institute, FMI) and chain restaurants (National Council of Chain Restaurants, NCCR) consolidated their recently established animal welfare expert committees to create a coordinated and uniform program. Following their lead, other retailers and food animal producers have adopted standards of their own.

However, when an affected industry defines, monitors, and enforces voluntary standards, it is vulnerable to charges of "the fox guarding the hen house." So in the spirit of Ronald Reagan's "trust but verify" admonition, third-party certification and labeling (in which the label is granted by an independent organization) have become increasingly common. Such labels allow consumers both in the United States and abroad to know that the products they buy are consistent with their concerns for environmental sustainability, social equity, and/or humane animal treatment. Some examples of third-party certification and labeling include Fair Trade certification of commodities, a designation that indicates sustainably grown coffee, for example, and the payment of a just wage to growers; and the Forest Stewardship Council's Certified Sustainable Forest Products have made significant inroads into the marketplace for lumber. Consumer preference for such labeling has been strong enough that many commodity producers and retailers seek out certification to protect their market share and increase market penetration.

Several third-party certification programs focus primarily on animal welfare. The largest of these is Certified Humane Raised and Handled. This International Standards Organization (ISO) Guide 65 certified labeling program, modeled on the Freedom Foods program established by the Royal Society for Prevention of Cruelty to Animals in the United Kingdom, has the support of 27 humane organizations around the world. Since its inception in 2003, it has grown to cover more than 14 million animals produced by 60 meat, poultry, dairy, or egg suppliers as well as 20 restaurants and supermarket chains that feature certified products.

All of these standards seek to address consumer concerns for the humane treatment of animals. Advocacy by animal protection groups has been effective in raising awareness in this area, and sensitivity to issues that affect animal well-being continues to grow.

Legislation

Reliance on voluntary standards alone is not likely to fully meet the public's concern for the welfare of industrial farm animals. Voluntary standards applied in other industries (forestry, for example) have been limited by the loopholes allowed in the standards. Similarly, because the food animal industry has an economic stake in ensuring that such voluntary standards result in the least cost, and consequently, additional measures are likely to be needed to ensure a decent minimally life for animals raised for food. Surveys such as those conducted by the Humane Society and the Farm Bureau . . . clearly reveal a growing social ethic among consumers that compels the animal agriculture industry to address public concerns about animal welfare.

At the present time, federal regulation of the treatment of farm animals is minimal, consisting of only two major laws. The first is the Twenty-Eight Hour Law, which was passed in 1873 and requires that, after 28 hours of interstate travel by rail, steam, sail, or "vessels of any description," livestock be unloaded and fed, watered, and rested for at least five consecutive hours before the resumption of transport. While generally thought of as a law to address animal cruelty, its motivation was in large part to reduce animal losses in transit. Strengthened in 1906 after publication of Upton Sinclair's *The Jungle,* the law was amended again in 1994 to apply to animals transported by "rail carrier, express carrier, or common carrier (except by air or water)." However, USDA did not agree to regulate truck transport (the major means of transport for livestock) until 2006, after animal protection groups protested (HSUS, "USDA Reverses Decades-Old Policy on Farm Animal Transport," 2006) and the courts ruled that USDA could no longer apply "regulatory discretion" to truck transport. The second federal law is the Humane Methods of Slaughter Act (HSA), which was passed in 1958 and stipulated that livestock be rendered insensible to pain before slaughter. The HSA did not cite poultry, however, so poultry processing plants are excluded from USDA enforcement.

All other attempts to pass federal laws setting standards for farm animal housing, transport, or slaughter have been unsuccessful, with the exception of the federal standards for the transport of slaughter horses, authorized under the 1996 Farm Bill. Indeed, few bills dealing with on-farm animal welfare regulation have been introduced in Congress and most have failed. This absence of regulation stands in sharp contrast to the federal oversight of certain mammals (including farm animals) used in biomedical research, teaching, and testing, the use and care of which are extensively regulated under the provisions of the 1966 Animal Welfare Act.

Perhaps because of the lack of federal regulation, there has been increasing emphasis on the introduction of state and local regulation. All states have some form of animal cruelty legislation and enforcement is becoming stricter, with more significant fines for violations. However, 25 states specifically exempt farm animals from animal cruelty laws, and in 30 states certain "normal" farm practices are exempted. Concerned citizens and advocates are therefore using mechanisms other than cruelty charges in an attempt to regulate or outlaw certain practices. For example, several states now have laws banning sow gestation crates: a voter referendum on a constitutional amendment banned them in Florida in 2002, a similar initiative (which also banned the use of veal crates) passed in Arizona in 2006, and the Oregon legislature also recently passed a state law banning crates. The production of foie gras was outlawed in California by legislative vote in 2004, and the city of Chicago in 2006 banned the sale of foie gras in restaurants. Several states have referendums on their ballots in 2008 that propose banning the use of battery cages to house laying hens.

In 1996, New Jersey became the first (and only) state to require its Department of Agriculture to write comprehensive standards for the "humane raising, keeping, care, treatment, marketing, and sale of domestic livestock." But the department's proposed regulations were not issued until 2004, and animal protection groups immediately criticized them as endorsing the status quo, although the preface to the standards makes it clear that the intent was to provide minimal requirements for the prosecution of animal cruelty cases. Animal protection groups have filed suit against the state of New Jersey, and it is unclear whether or not (or when) the proposed regulations will be finalized and enforced.

Commissioners' Conclusions

The Pew Commission on Industrial Farm Animal Production considers animal well-being an essential component of a safe and sustainable production system for farm animals. Food animals that are treated well and provided with at least minimum accommodation of their natural behaviors and physical needs are healthier and safer for human consumption.

After reviewing the literature, visiting production facilities, and listening to producers themselves, the Commission believes that the most intensive confinement systems, such as restrictive veal crates, hog gestation pens, restrictive farrowing crates, and battery cages for poultry, all prevent the animal from a normal range of movement and constitute inhumane treatment.

Growing public awareness and concern for the treatment of food animals has brought increased demands for standards to ensure at least minimal protection of animal welfare. These demands have been expressed through pressure on retail and restaurant operators for standards that can be audited and certified. The Commissioners believe that the demand for such standards will increase in the next several years and that it will be incumbent upon meat, poultry, egg, and dairy producers to meet that demand and demonstrate that food animals are treated humanely throughout their lifetimes, up to and including the method of slaughter. Further, producers who are able to incorporate animal husbandry practices that assure better treatment for animals are likely to benefit in increased profit and market share as consumers express their preference at the grocery store.

Source: "Animal Welfare." *Putting Meat on the Table: Industrial Farm Animal Production in America.* Washington, DC: Pew Commission on Industrial Farm Animal Production, 2008, pp. 31, 33, 35, 37–39. Used by permission of PEW Trusts.

ANALYSIS

Dramatic changes in animal agriculture have occurred during the past several decades. A shift has taken place from diversified farming, in which farmers, for instance, raised cows for milk production but also grew wheat (for production purposes but also to feed the cattle), to a more specialized, highly productive animal-production operation. The so-called industrial farm animal production (IFAP) industry involves a wide range of interested parties, both large and small, and including individuals, communities, private industry, and government regulators.

In 2008, the independent Pew Commission on Industrial Farm Animal Production (PCIFAP) was formed to examine key aspects of the farm animal industry.

According to the PCIFAP, the 15 commissioners represented diverse backgrounds and perspectives and come from the fields of veterinary medicine, agriculture, public health, business, government, rural advocacy and animal welfare. For instance, chair John W. Carlin grew up on a family-operated dairy farm in Saline County, Kansas. He also served as governor of that heavily agricultural state from 1979 to 1987. Animal welfare scholar Bernard Rollin, former U.S. secretary of agriculture Dan Glickman, and nutrition author and professor Marion Nestle were also among those who served on the Pew commission.

For two and a half years, the PCIFAP consulted with national experts and conducted an assessment of the industrial farm animal production industry's impact on public health, the environment, farm communities, and animal health and well-being. On April 29, 2008, the PCIFAP issued a final, thorough report entitled *Putting Meat on the Table: Industrial Farm Animal Production in America*. The work focused on how industrial farm animal production has affected four key areas: public health, the environment, animal welfare, and rural communities. The report included analysis and input from many different disciplines—including agricultural engineering, agronomy, animal sciences, biology, economics, ethics, food science, genetics, nutrition, and veterinary medicine. According to Carlin, "All Americans have a stake in the quality of our food, and we all benefit from a safe and affordable food supply. We care about the well-being of rural communities, the integrity of our environment, the public's health, and the health and welfare of animals."

The above excerpt from *Putting Meat on the Table: Industrial Farm Animal Production in America* focuses exclusively on animal welfare. Because highly specialized systems now consist of crop growers selling grain to feed mills that involve formulating engineered feeds to sell to farmers, consumers have become increasingly concerned that farm animals are afforded a decent life. But, unfortunately, according to Pew, "it can be difficult to define what actually constitutes a decent life for animals because doing so includes both ethical (value-based) and scientific (empirical) components."

The report covers issues related to animal confinement, natural animal behavior, feeding and nutrition, and pain and physical alteration. In addition, the report looks at the so-called "Five Freedoms" issued by the British government–based Farm Animal Welfare Council (FAWC) in 1997: (1) freedom from hunger and thirst; (2) freedom from discomfort; (3) freedom from pain, injury, or disease; (4) freedom to express normal behavior; and (5) freedom from fear and distress. The report also considers the self-adopted standards such companies as McDonald's and Walmart have taken and reviews various state and federal legislation that relates to animal welfare.

FURTHER READING

Carlin, John W. "Preface." *Putting Meat on the Table: Industrial Farm Animal Production in America*. Pew Commission on Industrial Farm Animal Production, accessed December 13, 2014. http://www.pewtrusts.org/en/research-and-analysis/reports/0001/01/01/putting-meat-on-the-table.

Field, Thomas G., and Robert E. Taylor. *Scientific Farm Animal Production: An Introduction to Animal Science*. 9th ed. Upper Saddle River, NH: Pearson Prentice Hall, 2008.

Kirby, David. *Animal Factory: The Looming Threat of Industrial Pig, Dairy, and Poultry Farms to Humans and the Environment*. New York: St. Martin's Press, 2010.

Norwood, F. Bailey, Pascal A. Oltenacu, Michelle S. Calvo-Lorenzo, and Sarah Lancaster. *Agricultural and Food Controversies: What Everyone Needs to Know*. New York: Oxford University Press, 2014.

Pew Commission on Industrial Farm Animal Production, accessed December 13, 2014. http://www.ncifap.org/.

"Pew Commission on Industrial Farm Animal Production." National Pork Producers Council, accessed December 13, 2014. http://www.nppc.org/issues/animal-health -safety/pew-commission-on-industrial-farm-animal-production/.

Pond, Wilson G., Fuller W. Bazer, and Bernard E. Rollin, eds. *Animal Welfare in Animal Agriculture*. Boca Raton, FL: CRC Press, 2012.

Rollin, Bernard E. *Farm Animal Welfare: Social, Bioethical, and Research Issues*. Ames: Iowa State University Press, 1995.

5

ANIMAL WELFARE FROM SEAWORLD TO A WORLD OF RISING SEAS

"THE ETHICS OF RIDING ATOP A WILD ANIMAL IN A SPANDEX SUIT WITH LOUD MUSIC BLARING CANNOT BE RECONCILED UNDER THE BANNER OF EDUCATION OR CONSERVATION"

- **Document:** Statement of Louis Psihoyos, executive director of the Oceanic Preservation Society, at *Marine Mammals in Captivity: What Constitutes Meaningful Public Education?*, a hearing before the House Committee on Natural Resources' Subcommittee on Insular Affairs, Oceans and Wildlife.
- **Date:** April 27, 2010.
- **Where:** Washington, D.C.
- **Significance:** When SeaWorld trainer Dawn Brancheau was drowned by a captive orca whale named Tilikum in February 2010, many wildlife conservation and animal rights organizations cited the tragedy as heartbreaking evidence that keeping killer whales, dolphins, and other marine mammals in captivity at theme parks, aquariums, and zoos was a horrible practice that needed to end. They pressed their case at a public hearing on the wisdom and ethics of marine mammal captivity held by a House of Representatives Subcommittee on Insular Affairs, Oceans, and Wildlife. In the following testimony, documentary filmmaker, photographer, and ocean conservationist Louis Psihoyos asserts that SeaWorld and other aquatic parks and aquariums should end all of their programs that require dolphins and orcas to spend their lives in artificial tanks rather than in the wild ocean habitat where they properly belonged.

DOCUMENT

I represent the Oceanic Preservation Society, founded 5 years ago to advocate on behalf of the oceans, and on a more personal note, the diving community.

Over 35 years I have been on nearly 1,000 dives around the world, as a photographic journalist, an Academy Award winning director and for my own recreation. And of the dozens of marine animal parks I've visited in the U.S. and around the world, none has come close to replicating the natural environment I have witnessed with my own eyes.

To know marine animals is to see them in their natural environment. Never once have I seen a dolphin flip, spit water at a human, wave goodbye with their flipper, or moonwalk. Professional divers would never feed, touch or attempt to ride an animal in the wild—it's one of the first lessons taught during dive certification—because they are not performers. They are rather, wild hunters, exceptional athletes, and some of the most social creatures on the planet. Rarely, if ever, have I witnessed a dolphin alone, or with as few members as I've seen in any dolphin park.

It is my firm belief that the way to understanding marine mammals is not achievable in a park setting. What we witness in a park setting most often—animals performing tricks because they want to be fed—is not animal behavior but rather a display of human dominance. In this way I contend that it is also false to represent to an audience in an amusement park setting, that they are becoming educated on real animal behavior. In my experience, there are ways of exposing animals to the public that do not involve putting them in a concrete enclosure. As a photojournalist and documentarian I have endeavored throughout my career to bring diverse creatures, peoples and environments to life for my audience, in a way that engenders connection, promotes conservation or at least a social awareness of my subject.

Encountering dolphins in the wild is one of the most exhilarating life experiences I have had as a diver or as a human. In the wild, the dolphin is dominant and controls the encounter. They can choose to approach, interact and disappear with more agility and grace than humans could ever hope to achieve underwater. Even our high-end equipment is of little novelty to these highly evolved creatures. In 2006 while diving with OPS Director of Expeditions Simon Hutchins, we came upon a pod of bottlenose dolphins in the Rangiroa atoll (part of the Tuamotu Island group in Polynesia). Rangiroa is the second largest atoll in the world; the tidal rush of water is epic, bringing in a host of other large animals. More than a dozen dolphins scanned us with sonar and swarmed around curiously and playfully for fifteen minutes before dashing off, much to our disappointment. At that moment we saw a great hammerhead shark headed straight for us, and the dolphin pod attacking it. Hammerhead sharks are some of the largest in the world, about 18 feet long, which is similar to the large great whites. I had seen pictures once of a great hammerhead with a gray reef shark in his mouth that made the reefer look like a child's toy. The bottlenose dolphins were large, about 8 feet long and weighed several hundred pounds, but they were dwarfed by the hammerhead.

Each pod member took turns ramming the shark away from us, in a manner quite violent, and wholly distinct from their interaction with us just moments before. Dolphins can easily outswim a shark, but instead they chose to attack it. In the wild, I have seen a pod support injured members by taking turns propping them afloat to breathe, and I've spoken to swimmers who have experienced the same life-saving phenomenon when they were drowning. Dolphins remain the only known wild animal throughout history to save the life of humans.

In oceans all over the world you will see pods of dolphins by the thousands jumping and frolicking. Playing on their agile talents, dolphin shows have trained dolphins in synchronized jumping, akin to circus acts, which have caused collisions resulting in injury and death for many dolphins in captivity. Again, this behavior is not something that occurs in the wild—despite an industry representative's claim that it is "an unfortunate, random incident"—it is clearly a result of being forced to do dangerous circus-like tricks twice a day, seven days a week.

Many dolphin species have larger brains than humans. All orca whales have larger brains than humans, and additionally, more convolutions of the gray matter allowing for sensory neurons—so they are more sensitive than us. Until recently,

Spindle cells—specialized brain cells involved in processing emotions and social interaction/organization—were thought to be the sole provenance of humans and the great apes. In 2006 the *New Scientist Journal* published a striking article when it was discovered that orcas also have spindle cells, and in the same area of the brain as humans. Interestingly, in accounting for their larger brain size, Orcas and other whales have even more spindle cells.

Orcas, like dolphins, similarly, are extremely social in resident pods; they stay with their mothers for life. For millions of years they have evolved to be social, forage for their collective food through cooperative hunting, and communicate with sonar in a complex environment using a full array of their senses to explore and travel far. It is hard to imagine that these animals are safer alone, in a confined pool, than they are with their pod. However, many public display facilities would have you believe that they provide superior nourishment and safety, a fact that is not substantiated, and only serves their own purposes.

Throughout the history of mankind there has never been a single documented case in the wild of an orca whale killing a human being, but the Sea World Orca, [Tilikum], who was taken from his mother in Iceland at the age of two, has killed three people in his lifetime. The educational benefit of these unfortunate facts should be to alert everyone involved in marine mammal captivity that they are in fact responsible for inducing abnormal behavior. In explanation, the industry has drawn parallels between orcas and other wild animals that are known to be dangerous, like lions. Lions are predatory animals that have been known to hunt and kill humans throughout history. However orcas have never hunted people and certainly not ever eaten people, including the deceased trainers.

A trainer will never suffice for a mother; these are mammals, who carried their baby to term, not fish laying multiple eggs. And we know that the only thing a dolphin habitat has in common with a concrete tank is the water, except there is a lot less water in Orlando and Las Vegas where Sea World dolphins are rented out. After a "Show" at many of the public display facilities, which are also members of AZA and The Alliance of Marine Mammals and Aquariums, I have witnessed dolphins baking in the tropical sun in shallow pools with no shade protection, and observed these otherwise gregarious social animals floating in isolation at the surface or dragging their rostrums around the edge of the concrete.

If the behavior of [Tilikum] was the aberrant behavior of one individual you could perhaps dismiss it as a statistical anomaly. However just two months before, on the day before Christmas, another Sea World orca, one of four rented out to an aquarium in the Canary Islands, killed another trainer. An article in *USA Today* last week highlighted a long history of trainers being maimed, injured and killed. It is irresponsible of those in the captivity industry to compare orcas and dolphins to playful happy pets who do tricks for food when it serves to entertain an audience, and then compare them to wild predatory animals when they need an explanation for extreme and aberrant behavior.

From dolphin collisions to orca attacks, the question is not whether but when the next tragedy for marine mammals in captivity will occur. The live experience does not constitute a necessary part of education. If our goal is to educate the public on marine mammals, to engender compassion and promote conservation, then we must think seriously about the "message" conveyed by marine mammal parks. We must think about how we educate, and how we make the greatest impact. It can be a subjective question, however, we do not find it necessary to furnish parks with deserts and arctic tundra in order to explain geography, nor to bring dinosaurs back from the dead to explain them.

One of my areas of expertise is the Mesozoic Era, or the mid-life of the planet, commonly known as the Age of Dinosaurs. I have done four stories for *National Geographic* on this era and by readership surveys conducted by the magazine, a few rank among the most popular stories in the magazine's history. I also authored a best-selling book, *Hunting Dinosaurs*, that was extremely popular with children and scientists alike. And although the last dinosaurs died 65 million years ago, public interest in them has never waned. And so, the argument that people must have first hand experience [with] these animals in order to appreciate them is not substantiated by the facts. We hold marine mammals on public display simply because we can.

The ethics of riding atop a wild animal in a spandex suit with loud music blaring cannot be reconciled under the banner of education or conservation because it goes against everything we are trying to teach our children about these animals. If provoked in the wild these encounters would and should result in arrest. Jacques Cousteau famously said, "There's about as much educational benefit studying dolphins in captivity as there would be studying mankind by only observing prisoners held in solitary." Viewing marine mammals in captivity tells us nothing of the animals' actual habits and behaviors.

What we see is animals becoming domesticated, losing their evolutionary edge, and above all being dominated. Public display facilities are misrepresenting themselves as educators because we haven't set up the legal structure to hold them to a higher standard.

Self Regulation: A Conflict of Interest

As children and adults we are admonished that feeding animals in the wild encourages and promotes abnormal behavior that may even result in personal injury or death. For these reasons, it is also illegal in many places. Neither is it allowable to feed wild animals in zoos, in fact you would be thrown out of any zoo if you did. Nonetheless many dolphin parks allow random feeding by paying customers. How is it that feeding wild animals is bad and dangerous but if they pay $70.00 to a dolphinarium it is education?

This is not education; it is, more accurately, a manipulation of fact for the benefit of purely financial enterprise. One of the founders of the Alliance of Marine Mammal Parks and Aquariums has been one of the world's largest dolphin traffickers. He provided animals from the infamous dolphin drive hunts in Taiji and Iki, Japan, to Sea World, the Indianapolis Zoo, a dolphin park in Hawaii and the U.S. Navy. I know quite a bit about Taiji. Over a three-year period I made seven trips to Taiji for the Academy Award winning film that I directed called *The Cove*. Our film was named for the now infamous secret cove in a Japanese National Park that is the site of the largest dolphin slaughter on the planet—it's also the center of the captive dolphin industry. Any dolphin originating from Taiji, seen performing in a public display facility or amusement park is, without question, the last surviving member of its pod. Every single one of its relatives, not chosen for the captive dolphin industry, would have been killed in the most violent way imaginable, which we went to great lengths to portray, in all its graphic accuracy. The economic underpinning of Taiji's dolphin slaughter is the trafficking of dolphins for public display facilities.

The law that allows for the public display of marine mammals was established without the benefit of scientific research that we have before us today. We know far more about these intelligent sentient creatures now than we did in 1972, and 1994. Ironically, much of what we have learned about their cognitive abilities was learned in zoo and aquarium research facilities. Therein lies a major conflict of interest for the industry: when you begin to understand what these animals are truly capable of and then continue to pull them out of the wild and force them to do tricks for our amusement, it says more about our intelligence than theirs.

It is prudent now that we consider whether these facilities would still constitute viable businesses if a larger role was established for education and the "circus shows" were banned altogether. Because while it may be said that public support for marine mammals increased over the last several decades, the same cannot be said for the environment in which the animals live. Environmental degradation has continued at an alarming rate. It can only be assumed that people are not making the connection that in order to protect these animals, we must first protect their environment. It seems no great coincidence that this disconnect was inspired by the false impression of sanctuary represented by public display facilities.

I strongly urge you today to take action in establishing regulated oversight of the education programs for public display facilities of marine mammals. Under the current law they have been allowed to become denigrated circus animals that serve our amusement rather than our education.

Source: Statement of Louis Psihoyos, Oceanic Preservation Society. In *Marine Mammals in Captivity: What Constitutes Meaningful Public Education?*, a hearing before the House Committee on Natural Resources' Subcommittee on Insular Affairs, Oceans and Wildlife, April 27, 2010. Committee on Natural Resources, 111th Congress Hearing Archives. http://naturalresources.house.gov/calendar/eventsingle.aspx?EventID=181362.

ANALYSIS

Like many other critics of SeaWorld and similar aquatic theme parks, Psihoyos condemned the practice of allowing commercial enterprises that publicly display marine mammals for profit to decide for themselves whether their displays had the necessary educational merit to receive protection under the Marine Mammal Act of 1992. He spent most of his time, however, hammering home his assertion that holding healthy dolphins and orcas in captivity was *never* a morally defensible practice. He supported this position by pointing out the complex social structures of wild dolphins and killer whales as well as their physiological and behavioral characteristics that suggest high intelligence.

Ultimately, the hearing failed to generate any new laws or regulations to tighten the licensing of marine mammal programs or otherwise restrict the use of dolphins, orcas, beluga whales, and other marine mammals in public exhibitions. Undeterred, animal rights activists—as well as some marine biologists and oceanographers—continue to call for bans on the capture and public display of marine mammals. To date, the U.S. Department of Agriculture's Animal and Plant Health Inspection Service, which regulates major marine park operations under the authority of the 1962 Animal Welfare Act, has shown little inclination to make changes, especially given the tremendous popularity of SeaWorld and similar parks. "If there are changes that need to be made, there's a set process," said one USDA spokesperson. "We want to take the best science available and the best input that comes in from the general public. We're a science-based agency, but as such still respond and are receptive to ideas that come in from all the interested stakeholders. It always comes down to ensuring that the animals are getting the proper care that they need" (Wright, 2010).

But while the licensing process did not undergo any changes, the Department of Labor's Occupational Safety and Health Administration (OSHA) did force reforms to SeaWorld's operations to better protect trainers from injury or death from orcas. After conducting an investigation into Brancheau's death, OSHA fined SeaWorld for workplace safety violations and imposed new restrictions on trainer interactions with killer whales, including the introduction of physical barriers between trainer and animal. SeaWorld appealed the OSHA ruling, but on April 11, 2014, a U.S. Appeals Court upheld OSHA's finding in a 2–1 ruling.

FURTHER READING

Blackfish Official Film Site. Accessed June 18, 2014. http://blackfishmovie.com/.

Hurley, Lawrence. "Court Upholds Ruling against SeaWorld over Trainer Safety," *Reuters*, April 11, 2014. http://www.reuters.com/article/2014/04/11/us-usa-courts-employment -idUSBREA3A19Q20140411.

"Killer Whale Care." SeaWorld.com, 2014. Accessed June 18, 2014. Available at http:// seaworld.com/en/truth/killer-whales/.

Kirby, David. *Death at SeaWorld: Shamu and the Dark Side of Killer Whales in Captivity.* New York: St. Martin's, 2012.

Norton, Brian G., Michael Hutchins, Elizabeth F. Stevens, and Terry L. Maple, eds. *Ethics on the Ark: Zoos, Animal Welfare, and Wildlife Conservation.* Washington, D.C.: Smithsonian Institution, 2012.

Rose, Naomi A., E. C. M. Parsons, and Richard Farinato. *The Case against Marine Mammals in Captivity.* 4th ed. Humane Society of the United States, World Society for the Protection of Animals, May 2009. Accessed June 18, 2014. http://www.marine connection.org/docs/The%20Case%20against%20Marine%20Mammals%20in %20Captivity%20%20%28HSUS%29.pdf.

"Who We Are." Oceanic Preservation Society, 2014. Accessed January 1, 2015. http://www .opsociety.org/about-ops.htm.

Wright, Jeffrey. "So Wrong, but Thanks for All the Fish: A SeaWorld Ethics Primer." *San Antonio Current*, April 14, 2010. Accessed June 18, 2014. http://www2.sacurrent .com/news/story.asp?id=71101.

"FIRSTHAND EXPERIENCE WITH ANIMALS IS THE BEST WAY TO CREATE A LASTING APPRECIATION AND RESPECT FOR ANIMALS"

- **Document:** Statement of Julie Scardina, curator at SeaWorld Parks and Entertainment, at *Marine Mammals in Captivity: What Constitutes Meaningful Public Education?*, a hearing before the House Natural Resources Committee's Subcommittee on Insular Affairs, Oceans and Wildlife.
- **Date:** April 27, 2010.
- **Where:** Washington, D.C.
- **Significance:** On February 24, 2010, SeaWorld trainer Dawn Brancheau was drowned by SeaWorld's orca whale Tilikum during a public performance. This tragedy, which marked the third human fatality attributed to Tilikum during the animal's captivity, prompted a House Subcommittee on Insular Affairs, Oceans, and Wildlife to hold a public hearing to (1) explore the educational advantage of keeping orcas, dolphins, and other marine mammals in aquarium settings and (2) to investigate whether the federal government should step in and issue licensing requirements for education programs at zoos and aquaria, both of which had become accustomed to an environment of self-regulation. The potential economic consequences of such a shift in the regulatory environment would be considerable for the 200 or so American zoos and aquaria licensed to keep and display marine mammals for educational and conservation purposes. Industry representatives who testified at the hearing thus asserted that federal oversight was unnecessary. They also claimed that their educational and conservation programs were extremely valuable in helping at-risk animals and in enlisting public support for policies to protect and preserve wild species. Following are excerpts from the testimony of SeaWorld curator Julie Scardina, who described the park's programs as a tremendous asset to marine mammal protection efforts.

DOCUMENT

There are approximately 200 zoos and aquariums currently licensed to keep and show marine mammals. Facilities need to prove that they offer education or conservation programs based on industry standards in order to be eligible for a license.

The National Marine Fisheries Service, which issues the permits, has never issued specific rules that define the standards, does not review the facility for compliance once the permit is issued and has never revoked a permit from such parks.

Trainer Mike Boos works with Shamu, a killer whale, following a performance at SeaWorld Cleveland in August 2000. Despite ongoing concerns of animal rights groups about animal captivity and calls to put education programs at zoos and aquariums under federal supervision, these institutions remain under the guidance of the Association of Zoos and Aquariums and the Alliance of Marine Parks and Aquariums. (AP Photo/Amy Sancetta)

The problem with that is that there is no independent oversight for what constitutes these programs, leaving the industry to self-regulate. Most of these facilities are run for a profit, making for an interesting conflict of interest.

SeaWorld Parks & Entertainment appreciates the Subcommittee's interest in education and conservation programs at zoological parks. And we understand that in anticipation of a proposed regulation covering the permitting processes under the Marine Mammal Protection Act, you have asked for SeaWorld to comment on the adequacy of the professionally recognized standards governing public display, whether the federal government should regulate the public education programs at zoos and aquaria, and how our public education programs are evaluated.

We believe the current standards encourage and require exceptional public education programs and that additional federal regulations are not needed. SeaWorld offers world class zoological experiences at our parks in Orlando, Florida, San Diego, California and San Antonio, Texas along with our Busch Gardens parks in Tampa, Florida and Williamsburg, Virginia. We thank the Committee for this opportunity to share information about SeaWorld and, particularly, its education and conservation programs.

SeaWorld has the largest zoological collection in the world—more than 65,000 animals, including nearly 200 endangered, threatened and at-risk species. We also have a 46-year history of leadership in wildlife conservation and education. The success of the parks' animal rescue and rehabilitation programs, educational programs and endangered species breeding programs are unparalleled in the world.

SeaWorld has a multi-faceted mission. Our parks are entertainment and education centers. We work hard to ensure that our patrons leave our facilities having had an enjoyable experience, and with greater knowledge of and appreciation for animals and the natural world. The "multiple facets" of our business are interrelated; entertainment, education and the research components all complement each other.

As an education, research and conservation center, we devote substantial resources to learning more about the animals in our care, both independently and in partnership with research facilities around the world. A key component of our conservation mission is to rescue, rehabilitate, and then release animals in need. We rescue and rehabilitate more marine animals than any other organization in the world.

Each year, more than 12 million people visit a SeaWorld park. Creating a connection between people and animals is the critical first step in educating our visitors about the importance of conservation. Since the first SeaWorld park opened in 1964, more than 525 million people have been brought closer to the marine environment at SeaWorld. In 2009 alone, SeaWorld conducted more than 500,000 hours of structured teaching involving more than half a million guests. The exhibits at SeaWorld are designed to inspire visitors to conserve our valuable natural resources by increasing awareness of the interrelationships between humans and the environment.

SeaWorld and Busch Gardens employ the largest and most-experienced team of veterinarians, trainers, and animal care specialists in the world. The parks also employ educators who teach a wide variety of programs. Those educators also reach millions of people who have never visited a SeaWorld park, through distance learning programs.

Conservation education is one of the key components of the accreditation process for the Association of Zoos and Aquariums (AZA) and the Alliance for Marine Mammal Parks and Aquariums (the Alliance). Our parks also meet the conservation education requirements and other standards of the American Camping Association.

SeaWorld's conservation efforts are not limited to its parks. In 2003 a non-profit foundation, the SeaWorld & Busch Gardens Conservation Fund, was created to further promote conservation. To date, the Fund has granted more than $6 million to 400 projects across 60 nations. The Fund's grantees are diverse, including global organizations such as World Wildlife Fund, The Nature Conservancy, Conservation International, as well as smaller, grassroots organizations. The Fund focuses its resources in four areas: species research, habitat protection, animal rescue and conservation education.

Conservation—Education

Education is a cornerstone of SeaWorld parks. We believe that firsthand experience with animals is the best way to create a lasting appreciation and respect for animals and the environment. Our animal attractions and exhibits are designed to inspire park visitors through multiple levels of learning opportunities, including exciting and entertaining marine animal shows, live interpretation, static graphics, video displays, and interactive learning tools. All SeaWorld education programs are consistent with AZA standards. In addition, half a million students and guests participate in in-park education programs, ranging from sleepovers and summer camps to school trips and behind-the-scenes tours. These hands-on, in-depth programs promote an appreciation of and stewardship for animals and the environment that cannot be replicated elsewhere. It is important to note that these programs bring people into contact with animals most will never see in the wild.

Consistent with AZA Standard 4.2.31, our educational reach extends into classrooms and homes across the U.S. and the world. SeaWorld's commitment to teachers is evidenced by our teacher workshop series and our extensive classroom resources, including species information books, teachers' guides, DVDs, posters, student incentives, and books for young learners. Several of these programs have been honored with Teachers' Choice Awards. Through partnerships with organizations such as the National Science Teachers Association (NSTA) and the National Marine Educators Association, SeaWorld and Busch Gardens help promote science teaching and learning. . . .

SeaWorld also rewards those who take action to make a difference. The "SeaWorld/Busch Gardens Environmental Excellence Awards" grants $80,000 to students and teachers across the U.S. who work at the grassroots level to protect and preserve the environment. Since 1993 this program has awarded more than $1.6 million to 130 schools in 43 states.

SeaWorld's educators have also created distance learning programs such as Shamu TV, an Emmy-award winning education series that is available to more than 50 million viewers each year. In addition, SeaWorld maintains the largest animal information Web site of any zoological organization at www.seaworld.org. ANIMALS features more than 4,000 pages of zoological, ecological, and conservation-minded materials—including multimedia—photo, video, and audio of species reference sources, classroom curriculum, conservation project calls-to-action, zoological career information, and environmentally focused family resources. In just two years, more than 12.5 million guests have visited ANIMALS at www.seaworld.org.

Finally, SeaWorld shares the concerns of many in Congress that American science education is losing ground to other nations. Like many zoos and aquariums around the country, we do our part to support and enhance students' exposure to the biological sciences by promoting direct interactions with both our animals and our research facilities, explaining the animals' roles in the marine ecosystem, and inspiring students to learn more about and become more active in conservation science.

Conservation—Rescue and Rehabilitation

For more than 46 years, SeaWorld and Busch Gardens have helped animals in need—whether ill, injured, abandoned or orphaned. More than 17,000 animals have been rescued through this program since 1970, including endangered and threatened species such as Florida manatees, sea turtles, sandhill cranes and gopher tortoises. SeaWorld and Busch Gardens are part of an animal rescue system

established by federal, state and local government agencies. SeaWorld and Busch
Gardens veterinarians and animal care specialists assist animals 24 hours a day,
7 days a week, 365 days a year. In 2009 alone, SeaWorld devoted more than $1.5 mil-
lion to rescue and rehabilitation of animals in need. Equally compelling is the "sweat
equity" freely donated by SeaWorld staff. A good example: cold-stunned sea turtles
all along the southeastern U.S. shoreline were assisted by SeaWorld staff. In coordination with state and federal officials—and in cooperation with marine and zoological organizations throughout the region—both SeaWorld and Busch Gardens
provided housing and critical care for more than 250 sea turtles. Manatees also are
suffering the effects of a harsh winter. SeaWorld has rescued a record high number
of manatees. Just recently, a team from SeaWorld Orlando released a manatee and
its calf that had been rescued in January.

Conservation—Research

SeaWorld and Busch Gardens work closely with leading scientists, including the
independent Hubbs-SeaWorld Research Institute (HSWRI). The non-profit
HSWRI was established by SeaWorld's founders in 1963. Its mission is "... to return
to the sea some measure of the benefits derived from it." Originally chartered as a
private non-profit organization, HSWRI has operated as a 501(c)(3) public charity
since 1998 and is recognized as a leader in marine conservation research around
the world. The SeaWorld & Busch Gardens Conservation Fund also provides millions of dollars to support these conservation efforts.

Studies of the animals in our care complement research efforts in the
field. . . . The scientific data gathered from killer whales in zoological settings is having an immediate impact on wild populations. . . .

[For example], over the past few years, the predatory behavior of killer whales has
moved into the forefront of public discussions. Between 1990 and 1998, largely due
to killer whale predation, scientists concluded that a single killer whale could con-
sume as many as 1,825 otters per year. Calculations of this kind depend upon understanding the predator's metabolic needs—information that is not available for killer
whales. Killer whales at SeaWorld are providing scientists from the University of
Central Florida with an opportunity to measure physiological parameters such as
heart rate, metabolic rate and thermal balance under controlled conditions, and to
evaluate how these parameters may be affected by age or body mass.

SeaWorld's killer whale breeding program has also made major contributions to
the understanding of killer whale biology, reproductive physiology and husbandry.

In a conservation sense, the killer whales at SeaWorld provide a living laboratory
for developing knowledge and techniques crucial to the survival of endangered or
threatened killer whale stocks.

Conservation—Breeding

SeaWorld is the global leader in the field of killer whale and dolphin reproduction including its pioneering work on killer whale artificial insemination. More than
80 percent of the marine mammals at SeaWorld were born in SeaWorld parks. . . .

The Accreditation Process

SeaWorld and Busch Gardens parks are accredited members of the Association of Zoos and Aquariums (AZA). SeaWorld parks also are accredited members of the Alliance for Marine Mammal Parks and Aquariums (Alliance). We are also accredited by 19 other respected national and international groups with specialties in education, conservation, and animal care. Examples include the National Marine Educators Association, the National Science Teachers Association, and the Society of Marine Mammalogy. Other organizations we work with include the American Veterinary Medical Association and the International Association for Aquatic Animal Medicine. All of these organizations together provide a greater breadth of expertise and experience on education than any federal program could hope to provide. Public education programs at zoos and aquaria [are] simply not an area which the federal government needs to regulate.

Recognizing that zoos and aquariums are constantly evolving and standards are continuously being raised, both AZA and the Alliance require accredited facilities to adopt and go through the entire accreditation process on a regular basis to prove it. AZA requires members to be accredited every five years. The alliance recertifies every five years. . . .

SeaWorld exhibits are regularly evaluated and improved based on our ongoing research programs and gains in conservation knowledge and practices. SeaWorld receives feedback daily from our own experts, outside experts, our conservation partners, and our patrons. Our ongoing research and mammal rehabilitation efforts continually inform our education programs and allow us to incorporate the most recent scientific information into our education program. We take pride in offering the public the best educational experience available about the animals in our collection and the natural world we live in.

Our accreditation demonstrates that we meet or exceed the AZA's and Alliance's education and conservation standards. Under the express language of the MMPA, as amplified by the statute's legislative history and as recognized by the National Marine Fisheries Service (NMFS) the federal agency that administers the MMPA for the Secretary of Commerce . . . SeaWorld satisfies the permitting requirement that we offer "a program for education or conservation purposes that is based on professionally recognized standards of the public display community."

Nationwide Study Evidencing the Efficacy of the Educational Programs of Accredited Members of the Public Display Community

Studies support the fact that accredited programs such as SeaWorld's are successful in educating the public. AZA conducts substantial research to gain a better understanding of how visits to AZA-accredited zoos and aquariums are valued by their visitors. AZA recently partnered with the Institute of Learning Innovation and the Monterey Bay Aquarium to conduct a three-year, nationwide study that investigated the impacts zoo or aquarium visits have on conservation attitudes and understanding of visitors. The results demonstrate that these visits enhance the understanding of wildlife and the conservation of the places in the wild where animals live. Key findings include:

- Visits to accredited zoos and aquariums prompt individuals to reconsider their role in the environmental problems and conservation action, and see themselves as part of the solution.
- Visitors believe zoos and aquariums play an important role in conservation education and animal care.
- Visitors believe they experience a stronger connection to nature as a result of their visit.

The study included a follow up with some participants seven to 11 months after their visit to determine the impact over time and a significant majority of visitors were able to talk about what they learned from their earlier visit.

The results of this comprehensive study will help institutions like SeaWorld and Busch Gardens develop even more effective exhibits and educational programs that help connect people with nature and encourage changes in attitude and behavior that advance conservation.

The Rescue and Rehabilitation of JJ

SeaWorld rescued, rehabilitated and released JJ, an orphaned gray whale calf beached near Los Angeles. SeaWorld animal care specialists and veterinarians rescued her, transported her to SeaWorld and spent the first few days in the water with her keeping her moving and feeding her a formula developed especially for her by SeaWorld nutritional experts. During JJ's rehabilitation at SeaWorld, she made remarkable progress. Within her first week, she gained 2.2 pounds per *hour* and ½ inch in length per day.

From the moment of her arrival at SeaWorld, all efforts were focused on improving her physical condition and preparing her for release. JJ's time at SeaWorld allowed the public to come into contact with this magnificent animal. An educational program about gray whales, their migration, conservation status, physiology, and other information, was displayed and educational specialists were made available to answer questions from the public.

JJ provided the scientific community with research opportunities never before imagined. Research on gray whale physiology, vocalizations, respiration and other studies by many of the world's leading experts in these fields was undertaken resulting in the publication of numerous scientific articles.

In March, 1998, SeaWorld released JJ back into the wild to join the northward migration of gray whales. JJ had grown from a frail infant weighing 1,670 pounds and measuring less than 14 feet to a healthy animal over 30 feet in length and weighing more than 18,000 pounds.

Conclusion

SeaWorld Parks & Entertainment appreciates this opportunity to share our perspective about how effective our educational and conservations programs are. We are proud of the work we do in educating the public about marine animals and the marine ecosystem and our hands-on efforts to conserve these treasured resources. Working in partnership with other zoos and aquaria, our environmental partners and the government, we are excited about the new discoveries and advances that lie ahead.

Source: Statement of Julie Scardina, SeaWorld Parks and Entertainment. In *Marine Mammals in Captivity: What Constitutes Meaningful Public Education?*, a hearing before the House Natural Resources Committee's Subcommittee on Insular Affairs, Oceans and Wildlife, April 27, 2010. Committee on Natural Resources, 111th Congress Hearing Archives. http://naturalresources.house.gov/calendar/event single.aspx?EventID=181362.

ANALYSIS

Scardina marshaled glowing descriptions of many different SeaWorld programs in order to reassure committee members and members of the public following the issue in the press about the value and high professional standards of SeaWorld's education and conservation initiatives. Her assertion that federal regulation of for-profit marine mammal programs for the public was both unnecessary and undesirable was echoed by other representatives of the zoo and aquarium industry, including Paul Boyle of the Association of Zoos and Aquaria and Rae Stone, who testified on behalf of the Alliance of Marine Mammal Parks and Aquariums.

The testimony of Scardina and her colleagues helped stave off calls from animal rights groups to place education programs at zoos and aquariums under direct federal supervision. Claims from some animal rights activists that Brancheau's death showed that SeaWorld's shows should be curtailed—or even ended altogether—were also rebuffed. As of 2014, licensing of educational and conservation programs at zoos and aquariums continued to be routed through the AZA and the alliance.

But while the licensing process did not undergo any changes, Brancheau's drowning convinced the Department of Labor's Occupational Safety and Health Administration (OSHA) to hold hearings to investigate whether SeaWorld's safety policies were deficient. OSHA ultimately concluded that the company had knowingly exposed its orca trainers to recognized hazards. The agency subsequently fined SeaWorld for workplace safety violations and imposed new safety measures governing trainer interactions with killer whales. SeaWorld appealed the OSHA ruling, but on April 11, 2014, a U.S. Appeals Court upheld OSHA's finding in a 2–1 ruling.

Tilikum, meanwhile, continued to perform at SeaWorld. He returned to Sea-World shows in March 2011, albeit under new measures that greatly restricted direct contact with humans. In 2013 Tilikum once again returned to the public spotlight when he became the focal point of *Blackfish*, a CNN documentary that excoriated SeaWorld for its treatment of Tilikum and other captive killer whales and its cavalier attitude toward trainer health and well-being. The documentary led several popular musical acts, from Willie Nelson to Heart, to cancel scheduled concerts at the Orlando theme park. *Miami Herald* columnist Carl Hiaasen weighed in as well.

"There's no denying that places like SeaWorld and the Seaquarium [in Miami] have educated millions of people about the beauty of orcas. Nor does the documentary leave any doubt that the trainers and vets who work directly with the whales care passionately for them. It doesn't change the fact that they exist in a state of extreme and stressful confinement. Imagine spending your whole life in a backyard swimming pool. Think you might get depressed every now and then? Bored out of your skull? Pissed off?" (Hiaasen, 2013).

FURTHER READING

Association of Zoos and Aquariums. "Accreditation." AZA.org, n.d. https://www.aza.org/accreditation/.

Hiaasen, Carl. "Misery of Captive Whales Portrayed in 'Blackfish.'" *Miami Herald*, December 14, 2013. http://www.miamiherald.com/opinion/opn-columns-blogs/carl-hiaasen/article1958509.html.

Hurley, Lawrence. "Court Upholds Ruling against SeaWorld over Trainer Safety," *Reuters*, April 11, 2014. http://www.reuters.com/article/2014/04/11/us-usa-courts-employment-idUSBREA3A19Q20140411.

"Killer Whale Care." *SeaWorld.com*, 2014. http://seaworld.com/en/truth/killer-whales/.

Kirby, David. *Death at SeaWorld: Shamu and the Dark Side of Killer Whales in Captivity.* New York: St. Martin's, 2012.

Norton, Brian G., Michael Hutchins, Elizabeth F. Stevens, and Terry L. Maple, eds. *Ethics on the Ark: Zoos, Animal Welfare, and Wildlife Conservation.* Washington, D.C.: Smithsonian Institution, 2012.

"THIS LAW PROTECTS BOTH ANIMALS AND FREE SPEECH BY FOCUSING SPECIFICALLY ON CRUSH VIDEOS, WHICH CLEARLY HAVE NO PLACE IN OUR SOCIETY"

- **Document:** Press release from the American Society for the Prevention of Cruelty to Animals (ASPCA) concerning the passage of the Animal Crush Video Prohibition Act.
- **Date:** December 10, 2010.
- **Where:** New York City.
- **Significance:** The ASPCA joined virtually every other animal rights organization in the country in applauding President Barack Obama's signature on a law designed specifically to outlaw the creation, sale, or marketing of so-called crush videos—footage of small animals being tortured to death by humans. The Animal Crush Video Prohibition Act was quickly crafted and passed after the Supreme Court ruled earlier in the year that another animal cruelty law used to prosecute producers and consumers of crush videos was unconstitutional.

DOCUMENT

ASPCA Commends New Animal Crush Video Law

President Obama's Signature of Animal Crush Video Act Helps Fight Animal Cruelty and Violence toward People

NEW YORK—The ASPCA® (The American Society for the Prevention of Cruelty to Animals®) expressed thanks to President Barack Obama for signing the Animal Crush Video Prohibition Act of 2010 into law and voicing his conclusive support for this important legislation. The new law prohibits the creation, sale and distribution of "crush videos" and carries with it a potential sentence of up to seven years in prison. Crush videos are generally sold over the Internet and typically contain graphic images of small animals being stomped to death by women in high heels.

Dr. Randall Lockwood, senior vice president of ASPCA Forensic Sciences and Anti-Cruelty Projects, who helped draft an amicus brief on the Supreme Court case and works to increase public and professional awareness of the connection between animal abuse and other forms of violence, issued the following statement on President Obama's signing:

"The ASPCA has long recognized the dangerous potential for animal cruelty to lead to more serious crimes. By banning crush videos, our federal government is potentially helping to protect the community from other serious crimes and sending a clear message to individuals seeking to profit from the suffering of helpless animals.

"This law protects both animals and free speech by focusing specifically on crush videos, which clearly have no place in our society."

The bill was drafted in response to the U.S. Supreme Court's ruling last April saying the 1999 federal law regarding the depiction of animal cruelty was too broad and violated the First Amendment. The Court left open a pathway for Congress to pass a more narrowed law targeting crush videos and exempting visual depictions of hunting, trapping, and fishing. The Senate recently gave its unanimous approval just days after the House took action on the bill.

Source: ASPCA press release "ASPCA Commends New Animal Crush Video Law," December 10, 2010, http://www.aspca.org/about-us/press-releases/aspca-commends-new-animal-crush-video-law. Copyright © 2014. The American Society for the Prevention of Cruelty to Animals (ASPCA). All Rights Reserved.

ANALYSIS

The Animal Crush Video Prohibition Act (P.L. 111-294) bans the creation, distribution, or sale of "animal crush videos," which depict acts of extreme animal cruelty for the purpose of providing sexual gratification or entertainment. This law replaced the Depiction of Animal Cruelty Act (P.L. 106-152), which was struck down as unconstitutional by the U.S. Supreme Court in April 2010. The details surrounding this legislation and the acts it prohibits raise serious questions about how much progress has been made in the effort to secure animal welfare or animal rights.

The selected excerpt, a press release from the American Society for the Prevention of Cruelty to Animals (ASPCA), focuses on the victory of reinstating legal protection against a very specific and disturbing form of animal cruelty—the intentional crushing (often by women's high-heeled shoes) of small animals, such as hamsters and guinea pigs, filmed and sold as entertainment for as much as $100 worldwide.

However, the ASPCA's official statement links the importance of the legislation to its potential value for human beings: "The ASPCA has long recognized the dangerous potential for animal cruelty to lead to more serious crimes. By banning crush videos, our federal government is potentially helping to protect the community from other serious crimes. . . ." Given that the "crush videos" involve the torture and killing of nonhuman animals, "more serious crimes" must refer to cruelty or acts of violence against human beings. This perspective is distinctly human-centered: what is deemed most noteworthy about the new law is the utility the law might have for human beings. Despite the logical and moral arguments of such animal rights philosophers as Tom Regan, the view persists that the interests and needs of human beings are ultimately of greater importance than the interests and needs of nonhuman animals.

Instead of creating a specific restriction on "crush videos," the original law against depictions of animal cruelty (P.L. 106-152) prohibited all video recordings of animal cruelty. However, the wording of the legislation would have allowed criminal prosecution of people who filmed legal hunting, trapping, and fishing activities. Therefore, the original law was ruled unconstitutional because it infringed on the right to free speech. While the ruling makes legal sense, the legal system operates with the underlying assumption that human beings are the only species that have fundamental rights, so human rights (including the right to free speech) always take precedence over the interests of other animals, even when the animal's "interest" is survival. The ASPCA spokesman quoted in the excerpt notes that the new law "protects both animals and free speech" (by exempting depictions of legal activities such as hunting), and, in that sense, the law is a victory, because it attempts to honor the rights of all while complying with established legal tradition.

According to the Humane Society of the United States (HSUS), there was "a massive resurgence of crush videos for sale on the Internet" after the original law against depictions of animal cruelty was overturned. It is a depressing fact that legislation against such grotesque forms of animal cruelty is still necessary. The Animal Crush Video Prohibition Act is as necessary as other laws prohibiting dangerous and morally offensive behavior (e.g., the distribution of child pornography); it is designed to protect a vulnerable group (voiceless, defenseless animals)—as well as society as a whole—against deviant individuals. Fortunately, like other legislation designed to curb deviant behavior, the Animal Crush Video Prohibition Act addresses a very small population of offenders. While even one "crush video" is too many, the "massive resurgence" of such videos, reported in 2010 while no prohibition was in effect, still represents a minority of people who find these depictions acceptable, entertaining, or sexually gratifying. (In 1999 the HSUS found about 3,000 "crush videos" available online; the HSUS reported that this video market disappeared shortly after the original prohibition went into effect.)

The rapid response of Congress after the original law was overturned offered encouraging proof that crush videos are widely recognized as works of horrific deviance. Acting as representatives of the people, the members of Congress—so fractious on virtually every other policy issue in the twenty-first century—were united in their effort to reestablish the legal prohibition against such works. The Supreme Court struck down the Depiction of Animal Cruelty Act in April 2010. By July 2010 the House of Representatives had already approved a new, modified law, H.R. 5566, which became the Animal Crush Video Prohibition Act, by a vote of 416–3 (the three dissenting votes included two representatives from Georgia and Representative Ron Paul of Texas, a presidential hopeful in 2012). After various revisions, H.R. 5566 received unanimous approval in the Senate in November 2010, and President Barack Obama signed the bill into law in December 2010.

FURTHER READING

"Animal Crush Video Protection Act." *Animal Welfare Institute*. https://awionline.org/content/animal-crush-video-prohibition-act.

"Animal Porn—Criminalized by Federal Law Again." *Constitutional Law Prof Blog*, December 14, 2010. http://lawprofessors.typepad.com/conlaw/2010/12/animal-porn-criminalized-by-federal-law-again.html.

"Bill to Crack Down on Animal Crush Videos Wins Final U.S. Senate and House Approval." *Humane Society of the United States*, November 19, 2010. http://www .humanesociety.org/news/press_releases/2010/11/bill_to_crack_down_on_animal.html.

"The Chain of Cruelty." *BBC News*, May 9, 2000. http://news.bbc.co.uk/2/hi/uk_news/ 741856.stm.

"18 U.S. Code § 48—Animal Crush Videos." *Legal Information Institute*. http://www.law .cornell.edu/uscode/text/18/48.

"Fifth Circuit Court of Appeals Upholds Federal Animal Crush Video Prohibition Act." *Humane Society of the United States*. June 13, 2014. http://www.humanesociety.org/ news/news_briefs/fifth_circuit_upholds_animal_crush_prohib_act_061314.html.

"House Vote 459—H.R. 5566: On Motion to Suspend the Rules and Pass, as Amended." *New York Times*. http://politics.nytimes.com/congress/votes/111/house/2/459.

"New Evidence Shows Animal Torture Videos Remain Available Online." *Humane Society of the United States*, July 29, 2010. http://www.humanesociety.org/news/press_releases/ 2010/07/new_evidence_shows_animal.html.

Pacelle, Wayne. "Federal Court Ruling on 'Crush Videos' Just the Latest to Affirm Value of Animal Protection Legislation."*A Human Nation: Wayne Pacelle's Blog*. June 16, 2014. http://hsus.typepad.com/wayne/2014/06/hsus-legal-team.html.

Perdue, Abigail, and Randall Lockwood. *Animal Cruelty and Freedom of Speech: When Worlds Collide*. West Lafayette, IN: Purdue University Press, 2014.

"Resurgence of Animal 'Crush' Videos Reinforces Need for Federal Depiction of Animal Cruelty Law." *Humane Society of the United States*, September 15, 2009. http://www .humanesociety.org/news/press_releases/2009/09/resurgence_of_animal_crush_videos _091509.html.

Ricaurte, Emma. "Son of Sam and Dog of Sam: Regulating Depictions of Animal Cruelty through the Use of Criminal Anti-Profit Statutes." *Animal Law* 16, no. 171 (January 10, 2013): 171–206. http://www.animallaw.info/journals/jo_pdf/lralvol16_p171.PDF.

Shafer, Meredith L. "Perplexing Precedent: *United States v. Stevens* Confounds a Century of Supreme Court Conventionalism and Redefines the Limits of 'Entertainment'." *Animal Legal & Historical Center*. http://www.animallaw.info/articles/arus19vill sportsentlj281.htm.

Williams, Mary Elizabeth. "The Dark World of Animal 'Crush' Films." *Salon*, April 18, 2014. http://www.salon.com/2014/04/18/the_dark_world_of_animal_crush_films/.

"THE EXPECTED BENEFITS FOR ANIMAL WELFARE AND FOR INNOVATIVE WAYS OF CARRYING OUT HUMAN HEALTH ASSESSMENT ARE LIKELY TO OUTWEIGH ANY NEGATIVE IMPACTS"

- **Document:** Press release from the European Commission and an accompanying question-and-answer sheet regarding a full European Union ban on animal testing for cosmetics.
- **Date:** March 11, 2013.
- **Where:** Brussels, Belgium.
- **Significance:** A complete ban on animal testing for the development of cosmetics gives animal rights activists hope that the same ban can occur elsewhere in the world, including the United States and Canada.

DOCUMENT

Full EU Ban on Animal Testing for Cosmetics Enters into Force

Today the last deadline to phase out animal testing for cosmetic products in Europe enters into force. As of today, cosmetics tested on animals cannot be marketed any more in the EU.

A Communication adopted by the Commission today confirms the Commission's commitment to respect the deadline set by Council and Parliament in 2003 and outlines how it intends to further support research and innovation in this area while promoting animal welfare world-wide.

European Commissioner in charge of Health & Consumer Policy, Tonio Borg, stated: *"Today's entry into force of the full marketing ban gives an important signal on the value that Europe attaches to animal welfare. The Commission is committed to continue supporting the development of alternative methods and to engage with third countries to follow our European approach. This is a great opportunity for Europe to set an example of responsible innovation in cosmetics without any compromise on consumer safety."*

The Commission has thoroughly assessed the impacts of the marketing ban and considers that there are overriding reasons to implement it. This is in line with what many European citizens believe firmly: that the **development of cosmetics does not warrant animal testing.**

The quest to find alternative methods will continue as **full replacement of animal testing by alternative methods is not yet possible.** The Communication published today outlines the Commission's contribution to the research into alternative methods and the recognition that these efforts must be continued. The Commission has made about **EUR 238 million available between the years 2007 and 2011 for such research.** The cosmetics industry has contributed as well, for example by co-funding the SEURAT [Safety Evaluation Ultimately Replacing Animal Testing] research initiative with EUR 25 million.

The leading and global role of Europe in cosmetics requires reaching out to trading partners to **explain and promote the European model** and to work towards the international acceptance of alternative methods. The Commission will make this an integral part of the Union's trade agenda and international cooperation.

Background

Directive 2003/15/EC introduced provisions in relation into animal testing into the Cosmetic Directive 76/768/EEC. Accordingly, **animal testing in the Union is already prohibited since 2004 for cosmetic products and since 2009 for cosmetic ingredients** ('testing ban'). As from March 2009, it is also prohibited to market in the Union cosmetic products containing ingredients which have been tested on animals ('marketing ban'). For the most complex human health effects (repeated-dose toxicity, including skin sensitisation and carcinogenicity, reproductive toxicity and toxicokinetics) the deadline for the marketing ban was extended to 11 March 2013.

Source: "Full EU Ban on Animal Testing for Cosmetics Enters into Force." March 11, 2013. Memo/13/188. http://europa.eu/rapid/press-release_IP-13-210_en.htm.

DOCUMENT

Questions and Answers: Animal Testing and Cosmetics

Cosmetic products range from everyday hygiene products, such as soap, shampoo, deodorant and toothpaste to luxury beauty items including perfumes and decorative cosmetics. These products are regulated at European level [Directive 76/768/EEC to be replaced as of July 2013 by Regulation 1223/2009/EU] in order to ensure consumer safety and to secure an internal market for cosmetic products.

The European Cosmetics and Toiletries industry is worth more than **EUR 70 billion**; this represents almost half of the global market for cosmetics. An estimated 184 000 people are directly employed by the cosmetics industry in the Union.

Animal testing for cosmetics is prohibited in the Union since March 2009. Before that 8988 animals were reported to be used for cosmetic purposes in the Union in 2004, a number that was reduced to 1510 animals in 2008 and to 344 animals in 2009. Animals used for testing for cosmetic purposes are rats, mice, guinea-pigs and rabbits. Any animal testing done for EU cosmetic purposes since 2009 is done outside the EU. Between 15000 and 27000 animals are estimated to be used outside the EU for this purpose yearly.

Is animal testing for cosmetics not already prohibited in Europe?
Yes, that is true: there can be **no animal testing for cosmetic purposes carried out in Europe**. Animal testing for finished cosmetic products is already banned since

2004, animal testing for cosmetic ingredients is banned since 11 March 2009 ('testing ban'). Since March 2009 it is also prohibited to market in the Union cosmetic products containing ingredients which have been tested on animals in order to meet the requirements of the Directive ('marketing ban').

But for the most complex tests the marketing ban deadline was extended to 11 March 2013. This means that for these tests companies could still carry out the tests outside the Union for cosmetic purposes and rely on the results for the safety assessment in the Union. This is not possible any more after 11 March 2013.

Why is animal testing carried out for cosmetics anyhow?
It is crucial to make sure that products that come into contact with our body day-by-day are safe for human health. Cosmetics are products that are used by consumers every day—there are estimates that **each consumer uses at least seven different cosmetics per day** and many of us will use more. Animal testing data is still needed to carry out this safety assessment—for example to establish whether or not a certain ingredient can cause skin allergy or contributes to the formation of cancer.

So is it possible to fully replace animal testing by other methods?
No, this is not yet possible in all cases. A lot of progress has been made, but there remains a lot to be done. Several alternative test methods have been validated by the European Union Reference Laboratory for Alternatives to Animal Testing (EURL ECVAM) and have subsequently been included in OECD Testing Guidelines and in the respective Union legal texts. For example, reconstructed human skin models exist to test whether an ingredient can cause skin irritation.

However, for the complex health effects that concern the whole human organism the situation is much more complicated. Important progress has been made here as well and methods have been validated or are undergoing validation that can then be used as building blocks within an overall testing strategy. Replacement will however not be achieved by replacing one animal test with one *in vitro* test and it is difficult to predict when full replacement will be possible [See "Alternative (non-animal) methods for cosmetics testing: current status and future prospects—2010"]. More research is needed.

What is being done to find alternative methods?
The Commission has made about EUR 238 million available between the years 2007 and 2011 for research into alternative methods to animal testing alone. The largest part of this budget, around EUR 198 million, was spent on projects through the 6th and 7th Framework Programmes. The second largest part was spent on the European Reference Laboratory for Alternative Methods to Animal Testing for its work on alternatives. The Communication adopted by the Commission today recognises the importance of continuing this research.

In addition, the cosmetics industry plays an active role in the development of alternatives. A very concrete example is the **SEURAT-1 initiative** ('Safety Evaluation Ultimately Replacing Animal Testing') in the field of repeated dose toxicity.

This project is jointly funded by the European Commission and the cosmetics industry, each of which [is] contributing a EUR 25 million between 2011 and 2015.
Will cosmetic products remain safe for consumers after March 2013?

Yes, the same safety standards as now apply. The marketing ban does not change the stringent safety assessment required under the Cosmetics legislation, an assessment which was strengthened in the new Cosmetics Regulation.

In cases in which it will not be possible to carry out a conclusive safety assessment because data is missing and because new animal data cannot be created for the purposes of cosmetics use, the respective ingredient should not be used.

Will the cosmetics I am used to disappear from the shelves as a result of the ban?
No, cosmetics on the market and for which the safety is already established are not affected by the ban and can continue to be placed on the market, historic animal data can continue to be relied on.

Will there be impacts on the cosmetics and cosmetic ingredients industry?
The Commission carried out an impact assessment [The Impact Assessment is available on the SANCO cosmetics website: http://ec.europa.eu/consumers/sectors/cosmetics/animal-testing/index_en.htm] to determine the impacts. It is clear that there will be some impacts on industry, as in certain cases it will not be able to carry out the required safety assessment and thus to use certain ingredients. The impacts, however, were difficult to quantify.

Overall, the Commission considers that the **expected benefits for animal welfare and for innovative ways of carrying out human health assessment are likely to outweigh any negative impacts**. The Commission will however closely monitor the impacts on the industry in the coming years and will continue to fund research into alternative methods and to work internationally towards acceptance of alternative methods in order to mitigate impacts.

With the full ban in place—can consumers be sure that cosmetics and cosmetic ingredients purchased in Europe were not subject to animal testing?
With the testing and marketing ban in force **there can be no new animal testing for cosmetics purposes in the Union**—be it for cosmetics products or ingredients thereof—and **it is no longer possible to simply carry out testing for these purposes outside the Union and then use the data here to substantiate the safety of cosmetics**. Consumers can therefore be sure that the cosmetic use of an ingredient in Europe cannot be the reason for any new animal testing.

However, the majority of ingredients that go into cosmetics are ingredients that are also in use in many other consumer and industrial products, such as in pharmaceuticals, detergents, food, paints etc. They may therefore be subject to animal testing requirements under these respective legal frameworks.

Source: European Commission. "Questions and Answers: Animal Testing and Cosmetics." March 11, 2013. IP/13/210. http://europa.eu/rapid/press-release _MEMO-13-188_en.htm.

ANALYSIS

The 100-plus-year battle to end animal testing in the European Union (EU) took a giant step forward on March 11, 2003, the final deadline for the full EU ban on animal testing for cosmetics. This battle began in 1898, when the British Union for the Abolition of Vivisection (BUAV) was founded by Frances Power Cobbe, a women's rights advocate and philanthropist. Cobbe proclaimed that vivisection is "a great moral offence, a great sin before God, [that] goes on in this land under the sanction of law." She had other powerful supporters, including Queen Victoria, who proclaimed that vivisection is "a disgrace to Christianity and humanity." As the decades passed, the BUAV's mission remained the same: to combat all forms of animal testing through legal, nonviolent channels, such as undercover investigations, legal challenges, funding research to find alternatives to animal testing, and supporting and promoting cruelty-free companies.

Nearly 100 years after its formation, the BUAV turned its focus to the issue of testing cosmetics on animals. Cosmetic products include everything from hygiene products, such as soap, deodorant, and toothpaste, to beauty products, such as perfumes and makeup. Although it is estimated that every person who purchases cosmetics uses seven different cosmetic products each day, the belief of many, according to a European Commission press release, is that "the development of cosmetics does not warrant animal testing." Note that this statement implies that animal testing by other industries, such as the medical industry, is warranted.

In 1990 the BUAV established the European Coalition to End Animal Experiments (ECEAE). Together, the BUAV and ECEAE organized rallies and marches throughout Europe to bring public awareness to the issue of cosmetics animal testing and to urge members of the European Parliament (MEPs) to vote for antivivisection measures in relation to cosmetics. In 1996, The Body Shop founder Anita Roddick and Chrissie Hynde, lead singer of The Pretenders rock band, along with nearly four million others, signed a petition to end animal testing of cosmetics; this petition was brought before the European Commission by the BUAV, ECEAE, and a group of MEPs.

It took another eight years, but in 2003, the EU established the Cosmetics Directive, which would bring to an end the practice of testing cosmetics on animals and prohibit the marketing of any cosmetic product that had been tested on animals. This directive was created to ensure consumer safety while also securing a market in the EU for cosmetic products.

The deadlines established by the directive took place over a period of years to give the industry time to develop and validate alternative, animal-free methods of testing the safety of cosmetic products. The first phase, effective as of 2004, banned animal testing of finished cosmetic products. However, this ban did not extend to the testing of individual ingredients of those cosmetics. The deadline for the ban on testing individual ingredients was in 2009, though that ban was made exempt for three types of tests (repeated-dose toxicity, reproductive toxicity, and toxicokinetics), because alternative methods had not yet been validated.

Between the 2004 and 2009 deadline, the number of rats, mice, guinea pigs, and rabbits used in the EU to test cosmetics dropped from 8,988 to 344. After 2009,

any animal cosmetic testing for cosmetics sold in the EU was performed on an estimated 15,000–27,000 animals outside the borders of the EU. The final cutoff date of
the ban was reached on March 11, 2013. This last deadline not only enforces the
ban on animal testing for cosmetics within the EU but also prohibits the sale and
marketing of any new cosmetic products that have been tested on animals, putting
an end to animal testing for any cosmetics sold within the EU.

Animal rights advocates are thrilled with this final ban. People for the Ethical
Treatment of Animals (PETA) offered a representative reaction, calling the ban a
"historic victory" and a "spectacular achievement." According to Silke Bitz, spokesperson for Doctors against Animal Testing, this ban is "the tip of the iceberg."
The hope is that the cosmetics industry will continue to lead the way in finding
new safety-testing methods that do not include animals and that will eventually lead
to an end to all forms of animal testing in all industries in the EU. (It is estimated
that 12 million animals are used for testing in the EU for everything from chemical
products to pharmaceuticals and medical research.) A promising alternative is the in
vitro approach, in which human stem cells are used to create skin cell models; this
method is already being used to detect skin irritants or corrosive substances. Because
human stem cells have the ability to differentiate into any type of cell, this research
method is "the way of the future," according to biologist Michael Oelgeschläger.
However, there are bureaucratic roadblocks, with each new method requiring validation and approval by both the scientific and political communities.

There are also certain loopholes in the ban. For example, a cosmetics company
can still use products that include ingredients tested on animals as long as those
tests were conducted by noncosmetic producers, such as the pharmaceutical or
food industry. If a European consumer wants to be sure that a product truly is free
of ingredients tested on animals, he or she should look for the Leaping Bunny
logo. Products with this logo are certified by the Coalition for Consumer Information on Cosmetics (the Leaping Bunny Program) as not having tested their
products or ingredients on animals, "regardless of any international regulatory
requirements."

From 2007 to 2011, the European Commission devoted about EUR 238 million
(US$320 million) for research into alternative testing methods. In addition,
Cosmetics Europe, the industry's European trade commission, has devoted considerable
time, effort, and money to research and develop alternatives while still supporting the
interests of the EUR 70 billion-a-year (US$91 billion) industry. Cosmetics Europe, in
conjunction with the European Commission, also funded the Safety Evaluation Ultimately Replacing Animal Testing (SEURAT-1) initiative, each contributing approximately EUR 25 million. The commission also conducted an impact assessment to
determine how this ban will affect the cosmetics industry. The assessment found that
although there will be consequences, the benefits to animals and the furtherance of
innovative ways to perform tests will outweigh any negative impacts.

One major challenge to the cosmetic industry's financial success, however, is the
fact that many developing nations, such as China, actually require animal testing of
all cosmetics sold in their country. Thus, companies that sell cruelty-free products in
the EU will have to test those products on animals outside the EU in order to maintain their markets in other countries. Animal rights activists have warned that this

situation can create a dynamic in which a consumer in Germany may buy a product created with no animal testing and yet still unknowingly help the bottom line of a company that still tests its products on animals to make sales in other parts of the world. Proponents of the EU ban state that they will work with such countries and encourage them to move away from animal testing. Their goal, according to EU commissioner for health and consumer policy Tonio Borg, is for the EU to set "an example [for other countries] of responsible innovation in cosmetics without any compromise on consumer safety." According to the organization Cruelty Free International, the advancements in alternate testing that have taken place in the EU provide a blueprint for other countries where animal testing for cosmetics is still allowed, such as the United States and Canada, to wean themselves off of all animal testing for cosmetics.

FURTHER READING

"Ban on Animal Testing." *European Commission*. http://ec.europa.eu/consumers/sectors/cosmetics/animal-testing/index_en.htm.

"The Cosmetic Directive's Ban on Animals in Testing." *Cosmetics Europe*. https://www.cosmeticseurope.eu/safety-and-science-cosmetics-europe/alternative-methods/the-cosmetics-directive-ban-on-animals-in-testing.html.

"Cosmetics and Animal Testing: A Historic Victory." *PETA: People for the Ethical Treatment of Animals*. http://www.peta.org.uk/features/new-cosmetics-law/.

Dickinson, Lynda. *Victims of Vanity: Animal Testing of Cosmetics and Household Products, and How to Stop It*. 2nd ed. Toronto: Summerhill Press, 1990.

Engebretson, Monica. "Celebrating the First Anniversary of the EU Ban on Animal Testing for Cosmetics." *Huffington Post*, March 19, 2014. http://www.huffingtonpost.com/monica-engebretson/celebrating-the-first-ann_b_4994028.html.

"EU Bans Sale of All Animal-Tested Cosmetics." *BBC*, March 11, 2013. http://www.bbc.com/news/world-europe-21740745.

"FAQ about the EU Cosmetics Testing Ban." *Leaping Bunny Program*. http://leapingbunny.org/eu2013/#.U6cNsaiSI8p.

Hamilton, Susan. "Reading and the Popular Critique in Science in the Victorian Anti-Vivisection Press: Frances Power Cobbe's Writing for the Victorian Street Society." *Victorian Review* 36, no. 2 (Fall 2010): 66–79.

Hester, R. E., and Roy M. Harrison. *Alternatives to Animal Testing*. Cambridge: Royal Society of Chemistry, 2006.

Kanter, James. "E.U. Bans Cosmetics with Animal-Tested Ingredients." *New York Times*, March 11, 2013. http://www.nytimes.com/2013/03/11/business/global/eu-to-ban-cosmetics-with-animal-tested-ingredients.html?_r=1&.

"Our History." *BUAV: The Campaign to End All Animal Experiments*. http://www.buav.org/about-us/our-history/.

"We Did It! Europe Bans Animal Testing for Cosmetics." *Cruelty-Free International*. http://www.crueltyfreeinternational.org/en/the-solution/animal-testing-for-cosmetics-in-europe-finally-set-to-end.

"WE HAVE STRENGTHEN[ED] OUR ABILITY TO ENFORCE HUMANE HANDLING LAWS AT LIVESTOCK SLAUGHTER FACILITIES NATIONWIDE"

- **Document:** Press release announcing new federal guidelines for the humane handling of livestock.
- **Date:** October 23, 2013.
- **Where:** Washington, D.C.
- **Significance:** The new guidelines implemented by the Food Safety and Inspection Service (FSIS) of the Department of Agriculture were designed to shore up perceived problems with industry adherence to the regulations contained in the Humane Methods of Slaughter Act, the primary legislation governing USDA-licensed cattle and hog slaughtering operations across the country.

DOCUMENT

Today, U.S. Department of Agriculture's Food Safety and Inspection Service (FSIS) will introduce new guidance—FSIS Compliance Guide for a Systematic Approach to the Humane Handling of Livestock—to support the Humane Methods of Slaughter Act. Proper implementation of this guidance will better ensure the humane treatment of livestock presented for slaughter, as it provides establishments a set of practices that will assist them in minimizing excitement, discomfort and accidental injury.

"We have taken significant measures over the last few years to strengthen our ability to enforce humane handling laws at livestock slaughter facilities nation-wide," said FSIS Administrator Al Almanza. "The guidance is one example of our commitment to the humane treatment of animals. We continue to implement improvements so that we have the best system possible."

This new guidance was developed to address the humane handling incidents cited in the spring 2013 Office of Inspector General report. As of this year, half of all live-stock slaughter establishments have adopted the systematic approach to humane handling, meeting the agency's strategic objective three years early. The agency will continue to implement additional best practices to support the humane treatment of animals.

In addition to this guidance, the agency is further equipping employees to prevent and respond to inhumane handing incidents by delivering a more practical, situation-based humane handling training to inspectors and veterinarians who verify and enforce humane handling requirements at hundreds of livestock slaughter establishments across the country. FSIS began delivering this enhanced training in 2010, and the agency will continue to deliver this training to new employees.

The training presents a variety of realistic animal-handling scenarios that employees may encounter, from truck unloading, to stunning, to post-stunning.

FSIS recently created a Humane Handling Enforcement Coordinator position, who oversees the agency's implementation and daily enforcement of humane handling requirements. Also, the agency created the Department-level Ombudsman position, who provides a neutral forum for the agency's field personnel and other stakeholders to report humane handling concerns that have not been addressed by the standard agency reporting mechanisms. For more information about the Ombudsman and for information on how to file a complaint, visit the Ombudsman Fact Sheet on the FSIS website.

Source: Boody, Elizabeth. "FSIS Issues New Guidance on Humane Handling." U.S. Department of Agriculture. Food and Safety Inspection Service. October 23, 2013. http://www.fsis.usda.gov/wps/portal/fsis/newsroom/news-releases-statements-transcripts/news-release-archives-by-year/archive/2013/nr-102313-01.

ANALYSIS

The treatment of livestock from birth to eventual slaughter has been a subject of scrutiny and criticism from animal welfare advocates for many years in the United States. One of the most venerable organizations concerned with this issue is the American Humane Association (AHA), which was founded in 1877 (in its early years the AHA had a dual mandate to fight for both child and animal welfare).

In 2000 the AHA created a set of animal welfare guidelines for the care and well-being of farm animals called the American Humane Certified program. Provisions contained in the American Humane Certified program seek to ensure that animals being used for food are raised and cared for under strict humane standards. According to the American Humane Association Web site, "in addition to providing proper medical care, diet, and water and keeping animals free from fear and distress, American Humane Certified producers must provide appropriate shelter for animals' comfort and rest and provide an environment that allows for the normal expression of the animal's behaviors." Examples of such an environment specifically mentioned by AHA include giving animals enough space to move around and lie down freely and allowing certain animals, such as hens and chickens, to be cage-free.

Another influential voice in this subject area has been Temple Grandin, an associate professor of animal science at Colorado State University, who has been studying animal welfare issues in agriculture for decades. She began auditing processing plants at the request of the U.S. Department of Agriculture and subsequently urged a host of operating reforms in slaughterhouse facilities. Some of her recommendations include the affixing of metal floor gratings to reduce slippage by cattle, implementation of centerline conveyors for comfortable transportation, and relaxed handlers, so the animals are more content and not stressed. These are fairly simple measures to implement that nonetheless allow for more humane treatment of animals that are killed so that their meat can be processed for human consumption.

The new USDA/FSIS guidelines took many of these measures into account and also provided training for employees to ensure that they are familiar with the various rules and regulations of the Humane Methods of Slaughter Act.

According to Dr. Lucy Anthenill, who in 2013 was appointed the USDA's humane handling enforcement coordinator, the new FSIS compliance guide was also supplemented with new training programs for inspectors and veterinarians to help them understand and improve the enforcement of humane handling requirements at hundreds of slaughter establishments across the country. FSIS also established a team of district veterinary medical specialists (DVMSs) to evaluate animal treatment at plant facilities across the country. According to Anthenill, "FSIS believes that humane treatment of animals for food is legally and ethically necessary and that these animals must be treated with . . . respect prior to arriving at our dinner tables" (Anthenill, 2014).

FURTHER READING

Anthenill, Lucy. "Counterpoint: For the Humane Treatment of the Animals We Eat." *Minneapolis StarTribune*, May 1, 2014. http://www.startribune.com/opinion/commentaries/257582911.html.

Bonné, Jon. "Can Animals You Eat Be Treated Humanely?" *NBC News*, June 28, 2004. http://www.nbcnews.com/id/5271434/ns/business-us_business/t/can-animals-you-eat-be-treated-humanely/#.U6SkpPldV8E.

Eisnitz, Gail A. *Slaughterhouse: The Shocking Story of Greed, Neglect, and Inhumane Treatment Inside the U.S. Meat Industry*. Amherst, NY: Prometheus Books, 2006.

Grandin, Temple, ed. *Improving Animal Welfare: A Practical Approach*. Cambridge, MA: CAB International, 2010.

Grandin, Temple, and Mark Deesing. *Humane Livestock Handling: Understanding Livestock Behavior and Building Facilities for Healthier Animals*. North Adams, MA: Storey Publishing, 2008.

"Temple Grandin: Humane Treatment of Livestock." Video. *Cooking Up a Story*. http://cookingupastory.com/temple-grandin-humane-tratment-of-farm-animals.

"Treatment of Farm Animals." *American Humane Association*. http://www.americanhumane.org/about-us/who-we-are/history/treatment-of-farm-animals.html.

"IT IS OUR MORAL RESPONSIBILITY TO PROTECT AND PRESERVE THE DIVERSE LIFE FORMS OUR FOREFATHERS KNEW IN ABUNDANCE"

- **Document:** "Who Speaks for the Sage Grouse?," an op-ed piece by Fort Lewis College professor Andrew Gulliford that appeared in the magazine *High Country News*.
- **Date:** Published in the January 9, 2014, issue.
- **Where:** The magazine is based in Paonia, Colorado.
- **Significance:** An impassioned writer looks at conflicts between finances and the environment, state and federal land control, and various political views as they pertain to the sage grouse and other endangered species.

DOCUMENT

Across the West, politicians and oil and gas industry spokesmen are wringing their hands, shaking their heads and saying "no" to Bureau of Land Management proposals to set aside large swaths of land for the greater sage grouse, and for federal plans to list the separate Gunnison sage grouse as an endangered species.

Colorado Gov. John Hickenlooper wants the BLM to "look at the public-private partnerships that have been so successful in Colorado as a model on how to get things done."

Perhaps. But who speaks for the sage grouse? What is at stake are thousands of square miles of the inter-mountain West because prime habitat for both species of grouse is also prime turf for oil and gas rigs and cattle. In Colorado's Mesa County, Commissioner Rose Pugliese said stringent federal management of the greater sage grouse "will kill us" economically. Commissioner Chuck Grobe in nearby Moffat County worries that $1.1 billion worth of minerals are at risk.

But things sound different in one part of the state's southwest. "San Miguel County wants to have U.S. Fish and Wildlife biologists make a determination based on science, not politics, as to whether the [Gunnison sage grouse] is threatened or endangered," said Commissioner Art Goodtimes. He added, "Losing another iconic Western species to extinction is a threat to the web of life, and the repercussions could have lasting consequences that we are not even aware of today."

In Utah, however, San Juan County residents are voicing their opinions in letters to the editor and at public meetings, and some people say the issue is really all about a government conspiracy. As Eric George complained, "The Gunnison sage grouse isn't the real issue here; no matter what the feds' PowerPoint presented. This is about corruption and usurpation of power, plain and simple."

No, it's not. If we can step back long enough from the rhetoric and the hand-wringing, we see that we are now in the third great age of extinction on this planet. Not since the dinosaurs disappeared have species been dying with such overwhelming

A male sage grouse fans his tail and puffs up his chest in a mating ritual. The sage grouse has been on a waiting list since March 2010 in its attempt to be classified as an endangered species. (Photos.com)

speed. Pulitzer Prize–winning scientist Edward O. Wilson explains, "The causes of extinction intensified throughout the 20th century. They are now the highest ever, and still rising. Almost one in four of Earth's mammal species and one in eight of the bird species are at some degree of risk."

This alarming and continuing story about extinction is all about our domination of nature and loss of habitat for all species. It's also about restraint. The Endangered Species Act of 1973, signed into law by President Richard Nixon, was one of our finest hours as Americans because the legislation represents humility. The law posits that we are only one species on this continent, and that it is our moral responsibility to protect and preserve the diverse life forms our forefathers knew in abundance and bequeathed to us.

Conservationist Aldo Leopold said it simply: "The first rule of intelligent tinkering is to save all the parts." Now there are believed to be fewer than 5,000 Gunnison sage grouse. As Westerners, we have moved into their habitat with our oil and gas rigs and our cows.

How ironic it is that across the West, the same ranchers who have been eager to pocket federal subsidies for *not* growing crops and for protecting habitat by joining the Conservation Reserve Program are now demanding the federal government get out of their lives. In San Juan County, Utah, Conservation Reserve Program payments since 1995 have exceeded $23 million. How much has been paid out across the West for the same purposes?

The sage-grouse controversy is just beginning. A federal listing of the Gunnison sage grouse as an endangered species may change the way the rural West does business, but what's wrong with that? Can't we take the long view? When we've pumped the natural resources dry and oil and gas are gone, what kind of world will we have left for our children's children?

Ranching has never been easy, and oil and gas revenues have financially propped up counties across the West. But as my hero, Republican President Theodore Roosevelt, said, "We're not building this country of ours for a day or even a year. It is to last through the ages."

Who speaks for the sage grouse? That is something every one of us has an obligation to do.

Source: Gulliford, Andrew. "Who Speaks for the Sage Grouse?" *High Country News*, January 9, 2014. https://www.hcn.org/wotr/who-speaks-for-the-sage-grouse. Used by permission of Andrew Gulliford.

ANALYSIS

This essay, which urges federal protection for two species of sage grouse that inhabit parts of the western United States, illustrates how economics and politics have come to dominate the animal rights debate in the twenty-first century.

The author, Andrew Gulliford, is a professor of history and environmental studies at Fort Lewis College in southwest Colorado, one of only two areas in the United States where Gunnison sage grouse remain. Gulliford argues not only that human interests should not outweigh the interests of other species but that preservation of endangered species actually is of lasting and enormous benefit to humankind.

Gulliford states that the Endangered Species Act reflects "our moral responsibility to protect and preserve the diverse life forms our forefathers knew in abundance and bequeathed to us." But Gulliford's piece does not focus only on the morality or philosophical underpinnings of arguments for animal rights. He also highlights the conflict between financial and environmental interests, the conflict between state and federal control over lands, and the conflicting political views in the regions where sage grouse live.

The excerpt provides a quick sketch of local politics in the two areas where Gunnison sage grouse live. In San Miguel County, a strongly Democratic county in southwestern Colorado, the people want "science, not politics" to determine whether the Gunnison sage grouse needs protection. (Scientists agree that the species is at risk for extinction; scientific studies indicate the sage grouse requires protection to survive.) Nearby San Juan County, in southeastern Utah, is heavily Republican and favors state-level decision making on the sage grouse issue. Under such a scenario, the state's industry-friendly political environment would probably preclude the introduction of major environmental protections for the sage grouse.

Although Gulliford leans toward the Democratic view, he tries to rise above the political argument by pointing out that "extinction is all about our domination of nature and loss of habitat for all species." With this statement, he echoes animal rights philosophers who emphasize both the connection and the responsibility human beings have to other species. Gulliford goes on to say, "Can't we take the long view?" While he recognizes that real financial sacrifices will be required, Gulliford asks people in the ranching, oil, and gas industries to put long-term interests above short-term gains, to protect the sage grouse for the sake of all species, including the human species.

The Endangered Species Act gives the federal government authority to acquire land for the conservation of listed species (i.e., species officially listed as endangered). The two species of sage grouse discussed in this passage are currently candidates for listing; this means they are on a waiting list behind other species that are believed to face a more immediate threat of extinction. The greater sage grouse has been on the waiting list since March 2010; the Gunnison sage grouse was added to the waiting list in September 2010. As long as the two species are only on the waiting list, federal authorities cannot set aside land for the birds' protection. People who use the land in question—ranchers and oil and gas developers—have a strong financial interest in maintaining the status quo, keeping the land unprotected by having the sage grouse on the waiting list. To accomplish this, they vote for political representatives who will defend the financial interests at stake.

The battle over sage grouse protection continues. The U.S. Fish and Wildlife Service proposed the Gunnison sage grouse as an endangered species in January 2013, moving the species one step closer to leaving the waiting list. Since then, however, the deadline for a final decision has been extended repeatedly, sometimes for additional public comment and sometimes for additional scientific data—both driven by the political controversy. In March 2013, ornithologist John W. Fitzpatrick said, "It is urgent that the Gunnison sage grouse be listed as an endangered species immediately." Nevertheless, the delays continued, and in April 2014, a bill (H.R. 4419) was introduced to prohibit the federal listing of greater sage grouse as an endangered species for the next 10 years, with the stipulation that states would be responsible for the birds' protection during that time. In May 2014, less than a week before the deadline for a final decision on listing the Gunnison sage grouse as an endangered species, the timeline was extended by an additional six months.

FURTHER READING

Broder, John M. "No Endangered Status for Plains Bird." *New York Times*, March 5, 2010. http://www.nytimes.com/2010/03/06/science/earth/06grouse.html.

"Colorado Prepared to Sue over Gunnison Sage-Grouse." *KUSA-TV*. http://www.9news .com/story/news/local/2014/04/22/colorado-gunnison-sage-grouse/8006049/.

"Farm Bureau Supports Sage Grouse Protection Act." *WNAX Radio*. http://wnax.com/news/ 180081-farm-bureau-supports-sage-grouse-protection-act/.

Fitzpatrick, John W. "Newly Discovered, Nearly Extinct." *New York Times*, March 6, 2013. http://www.nytimes.com/2013/03/07/opinion/the-plight-of-the-gunnison-sage-grouse .html?_r=0.

"FWS Lists Sage-Grouse as Candidate Species." *Wildlife Management Institute*. http://www .wildlifemanagementinstitute.org/index.php?option=com_content&view=article&id =435:fws-lists-sage-grouse&catid=34:ONB%20Articles&Itemid=54.

"Greater Sage Grouse Range Map." *South Dakota Birds and Birding*. http://sdakotabirds.com/ species/maps/greater_sage_grouse_map.htm.

"Gunnison Sage-Grouse." *Endangered Species*. U.S. Fish & Wildlife Service. http://www.fws. gov/mountain-prairie/species/birds/gunnisonsagegrouse/.

"Gunnison Sage-Grouse *Centrocercus minimus* ESA Status: Proposed for Listing." *Wild Earth Guardians*. http://www.wildearthguardians.org/site/PageServer?pagename=species _birds_gunnison_sage_grouse#.U6EYrbEmPT0.

Knick, Steven T., and John William Connelly, eds. *Greater Sage-Grouse: Ecology and Conservation of a Landscape Species and Its Habitats*. Berkeley: University of California Press, 2011.

Sage Grouse Initiative. http://www.sagegrouseinitiative.com/.

"Text of the Sage-Grouse and Endangered Species Conservation and Protection Act." *Govtrack.us*. https://www.govtrack.us/congress/bills/113/hr4419/text.

"MANY SPECIES DECIMATED BY ILLEGAL TRADE AND OTHER THREATS, SUCH AS HABITAT LOSS, ARE NOW IN DANGER OF EXTINCTION"

- *Document:* The National Strategy for Combating Wildlife Trafficking, issued by the White House.
- *Date:* February 2014.
- *Where:* Washington, D.C.
- *Significance:* This document demonstrates U.S. commitment to fighting wildlife trafficking by "strengthen[ing] enforcement," "reduc[ing] the demand for illegally traded wildlife," and "expand[ing] international cooperation and commitment."

DOCUMENT

National Strategy for Combating Wildlife Trafficking Executive Summary

The National Strategy for Combating Wildlife Trafficking establishes guiding principles and strategic priorities for U.S. efforts to stem illegal trade in wildlife. This Strategy positions the United States to exercise leadership in addressing a serious and urgent conservation and global security threat. It calls for strengthening the enforcement of laws and international agreements that protect wildlife while reducing demand for illegal wildlife and wildlife products. It affirms our Nation's resolve to work in partnership with governments, local communities, nongovernmental organizations, the private sector, and others to strengthen commitment to combating wildlife trafficking.

The United States will advance three strategic priorities to combat wildlife trafficking.

1. **Strengthen Enforcement**—We will improve efforts in the United States to stop illegal trade in wildlife and to enforce laws prohibiting wildlife trafficking. We will use administrative tools to address the dramatic increase in illegal elephant ivory and rhino horn trade. We will improve coordination and prioritize wildlife trafficking across enforcement, regulatory, and intelligence agencies. We will integrate wildlife trafficking, where appropriate, with other U.S. efforts to combat transnational organized crime. We will also help improve global enforcement efforts by supporting partner countries to build enforcement capacity. We will provide assistance for field-level wildlife and protected area management and enforcement, and also assist and participate in multinational enforcement operations targeting illegal trade in wildlife. We will work to dismantle trafficking networks and prevent others from assuming their illegal activities.

2. **Reduce Demand for Illegally Traded Wildlife**—We will raise public awareness of the harms done by wildlife trafficking through outreach in the United States and public diplomacy abroad to dissuade consumers from purchasing illegally traded wildlife. Criminals will continue to kill wildlife and traffic in contraband as long as the potential profits remain so high. We must enlist individual consumers in our country and other nations in this fight by educating them about the impacts of wildlife trafficking, on people as well as wildlife, and encouraging them to examine their purchasing patterns.

3. **Expand International Cooperation and Commitment**—Through our diplomacy, we will mobilize global support for, and encourage partners to actively participate in, the fight against wildlife trafficking. We will strengthen implementation of international agreements and arrangements that protect wildlife. We will build partnerships with governments, intergovernmental organizations, nongovernmental organizations, local communities, and the private sector to address this issue to develop and implement innovative and effective approaches to combating wildlife trafficking.

Advancing these strategic priorities will require a whole-of-government approach that marshals and strategically applies Federal resources. It demands innovative and science-based analytical tools and inclusive information sharing. And, it requires strengthening relationships and partnership to develop and implement strategies for dealing with all aspects of wildlife trafficking. Now is the time for effective solutions to combat wildlife trafficking.

Introduction

In the past decade, wildlife trafficking—the poaching or other taking of protected or managed species and the illegal trade in wildlife and their related parts and products—has escalated into an international crisis. Wildlife trafficking is both a critical conservation concern and a threat to global security with significant effects on the national interests of the United States and the interests of our partners around the world.

As President Obama said in Tanzania in July 2013, on issuing a new Executive Order to better organize United States Government efforts in the fight against wildlife trafficking, wildlife is inseparable from the identity and prosperity of the world as we know it. We need to act now to reverse the effects of wildlife trafficking on animal populations before we lose the opportunity to prevent the extinction of iconic animals like elephants and rhinoceroses. Like other forms of illicit trade, wildlife trafficking undermines security across nations. Well-armed networks of poachers, criminals, and corrupt officials exploit porous borders and weak institutions to profit from trading in illegally taken wildlife.

We know that the United States is among the world's major markets for wildlife and wildlife products, both legal and illegal. In Asia, increased demand for ivory and rhino horn stems from a rapidly expanding wealthy class that views these commodities as luxury goods that enhance social status. As a result, we have seen an increase in ready buyers within Africa who serve as dealers to clients in Asia.

Increased demand for elephant ivory and rhino horn has triggered dramatic and rapid upticks in poaching in Africa. Criminal elements of all kinds, including some terrorist entities and rogue security personnel—often in collusion with government officials in source countries—are involved in poaching and transporting ivory and rhino horn across Africa. We assess with high confidence that traffickers use sophisticated networks and take advantage of jurisdictions where public officials are complicit in order to move elephant ivory and rhino horn from remote areas to markets and ports, perpetuating corruption and border insecurity, particularly in key eastern, central, and southern African states. Some of these networks are likely the same or overlap with those that also deal in other illicit goods such as drugs and weapons.

Poaching presents significant security challenges for militaries and police forces in African nations, which are often outgunned by poachers and their criminal and extremist allies. Moreover, wildlife trafficking corrodes democratic institutions and undermines transparency. Corruption and lack of sufficient penal and financial deterrents are hampering these governments' abilities to reduce poaching and trafficking. Material and training, legal, and diplomatic support could have a significant impact on the trajectory of the illicit rhino horn and ivory trades, and would also represent a relatively cost-effective way to gain new insights into the behavior of implicated criminal groups and associated trafficking networks. However, the widespread complicity of military and government officials in the trade hinders potential partnerships.

Why Now?

The scale and scope of wildlife trafficking continue to grow at an alarming rate, reversing decades of conservation gains. Wildlife trafficking threatens an increasing variety of terrestrial, freshwater, and marine species, including but not limited to: elephants, rhinos, tigers, sharks, tuna, sea turtles, land tortoises, great apes, exotic birds, pangolins, sturgeon, coral, iguanas, chameleons, and tarantulas. Wildlife trafficking is facilitated and exacerbated by illegal harvest and trade in plants and trees, which destroys needed habitat and opens access to previously remote populations of highly endangered wildlife, such as tigers. In addition, illegal trafficking of fisheries products, among others, threatens food supplies and food security. Many species decimated by illegal trade and other threats, such as habitat loss, are now in danger of extinction. Wildlife trafficking jeopardizes the survival of iconic species such as elephants and rhinos. Now is the time for greater action, before such losses become irreversible.

The United States has long placed great value and importance on conserving wildlife resources within and beyond our borders. Federal law has protected some of this Nation's species from poaching and illegal commercialization for more than a century. As the first Nation to ratify the Convention on International Trade in Endangered Species of Wild Fauna and Flora (CITES) in 1974, the United States has consistently stood with countries around the world in combating wildlife trafficking and protecting natural resources.

Conservation efforts to protect biodiversity and preserve functioning ecosystems are critical to secure economic prosperity, regional stability, and human health around the world. Wildlife trafficking now threatens not only national and global wildlife resources but also national and global security. This reality requires that we strengthen our efforts at home and abroad and ensure that the agencies tasked with this work have adequate resources, appropriate authorities, and the necessary partnerships to do it well.

This strategy sets forth a broad and time-sensitive course of action. This crisis must be addressed aggressively and quickly, or it will be too late.

U.S. Strategic Priorities

We have identified three strategic priorities to respond to the global wildlife trafficking crisis and address related threats to U.S. national interests:

1. Strengthen enforcement;
2. Reduce demand for illegally traded wildlife; and
3. Build international cooperation, commitment, and public-private partnerships.

To meet these strategic goals, we will expand United States Government leadership guided by the following principles.

- **Marshal Federal Resources for Combating Wildlife Trafficking** by elevating this issue as a core mission of all relevant executive branch agencies and departments and ensuring effective coordination across our government.
- **Use Resources Strategically** by identifying common priorities and strategic approaches and by coordinating and harmonizing funding and programs across agencies to maximize strategic impact and minimize duplication of efforts.
- **Improve the Quality of Available Information** by developing and using innovative and science-based tools to gather and appropriately share the information needed to fight wildlife trafficking and to assess and improve our and our partners' efforts.
- **Consider All Links of the Illegal Trade Chain** in developing and evaluating strategies to establish strong and effective long-term solutions that address all aspects of wildlife trafficking, from poaching and transit through consumer use.
- **Strengthen Relationships and Partnerships** with the many public and private partners who share our commitment and our belief that continued coordination among nations, as well as with nongovernmental organizations and the private sector, are key to stopping wildlife trafficking. . . .

Conclusion

This Strategy recognizes that we must redouble our efforts to address wildlife trafficking now if we are to preserve species and promote global peace and economic stability. The actions needed to disrupt and deter wildlife trafficking are clear, as are the consequences of failing to act both quickly and strategically in response to this multidimensional threat. The United States must curtail its own role in the illegal trade in wildlife and must lead in addressing this issue on the global stage. By working across Federal departments and agencies, the Presidential Task Force on Wildlife Trafficking, in consultation with the Advisory Council, will implement this strategy and collaborate where appropriate with the nongovernmental organizations and the private sector to ensure success. We can strengthen and expand enforcement and demand reduction efforts and promote and secure global commitment and cooperation in combating wildlife trafficking. In all of our endeavors, we must foster and strengthen partnerships with other governments, the nonprofit conservation community, and the private sector. No one country can tackle these issues on its own. This is a global challenge that requires global solutions. It is only by working together that we can develop effective solutions to combat wildlife trafficking and protect our natural resources for future generations.

Source: White House. National Strategy for Combating Wildlife Trafficking, February 11, 2014. http://www.doi.gov/news/upload/NationalStrategyWildlifeTrafficking.pdf.

ANALYSIS

This document, published in February 2014, shows how the interests of human beings and the interests of other species are intricately connected in real-world matters, not just in animal rights philosophy. The excerpt is a broad summary of a federal plan to stop illegal trade in wildlife and wildlife products. The selected passage reaffirms the U.S. commitment to protecting wildlife and provides a sketch of how complex and challenging that goal has become in the twenty-first century.

The excerpt describes wildlife trafficking as "both a critical conservation concern and a threat to global security." The connection between wildlife trafficking and global security is complicated. (The idea is discussed in detail in *International Illegal Trade in Wildlife: Threats and U.S. Policy,* a report prepared for Congress in early 2009.) However, as the excerpt indicates, illegal trade in wildlife—like other forms of illegal trade—can involve multiple international and criminal links. And because wildlife trafficking is so profitable, it is particularly problematic in poor countries, where some of the greatest and most exotic wildlife resources exist. For example, traffickers frequently bribe low-paid border security officials to not intercede in the transport of illegally taken wildlife. As noted in the excerpt, traffickers and terrorists may sometimes be part of the same group, using the profits from illegal wildlife trade to buy weapons and fund various dangerous activities. In this sense, the "enemies" of the animals may also be the enemies of international security and global peace.

On the same day the National Strategy for Combating Wildlife Trafficking was published, the United States announced a ban on ivory sales within U.S. borders. The ban was a response to a recent and rapid increase in the poaching of elephants for their tusks. The press release announcing the ban states that global trade in illegal ivory "has more than doubled since 2007," with an estimated 35,000 elephants killed in 2012. This increase in poaching corresponds to increasing poverty and desperation in African nations where elephants live and increasing demand for ivory from wealthier nations, such as China and the United States. Along with conservationists around the world, some Africans want their wildlife resources to be protected, both for altruistic purposes and because such wildlife is a big draw for tourism. But poverty drives other Africans to trade in wildlife and exotic animal parts that are in high demand (in wealthier countries). Poverty and political motivations drive others to join rebel groups, which may fund their activities with profits from wildlife trafficking. The fate of the elephants is thus directly linked to economic imbalances and political turmoil among human beings.

The newly announced U.S. ban on commercial ivory trade is one example of the effort to strengthen enforcement of laws prohibiting wildlife trafficking. By banning forms of ivory trade that were previously exempt from prohibitions, the U.S. government hopes to further reduce the role the United States plays in wildlife trafficking. For example, illegal ivory may be routed through individuals in the United States who act as middlemen between poachers in Africa and buyers in Southeast Asia. By creating strict rules for the exchange of ivory already in the United States, the government hopes to break links in the international wildlife trafficking chain.

The U.S. government is also enforcing stronger penalties for illegal wildlife trade. In May 2014, just three months after the National Strategy for Combating Wildlife Trafficking was published, a New Jersey–based smuggler of elephant ivory and rhino horn was sentenced to 70 months in jail, one of the longest sentences ever handed down in a U.S. court for wildlife trafficking.

Reducing demand for illegally traded wildlife—the second strategic priority listed in the excerpt—would theoretically reduce the profits and therefore the motivation of wildlife traffickers and poachers. However, a *Smithsonian* article on illegal wildlife trade in South America points out that "the rarer the species, the more valuable it is to poachers—which only puts more pressure on the few remaining specimens." In other words, as a species gets closer to extinction, demand (and prices) can be expected to rise. This fact suggests that greater conservation efforts, designed to increase the populations of vulnerable species, will be a necessary part of any plan to reduce demand for illegally traded wildlife.

The excerpt repeatedly mentions the need for cooperation among all nations in the fight against wildlife trafficking. In addition to having its own animal and wildlife protection laws (e.g., the Lacey Act, the Animal Welfare Act, and the Endangered Species Act), the U.S. government abides by international agreements on wildlife conservation. The source document for this excerpt notes that CITES (the Convention on International Trade in Endangered Species of Wild Fauna and Flora) is "the principal international agreement that specifically addresses unsustainable and illegal wildlife . . . trade." Yet participating nations sometimes violate CITES regulations. For example, Japan, Norway, and Iceland have all continued to hunt whales, despite the CITES prohibition against whale hunting.

Violations of the CITES agreement create a conflict between U.S. strategic priorities in combating illegal wildlife trade: international cooperation and diplomacy versus enforcement of wildlife trade laws. In April 2014, President Barack Obama chose not to impose sanctions on Iceland for its illegal whale hunting, opting for continued diplomatic pressure instead. Animal rights advocates and conservationists expressed disappointment with this decision, complaining that it favored political interests over animal interests. However, defenders of the decision indicated that it reflected a belief that careful and long-term cultivation of international relationships are the most promising route to winning the global battle against the illegal trade in wildlife.

FURTHER READING

"African Elephant Conservation Fund." *U.S. Fish & Wildlife Service*, December 2013. http://www.fws.gov/international/pdf/factsheet-african-elephant.pdf.

Bergman, Charles. "Wildlife Trafficking: A Reporter Follows the Lucrative, Illicit and Heartrending Trade in Stolen Wild Animals Deep into Ecuador's Rain Forest." *Smithsonian*, December 2009. http://www.smithsonianmag.com/people-places/wildlife-trafficking-149079896/?no-ist.

Edmonds, Molly. "President Obama Forgoes Sanctions over Iceland Whaling." *World Wildlife Fund*, April 1, 2014. https://www.worldwildlife.org/press-releases/president-obama-forgoes-sanctions-over-iceland-whaling.

"Elephant Management." *Kavango-Zambezi Transfrontier Conservation Area*. http://www.kavangozambezi.org/elephant-management.

"Fact Sheet: National Strategy for Combating Wildlife Trafficking & Commercial Ban on Trade in Elephant Ivory." *White House*, February 11, 2014. http://www.whitehouse.gov/the-press-office/2014/02/11/fact-sheet-national-strategy-combating-wildlife-trafficking-commercial-b.

Karimi, Faith. "Poachers Kill Beloved Kenyan Elephant Known for Giant Tusks." *CNN*, June 15, 2014. http://www.cnn.com/2014/06/15/world/africa/kenya-satao-famous-elephant/.

"Law Enforcement Stories and News Releases." *U.S. Fish & Wildlife Service, Office of Law Enforcement*. http://www.fws.gov/le/stories.html.

Martin, Rachel. "Conservationist Shot in Africa's Oldest Nature Preserve." *NPR*, April 20, 2014. http://www.npr.org/2014/04/20/305162821/conservationist-shot-in-africas-oldest-nature-preserve.

Omer, Amal. "WWF: Stiff Sentence for Rhino Horn Smuggler Is Game Changer in Wildlife Trafficking Fight." *World Wildlife Fund*, May 28, 2014. https://www.worldwildlife.org/press-releases/wwf-stiff-sentence-for-rhino-horn-smuggler-is-game-changer-in-wildlife-trafficking-fight.

Pacelle, Wayne. "Stop U.S. Hunters from Killing the Elephants." *CNN*, June 27, 2014. http://www.cnn.com/2014/06/26/opinion/pacelle-elephant-poaching/index.html?hpt=hp_t3.

Portman, Rob. "Elephants Slaughtered for Trinkets and Terrorism." *CNN*, February 8, 2014. http://www.cnn.com/2014/02/08/opinion/portman-elephants/index.html.

"The President's Advisory Council on Wildlife Trafficking." *U.S. Fish & Wildlife Service*, June 9, 2014. http://www.fws.gov/International/advisory-council-wildlife-trafficking/pdf/advisory-council-recommendations-06-09-14.pdf.

"Press Release: Interior Announces Ban on Commercial Trade of Ivory as Part of Overall Effort to Combat Poaching, Wildlife Trafficking." *U.S. Department of the Interior*, February 11, 2014. http://www.doi.gov/news/pressreleases/interior-announces-ban

-on-commercial-trade-of-ivory-as-part-of-overall-effort-to-combat-poaching-wildlife
-trafficking.cfm.

Siber, Kate. "The One Use of Drones Everyone Can Agree on, Except for Poachers."
Smithsonian, March 13, 2014. http://www.smithsonianmag.com/science-nature/one
-use-drones-everyone-can-agree-except-poachers-180950078/?no-ist.

Traffic: The Wildlife Trade Monitoring Network. http://www.traffic.org/trade/.

"Wildlife Trafficking." *U.S. Fish & Wildlife Service, International Affairs.* http://www.fws.gov/
International/wildlife-trafficking/index.html.

Wyatt, Tanya. *Wildlife Trafficking: A Deconstruction of the Crime, the Victims, and the
Offenders.* Basingstoke: Palgrave Macmillan, 2013.

Wyler, Liana Sun, and Pervaze A. Sheikh. *International Illegal Trade in Wildlife: Threats and
U.S. Policy.* Washington, D.C.: Congressional Research Service, 2009. https://www
.hsdl.org/?view&did=38656.

"Zhifei Li Pleads Guilty in New Jersey to Running International Rhino Horn Smuggling
Ring." *Huffington Post*, December 19, 2013. http://www.huffingtonpost.com/2013/12/
19/zhifei-li-guilty-nj-rhino-horn_n_4474402.html.

"MANY SPECIES MAY NOT BE ABLE TO KEEP PACE WITH CLIMATE CHANGE ... THUS LEADING, IN SOME PLACES, TO LOCAL EXTINCTIONS OF BOTH PLANTS AND ANIMALS"

- **Document:** Excerpt from a chapter on the impact of climate change on plants and animals from the U.S. Global Change Research Program's *Third National Climate Assessment*.
- **Date:** May 2014.
- **Where:** Washington, D.C.
- **Significance:** This excerpt from the National Climate Assessment, which reports every four years on the state of scientific knowledge about climate change and its effect on various regions of the United States, addresses the potential impact of global warming on plants and animals, including the possibility of extinction. The assessment was prepared under the auspices of the U.S. Global Change Research Program (USGCRP), which was established in 1989 and mandated by Congress to "assist the Nation and the world to understand, assess, predict, and respond to human-induced and natural processes of global change." The 2014 assessment, the third of its kind, was assembled by more than 300 experts and a Federal Advisory Committee (including representatives of two oil companies). It was extensively reviewed prior to publication by experts from various federal agencies as well as a special panel of the National Academy of Sciences. According to the *New York Times*, the third National Climate Assessment (the first two were published in 2000 and 2009, respectively) "is by far the most urgent in tone, leaving little doubt that the scientists consider climate change an incipient crisis" (Gillis, 2014).

DOCUMENT

Key Message 3: Plants and Animals

Landscapes and seascapes are changing rapidly, and species, including many iconic species, may disappear from regions where they have been prevalent or become extinct, altering some regions so much that their mix of plant and animal life will become almost unrecognizable.

Vegetation model projections suggest that much of the United States will experience changes in the composition of species characteristic of specific areas. Studies applying different models for a range of future climates project biome changes for about 5% to 20% of the land area of the U.S. by 2100. Many major changes, particularly in the western states and Alaska, will in part be driven by increases in fire frequency and severity. For example, the average time between fires in the Yellowstone National Park ecosystem is projected to decrease from 100 to 300 years to less than 30 years, potentially causing coniferous (pine, spruce, etc.) forests to be replaced by woodlands and grasslands. Warming has also led to novel wildfire occurrence in ecosystems where it has been absent in recent history, such as arctic Alaska and the southwestern deserts where new fires are fueled by non-native annual grasses (Ch. 20: Southwest; Ch. 22: Alaska). Extreme weather conditions linked to sea ice decline in 2007 led to the ignition of the Anaktuvuk River Fire, which burned more than 380 square miles of arctic tundra that had not been disturbed by fire for more than 3,000 years. This one fire (which burned deeply into organic peat soils) released enough carbon to the atmosphere to offset all of the carbon taken up by the entire arctic tundra biome over the past quarter-century.

In addition to shifts in species assemblages, there will also be changes in species distributions. In recent decades, in both land and aquatic environments, plants and animals have moved to higher elevations at a median rate of 36 feet (0.011 kilometers) per decade, and to higher latitudes at a median rate of 10.5 miles (16.9 kilometers) per decade. As the climate continues to change, models and long-term studies project even greater shifts in species ranges. However, many species may not be able to keep pace with climate change for several reasons, for example because their seeds do not disperse widely or because they have limited mobility, thus leading, in some places, to local extinctions of both plants and animals. Both range shifts and local extinctions will, in many places, lead to large changes in the mix of plants and animals present in the local ecosystem, resulting in new communities that bear little resemblance to those of today.

Some of the most obvious changes in the landscape are occurring at the boundaries between biomes. These include shifts in the latitude and elevation of the boreal (northern) forest/tundra boundary in Alaska; elevation shifts of the boreal and sub-alpine forest/tundra boundary in the Sierra Nevada, California; an elevation shift of the temperate broadleaf/conifer boundary in the Green Mountains, Vermont, the shift of temperate the shrubland/conifer forest boundary in Bandelier National Monument, New Mexico, and upslope shifts of the temperate mixed forest/conifer boundary in Southern California. All of these are consistent with recent climatic trends and represent visible changes, like tundra switching to forest, or conifer forest switching to broadleaf forest or even to shrubland.

As temperatures rise and precipitation patterns change, many fish species (such as salmon, trout, whitefish, and char) will be lost from lower-elevation streams, including a projected loss of 47% of habitat for all trout species in the western U.S. by 2080. Similarly, in the oceans, transitions from cold-water fish communities to warm-water communities have occurred in commercially important harvest areas, with new industries developing in response to the arrival of new species. Also, warm surface waters are driving some fish species to deeper waters.

Warming is likely to increase the ranges of several invasive plant species in the United States, increase the probability of establishment of invasive plant species in boreal forests in south-central Alaska, including the Kenai Peninsula, and expand the range of the hemlock wooly adelgid, an insect that has killed many eastern hemlocks in recent years. Invasive species costs to the U.S. economy are estimated at $120 billion per year, including substantial impacts on ecosystem services. For instance, the yellow star-thistle, a wildland pest which is predicted to thrive with increased atmospheric CO_2, currently costs California ranchers and farmers $17 million in forage and control efforts and $75 million in water losses. Iconic desert species such as saguaro cactus are damaged or killed by fires fueled by non-native grasses, leading to a large-scale transformation of desert shrubland into grassland in many of the familiar landscapes of the American West. Bark beetles have infested extensive areas of the western United States and Canada, killing stands of temperate and boreal conifer forest across areas greater than any other outbreak in the last 125 years. Climate change has been a major causal factor, with higher temperatures allowing more beetles to survive winter, complete two life cycles in a season rather than one, and to move to higher elevations and latitudes. Bark beetle outbreaks in the Greater Yellowstone Ecosystem are occurring in habitats where outbreaks either did not previously occur or were limited in scale.

It is important to realize that climate change is linked to far more dramatic changes than simply altering species' life cycles or shifting their ranges. Several species have exhibited population declines linked to climate change, with some declines so severe that species are threatened with extinction. Perhaps the most striking impact of climate change is its effect on iconic species such as the polar bear, the ringed seal, and coral species (Ch. 22: Alaska; Ch. 24: Oceans). In 2008, the polar bear (*Ursus maritimus*) was listed as a threatened species, with the primary cause of its decline attributed to climate change. In 2012, NOAA determined that four subspecies of the ringed seal (*Phoca hispida*) were threatened or endangered, with the primary threat being climate change.

Source: Groffman, Peter M., Peter Kareiva, Shawn Carter, Nancy B. Grimm, Joshua Lawler, Michelle Mack, Virginia Matzek, and Heather Tallis. "Ch. 8: Ecosystems, Biodiversity, and Ecosystem Services." In *Climate Change Impacts in the United States: The Third National Climate Assessment.* Edited by Jerry M. Melillo, Terese (T. C.) Richmond, and Gary W. Yohe. Washington, D.C.: U.S. Global Change Research Program, 2014, 195–219.

ANALYSIS

This excerpt discusses how climate change threatens wildlife by changing the balance in ecosystems worldwide. Changes in temperature and precipitation have immediate effects on plant life, and changes in plant life inevitably affect animal species. The selected passage provides examples to show that climate change is a scientific reality that is putting wildlife at risk—and creating economic problems for human beings as a direct result. This analysis confirms statements made by animal rights advocates in the 1980s—namely, that the interests of human beings, nonhuman animals, and the environment are all linked together.

One of the most important details noted in this excerpt is the rate of climate change. Although successful species must continually adapt to a changing environment, they cannot necessarily match the rapid pace of climate change or survive destructive events related to changes in climate. The Anaktuvuk River Fire, cited in this excerpt, is an example of how a single, relatively brief event (a wildfire) can quickly cause damage far beyond measurable acreage: the fire, which occurred in the North Slope area of Alaska, released an amount of carbon dioxide (CO_2) that had taken the tundra 25 years to absorb. CO_2 is one of the "greenhouse gases" known to contribute to increasing global temperatures; the Anaktuvuk River Fire is just one part of the cycle of climate change. In this cycle, increasing temperatures cause increasingly frequent and severe fires, which destroy plant life and habitat; plants can absorb CO_2, but the destruction of plant life means too much CO_2 builds up in the atmosphere, raising temperatures even higher and starting the cycle over again. All of these changes harm animal species, damaging or destroying their habitats and threatening their survival.

This excerpt shows how damage to habitat that sustains both wildlife and commercial livestock also causes economic harm to human beings. Specifically, the excerpt notes that damages from climate change negatively affect commercial interests such as fishing, ranching, and farming. Ironically, since intensive industrial ranching and farming practices have been identified as significant contributors to climate change, they are in fact playing a significant role in jeopardizing their own financial security. For example, worldwide, CO_2 emissions from livestock production make up about 14 percent of all CO_2 emissions related to human activities. As atmospheric CO_2 levels rise, so do temperatures, and higher temperatures damage desirable plant life, allowing invasive plant species to encroach on ranchland. Ranchers then have to spend increasing amounts of money on weed control; scarce, valuable water is also wasted, taken up by invasive plants that have no agricultural value. Farming and ranching practices have long been criticized by animal rights advocates, who object to both the treatment of the animals and the detrimental environmental effects of many ranching and farming operations. The examples provided in the excerpt suggest that presently dominant forms of ranching and farming may be environmentally and economically unsustainable if climate change continues on its current trajectory.

CO_2 emissions and global warming also have significant impact on aquatic environments, especially the oceans. As the water gets warmer, fish must relocate (if possible) or die out, potentially leaving other aquatic species without a food source. In addition, the acidity of seawater has risen because the oceans have absorbed large amounts of CO_2, generated by increasing industrial activity. Because of these changes, the oceans' ability to absorb CO_2 is expected to decrease over time, accelerating the effects of climate change on land and water. The 2014 National Climate Assessment noted that climate change has already threatened or endangered a wide range of marine species, from coral to ringed seals. The polar bear offers a dramatic example of the effects of climate change, because people can visualize the problem: as the ocean temperature rises, polar bears must hunt from smaller and smaller platforms of melting sea ice. Their habitat is visibly changing and gradually disappearing, as are the habitats of many other species.

The excerpt makes two references to the visible effects of climate change, stating that in some regions the "mix of plant and animal life will become almost unrecognizable" (compared to existing conditions) and "new communities [will] bear little resemblance to those of today." The excerpt also includes references to "iconic species," including the saguaro cactus and the polar bear. Discussing changes that people can actually see and mentioning species that people easily recognize are ways to draw the public's attention to the problem and persuade people that climate change is a reality and a risk to "life as we know it." This is important because the subject of climate change (sometimes referred to as "global warming") continues to be controversial. Like other issues that relate to animal rights, climate change inspires strong feelings about the relative value of human interests and nonhuman animal interests. Those who believe that human beings have a right to use animals and the rest of the natural environment as they wish resist the idea that people might need to curtail their familiar habits or activities in order to preserve the planet or save its animals. While this excerpt does not attempt to directly argue the point, the information provided supports the message of animal rights advocates who believe that protecting the human race from global warming cannot be accomplished without also saving the ecosystems on which animals and plants, both wild and domestic, depend for their existence.

FURTHER READING

"Climate Change." *How to Do Animal Rights*. http://www.animalethics.org.uk/i-ch8-7 -climatechange.html.

"Climate Change and Animal Welfare." *Eurogroup for Animals*. http://eurogroupforanimals. org/files/otherpolicies/downloads/205/rbclimate_change_and_animal_welfare.pdf.

"Climate Change Effects on Ocean Animals." *New England Aquarium*. http://www.neaq.org/ conservation_and_research/climate_change/effects_on_ocean_animals.php.

"Climate Change Linked to Decline in Native Trout." *GlobalChange.gov*, June 17, 2014. http://www.globalchange.gov/news/climate-change-linked-decline-native-trout.

Darwall, Rupert. *The Age of Global Warming: A History*. London: Quartet Books, 2013.

"Effects on Wildlife and Habitat." *National Wildlife Federation*. http://www.nwf.org/Wildlife/ Threats-to-Wildlife/Global-Warming/Effects-on-Wildlife-and-Habitat.aspx.

"Emerging Consensus Shows Climate Change Already Having Major Effects on Ecosystems and Species." *U.S. Geological Survey*, December 18, 2012. http://www.usgs.gov/ newsroom/article.asp?ID=3483&from=rss_home#.U7Gu87EmPT0.

"Fact Sheet." *National Fish, Wildlife, & Plants Climate Adaption Strategy*. http://www .wildlifeadaptationstrategy.gov/pdf/New_Strategy_Factsheet.pdf.

Gillis, Justin. "U.S. Climate Has Already Changed, Study Finds, Citing Heat and Floods," *New York Times*, May 6, 2014. http://www.nytimes.com/2014/05/07/science/earth/ climate-change-report.html?_r=0.

"Global: Put Small-Scale Farmers on the Climate Change Talks Agenda." *IRIN*, April 2, 2009. UN Office for the Coordination of Humanitarian Affairs. http://www.irinnews .org/report/83763/global-put-small-scale-farmers-on-the-climate-change-talks-agenda.

"An HSUS Report: The Impact of Animal Agriculture on Global Warming and Climate Change." *Humane Society of the United States*. http://www.humanesociety.org/assets/ pdfs/farm/animal-agriculture-and-climate.pdf.

"IAB News Release: Largest Recorded Tundra Fire Yields Scientific Surprises." *Institute of Arctic Biology*, July 27, 2011. http://www.iab.uaf.edu/news/news_release_by_id.php? release_id=94.

McKibben, Bill, ed. *The Global Warming Reader: A Century of Writing about Climate Change*. New York: Penguin Books, 2011.

"National Strategy Will Help Safeguard Fish, Wildlife and Plants in a Changing Climate." *GlobalChange.gov*, March 26, 2013. http://www.globalchange.gov/news/national -strategy-will-help-safeguard-fish-wildlife-and-plants-changing-climate.

Nellemann, Christian, Emily Corcoran, Carlos M. Duarte, Luis Valdés, Cassandra De Young, Luciano Fonseca, and Gabriel Grimsditch, eds. *Blue Carbon: A Rapid Response Assessment*. Arendal, Norway: United Nations Environment Programme, 2009. http:// dev.grida.no/RRAbluecarbon/pdfs/Blue_Carbon_Low_Res_2009-11-25.pdf.

"New Report Suggests Earth on the Brink of a Great Extinction." *PBS NewsHour*, June 1, 2014. http://www.pbs.org/newshour/bb/new-report-suggests-earth-brink-great -extinction/.

"New Report Summarizes Climate Change Impacts on U.S. Oceans, Marine Resources." *GlobalChange.gov*, September 20, 2013. http://www.globalchange.gov/news/new -report-summarizes-climate-change-impacts-us-oceans-marine-resources.

Rice, Doyle. "Study: Many Mammals Won't Be Able to Outrun Climate Change." *USA Today*, May 14, 2012. http://content.usatoday.com/communities/sciencefair/post/2012/ 05/climate-change-global-warming-mammal-species-migration/1#.U7G5Y7EmPT1.

"Species Threatened by Climate Change." *World Wide Fund Global*. http://wwf.panda.org/ about_our_earth/aboutcc/problems/impacts/species/.

"A Student's Guide to Global Climate Change." *U.S. Environmental Protection Agency*. http://www.epa.gov/climatestudents/impacts/effects/ecosystems.html.

"Tackling Climate Change through Livestock." *Food and Agriculture Organization of the United Nations, Agriculture and Consumer Protection Department, Animal Production and Health*. http://www.fao.org/ag/againfo/resources/en/publications/tackling _climate_change/index.htm.

BIBLIOGRAPHY

"Animal Fighting Facts." *Animal Legal Defense Fund*. http://aldf.org/resources/laws-cases/ animal-fighting-facts/.

Appleby, Michael C., Joy A. Mench, I. Anna Olsson, and Barry O. Hughes, eds. *Animal Welfare*. 2nd ed. Cambridge, MA: CABI Publishing, 2011.

Babb, Earl B., Leonard C. Hare, and Tadlock Cowan. *Animal Welfare: Select Issues and Management Considerations*. New York: Nova Science Publishers, 2013.

Baur, Gene. *Farm Sanctuary: Changing Hearts and Minds about Animals and Foods*. New York: Simon & Schuster, 2008.

Bayne, Kathryn, and Patricia V. Turner, eds. *Laboratory Animal Welfare*. Bethesda, MD: National Institutes of Health, 1985.

Bekoff, Marc. *Animals Matter: A Biologist Explains Why We Should Treat Animals with Compassion and Respect*. Boston: Shambhala, 2007.

Bekoff, Marc, and Carron A. Meaney. *Encyclopedia of Animal Rights and Animal Welfare*. 2nd ed. Santa Barbara, CA: Greenwood Press, 2010.

Bergman, Charles. "Wildlife Trafficking: A Reporter Follows the Lucrative, Illicit and Heartrending Trade in Stolen Wild Animals Deep into Ecuador's Rain Forest." *Smithsonian*, December 2009. http://www.smithsonianmag.com/people-places/ wildlife-trafficking-149079896/?no-ist.

Best, Steven, and Anthony J. Nocella. *The Animal Liberation Front: A Political and Philosophical Analysis*. New York: Lantern Books, 2011.

Brown, Jenny. *The Lucky Ones: My Passionate Fight for Farm Animals*. New York: Avery, 2012.

Cheeke, Peter R. *Contemporary Issues in Animal Agriculture*. 3rd ed. Upper Saddle River, NJ: Prentice Hall, 2004.

"Christianity: Animal Rights." BBC. http://www.bbc.co.uk/religion/religions/christianity/ christianethics/animals_1.shtml.

Cohen, Carl, and Tom Regan. *The Animal Rights Debate*. Lanham, MD: Rowman and Littlefield, 2001.

Committee for the Update of the Guide for the Care and Use of Laboratory Animals. *Guide for the Care and Use of Laboratory Animals*. Washington, DC: National Academies Press, 2010.

Conn, P. Michael, and James V. Parker. *The Animal Research War*. New York: Palgrave Macmillan, 2008.

Curnutt, Jordan. *Animals and the Law: A Sourcebook*. Santa Barbara, CA: ABC-CLIO, 2001.

Dawkins, Marian Stamp. *Why Animals Matter: Animal Consciousness, Animal Welfare and Human Well-Being*. New York: Oxford University Press, 2012.

Dickinson, Lynda. *Victims of Vanity: Animal Testing of Cosmetics and Household Products, and How to Stop It*. 2nd ed. Toronto: Summerhill Press, 1990.

Dickson, Barnabas, and Jon Hutton, eds. *Endangered Species Threatened Convention: The Past, Present and Future of CITES, the Convention on International Trade in Endangered Species of Wild Fauna and Flora*. Hoboken, NJ: Taylor and Francis, 2013.

Doub, J. Peyton. *The Endangered Species Act: History, Implementation, Successes, and Controversies*. Boca Raton, FL: CRC Press, 2012.

"Ecoterrorism: Extremism in the Animal Rights and Environmentalist Movements." *Anti-Defamation League*. http://archive.adl.org/learn/ext_us/ecoterrorism.html.

Eisnitz, Gail A. *Slaughterhouse: The Shocking Story of Greed, Neglect, and Inhumane Treatment Inside the U.S. Meat Industry*. Amherst, NY: Prometheus Books, 2006.

Fairclough, Caty. "Shark Finning: Sharks Turned Prey." *Ocean Portal*. Smithsonian National Museum of Natural History. http://ocean.si.edu/ocean-news/shark-finning-sharks-turned-prey.

"Farmed Animals and the Law." *Animal Legal Defense Fund*. http://aldf.org/resources/advocating-for-animals/farmed-animals-and-the-law/.

Farm Sanctuary. *Life behind Bars: An Introduction to Factory Farming*. Watkins Glen, NY: Farm Sanctuary, 2002.

Francione, Gary L. *Animals as Persons: Essays on the Abolition of Animal Exploitation*. New York: Columbia University Press, 2008.

Francione, Gary L. *Introduction to Animal Rights: Your Child or the Dog?* Philadelphia: Temple University Press, 2000.

Francione, Gary L. *Rain without Thunder: The Ideology of the Animal Rights Movement*. Philadelphia: Temple University Press, 1996.

Francione, Gary L., and Robert Garner. *The Animal Rights Debate: Abolition or Regulation?* New York: Columbia University Press, 2010.

Government Accountability Office (GAO). *Endangered Species: Time and Costs Required to Recover Species Are Largely Unknown*. Washington, DC: GAO, 2006. http://www.gao.gov/assets/100/94110.pdf.

Grandin, Temple, ed. *Improving Animal Welfare: A Practical Approach*. Cambridge, MA: CABI, 2010.

Grandin, Temple, and Mark Deesing. *Humane Livestock Handling: Understanding Livestock Behavior and Building Facilities for Healthier Animals*. North Adams, MA: Storey Publishing, 2008.

Hawthorne, Mark. *Striking at the Root: A Practical Guide to Animal Activism*. Washington, DC: Changemakers, 2007.

Hester, R. E., and Roy M. Harrison. *Alternatives to Animal Testing*. Cambridge, UK: Royal Society of Chemistry, 2006.

Iacobbo, Karen. *Vegetarian America: A History*. Westport, CT: Praeger, 2004.

Joy, Melanie. *Why We Love Dogs, Eat Pigs, and Wear Cows: An Introduction to Carnism*. San Francisco, CA: Conari Press, 2010.

Kirby, David. *Animal Factory: The Looming Threat of Industrial Pig, Dairy, and Poultry Farms to Humans and the Environment*. New York: St. Martin's Press, 2010.

Kirby, David. *Death at SeaWorld: Shamu and the Dark Side of Killer Whales in Captivity*. New York: St. Martin's, 2012.

Kowalski, Gary A. *The Souls of Animals*. 2nd ed. Novato, CA: New World Library, 2007.

Laufer, Peter. *No Animals Were Harmed: The Controversial Line between Entertainment and Abuse*. Guilford, CT: Lyons Press, 2012.

Liddick, Donald, R. *Eco-Terrorism: Radical Environmental and Animal Liberation Movements*. Westport, CT: Praeger, 2006.

Linzey, Andrew, and Paul A. B. Clarke. *Animal Rights: A Historical Anthology*. New York: Columbia University Press, 2004.

Matsumoto, Sarah, Cara Pike, Tom Turner, and Ray Wan. *Citizens' Guide to the Endangered Species Act*. San Francisco: Earthjustice, 2003. http://earthjustice.org/sites/default/files/library/reports/Citizens_Guide_ESA.pdf.

Mech, L. David. "The Challenge of Wolf Recovery: An Ongoing Dilemma for State Managers." *Wildlife Society News*, March 22, 2013. http://news.wildlife.org/featured/the-challenge-of-wolf-recovery/.

Morgan, Gilbert E., and Deavon Hill, eds. *The Lacey Act: Federal Regulation and Protection of Wildlife and Plants*. New York: Nova Science Publishers, 2012.

Musiani, Marco, Luigi Boitani, and Paul Paquet, eds. *A New Era for Wolves and People: Wolf Recovery, Human Attitudes and Policy*. Calgary, AB: University of Calgary Press, 2009.

Newkirk, Ingrid. *Free the Animals: The Amazing True Story of the Animal Liberation Front*. New York: Lantern Books, 2000.

Newkirk, Ingrid. *The PETA Practical Guide to Animal Rights: Simple Acts of Kindness to Help Animals in Trouble*. New York: St. Martin's Griffin, 2009.

Nie, Martin A. *Beyond Wolves: The Politics of Wolf Recovery and Management*. Minneapolis: University of Minnesota Press, 2003.

Norton, Brian G., Michael Hutchins, Elizabeth F. Stevens, and Terry L. Maple, eds. *Ethics on the Ark: Zoos, Animal Welfare, and Wildlife Conservation*. Washington, DC: Smithsonian Institution, 2012.

Owen, David. *Shark: In Peril in the Sea*. Crows Nest, NSW: Allen & Unwin, 2009.

Panaman, Roger, *How to Do Animal Rights* (blog), April 2008, http://www.animalethics.org.uk/index.html.

Perdue, Abigail, and Randall Lockwood. *Animal Cruelty and Freedom of Speech: When Worlds Collide*. West Lafayette, IN: Purdue University Press, 2014.

Phelps, Norm. *The Longest Struggle: Animal Advocacy from Pythagoras to PETA*. New York: Lantern Books, 2007.

Pickering, Leslie James. *The Earth Liberation Front, 1997–2002*. 2nd ed. Portland, OR: Arissa Media Group, 2007.

Pipe, Sheryl L. "Animal Rights and Animal Welfare." *Learning to Give*. http://learningtogive.org/papers/paper360.html.

Pluhar, Evelyn B. *Beyond Prejudice: The Moral Significance of Human and Nonhuman Animals*. Durham, NC: Duke University Press, 1995.

Pond, Wilson G., Fuller Warren Bazer, and Bernard E. Rollin. *Animal Welfare in Animal Agriculture: Husbandry, Stewardship and Sustainability in Animal Production*. Boca Raton, FL: CRC Press, 2012.

Potter, Will. "Analysis of the Animal Enterprise Terrorism Act (AETA)." *Green Is the New Red*. http://www.greenisthenewred.com/blog/aeta-analysis-109th/.

Preece, Rod. *Brute Souls, Happy Beasts, and Evolution: The Historical Status of Animals*. Vancouver: University of British Columbia Press, 2005.

Preece, Rod. *Sins of the Flesh: A History of Ethical Vegetarian Thought*. Vancouver: University of British Columbia Press, 2008.

Regan, Tom. *Animal Rights, Human Wrongs: An Introduction to Moral Philosophy*. Lanham, MD: Rowman and Littlefield, 2003.

Regan, Tom. "Animal Rights 101," *Tom Regan Rights & Writes* (blog), 2014. http:// tomregan.info/essays/animal-rights-101/.

Regan, Tom. *The Case for Animal Rights*. Updated ed. Berkeley: University of California Press, 2010.

Regan, Tom. *Empty Cages: Facing the Challenge of Animal Rights*. Lanham, MD: Rowman & Littlefield, 2004.

Regan, Tom, Gary Francione, and Ingrid Newkirk. "Point/Counterpoint—Point: A Movement's Means Create Its Ends / Counterpoint: Total Victory, Like Checkmate, Cannot Be Achieved in One Move." *The Animals' Agenda*, January/February 1992, pp. 40–45. http://arzonetranscripts.files.wordpress.com/2011/06/point_counterpoint -regan_francione_newkirk.pdf.

Robbins, John. *Diet for a New America*, xiii–xvii. Walpole, NH: Stillpoint Publishing, 1987.

Rollin, Bernard. *Animal Rights & Human Morality*. 3rd ed. Amherst, NY: Prometheus Books, 2006.

Rollin, Bernard. *Farm Animal Welfare: Social, Bioethical, and Research Issues*. Ames: Iowa State University Press, 1995.

Rollin, Bernard. *Science and Ethics*. New York: Cambridge University Press, 2006.

Rose, Naomi A., E.C.M. Parsons, and Richard Farinato. The Case against Marine Mammals in Captivity. 4th ed. Humane Society of the United States, World Society for the Protection of Animals, May 2009. http://www.marineconnection.org/docs/The%20Case %20against%20Marine%20Mammals%20in%20Captivity%20%20%28HSUS%29.pdf.

Shprintzen, Adam D. *The Vegetarian Crusade: The Rise of an American Reform Movement, 1817–1821*. Chapel Hill: University of North Carolina Press, 2013.

Sinclair, Upton. *The Jungle*. New York: Doubleday, 1906.

Singer, Peter. *Animal Liberation: The Definitive Classic of the Animal Movement*. Updated ed. New York: HarperCollins, 2009.

Singer, Peter. *The Animal Liberation Movement: Its Philosophy, Its Achievements, and Its Future*. Nottingham, England: Old Hammond Press, 1985.

Singer, Peter, ed. *In Defense of Animals*. New York: Basil Blackwell, 1985.

Slater, Lauren. "Wild Obsession: The Perilous Attraction of Owning Exotic Pets." *National Geographic*, April 2014. http://ngm.nationalgeographic.com/2014/04/exotic-pets/ slater-text.

Smith, Wesley J. *A Rat Is a Pig Is a Dog Is a Boy: The Human Cost of the Animal Rights Movement*. New York: Encounter Books, 2012.

Spencer, Colin. *The Heretic's Feast: A History of Vegetarianism*. Hanover, NH: University Press of New England, 1995.

Sunstein, Cass R., and Martha Craven Nussbaum. *Animal Rights: Current Debates and New Directions*. New York: Oxford University Press, 2004.

Tompkins, Ptolemy. *The Divine Life of Animals: One Man's Quest to Discover whether the Souls of Animals Live On*. New York: Crown, 2010.

Waldau, Paul. *Animal Rights: What Everyone Needs to Know*. New York: Oxford University Press, 2010.

Walsh, Edward. "The Animal Enterprise Protection Act: A Scientist's Perspective Brings the Law into Focus." *National Animal Interest Alliance*. http://www.naiaonline.org/articles/ article/the-animal-enterprise-protection-act-a-scientists-perspective-brings-the-la.

Williams, Erin E., and Margo DeMello. *Why Animals Matter: The Case for Animal Protection*. Amherst, NY: Prometheus Books, 2007.

Wilson, Scott. "Animals and Ethics," in *Internet Encyclopedia of Philosophy*. http://www.iep .utm.edu/anim-eth/.

INDEX

ABOUT THE AUTHOR

LAWRENCE W. BAKER is an independent publishing professional with more than three decades of experience in reference, academic, and trade publishing. He has been a project editor, writer, copyeditor, proofreader, and indexer for hundreds of books in his career. He earned his Bachelor's degree in communications from the University of Michigan. He is also a graduate of the Denver Publishing Institute and is currently a visiting faculty member there, where he presents the "Reference Publishing in the Digital Age" session.